✓ W9-AQD-465

spatial foundations of urbanism
second edition

dean s. rugg
university of nebraska

LESLIE DIENES
Department of Geography

wcb
wm. c. brown company publishers
dubuque, iowa

To
the family
and
our
many trips
together

Contents

LESLIE DIENES
Department of Geography

Preface

One hesitates to change the first edition of a textbook because the existing format obviously has appealed to a certain number of people. The inclusion of concepts dealing with cities in other cultural areas was especially well received in the earlier edition and, therefore, this focus has been retained. Yet, my feeling and the sentiment of evaluations received over several years was that the book needed some changes in line with progress in Urban Geography. These alterations were most necessary in Chapters 4 and 5 where newer concepts were lacking. For example, the topic of interaction between and within cities required more explicit treatment. In addition, the idea of an urban system was required to supplement the central-place concept. The physical environment of cities has been a topic of interest in recent years and thus it seemed a good idea to expand Chapter 3 to include some of the interrelationships within an urban ecosystem. Finally, Chapters 2 and 6 required some revision and updating. In short, the book has been rather thoroughly revised.

The author asked himself, however, if some systematic methodology could be introduced that would provide a uniform approach to explaining the spatial foundations of urbanism. Such an approach is deemed necessary because an introductory book on Urban Geography cannot cover all topics but must be selective. Therefore, an approach that seems to fit the modern idea of geography as a discipline was adopted—that of comparing theory with reality. Throughout the book conceptual models, which geographers have developed, are offered on a selective basis to explain the processes of urban spatial organization characteristic of cities in general. These models are then tested in real world situations. In many cases, the test represents only a partial answer as to whether or not the theory is acceptable. However, I feel strongly that such an approach offers a logical method of comparing regional differences between urban areas. The student starts with similarities and thus has a framework against which reality can be measured. The regional exception can be more readily identified and the reasons for this deviation from theory can be explained. I have used this method in my introductory Urban Geography classes for some time and have found it successful. By applying these concepts to real world situations in the immediate area, the student can better understand the processes of urban spatial organization together with the reasons for differences between theory and reality. This approach is utilized also in the chapters dealing with the city in history and comparative urbanism where generalizations or models are introduced as frameworks of understanding. Throughout the book the amount of quantification is minimized but introduced where appropriate. For example, the increasing sophistication of tests made of the Christaller model are explained using approaches developed by Smailes, Brush, and Berry and his colleagues. In summary, these changes in the second edition of *Spatial Foundations of Urbanism* bring it more closely in line with progress in geography as a discipline, and allow it to be used either as an introduction to more rigorous work in urban studies or as a supplementary source for general courses. The philosophy of this approach is explained more fully in Chapter 1.

Appreciation is expressed to many colleagues and students who have contributed either directly or indirectly to the first and second editions of the book. I owe special thanks to John Adams, John Brush, Karel Kansky, and Roger Zanarini for reading portions of the second edition. I am also indebted to the publisher for patience during my efforts to improve on the first edition. Thanks are due to Tim Keelan and Kent Heermann for the maps. Finally, my wife, June, has contributed immeasurably to the completion of the revision.

Lincoln, Nebraska   DEAN S. RUGG

SPATIAL DIMENSIONS OF URBAN PROBLEMS, THE CHANGING ORGANIZATION OF URBAN SPACE, AND URBAN CLASSIFICATIONS

SPATIAL DIMENSIONS OF URBAN PROBLEMS

Writing after the first World War, Jean Brunhes (1920, 196), the well-known French geographer, noted that "There is doubtless no human fact which has more quickly and powerfully changed the face of the earth than the recent and prodigeous growth of cities." In those days the city represented the largest unit in the settlement fabric of the earth, and Brunhes undoubtedly would be astonished today to see the new forms represented by metropolitan areas, conurbations, and even megalopolii. The force behind these new forms is urbanization, the process whereby more and more people come to reside in cities, seeking the opportunities that they perceive to exist there. The urbanization process is one of population concentration and it proceeds in two ways: the multiplication of points of concentration and the increase in size of individual concentrations.

This strong trend toward urbanization appears to be universal, although the process may vary between different cultures. In most advanced countries of the world, regardless of the political system, one-half to two-thirds of the population live in cities. In the United States, about 70 percent of the population is considered urban and some 180 million people are concentrated in more than 275 larger nucleated settlements covering less than two percent of the land. It is estimated that the total world urban population will double in the next generation. However, the rate of increase of urban dwellers in advanced countries is slowing down and the most startling changes are beginning to occur in the underdeveloped countries. Although the degree of urbanization still is relatively low in these areas, city populations are increasing at rates much higher than cities in industrial countries did during their early expansion. This is because birth rates are high in such urban areas and supplement the rural-urban migration. In Costa Rica 44 percent of the growth of towns and cities between 1927 and 1963 was due solely to the country's general population increase. It is almost impossible to imagine the future population and areal extent of cities in China or India which are urbanizing from base populations of approximately 800 and 600 million, respectively.

This world trend of urbanization has taken place since 1800 and has affected cities of all sizes. The proportion of the world's population living in cities of over 20,000 rose from 2.4 percent in 1800 to over 32 percent in 1970; it is expected to be 45 percent by the year 2000 and 90 percent by 2050. In 1800 there were apparently less than 50 cities with over 100,000 inhabitants; now there are over 1,350. Only 11 "primate" cities of 1 million or more existed in 1900 but in 1970 there were 173 which included 12 percent of the world population (Davis, 1969). In other words, one person in thirteen now lives in a city of over 1 million inhabitants. Further up the scale are the large agglomerations of over 3 million people of which there are now some 35. These urban areas are so large in population and area that the term "city" is no longer applicable.

A startling effect of this rapid urbanization is the transfer of rural land into urban uses. It is estimated that in the United States over one million acres a year of rural land around cities is developed for urban use. The increasing demand for land on the edge of our cities causes a rise in prices and makes speculation profitable. Owners find it advantageous to withhold land from use, paying minimal taxes in anticipation of selling later for greater profits. Subdividers, therefore, are forced to "leapfrog" this land and acquire parcels farther out from the central city. The result of such land policies is urban sprawl. Belser (1954, 23) states that in Santa Clara County, California less than ten square miles of such land was turned into subdivisions in the decade after World War II, but actually the entire valley floor of the upper section of the County, an area of approximately 200 square miles, was permanently committed to urban development because of the dispersal of the subdivisions throughout the area. Since then the spread of settlement has been so widespread that planners are recommending the curtailment of incentives to attract industry (see fig. 1.1). With a 1970 population in the County of over one million (over three times that of 1950), the feeling is that growth for growth's sake is no longer desirable. The high price of land, insufficient taxes and services, mixture of governing districts, and worsening environmental problems all led to a decision by the Board of Supervisors to concentrate on assisting the people that already live there and not to worry about attracting more.

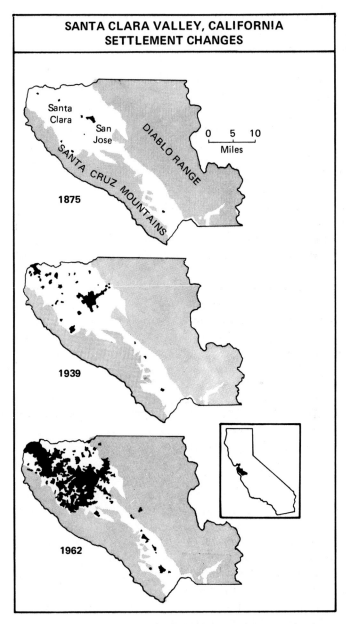

FIGURE 1.1. The spread of settlement in the Santa Clara Valley since 1875. Growth accelerated after World War II and today the area illustrates the effects of uncontrolled urban sprawl. (From *A Geography of Mankind* by Jan O. M. Broek and John W. Webb. Copyright © 1968 by McGraw-Hill, Inc., used with permission of McGraw-Hill Book Company.)

This example helps to illustrate that urbanization brings common problems that have *spatial* dimensions. Some of these problems are:

Organizing political space, especially in metropolitan areas where size and fragmentation are evident.
Preserving the central city in the face of suburban expansion.
Developing a diversified economic base.
Preserving historical landmarks.
Forming a stable relationship with the physical environment.
Establishing a consistent land use and growth policy.
Coping with intraurban transportation problems.
Eliminating areas of blight and/or segregation.

Different cultures have approached these problems in varying ways which reflect specific human consequences of urbanization (Berry, 1973). In the United States, the individualistic tradition led to an urbanization that was essentially developed by private interests. Cities here reflect the world's leading technology in their skyscrapers, subdivisions of single-family houses, shopping centers, and intraurban expressways. At the same time, however, problems exist which stem in great part from an individualistic approach to land development and control. The *spatial* dimensions of such problems are related to the fragmentation of political control, especially the dichotomy that exists between central city and suburbs in metropolitan areas. This dichotomy is reflected in strong social-economic contrasts that have developed as Whites and higher income residents have moved to the suburban ring. The central cities have become increasingly Black and low-income in structure, unable to finance minimum municipal services. The test case was a bankrupt New York City. The racial problem is reflected in the spatial phenomenon of busing, a movement which increases the White exodus. Efforts to force more low-income housing in the suburbs have been held unconstitutional. At the same time, rapid growth of individual suburbs has led to attempts at restricting expansion, a decision that was upheld for Petaluma, located on the outskirts of San Francisco. Finally, the central city-suburban dichotomy has made difficult the solution of *regional* problems of pollution, transportation, and public works. The overall impact of urban problems in the United States has led to considerable federal involvement through special legislation and activities of the Department of Housing and Urban Development. However, governmental impact (e.g., urban renewal) is only intended as complementary to the private enterprise tradition.

Urbanization in other parts of the world has brought similar problems but the cultural responses are different, in part because the spatial dimensions vary. Berry (1973, 164-5) suggests that these responses can be arranged along a cultural spectrum in which there is increasing public involvement in managing urbanization in order to change the nature of its perceived 19th Century consequences. In the Third World, urbanization is proceeding faster than industrialization so that cities are unable to handle the rapid influx of rural migrants. Concentration of population tends to build up in primate cities which are characterized by contrasts between Western sections, often of colonial origin, and squatter settlements housing the migrants. Although governmental urban planning is a goal, the public sector is small and dependency on external economic support makes some aspects of capitalism necessary. In Western Europe public involvement in planning is accepted because the impacts of urbanization are not diffused in space as they are in the United States. People live at higher densities because they lack mobility to locate where they wish or because agricultural land must be preserved. Such densities place tremendous pressure on the environment, and planning agencies are involved in problems of public transportation, green space, and pollution. The preservation of historic urban landscapes are important to the tourist industry. Finally, public control of urbanization reaches the ultimate in Socialist countries where "collective" institutions reflect the ideology of Marxism-Leninism. Here the government controls the political and economic aspects of life in order to create a city that not only lacks the problems of those in capitalistic society but also possesses social characteristics that fit the egalitarian ideology. The lack of consumer goods, including automobiles, tends to produce a different sort of city, but most of the problems mentioned above exist. Not surprisingly, the effects on the environment of pressures to increase production are similar to those in capitalistic societies.

THE APPROACH: SPATIAL FOUNDATIONS OF URBANISM

The urban problems mentioned above have spatial foundations. In order to carry out the specialized functions that a society requires, such as production and exchange of goods, man has organized the functions spatially around a series of nodes called cities. As these nodes have increased in size, the spatial organization of functions within them also has become necessary. The primary spatial component of this organization is relative location as man tries to overcome the friction of distance. Geographers have been concerned with the description and explanation of the spatial patterns that have emerged as a result of this organization. Historically, two approaches have been utilized.

TWO APPROACHES TO URBAN GEOGRAPHY. Until the 1950's, urban geography was largely descriptive since cities tended to be analyzed as static and unique entities rather than as examples of dynamic processes that tend to repeat themselves. For example, a geographer might be inclined to examine "The Retail Trade of City X" with little attempt at focusing on a problem characteristic of retail trade in cities in general, i.e., the decline of the CBD. Although concepts were important in these early studies they were often subdued in comparison with the attempt to illustrate differences. The reason for this emphasis on differences, it seems, was the lack of training among geographers in a statistical-mathematical methodology that would enable them to test rigorously hypotheses concerning cities that could be applied to many urban areas. Thus, for example, primacy was developed as a geographical concept by Mark Jefferson in 1939, but was presented descriptively rather than as an accepted proposition that could be developed as a part of spatial theory. The same is true of the central-place concept which, although actually tested in the 1930's by Christaller, was treated in early stages descriptively by Smailes and Brush. In other words, it was difficult for early conceptual work in urban geography to be applied to classes of cities. Instead, geographers tended to rely on traditional methods of field work and historical sources, techniques which tended to focus on the individual case. No real body of theory was being developed which could provide a framework of investigation for any city. In this writer's view, this early neglect of theory resulted largely from the lack of a comprehensive methodology characteristic of the other social sciences.

After 1955 this gap in training was remedied as geographers began to work more on the boundaries of their field where they came in contact with urban climatologists, sociologists, psychologists, and economists. In order to interact with these specialists, they found it necessary to adopt the methodology of testing hypotheses and developing theory common to the social sciences. Now, "The Retail Trade of City X" might be rephrased as "The Decline of the Central Business District: The Case of City X." A problem is implied regarding cities in general about which hypotheses can be formulated and tested. In other words, cities are not haphazard but are the product of systematic processes. Gradually, by the mid-1970s most Departments of Geography at universities included quantitative methods as a part of normal graduate and even undergraduate training. Techniques of analysis, including especially those of statistical inference used for hypotheses testing, were applied to urban locational problems. As a result, a body of theory relating to urban spatial structure evolved. Explanation and prediction of processes behind this structure supplemented description. Finally, the roles of perception and individual spatial behavior in decisions relating to urban processes came to supplement the focus on spatial structure.

These changes in approach to urban geography were part of an overall transformation of geography that has been termed the "quantitative revolution." The revolution did not come easily. Many older geographers, not trained in these methods, felt alienated and opposed the changes. And their protests were not without justification. Many of the early hypotheses posed by the "new" geographers were either focused on trivial relationships between spatial phenomena or were poorly defined and structured. The written interpretation of methodological computations was often brief or inadequately presented. Most significant, however, was the frequent omission of references to the cultural factors. Urban processes were often assumed to be uniform in all places and cross-cultural comparisons were lacking. The American or Western models of urbanization became common but less was known of European, Socialist, or Third World models. Such differences around the world seem to require a return to the older methods of field work and historical investigation as supplementary to the quantitative approach.

This writer believes that the basic problem with the early approach to urban geography was that a preoccupation with reality *preceded* one of theory. Logically, the two should be handled together, especially through the use of models which represent abstractions of reality (Garner, 1968). Once a theory is tested and accepted, it can be used as a frame of reference against which reality can be measured and, if necessary, again modified. The primary advantage of this approach is that areal differentiation, which remains a major goal of geography, is facilitated because of the opportunities for making regional *comparisons.* In the past a city was investigated with little real knowledge of whether or not it was typical. Thus, urban geography should be able to advance as a field of study where theory and reality are studied *together,* with the former being continuously *applied* to the latter. A penetrating study of an individual city utilizing theory can be very useful as a background to planning, e.g., the volume on Vienna, Austria prepared by Bobek and Lichtenberger (1966).

APPROACH USED IN THIS BOOK. The approach used in this book will employ this philosophical idea of combining theory with reality. Selected geographical, or spatial, foundations of urbanism are presented as a theory or generalization followed by its applications in reality. Only a moderate amount of quantification will be introduced owing to space and to the belief that most students taking introductory urban geography are more interested in the concepts than in the statistical or mathematical basis. In some cases, notably the chapters on historical and comparative urban geography, generalizations or models are presented that require further testing. This book is aimed at stimulating thought about selected spatial foundations of urbanism rather than *covering* all major topics. In this sense, it differs from other current books in the field.

The chapters reflect the spatial foundations of urbanism. In the balance of this chapter the changing organization of political space is analyzed with an emphasis on the problems connected with the underbounded nature of the North American city. The problem of classifying cities is also discussed briefly. Chapter 2 is a summary of the history of urban development from a spatial point of view; certain generalizations or principles are stated which seem to reflect best the contributions that these periods made to urban spatial organization, contributions that persist today in many parts of the world. In the third chapter, the ecological foundation of cities is examined from a spatial point of view utilizing generalizations that illustrate man's impact on his urban environment with consequent feedbacks. Chapters 4, 5, and 6 focus on three spatial foundations connected with the external relations of cities—interaction, the central-place system, and the total urban system. In chapters 7, 8, and 9, the focus shifts to the internal characteristics of cities and again three spatial foundations are examined—movement, expansion, and location. Chapters 10, 11, and 12 include a selective examination of cities in other cultures—specifically the models found in Western Europe, communist countries, and the Developing World. Finally, in chapter 13 the spatial foundations of urbanism are summarized.

THE CHANGING ORGANIZATION OF URBAN SPACE

The sharp dichotomy between the rural countryside and the city, which was so long a part of the American scene, is now disappearing as the entire hierarchy of settlement begins to appear urban. The term "urban," which means "of the city," is a broad term used to designate the nucleated forms of settlement which are similar or related to those of the city. In the same way, the term "suburban" refers to a form which is not quite urban (the way our suburbs frequently are). This hierarchy of American nucleated settlement, which includes hamlet, village, town, city, metropolitan area, and conurbation, is actually a continuum of urban forms, and precise definitions of each are difficult. In the past the smaller units—hamlet, village, and town—were rural. Now the scene is changing because, as Ottoson (1967, 8) states, farmers are becoming urbanized.

They have more business, social, and cultural connections with the outside world. They have more knowledge about the world around them and how they fit in. They are tending to identify more and more with business and to think of themselves less as laborers.

This new approach to farming has affected the pattern of urban settlement in the "rural" countryside. The smallest units decline in importance and even disappear while the larger ones grow. The "rural" towns come to possess larger business districts and individual retail outlets because they draw support from a larger area via the automobile. Housing subdivisions may appear and the consolidation of churches and schools is apparent in new and larger structures. These towns are also becoming more specialized as agricultural supply centers for such items as lumber, building materials, hardware, and farm equipment. Finally, the towns are in regular contact with larger cities via an improved highway network and the television medium. At the same time, the political power of the countryside is decreasing through reapportionment.

The cities are also affecting the "rural" countryside. Hart (1967, 64) states that some nine million Americans moved to new "nonfarm" homes in rural areas in the decade 1950-60. Land along many paved highways within commuting distance of metropolitan areas is quickly filling up with nonfarm houses and commercial establishments. Supplementing this permanent movement of people to the countryside is the periodic movement of "suitcase" and "sidewalk" farmers, who operate out of cities, either periodically or daily.

Complementing the urbanization of the rural countryside as a spatial aspect of the American scene is the changing form of the city itself. Until the 1940s, the individual city was supreme. Although it often was surrounded by suburbs, it was not until recent years that the central cities began to be threatened by the widespread decentralization of functions to the suburbs and by the evolution of larger metropolitan areas. In fact, these metropolitan areas have even coalesced in many cases. In order to clarify these changes in the nucleated forms at the upper end of the urban hierarchy, it will be helpful to look at six spatial concepts, all elements of the changing urban scene, which are to be used frequently in this book (see fig. 1.2):

City—the legal unit.
Urbanized area—the built-up area.
Metropolitan area—the city and surrounding counties.
Conurbation—the coalescing of urbanized areas.
Rural-Urban Fringe—the area outside the urbanized area.
City Region—the area of influence of the city.

CITY. A city is hard to define, largely because it is a member of a continuum of nucleated settlements that grade into one another. One

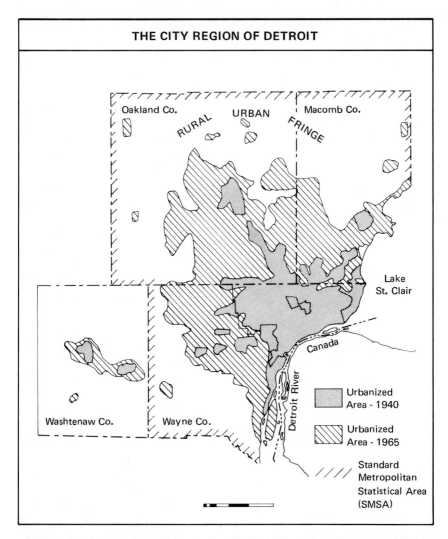

THE CITY REGION OF DETROIT

Oakland Co.   URBAN   Macomb Co.

RURAL   FRINGE

Lake
St. Clair

Canada

Detroit River

Urbanized
Area - 1940

Urbanized
Area - 1965

Standard
Metropolitan
Statistical Area
(SMSA)

Washtenaw Co.   Wayne Co.

FIGURE 1.2. The primary components of the Detroit City Region, The SMSA is made up of three counties. Detroit, as a part of Wayne County, includes several incorporated enclaves such as Hamtramck. (Source: R. Sinclair, *The Face of Detroit,* National Council for Geographic Education, 1970, fig. 10.)

recognizes general contrasts between hamlet, village, town, and city, yet the differences are not sharp between adjacent members of the continuum. Many different concepts exist as to just what sets a city off from smaller nucleated settlements. A first step in definition is made by examining the derivation of the term. Other important variables in a definition are size and the presence of nonagricultural functions. Wirth, however, feels the city is a "way of life" while Childe and Mumford are concerned with the institution as a creator and carrier of civilization. Finally, in contrast to smaller settlements, a city is generally incorporated as a legal unit, a "status" that is reflected in the charter expressing rights and obligations of residents. Each of these ideas concerning the city can be examined briefly.

The term "city" is thought to be derived from Latin and French words. A Latin term, *civitas,* meaning a union of citizens, was applied first to settled areas of the Roman Empire, which often later became ecclesiastical districts in medieval Europe. Only later was the term transferred from a region to the town within it, eventually becoming restricted to the latter. In France this ecclesiastical nucleus was called a *cité* and apparently our word city is partially derived from it. Gradually other terms like *ville* (French), *Stadt* (German), and town (English) developed with the word "city" or *cité* reserved for the old core. Even today the oldest part of London is called "The City." However, recent popular and legal use, especially in the United States, tends towards use of the term "city" for a large concentration of people with a certain distinction in size, degree of functional specialization, and legal status as differentiated from a town.

Few will argue with the fact that a city has a larger size and a greater degree of functional specialization than a town but it is difficult to separate the two units precisely. One might agree that a settlement with over 25,000 inhabitants is probably a city but 2,500 is certainly questionable. Yet the latter is the definition used by the Bureau of the Census, for in the United States most urban areas above this size exhibit the functional diversification that is characteristic of large-scale urban life. In a real sense, American settlements of 2,500 inhabitants might be called towns but in a statistical sense there has to be a break-off point between rural and urban dominance, and in the United States this is found in increasingly smaller settlements as the urbanization of the countryside becomes more evident. In Europe and other areas of the world, the separation of rural from urban is different because most farmers live in nucleated instead of dispersed settlements, often quite large ones (30,000 or more in Hungary). These settlements are called rural villages and towns, and they have few specialized nonagricultural functions that we associate with the term city. These remarks illustrate the problem of using mere size as a criterion for city, particularly when size is not accompanied by functional change.

The term "city," however, does seem to imply a lack of rural characteristics and the development of a diverse group of interdependent specialists who are engaged in nonagricultural activities. As pointed out in the next chapter, Childe (1950) feels that the "urban revolution" in Mesopotamia involved the development of a group of people within the city, freed from subsistence agricultural activity, who could interact and create the innovations in engineering, technology, religion, and the arts which we call civilization. Accompanying these urban innovations was progress in the organization of space from a city through a series of closer political, economic, and social relationships with external areas.

Supplementing attempts to define the city on the basis of size, functional specialization, and regional organization is the concept of a city as a peculiar "way of life." Such an approach is appealing but leads to controversy. In his classic study—*Urbanism as a Way of Life*—Louis Wirth (1938) states the hypothesis that as nucleated settlements become larger, patterns of social organization change. The three main features of Wirth's "city" are large size, high population density, and a heterogeneous population. In general his thesis was that in contrast to villages, which are developed in rural areas by homogeneous folk societies, large cities with dense populations tend to be composed of heterogeneous individuals who have trouble establishing stable relationships to society because of varying backgrounds, attitudes, occupations, and mobility. Competition and exploitation, he states, replace cooperation and assistance. Therefore, the average person tends to become alienated to the society, and he has difficulties in identification and participation except through organized groups. Some of these groups become segregated and frictions develop. According to Wirth, the disorganization characteristic of this "way of life" is true of all large settlements regardless of culture values and technology.

It is obvious that this pattern of social relationships is recognizable in large American cities but it is perhaps going too far to define a city on this basis. Although elements of alienation and lack of participation are characteristic of the large city, some sociologists point out that disorganization is not necessarily predominant. Apparently evidence exists which shows not only complex urban networks of social interaction but also considerable social adjustment of the individual to urban society. Furthermore, it is rather obvious that the variety of social contacts in a large city is not necessarily a disadvantage to the people living there. However, Berry (1973, 164) feels that Wirth's "city" is more characteristic of 19th Century cities than of the 20th Century metropolitan area. This contrast is discussed in chapter 2.

Another problem connected with defining a city as a "way of life," according to Sjoberg (1960, 13-15), is the lack of cross-cultural possibilities, i.e., it is not applicable to large cities of the "developing world" where authorities have discovered varying social patterns of organization existing side by side in one community rather than the one dominant pattern of disorganization set forth by Wirth. Sjoberg feels that technology is the main variable separating what he calls industrial and preindustrial cities, both of which cross cultural lines.

Still another approach to the definition of a city is developed by using legal status as a criterion. Most cities are incorporated, that is, they are established as legal units within a state through a charter giving the citizens power to govern, levy taxes, and provide services for the inhabitants. This idea of city "status" goes back to the Middle Ages when the residents of a feudal town gained certain rights through the charter granted by the lord. The towns receiving this charter became cities in a "legal" sense. Today "city status" varies by country. In the United States, there are often various classes of cities, mostly incorporated, which are based on size of population. Large urban units that remain unincorporated do so for a reason, often because of tradition or tax advantages. However, in the hierarchy of urban centers, the term "city" generally refers to the incorporated unit (see fig. 1.2).

A definition of a "city" which incorporates the ideas mentioned above should include the following ideas: development of specialized functional groups capable of creating and transmitting civilization; integration of regional activities for areas of different size; provision of social contacts between heterogeneous and homogeneous individuals and groups; and, maintenance of an administrative organization for a large group of people living in close association. A definition (Hallenbeck, 1951, 32) of the city incorporating these points might read:

> A city is a community consisting of a large concentration of people in a limited area activated by the production of manufactured goods and/or the distribution of various goods and services and involving a complicated social and political organization.

In recent years the landscape of the American city has changed. Ignoring the subdivisions, shopping centers, and industrial parks which are more characteristic of the suburbs and rural-urban fringe, we find the central core is undergoing great alteration. With the decentralization of retail functions, the office building has become relatively more important. One has only to visit any major American city to note the new skyscrapers that are referred to by some people as monuments to the corporation—a remark that provides a clue to the processes going on in our city center. Along with the office buildings, one sees larger retail stores, civic centers of governmental buildings, high-rise apartment houses and parking garages, and low-cost housing. Many of these new form elements of the city center are components of urban renewal plans designed to improve the old zone of deterioration surrounding the Central Business District—an environment that encourages crime and segregation (see fig. 1.3). Much of our attention with respect to the urban crises of the 1960s and 1970s is focused on the core areas of our cities.

FIGURE 1.3. The Civic Center of Downtown Los Angeles is one of the largest urban redevelopment areas in the United States. Although governmental office buildings dominate, the music center is an important focal point for the entire metropolitan region. A newer redevelopment project—Bunker Hill—is located nearby. Note the smog characteristic.

URBANIZED AREA.   The urbanized area refers to the built-up area, the actual brick-and-mortar unit viewed so vividly from an airplane (see fig. 1.2). In America the urbanized area generally extends beyond the legal incorporated central city, that is, the city is "underbounded" with respect to actual growth; such a situation contrasts with cities of Europe where "overbounded" cities often possess political boundaries that follow commune limits and thereby give the city plenty of "elbow room."[1] The American underbounded model is shown in fig. 1.2 with the city limits of Detroit lagging behind the built-up area. The concept of an "urbanized area" was developed by the United States Bureau of the Census to handle the variety of suburban units which exist outside the city limits of an "underbounded" city. These units may be smaller, older towns which have been engulfed by the expanding city and which, up to now, have resisted annexation. Such urban units may consist also of var-

1. The "town" of New England resembles the commune (township) unit of Europe. A European city is often part of a commune and the presence of this rural land causes it to be "overbounded."

ious unincorporated areas which fall within the county's administrative structure.

It is the diversity of suburban units which has resulted in many of our urban problems today. Although tied economically and socially to the central city, these units continue to operate independently, often without adequate tax base or utilities. The county units exhibit such things as unpaved streets and lack of bus and fire services. Many units are merely dormitory suburbs, dominated by residential areas, without any real diversification of functional support for the many services required. The landscape is a mixture of old and new forms although increasingly the subdivision, shopping center, industrial district, freeway, and airport predominate (see fig. 1.4). In order to measure and investigate this suburban zone, the Bureau of the Census has established rules which permit the precise delimitation of the "urbanized area." Included are incorporated and unincorporated areas which are contiguous to the central city and have a certain density of dwellings or population; non-contiguous units are included if they have given densities and are located less than 1.5 miles from the main urbanized area.

Most large American cities are underbounded and the political fragmentation resulting from this situation usually prevents a coherent

FIGURE 1.4. On the western outskirts of Omaha are found three of the new urban forms of America—subdivision, freeway, and planned industrial district. (Courtesy of the Wurgler Co., Inc., Omaha, Nebraska.)

approach to regional urban problems. Although the suburbs retain the advantage of local control, the disadvantage of overlapping jurisdictions seems to be more important in the long run. This is especially evident when urbanized areas cross state lines. Nevertheless, changes to an over-bounded structure are resisted, even some form of city-county consolidation.

METROPOLITAN AREA.   A third element in the urban landscape is the metropolitan area, which represents an attempt to look at the city and the area surrounding it (see fig. 1.2). Although the term is used in a general way to refer to an expanding city with its suburbs, the Bureau of the Census has attempted to be more explicit in order to measure aspects of metropolitan growth. Therefore, recent censusing has employed the terms Standard Metropolitan Area (1950) and Standard Metropolitan Statistical Area (1960 and 1970). These two variations of the metropolitan area concept are, with minor variations, essentially the same. The SMA or SMSA includes one or more central cities plus those contiguous counties that have more than 75 percent of their population engaged in nonagricultural activities. Certain criteria of integration between city and counties also must be met.[2] It is apparent then that the SMSA of 1960 and 1970 includes the "urbanized area" (also a census unit for certain purposes) and additional rural land as well, since complete counties are used. This statistical unit not only provides for excellent data, since counties are used, but also represents a realistic social and economic unit. It is evident that a large proportion of the people in the surrounding counties is tied to the central city in terms of work, specialized shopping, or cultural-social activities. In essence the metropolitan area represents the built-up area and its immediate trade region. Generally, political control within the American metropolitan area is fragmented.

CONURBATION AND MEGALOPOLIS.   A fourth concept in the continuum of urbanism is the conurbation. This term was developed to describe the increasing complexity of an urban landscape when two or more metropolitan areas merge or coalesce (see fig. 1.5). It was coined by that early pioneer in British planning, Patrick Geddes, in an attempt to describe the coalescing of cities in parts of this densely populated island. Freeman (1966) has separated the series of British urban landscapes into a number of major and minor units. An increasing percentage of Britain's population is found in these merging metropolitan areas

---

2. City, urbanized area, and SMSA in New England cannot be easily compared to these units in other parts of the United States because of a unique political structure.

FIGURE 1.5. Los Angeles is an example of the coalescence of several metropolitan areas and other centers into one continuous built-up region of nine million people. The primary urban nuclei are Los Angeles, Santa Monica, San Fernando, Pasadena, San Bernardino, and Long Beach. (Courtesy of Department of City Planning, Los Angeles, 1970.)

as people move there from smaller cities and from rural areas. The advantages of concentration for industry and other commercial activities is evident in the variety of services available. Other parts of Britain suffer from this trend which is well described by Chisholm (1964) in his article "Must We All Live in Southeast England?" At the same time, decentralization is very much a force within these conurbations since centrifugal movement from central city to suburb represents adjustments to lack of living space near the core areas of the separate metropolitan areas.

The United States also possesses growing conurbations in spite of the vastness of the country. Therefore, planners speak of the great future "strip cities" along the Atlantic coast, Mohawk Valley, Lakes Erie and Michigan, and parts of the Pacific coast. The greatest of these is the series of conurbations called Megalopolis, which stretches from Boston to Washington, D.C. and today includes some 40 million people (Gottmann, 1961). In 1960 the Bureau of the Census officially recognized the existence of such areas and the measurement of them by defining Standard Consolidated Areas (SCA) for New York and Chicago. Each SCA consists of the SMSA's of the region plus urbanized counties if applicable. For example, the New York SCA consists of the SMSA's of New York, Newark,

Jersey City, and Paterson-Clifton-Passaic in addition to Middlesex and Somerset Counties of New Jersey. Additional SCA's have been recognized since 1970. The delimitation of such regions recognizes the reality of the conurbation and permits its analysis and differentiation, especially by SMSA's.

RURAL-URBAN FRINGE.   A concept closely related to those mentioned above is that of the rural-urban fringe, a term designating the zone of land outside the urbanized area which is gradually being built over (see fig. 1.2).[3] It is the rural portion of the Standard Metropolitan Statistical Area which is actually the area of transition between urban and agricultural land use. This is county land, for the most part unincorporated and rural. Dwellers benefit from low taxes but are forced to rely on wells, septic tanks, and inadequate fire and police protection. However, the automobile permits the inhabitants to establish relationships with the city or suburban areas.

Perhaps the major characteristic of the rural-urban fringe is the sprawl of land use, a feature that will be discussed later in this book. Urban settlement is scattered throughout the area with gaps separating the elements of land use. These elements are both old and new. The older ones consist of villages and hamlets, industries such as foundries, utilities such as water and gas, concrete and gravel construction areas, and highway strip developments oriented to the automobile. The newer elements include housing subdivisions, shopping centers, industrial and warehousing districts, freeways, and major airports. The open areas, often leapfrogged by these developments, consist of rural land, either farmed parttime or held for speculation. This rural-urban fringe evolves in a hit-or-miss fashion because there is often little planning done in the unincorporated areas of counties, in contrast to that done in the incorporated city and suburbs (see fig. 1.6).

CITY REGION.   A final concept worthy of mention in this introductory chapter is that of the "city region," which represents the entire zone of influence of the city (see fig. 1.2). As we shall see later in this book, the growth of the city depends on the support derived from external areas. Part of this support comes from the immediate surroundings, i.e., both the suburbs of the urbanized area and the rural-urban fringe out to the limits of the metropolitan area. However, the city also depends on a series of more distant external relations which are responsible for bring-

3. The term "rural-urban fringe" is sometimes confused with the term "urban fringe," a Bureau of the Census concept referring to that portion of the Urbanized Area lying outside the central city.

FIGURE 1.6. The sprawl of New York City now encompasses large portions of Long Island and New Jersey. Extensive water bodies restrict accessibility. (Courtesy of The Port of New York Authority.)

ing in goods and money. The latter is derived from the sale of goods and services which are produced in the city. The city, therefore, possesses a series of graded influences which extend out to different limits. For example, the commuting range may be ten miles while the shopping influence may be farther, depending on the type. The range of support for the high school and the circulation of the newspaper represent additional supporting areas. Finally, manufacturing plants may draw on raw materials from quite distant areas and sell them afar as well. It is evident that one city has a considerable variety in the extent of its external areas of support, especially in the flow of goods, people, and ideas. This range of influence has been called by various names including hinterland, supporting or tributary area, urban field, or city region—the important characteristic being the degree of centrality or nodality affected by the urban unit. A city region reflects a realistic organization of space in the modern era that has made county and even state boundaries obsolete.

The influence of the city on its region decreases with distance because other cities are also competing with it for hinterland support. What is important to emphasize, however, is that this competition takes place at different levels. There are hamlet regions, village regions, town regions, city regions, big city regions, etc. For example, a village will compete with a city in that it possesses a food store, tavern, and garage which are able to draw people from the countryside dominated by the city. To carry the thought further, the town and city may compete for the village that lies halfway between them since village residents can choose between the two for certain shopping needs. Further up the hierarchy, a city also will tend to compete with other cities in terms of shopping facilities, newspapers, and manufacturing sites.

Today the hierarchy of urban settlements is based largely on economic factors, emphasized by the way in which the automobile has pulled centers closer together. City regions have outgrown their administrative framework which was established at a time when mobility was restricted. In many ways the county and even the state are outmoded as political and administrative units. In the New York metropolitan area, county and state lines are largely meaningless. Nebraska, a state of only 1.5 million, has ninety-three counties, over ten of which have less than 2,000 people each. Although the tradition of states and counties enables them to resist attempts at change, the need for more realistic divisions is made evident by recent moves toward legislative reapportionment and the reorganization of school districts.

This complexity of the hierarchy of settlements has been influential in bringing about a considerable degree of theoretical work on central places, work which has helped to make geography a more diversified discipline. Mention of this work will be made in later chapters.

CLASSIFYING CITIES

People want to put labels on cities. This goal is normal as a way of summarizing a city's characteristics, especially its economic functions. However, it is difficult to pigeon-hole cities objectively. They not only vary in size but also their degree of political fragmentation makes overall generalizations difficult. Most classifications have, out of necessity, been based on employment data, which represents perhaps the most objective way of getting at functional differentiation within a city. The most recent methods have been quite statistical with the goal of deriving, if possible, certain patterns of regularity in the functional structure of cities. The emphasis, therefore, has shifted from studying the city as an adjunct to regional geography to that of systematic analysis of the city itself. Such an approach not only has greater theoretical implications but also is of greater practical use to the planner. Largely for these reasons, the early classifications have been criticized as ends in themselves rather than as means to the understanding of cities. Hadden and Borgata (1965, 17) point out, for example, that "Little is gained . . .if a city is identified as a retailing center unless this information allows us to predict something else about the city. But very little has been done to relate the functional categories to other characteristics of cities." For this reason the following discussion will include mention of two examples of the early classifications plus a more recent one which with the help of modern computer methods has attempted to relate functions to social and economic characteristics of cities.

THE HARRIS AND NELSON CLASSIFICATIONS. Essentially, the early classifications of cities utilize data on functions *in the city,* i.e., employment, to work out the degree to which a city will emphasize one or more functions. Chauncy Harris (1943) did this for American cities using census and other data, and since that time his classification has been revised and improved. Basically, it is an attempt to develop a mutually-exclusive classification, i.e., to determine the activity of greatest importance in each city to the exclusion of all other forms of activity. Nine types of cities were described as follows: (1) retailing; (2) wholesaling; (3) diversified; (4) transport; (5) manufacturing; (6) mining; (7) educational; (8) resort or retirement; and (9) others, e.g., political capitals and military centers (see fig. 1.7).

Since all cities have several functions, Harris' basic problem was to devise a procedure for making the classification mutually exclusive. What criteria should be used for determining the break-off points between one class and another for the 988 cities of over 10,000 population? He recognized that some activity groups are generally more important than others. For example, the average proportion of the American urban labor force engaged in manufacturing is about 27 percent while in wholesaling it is only 4 percent. Obviously, cities with these employment percentages would be only average, but at the same time, these national averages do provide a key to limiting criteria. Furthermore, Harris realized that much of the employment in the different activities is non-basic and he wished to emphasize the basic proportions. When cities have unusually high proportions in the various activities, as compared to the national average, then the activity is probably more basic to city support. Utilizing these ideas, Harris established rather arbitrary and varying criteria for different functions as a method of eliminating all but one function which would represent the predominant economic activity in the city. Therefore, under his system a city can be classified as a "wholesale city" when the number employed in wholesaling is at least 20 percent of the total employed in manufacturing, retail, and wholesale activities, and when this number also makes up at least 45 percent of the number employed in retail alone; again, 15 percent or more employed in mining is sufficient to qualify as a "mining" city, while a city is "educa-

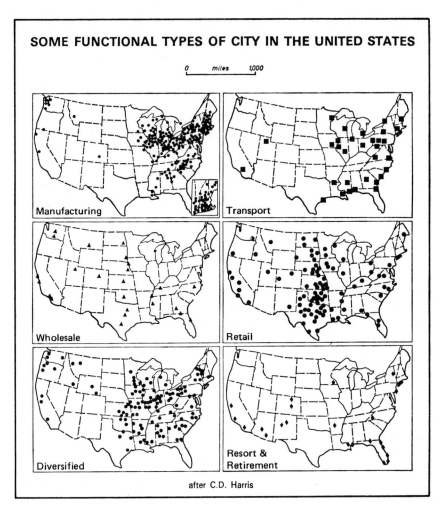

FIGURE 1.7. The distribution of United States cities according to Harris' classification. Note the cluster of manufacturing cities in the northeastern part of the country near raw materials, energy, labor, and markets. Cities that are predominantly retail or wholesale are widely distributed but many occur in agricultural regions. (Reprinted with permission from the *Geographical Review*, Vol. 33 [1943], and copyrighted by the American Geographical Society of New York. Reprinted in James H. Johnson, *Urban Geography*, Pergamon Press, 1967.)

tional" if the college enrollment equals at least 25 percent of the population of the city.

This kind of classification has the advantage of pigeonholing every city into a class. Harris found this helpful in mapping the distribution of cities and making generalizations about their locations. For example, the manufacturing belt appeared as a region in the northeast part of the

United States while retail and wholesale cities tended to be important along the eastern margins of the Great Plains, where agriculture is predominant. However, this single-function aspect can be a straitjacket in terms of reality since most cities are multi-functional; for example, a small university can dominate a small city while a great university like Chicago is lost among other city activities. In an absolute sense, New York is perhaps the greatest single manufacturing, transport, retail, and wholesale center in the United States and one might not be satisfied with Harris' classification as merely "Diversified."

Howard Nelson (1955), a geographer like Harris, attempted to remedy the unifunctional deficiency of the earlier classification by developing one that is multifunctional. He, too, was bothered by the criteria for separating the classes and therefore decided to handle this statistically. Functional significance is derived by means of a standard deviation (here referred to as SD) from the average employment in nine urban functions for the United States. For example, he found that the average American city in 1950 had 27.07 percent of its labor force engaged in manufacturing. The standard deviation of the mean for manufacturing employment is 16.06 percent, a figure that represents a statistical unit for the degree of variation from the mean. This deviation gave Nelson a means of measuring those cities which were most predominantly manufacturing, i.e., those that were one, two, or three standard deviations *above* the average. He did the same for retail trade, but here found the average was 19.23 percent and the SD 3.63 percent. Computing averages and SD's for all nine functions, he established a basis for a multifunctional classification. Utilizing this method, New York City is F2 or a financial city of two SD's; on all other functions it is either average or below for the United States as a whole. Table 1.1 gives examples of classifications for major American cities under both Harris and Nelson.

Several major advantages are represented by this approach. In the first place, a standard statistical technique is utilized to find the boundaries between classes. Although one might argue that the use of an SD is itself arbitrary, the method is a mechanical one which can be checked and which avoids the subjectivity of Harris' criteria. Secondly, it gives a perhaps more realistic portrayal of the functions of American cities in that several functions will show up if employment in various categories is significantly greater than that for the average United States city. For example, New Orleans is TWF (one SD in transport, wholesale, and financial functions). Therefore, this classification is a useful way of recognizing that these activities in cities are not mutually exclusive. However, such an approach has three major disadvantages: first, regional analysis is handicapped unless a large number of maps are used; second, use of deviations (see R. H. T. Smith, 1965, 543) from the average breaks up

TABLE 1.1
Classification of Selected Cities by Harris and Nelson

City	Harris (1930, 1935)*	Nelson (1950)**
Ann Arbor, Mich.	E	Pf3
Butte, Mont.	S	Mi3
Chicago, Ill.	D	F
Denver, Colo.	W	WF
Los Angeles, Calif.	D	F
Lowell-Lawrence, Mass.	M¹	Mf
New Orleans, La.	T	TWF
New York—NE New Jersey	D	F2
Phoenix, Ariz.	X	PsWF
Pittsburgh, Pa.	M	D
San Francisco, Calif.	W	F2
Tulsa, Okla.	R	F

*Classification based on metropolitan districts wherever possible.
Key to Symbols:

E—Education	W—Wholesale	T—Transportation
S—Mining	M¹—Manufacturing	X—Resort and Retirement
D—Diversified	(special)	R—Retail
	M—Manufacturing	
	(normal)	

**Classification based on urbanized areas wherever possible.
Key to Symbols:

Pf—Professional service	W—Wholesale	Ps—Professional service
Mi—Mining	Mf—Manufacturing	D—Diversified
F—Finance, insurance,	T—Transportation	R—Retail (not represented
and real estate		in table)
		Pb—Public Administration
		(not represented in table)

groupings of cities with similar characteristics (see fig. 1.8); and third, correlating types of functions of cities with the economic and social characteristics of their inhabitants is made difficult.

Owing to the importance of relating functional categories to other characteristics of cities, Nelson (1957) attempted this in a follow-up to his original article. Census data for the respective cities were correlated with the functions involved. He looked at manufacturing cities and discovered that during the 1940-50 decade they grew more slowly than cities of other types. Nelson also found that the proportion of the population in the labor force tended to be high for manufacturing cities, and median income high also. On the other hand, the educational level tended to be lower than for other classes of cities. Such studies reveal new information about the pattern of urban development over a period of time and

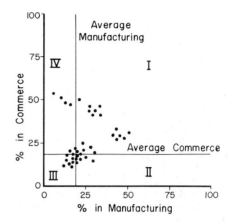

FIGURE 1.8. This figure illustrates how cities tend to group on the basis of similar characteristics. In this case, inclusion of the cities with above average employment in manufacturing and commercial activities tends to break up a group. (Source: R.H.T. Smith, "Method and Purpose in Functional Town Classification," *Annals of the Association of American Geographers,* 55 [1965]: 543.)

should lead to research aimed at explaining *why* different functional types of cities exhibit varying characteristics.

THE MOSER AND SCOTT CLASSIFICATION. The Harris and Nelson classifications are based on employment data that are readily available. As mentioned above, however, these classifications do not adequately describe other population characteristics of cities such as size, density, and age, or various social and economic characteristics of sex, race, income, education, disease, rate of crime, and welfare support. Housing areas also vary considerably within a city, and political tendencies may be evident in certain sections. Therefore, a truly representative classification of cities should be based on this type of data. How to handle it is the problem; the use of a large computer is the answer.

Moser and Scott (1961) have attempted one of the first classifications of cities to be based on a large variety of social and economic data. The method used is a multivariant statistical technique known as component analysis. Fifty-seven variables within the 157 British cities of over 50,000 population are reduced to four components through their basic similarities. For example, industrial cities of a certain age may exhibit similarities, such as lower income groups, large families, substandard housing, and a liberal political orientation. In this classification the greatest amount of correlation is accounted for by the components of social class (i.e., occupation), population change for two different periods, and urban overcrowding. To classify the towns scatter diagrams were prepared using the form components as axes and plotting the towns as points. Clearly, the closer any two points in the diagram came, the more similar were the towns. Then, by inspection, fourteen groups of towns (clusters of points) were identified.

However, the development of functional types is secondary to the achievement of rendering comprehensible a vast body of statistical material about the city. The variation of cities from an "average," a factor so important in the Harris and Nelson classifications, is ignored and instead cities are grouped together on the basis of possession of a considerable number of social and economic similarities. The classification, therefore, reflects many different aspects of urban life although it is obvious that occupation is still a basic criterion in any city. Moser and Scott found that their classification corresponds quite well to a common-sense knowledge of British cities. However, since the four components from which the classification is derived only account for 60 percent of the total variation between the 57 variables, further refinement of the process is possible and necessary.

A detailed classification like that of Moser and Scott can lead also to certain conclusions regarding regional geography and, therefore, assist regional planning. For example, it appears that the urban areas of northern and southern England differ: those in the north are characterized by a higher proportion of working-class people, less dynamic growth, and greater overcrowding.

CONCLUSION

A primary purpose of this introductory chapter has been to demonstrate that the spatial basis for urbanism is continually changing. Definitions for the city as we knew it 30 years ago are out of date. The city as a "lone" independent unit in the countryside is losing its identity as the latter becomes urbanized and as metropolitan areas develop and expand. A natural question arises: what will the future city look like? In many parts of the world supercities or megalopolii are appearing. Is this trend inevitable? Jones (1966, 64-68) points out that London, now 12 million, has reacted in three different ways to today's rapid and chaotic growth: attempting to limit city growth by recognizing green belts; undertaking to decentralize population and industry by creating new towns; and planning of city "neighborhoods." Which one is correct? Perhaps it is a combination of all three. It seems certain that planning, both city and regional, will play an increasing role in urban development. Analysis of these rapid changes in our urban areas of today provides a challenge to the many disciplines which are interested in the city. One of these disciplines—geography—can contribute to the understanding of the spatial foundations of urbanism and its problems.

CHAPTER **2**

SPATIAL ELEMENTS
IN THE HISTORY
OF URBANISM

While cities as such are very old, the urbanization trend is relatively new. People began to live in cities over five thousand years ago, but only in the last 100 years have large proportions of the populations of national states come to live in cities and urbanized areas. A look at the geographical basis of the history of urbanism should therefore include the spatial concepts behind both of these phenomena—city development and urbanization. These concepts are particularly well represented in European cities which not only exhibit a variety of urban forms but also have influenced indirectly the patterns of many large cities throughout the world. Most large cities of Asia, Africa, and North and South America were developed partly under the stimuli of European settlement and trade. An understanding of the modern city today, therefore, requires some insight into the historical periods of its development with special emphasis on the spatial factor.

The general hypothesis utilized in this chapter can be stated as follows: *"Historical changes in urban spatial organization reflect in great part the degree of control exercised by collective vs. elite groups."* Cities have grown in size as their external relations have been extended by a transport technology which permitted distant resources and markets to be tapped. Ideas and innovations also diffused into cities from greater distances and in shorter times. With this enlargement of the city and its area of influence, strong rulers assumed control, and the collective group found it increasingly difficult to either participate in decision-making or share in the quality of life made possible by cities. Only at certain times, as in Greece or in the Medieval city, does it appear that greater degrees of collective participation took place. Thus one way of looking at the different periods of urban development is to view each in terms of the interplay of collective and elite control, particularly with reference to spatial organization. As an aid to this approach, a series of sub-hypotheses relating to the main one are presented for each historical period. Although these sub-hypotheses refer to specific periods, it is possible to see examples of them in many parts of the world today.

1. The external relations of a village are limited but its collective control is excellent.
2. Control shifted to the elite group in Mesopotamia when spatial organization was enlarged and the first true city emerged.
3. In Greece the pendalum for collective control shifted back to citizen group but lasting external relations between city states were lacking.
4. Rome sacrificed collective control to organize space on a continental scale but its external relations to other cities were one-way in direction.
5. In the Middle Ages, the city once again reflected elements of collective control as the craftsmen and merchants used trade as a means of sharing power with the nobles and clergy.
6. The Renaissance and Baroque city of the national state again illustrated elite control by rulers who left their mark through authoritarian civic design.
7. Elite control of a different type was evident in the large industrial city which benefitted from world-wide external relations and a new technology of production.
8. The modern metropolitan area or conurbation reflects in great part continued elite control of spatial organization although the suburb retains elements of collective activity.

THE SINGLE CITY

THE EXTERNAL RELATIONS OF A VILLAGE ARE LIMITED BUT ITS COLLECTIVE CONTROL IS EXCELLENT.   The city has its roots in the social characteristics of man. Certain basic social forces pull people together, and it is believed that during the Stone Age permanent meeting places became established at favored spots to worship, obtain water, bury the dead, or exchange articles. In time this regular association expanded into a village, the first systematic attempt at a permanent agglomerated settlement. With this permanence came the organization of space around the village for its support in terms of food and its security in terms of rivals. The settlement was subsistent in nature and there was little time for anything but food production, although the advance from chipped to polished tools implied progress in the direction of a division of labor. Creativity, however, was lacking.

Mumford (1961, 3-20) feels that the outstanding marks of the village were its communal spirit and sense of participation. Although a common kinship was frequently present, the village spirit was apparently deeper than this. Everyone was dependent on others in the village for carrying out tasks that could only be done in cooperation—whether planting crops, building a residence, or defending the site. Certain primary bonds existed between the residents who also possessed a basic loyalty to this particular village as distinguished from others. All members of the community participated in the government which was controlled by a council of elders. The village also contained the faint beginnings of functional specialization which later became a basic characteristic of the city. It is important, therefore, to emphasize the contributions made by the village—not only the embryonic forms of urban development but, more significantly, the sense of social association and the diffusion of power which are symbols of collective control. As the city began to evolve, these attributes of the village became harder and harder to preserve although similar features are seen in the Greek "polis," the medieval city, the New England "town," the "neighborhood," and the suburb.*

CONTROL SHIFTED TO THE ELITE GROUP IN MESOPOTAMIA WHEN SPATIAL ORGANIZATION WAS ENLARGED AND THE FIRST TRUE CITY EMERGED. The transformation of village to city, or what Childe (1950) calls the "urban revolution," involved the development of a group of people that could interact and create civilization. In other words, the village lacked the specific characteristics which would permit the evolution of nonagricultural functions leading to the advancement of mankind. As food surpluses became possible, people were freed to engage in specialized activities such as architecture, handicraft, religion, recording, astronomy and other sciences, the arts, writing, trade, and military security. The village settlement thereby expanded into a larger unit comprising people engaged in various complementary functions. This new division of labor involved social interaction and the organization of the supporting area, both facilitated by *groupings* of people in larger settlements. However, a different form of control was necessary in order to carry out such a transformation. A strong king, evolving from the hunter chieftain of the Stone Age, was the main institution responsible for changing the agricultural village economy to that of a more diversified city economy. The city became the chief means for creating, storing, and transmitting civilization but control had *shifted* from collective to elite group. Central power was necessary in order to establish order over the complex new organization and the surrounding countryside. The strong ruler was frequently sanctioned by the priest and together they controlled the food supply, established taxes and capital, and monopolized all the new functions of crafts, trade, administration, construction, and war.

Gradually, special forms developed in the city which reflected the new functions, largely controlled by the elite group. Within a walled city the most significant area was that comprised of the palace, temple, and granary—later supplemented by barracks, prison, courts, and administration buildings. This area was isolated physically and socially from the remainder of the city, resulting in a rather permanent functional differentiation which we still find in cities today. Externally, the ruling group sponsored war as a means of perpetuating and extending power, procuring raw materials, and securing sacrificial victims for the gods.

Sjoberg (1965) states that this type of city developed about the same time in four different areas of the world—Mesopotamia, Egypt, the Indus Valley, and China.[1] These areas were characterized by similar natural environments—a fertile river valley where alluvial soils were renewed periodically by floods and water was controlled for irrigation purposes. In addition, these rivers—Tigris-Euphrates, Nile, Indus, and Yellow—served as transport routes, facilitating external contacts in terms of ideas and raw materials, e.g., copper. Such new contacts represent early attempts at the organization of space. Both irrigation and river transportation helped the accumulation of a food surplus which was a first requirement for an evolving concentration of people. The degree of cooperation required to control the important water resources derived partly from the communal village tradition but even more from the regimentation imposed by the ruler. Mumford (1961, 84-89) has emphasized the vast difference between the cities of Mesopotamia and Egypt. The former was the true "fortress city" with a strong king in ruthless control of the city, intimidating the subjects to serve the gods. In Egypt, however, the people apparently lived in open villages along the Nile, separate from but under the control of strong pharaoh rulers in the royal centers such as Thebes and Memphis. One must presume from this that people in the Nile Valley felt secure and were free to interact with each other. Although the Pharaoh was supreme, the people lived in almost autonomous self-governing communities, thereby preserving elements of collective control from the village tradition. The ruler pro-

---

1. A fifth area of urban development emerged somewhat later—in Mesoamerica. However, authorities disagree as to the extent of the urbanization. The Toltec religious center of Teotihuacán (first millenium A.D.) is believed to have had a population of 100,000. Aztec centers at the time of the Spanish conquest—notably Tenochtitlán, Texcoco, and Tlacapan—also apparently possessed the attributes of cities (see Sanders and Price, 1968, 151-53). On the other hand, the degree of urbanism in the Mayan area is still being revealed by investigations although their achievements in mathematics and astronomy argues for the presence of the interaction found in cities.

vided the necessary security and attraction—indeed the Pharaoh was a living god and personified the good life which the people were to enjoy in immortality. In summary then, the Mesopotamian city was an institution of intimidation symbolized by the wall while the Egyptian city, although centrally located, preserved elements of collective life.

The Mesopotamian city, as described by Herodotus and excavated in recent years, was small in area and population—ranging from one-half to two square miles and including between two thousand and twenty thousand people (see fig. 2.1). As Woolley (1954, 107, 175) points out, this city must have looked very much like a Middle Eastern city of today, with the same network of narrow, winding streets, the same one-two- and three-story houses, the same inner courts, and finally the step-pyramid of the "ziggurat" dominating all, as the mosque towers do today. Beyond the walled but spacious temple precinct spread a series of more or less coherent neighborhoods in which smaller shrines and temples served the householder. These temple communities (or "neighborhood units") included priests, officials, gardeners, craftsmen, stonecutters, merchants, slaves, and serfs.

In terms of movement technology, these agglomerations were "pedestrian" cities, an expression Boal (1967) has used to differentiate the compact pattern of early urban areas from the "axial" one of railroad cities developed during the Industrial Revolution and from the more "flexible" city dominated by the automobile. Distances covered by people on foot were short thus setting a limit to the radius of town development. Furthermore, the pattern of movement was varied thus making possible a plan of irregular narrow streets. In such a spatial situation, the controlling elite group often occupied residences near the center of the settlement because it gave them access to the important locations. This pattern is still evident in the preindustrial city today, and it was dominant in the cities of Greece, the Roman Empire, and the medieval and Renaissance-Baroque periods.

The elite control of the Mesopotamian city was aimed at a diversification of functions. The main process was a division of labor that led to considerable progress in technology and science. In a sense the interdependence and complementarity of functions produced an organic solidarity in the city that seems to differentiate it from the mutual cooperation of the village. Creativity was a monopoly of the ruler, and the rulers of Sumer made distinct contributions to city form through sponsorship of groups which developed massive brick architecture, astronomy, writing, military organization, irrigation, and manufacture. The mass of people, however, did not benefit from all this progress as much as they might have. In the first place, the degree of specialization certainly did

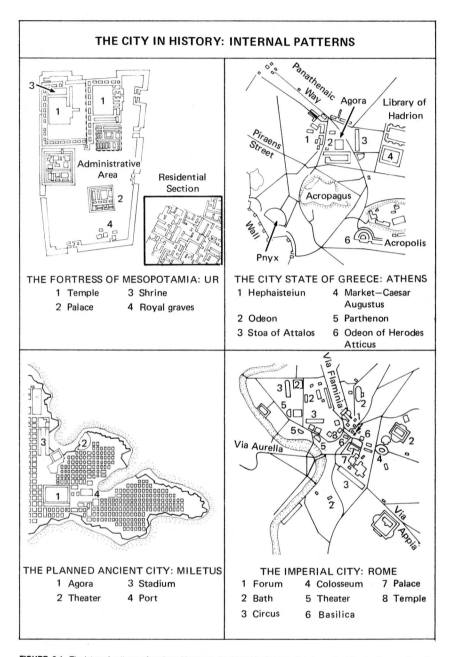

THE CITY IN HISTORY: INTERNAL PATTERNS

THE FORTRESS OF MESOPOTAMIA: UR

1 Temple	3 Shrine
2 Palace	4 Royal graves

THE CITY STATE OF GREECE: ATHENS

1 Hephaisteiun	4 Market—Caesar Augustus
2 Odeon	5 Parthenon
3 Stoa of Attalos	6 Odeon of Herodes Atticus

THE PLANNED ANCIENT CITY: MILETUS

1 Agora	3 Stadium
2 Theater	4 Port

THE IMPERIAL CITY: ROME

1 Forum	4 Colosseum	7 Palace
2 Bath	5 Theater	8 Temple
3 Circus	6 Basilica	

FIGURE 2.1. The internal patterns of ancient cities were dominated by fortress, temple, and public structures such as the theater, circus, arena, and agora-forum. In most cases these patterns developed irregularly over a long period, although Miletus provides an exception.

not help develop the "well-rounded" person. Secondly, freedom for self-direction, a trait of the village which is generally necessary to creativity and to the enjoyment of the good life, was not part of the city environment since the people were dependent upon the ruler. A contradiction therefore existed in Mesopotamia in that urban material progress did not necessarily lead to the diffusion of the good life for the collective group—a lesson we are to see repeated throughout urban history. Civilization was advanced and transmitted in the Mesopotamian city through a social process that involved a new series of institutions for human interaction. However, certain authorities state that with these advances man became depersonalized and insecure—more of a spectator than a participant. The city became a base for expansion in wealth and power for the ruler as the region of exploitation became larger and the subjects became enslaved in supporting it. The material elements came to dominate the nonmaterial aspects of the Mesopotamian city. In Egypt the two were in greater balance.

In terms of urban development, this period of emerging cities in Mesopotamia, Egypt, and the Indus Valley cannot be overemphasized. Childe (1950) has called it the "urban revolution" because of the functional contrasts between the city and the earlier village. Archeologists have been able to deduce that these cities became bigger than any settlements before, largely because a food surplus—based on irrigation, stock-breeding, and fishing—supported new groups of specialists. The resulting division of labor is seen in the remains of palaces, temples, granaries, tools, accounting tables, calendars, statues, and other items that have been uncovered. As shown by the dependence of the specialists on the rulers, the "new city" was held together by a functional complementarity and interdependence that was different from the mutual cooperation and sense of participation so important in the village. Social stratification of society was now apparent. It would appear, therefore, that the "urban revolution" in the Near East represents not only a new series of relationships between man and his environment but also changes in man's interaction with his fellows.

IN GREECE THE PENDALUM FOR COLLECTIVE CONTROL SHIFTED BACK TO CITIZEN GROUP BUT LASTING EXTERNAL RELATIONS BETWEEN CITY STATES WERE LACKING. In contrast to the elite control of the Near East settlements, the Greek city of the fifth century B.C., especially Athens, represents progress toward collective action. This collective tradition, partially derived from the village, was apparent in two principal forms of city life "participated" in by the citizen—first, the control of political life and, second, the creativity of art and science that remains unsurpassed in human history. It is necessary to examine briefly both of these aspects of collective action which were so important to the Greek "polis" and which were so often found lacking in later cities of history.

Why should collective political control of the individual city have emerged so strongly in Greece when the earlier cultures of Crete and Mycenae followed the elite trend established in the Near East? In part this seems to be related to the nature of the Hellenic environment and to the limited external relations of Greek cities. Due to their rugged topography, the Greek peninsula and islands did not lend themselves to central control, either of a city state over a sizeable hinterland, or of one city state over another. Each city was almost a natural fortress and isolated by water or terrain from other cities. The countryside was inhospitable and sparsely populated—a strong ruler would gain little from exploiting it in contrast to the richly settled river plains discussed earlier. The Greek "polis," therefore, had less need for strict overall control and a loose form of organization evolved.

A second factor in the collective political control of Greek cities was that an important segment of the "polis" had the status of citizen, free to participate in the control of their city. The evidence shows that this group was, strictly speaking, still a minority of the total population and pure democracy did not exist. Yet one must not minimize the progress represented by the very existence of such a group and its ability to participate in and contribute to urban development. The citizen had all the opportunities to express his views in the "agora" which served as a public meeting place. Some of the advantages of the village were retained, therefore, and the popular assembly meeting on the Pynx resembles the ancient meeting of village residents led by the council of elders. Such citizen control was more effective since the city never became too large. It was recognized that beyond a certain point the degree of collective participation would be lost. Furthermore, the rocky unproductive hinterland would only support a city of limited size. These limitations help to explain the systematic Greek colonization program which, in part, was aimed at relieving the overburdened "polis."

A second question relates to the reasons why the Greek city should have experienced the great collective burst of creativity that has affected so much of later Western civilization. Here again the lack of a need for strict political control, which was mentioned above, would lead to considerable personal independence and leisure time. This time was devoted not only to political participation but also to activity in art, drama, religion, mathematics, and philosophy. The result was a broadly developed person rather than the narrow specialist. The citizen's desire to use his time in trading activities was not strong, and commerce was left to noncitizens, frequently foreigners. However, such creativity required more stimuli than the association between citizens of one "polis" could provide. Mumford (1961, 133-44) seems to feel that it was in part the special external relations of all Greek cities to three special centers which provided for regular intercity association and cultural interchange. The first of these centers, Olympia, was the home of the Olympic games and stimulated the creation of the gymnasium, which was not only an athletic hall but a center of education. The second center, Delphi, held the chief shrine and sacred oracle of Apollo, a great civic and unifying influence. The Greek theater, here and elsewhere, arose out of religious festivals sanctioned by Delphi, and the tragic drama dealt with problems of human development apparent in the new urban order. The third center of creative development, Cos, was famous as a great health resort and sanitarium where the followers of Hippocrates sought to cure disease and promote public health and hygiene. These three centers—Olympia, Delphi, and Cos—brought all Greeks together to promote much of their creativity, and also served to break down to some extent the isolation and parochialism characteristic of each "polis."

Therefore, during the great period of Greek civilization, the city evolved incorporating the tradition of the village rather more than that of the strong fortress and, more specifically, facilitating greater collective control at the expense of the elite group. In later stages of urban development the patterns of control will shift back and forth between collective and elite groups. Such a theme, touched on by Mumford and other writers, seems worthy of further development and will be utilized below. Early Greek emphasis was on the social benefits of the city rather than on physical forms, a mistake which we have often reversed today in our modern city where some persons may have little chance for participation, identification, and association. The Greek "polis," therefore, did much for the city "idea" but less for the brick-and-mortar settlement. Many individual buildings or areas such as the temple, "agora," gymnasium, theater, and sanitarium were outstanding but planned order was lacking (see fig. 2.1). The "agora," the chief meeting place (and market), gained in importance at the expense of the "acropolis," reflecting the rise of collective over elite control, as the "agora" attracted the functions of government, law, commerce, industry, and sociability. In layout, the Greek city did not express any unity similar to that seen in individual buildings. Both "agora" and "acropolis" expressed an accumulation of traditional relationships rather than a fresh all-embracing order (see fig. 2.2). Each public structure in the Greek city was self-contained, self-sufficient, equal and independent—not subordinate in

FIGURE 2.2. The acropolis of Athens is a famous urban landmark of history. Located on this hill is the temple of Athena (Parthenon) while at its base lie the theaters of Dionysus and Herodes Atticus.

any hierarchic kind of order. In this sense, the city symbolized the people, actually the free citizen. <u>The rest of the city was not only unplanned but unattractive and unhygienic.</u> As Dicaearchus (see Müller, 1855, 97) observes:

> The city is dry and ill-supplied with water. The streets are nothing but miserable old lanes, the houses mean, with a few better ones among them. On his first arrival a stranger would hardly believe that this is the Athens of which he has heard so much.

There was no paving to keep down the mud in spring or the dust in the summer. <u>Sanitary facilities were scandalous and only the fact that cities were small made the situation tolerable; in the largest, Athens, with one hundred thousand inhabitants, conditions were deplorable.</u> Such living conditions seem an anomaly for a great city until it is recalled that here is a culture where a village is making the transition to city and trying to retain the advantages of both. <u>The Greek citizen was free from the requirements of subsistence and he also was free from materialistic zeal. His desire was to participate in the political and social life of the community and, therefore, village values were responsible for village forms and sanitation.</u> In the Hellenistic and Roman city, the urban forms and facilities progressed to city level but something of the village collective tradition died as well.

The Greek city represents an important step in the development of urbanism. In Mesopotamia elite control eliminated the collective aspects of the village while in Egypt the village was retained but within limits set by the elite group. In Greece, the urban unit grew larger but village traditions of participation and individual development were still basic to the community. However, as the "polis" increased in size it became harder and harder to retain these important village attributes. Citizen status was not extended to large proportions of the population, especially the non-Greeks who came to control much of the increasing commercial activity. The free citizen looked down on commercial activities, and his image of the city's collective life did not include the trader, banker, handworker, and shopkeeper—all of whom contributed to the surpluses so necessary to city growth. Stable economic and political relationships to other areas—the basis of urban growth—were never established by the citizens of the Greek "polis." If the new economic class had been a true collective participant in the city, possibly the reciprocal relationships of long-distance commerce would have replaced the exploitation by Athens of her economic rivals when her own growth of population demanded a widening of the whole field of joint effort for the common good. Instead, the Greek states remained politically at odds with one another, and the failure to use representative government and to widen collective urban control as members increased meant that elite control in the form of oligarchy or strong ruler was substituted for the collective influence.

At an early stage of human history, therefore, a basic problem confronting the city was that of size. The smaller the city in size, the better the participation by the people in all aspects of political and cultural life. Little need exists for emphasis on planned order within the city when the limited size means that problems of accessibility and living conditions can be solved. However, such a city is necessarily limited in its growth. Once its external basis for support is extended through commerce, government, and war, it will increase in population. With this increase will come less possibility for the village traditions of participation and more need for planned order. Since the collective response is decreased, such order will take place through elite groups and the city pattern will increasingly be a result of individual decisions. Perhaps this is the penalty a city must pay for size but it would appear that one ideal of the city, then and now, is to maximize the collective participation tradition of the village and yet continue the functional diversification and economic opportunity of the city.

The Hellenistic city of Asia Minor reflects this basic problem, and it was solved at the expense of collective participation. In the fourth century B.C., city forms developed by strong rulers reached a height never seen before, but the life of the individual was sterile and unproductive. Unlike the Greek "polis," the city became less a stage for drama in which every citizen had a role than a show place for power. Commerce was now a recognized part of urban life and its expansion had been helped by the inventions of coined money and the written alphabet. The strong ruler could focus the entire resources of the city involuntarily on the creation of a planned order. The best example is Miletus in Asia Minor where a comprehensive plan for the organization of urban space was developed utilizing four elements: rectangular grid pattern, wide streets for traffic (especially parades), geometric "agora" with colonnade, and separation of city into neighborhood units (see fig. 2.1). Only a strong central planner could establish such a pattern, but one might ask to what extent these forms were representative of the creative ideas of the collective community?

ROME SACRIFICED COLLECTIVE CONTROL TO ORGANIZE SPACE ON A CONTINENTAL SCALE BUT ITS EXTERNAL RELATIONS TO OTHER CITIES WERE ONE-WAY IN DIRECTION. The development of Rome as an imperial city continued the trend established in Hellenistic times as cities came to emphasize form more than social associations. This trend, of course, is related to the increasing loss of collective control as the rule of the elite group became more important. The emperor had the force needed to create new forms like the forum and arena in addition to the power to create new towns bound together by an intricate network of administration and roads. However, the sense of participation by residents in city control and in creative development was stifled. One wonders how this change in emphasis occurred.

The answer seems to lie again partly in the external relations of Rome. In contrast to Greek cities which managed to retain many of the attributes of the village, Rome became too large. As the first true imperial city, it drew on support from an area of continental proportions, a truly new phenomenon in the history of urban development. All roads led to Rome and the result was overgrowth as all the functions of administration, commerce, and even culture were centralized in this one center. A dozen Romes would have been preferable to one. At some point in its growth, the city lost contact with the residents, and few possibilities existed for continued collective participation. Instead the city became an instrument of power and exploitation, suppressing not only the creative ability of individual residents, but the independent aspects of provincial cities as well. The entire system had no basis for self-control. When the provinces were attacked, Rome suffered. When a provincial city was isolated from Rome, it could not stand alone. The result of the centralization of functions in Rome itself was increasing internal expansion which in turn led to the loss of many true social attributes of the city, especially freedom for the individual to participate in its control and to develop his own potential. The external basis for the support of a large city can be created, whether it be by the imperial relations of Rome or the commercial ties of London. The question is whether or not there are limits beyond which the quality of the city in terms of orderly civic cooperation begins to break down. This is the negative contribution of Rome to the history of urbanism—the illustration of the problem of rationalizing urban quantity, as a product of organizing space, with urban quality, as an environment in which man reaches his full creative potential.

Internally, everything in Rome was colossal in keeping with its function as the center of an empire. New urban forms were created and existing ones were universalized and adopted in all cities. Engineering contributions were especially noteworthy in the wide use of sewers, aqueducts, and paving. In its great public structures Rome attempted not merely to cope with large numbers of people but to give the mass culture an appropriate urban "front" reflecting imperial significance (see fig. 2.1). The forum represented a new concentration of functions (much as our Central Business District does today), to include meeting place, shrine, palace, halls of justice, council houses, and market. The houses of the patricians represented the height of Roman engineering in terms of space, air, sanitation, and heat. In direct contrast was the housing of a vast mass of the population characterized as overcrowded tenements which were not only unsafe and unheated but also lacked sewage pipes, toilets, and air.

Two new forms—bath and arena—were added to the urban landscape during this period. These two objects tell us something about the character of the Roman populace: they illustrate that the leisure time of the citizen was focused not on development of mind and body as in Greece but on gratification of the senses. The bath, while cleansing the body, also helped to fill the day. More illustrative of the non-productive use of time in Rome was the importance of watching chariot races in the circus or rituals of extermination in the colosseum (see fig. 2.3). The tourist today, when visiting Rome or Nîmes, may contemplate the similarity between the pull of the arena and that of football or boxing. It is possible to go one step further and trace back to Rome certain aspects of our mass urban culture such as the tenement, strip tease, and freeway.

One must not minimize the accomplishments of the Romans. The creation of a city of one million people covering an area of 5,000 acres was a tribute to administration, law, and engineering. Perhaps even more impressive was the creation of a new landscape of urbanism over

FIGURE 2.3. The Colosseum and Arch of Constantine symbolize the grandeur of the imperial city of Rome. (Courtesy of Italian Government Travel Office.)

Western Europe. The tragedy was that Rome never found a means of diffusing its power and order so as to make the whole Empire a balanced intercommunicating system in which there would be two-way intercourse and communication between the component urban and regional parts. (One sees the same result in part in highly centralized states today like the Soviet Union.) More urban self-government and regional autonomy would have benefited not only the Empire but also Rome itself since in a decentralized administration the city would not have had to carry everything on its shoulders. It is possible that a smaller Rome might have facilitated greater individual participation in control and creativity. Rome and the Greek "polis," therefore, illustrate two examples of one urban problem—finding a balance between the rule of the elite with its efficiency in organization of space, and the participation of the collective group, with its opportunities for involvement and creativity. Greece managed to keep the collective values but never established any real relations to external areas, other than those of trade and colonization in the Mediterranean Sea. Rome utilized elite power to control an Empire but lost certain internal qualities. Apparently, large cities and extended external relations are incompatible with qualities of the village. Can collective control and participation by all groups be retained as a city increases in size through expanded external support? The Middle Ages were the setting for a second attempt to establish collective city control which went even beyond that of the Greeks.

IN THE MIDDLE AGES, THE CITY ONCE AGAIN REFLECTED ELEMENTS OF COLLECTIVE CONTROL AS THE CRAFTSMEN AND MERCHANTS USED TRADE AS A MEANS OF SHARING POWER WITH NOBLES AND CLERGY. With the fall of Rome the central stimulus for founding and establishing administrative-military cities disappeared. The goal of the barbarian invaders, however, was not necessarily to destroy the Roman Empire but to occupy and utilize it. Although the central organization was lacking, trade continued, especially an exchange based on the Mediterranean Sea. Interaction between Byzantine East and the West continued, and even in the eighth century Marseilles was the great port of Gaul, stimulating economic growth in other parts of Charlemagne's Empire. However, the Frankish Empire was largely land-based and in the ninth century, when the Moslems closed the Mediterranean, feudalism became the predominate characteristic of Europe.

As feudalism evolved, clergy and lord divided the power. The link between classic and medieval city was provided by the church. The diocese replaced the Roman province, and the episcopal center (*civitas*) became the driving force in the agglomerated settlements of the Holy Roman Empire. The most significant institution in keeping the social ideas of the past alive was the monastery, often fortified, which maintained the literature and improved on the practices of Roman agriculture and Greek medicine. Indeed, the clerical institutions of these episcopal centers—monasteries, almshouses, schools, and hospitals—included a very high proportion of the total population. Supplementing the agglomerated episcopal center was a second power of the feudal period—the lord or prince—whose power finally led to the break up of the Carolingian Empire. Residing in a castle ("Burg") or manor house in or near the episcopal center, the lord found his power in the rural landscape, in the ownership of land, including demesne, and in control over the peasants. Such a division of power—urban clergy and rural lord—was responsible for a certain amount of stability within a limited area, but little growth or creativity was possible. The organization of space was lacking—either in terms of relations between cities or the conquest of the landscape. Each feudal area was a world unto itself, and Roman buildings, roads, bridges, clearings, and drainage canals gradually disappeared. The market was strictly local in its influence on the hinterland and the economy was subsistence in nature.

A third group, however, which rose to challenge the power of the clergy and lords, symbolized the evolution of the medieval city; in fact, this new group—a middle class—became responsible for completely new characteristics of city development. In the cities of Mesopotamia, Egypt, and the Roman Empire, the merchants and craftsmen were not equal members of society but generally were tolerated or sponsored to the degree that was necessary. Even in the Greek "polis," this group was made up of non-Greeks, and commercial activities were not accepted as an occupation for the regular citizens. Beginning in the ninth century, however, the episcopal or "Burg" centers of feudalism witnessed the development of a middle class dominated by traders and craftsmen. The origin of this group is subject to conjecture but it is reasonable to assume that in certain cities, especially trade centers and ports, a surplus of people accumulated. Some may have drifted in from distant places, attracted by opportunities for security and profit. Others may have escaped from the bondage of peasant serfdom in the surrounding countryside. Birth rates in the settlements apparently increased also, while death rates were reduced. At the same time, agricultural improvements, especially the extension of arable area and the systematic application of manure, were responsible for greater surpluses of food to feed this increased population which had been diverted to activities other than agriculture and religion. The most significant of these activities were crafts and trade.

The growth of the medieval city stemmed largely from the rise of this middle class group capable of challenging the power of the lords and clergy. As this group increased in numbers it became important to the other groups in terms of the services it performed for the settlement, such as defense in time of need. Its most important service, however, was the import and export of goods, bringing wealth into the town, and thereby providing a basis for urban growth. The institution responsible for this economic growth was the guild, a series of associations designed to protect workers in different crafts and trade, e.g., weavers and brass workers. These groups also became health and old-age insurance societies, dramatic groups, and educational institutions. The production of certain goods like cloth and metal wares increased, and surpluses became available for sale over long distances, a development not realized under the old demesne system with its peasant-artisan serfs.

The result of the rise of this new class was a contract between lords and middle class recognizing the new balance of power which existed. This contract took the form of a *charter* from the lord which gave the middle class certain individual and group rights in return for certain obligations. Specifically, the people had freedom to participate in government and to move from area to area, the latter being an important consideration in the development of trade. Under the charter, the group could also bear arms, hold regular markets, and organize a town council and court. The special court was particularly important in providing the new citizen with a form of protection he had never possessed under feudalism. In return for these rights, the middle class had certain obligations to the city such as participation in defense, police, and fire fighting in addition to the payment of taxes and rent. Moreover, the indirect benefits of the commercial activity to lord and clergy were significant. The granting of a charter to the medieval town incorporating legal rights and obligations, therefore, was an important event in city evolution since the charter remains an essential characteristic of the modern city. It represents the birth of town law. With this charter came also the idea of incorporation by which the city was itself considered a unit subject to legal action. We find then that by the eleventh century the medieval city exhibited a greater degree of collective participation and control than any form of agglomerated settlement up to that time. It was not only a communal association of citizens with mutual rights and obligations like the village but also a legal corporate unit organized to protect those rights and obligations.

Prior to the development of this communal corporate unit, a necessity for city-making had already existed. Its coming helped to *force* agreement on a charter which represented a balance between the three main powers. This necessity was apparently both political and economic, but which came first? Mumford (1961, 253-55, 262-65) feels that the political necessity came first because of the paramount importance of military considerations in feudal times. The lord, first of all, required fortresses for defense against many enemies and the people of these fortified settlements represented a cheap substitute for a standing army. By granting the inhabitants of these cities certain rights in return for their willingness to defend the city, a bargain in the balance of urban power was made. Only after these political rights were secured and security in the countryside became possible, could economic expansion take place, i.e., surpluses of products could be produced and trade could tap distant hinterlands for raw materials and markets. Money or capital, therefore, was brought into the city and supplemented land as a source of wealth and production.

For Mumford, therefore, the revival of trade could not come first— not without the prerequisites of security, goods, and market. In other words, trade, especially long distance trade which expanded the external hinterlands of cities, had to have a basis. Pirenne (1925), on the other hand, believes these earlier walled strongholds with communal associations were not cities, and only applies the term to urban communities that fostered long-distance trade and harbored a large mercantile middle class. For him, the economic aspects had to come before cities really existed. The writer feels that it is difficult to say which came first—the political or economic aspects of city development—for the charter granting rights was derived perhaps as much from the wealth possible under a stimulated trade as from the need for a citizenry to participate in the defense of the city. Therefore, security, trade, and charter probably evolved practically simultaneously to produce a new form of city with collective participation and distant trade connections. It is apparent that the factors conditioning medieval urban development are so varied, especially in terms of local conditions, that a single thesis of explanation is inadequate. It does appear, however, that in the medieval period, the three groups—lords, clergy, and middle class—were in relative balance. Each needed the others and so power was shared. Only later did the individual lord or prince feel strong enough to suppress his rivals and develop the national state.

The new chartered city of the Middle Ages spread over Europe from bases in the Mediterranean, the North Sea, and the Baltic Sea. An expanding network of external relations between European cities was founded primarily on trade, both by land and sea, while the political and religious ranges of influence remained largely regional (duchy and diocese). The early impetus to trade came from the Mediterranean, especially from Venice, which maintained contact with Constantinople. Other cities of the Italian peninsula like Genoa and Pisa also helped in the reduction of the power of the Moslem Empire, and the opening up of the Mediterranean once more to trade. The cities of the Italian plain such as Milan and Verona also began to develop manufactures and to spread their external connections over the Alps. In the Baltic and North Seas, commercial activities increased. The Norse turned from raiding to settlement and penetrated deep into Russia. Later certain cities of these northern seas banded together as the Hanseatic League to promote commercial relations. However, the biggest land base for northern European industry and trade in the Middle Ages was Flanders, where high quality cloth was supplied via Bruges and Ghent to an ever-widening market. Other centers of northwestern Europe such as Liège, Amsterdam, and Cologne profited by their accessibility to sea traffic, either directly or via the Scheldt, Meuse, and Rhine Rivers. Gradually a network of contacts between cities spread north from the Mediterranean and south from the North and Baltic Seas (see fig. 2.4). Certain cities in

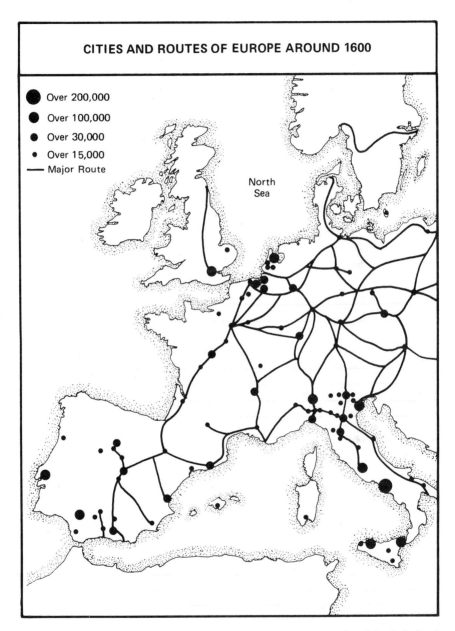

FIGURE 2.4. The cities of Europe around 1600. Primary routes across the continent were north-south from the North and Baltic Seas to the Mediterranean. (Source: After a map by K. Olbricht in *Petermanns Geographische Mitteilungen*, Nov.-Dec. 1939. By permission of the publishers—VEB Hermann Haack, Geographische—Kartographische Anstalt, Gotha/Leipzig.)

the Champagne such as Troyes and Provins, located on main routes between Venice and Ghent, became the site of famous periodic fairs. Other
routes spread north and south over Europe as well as east and west. Such
an expansion of trade influenced the establishment and growth of some
twenty-five hundred new towns during the eleventh through the fourteenth centuries. This period was the greatest attempt at the organization of space since the Roman Empire, but these towns possessed considerably more functional diversity and autonomy than the administrative-
military camps organized from Rome.[2] Instead of an Empire organizing
space from one large center many centers developed, most of them
stimulated by the participation and control exercised by a large proportion of the residents. This growth of cities in the Middle Ages
represents a new attempt by men to organize space in terms of relationships with larger hinterlands and especially between cities on a mutual
rather than authoritarian basis. The basis for authority existed but the
princes and lords were not yet strong enough to organize the national
state.

The internal development of this medieval city took place over a long
time and at different rates, depending on location. The loss of population from war and disease plus the restricted extent of supporting hinterland in feudal times kept the city size rather small by today's standards
(Russell, 1958). Venice was a large city with over 100,000 and Paris,
Florence, Bruges, and Ghent were comparable. However, the average
was probably closer to 10,000-30,000. The density of population and
buildings was high, especially since the wall restricted expansion. Land
was viewed as a commodity of importance to the city as a whole, to be
rented but not widely bought and sold as in later periods. City plans were
either irregular or regular, depending on whether they had evolved
gradually or were planned settlements. The former were more prevalent
in western Europe while the latter frequently represented either systematic Germanic colonization in Slavic areas of eastern Europe
(Königsberg) or "bastide" towns in conquered areas (Montauban).

The internal forms of the irregular medieval city provide clues as to
its evolution (see fig. 2.5). This evolution begins with the architectural
forms representing the three major groups in the city—lords in their
castle, clergy in their cathedral and monastery, and middle class
through market square, guild hall, and town hall (see fig. 2.6). The early
orientation was to the castle and/or cathedral through narrow streets

2. Josiah Russell, "The Metropolitan City Region of the Middle Ages," *Journal of Regional
Science* 2(Fall 1960): 55-70. Russell presents evidence to suggest that the medieval city region formed a unit in a regular network of settlements characterized by a hierarchical
structure and a hexagon pattern of distribution.

THE CITY IN HISTORY: INTERNAL PATTERNS

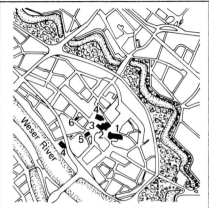

THE MEDIEVAL CITY:
BREMEN

1 Cathedral   4 Church
2 City Hall   5 Schutting

THE RENAISSANCE-BAROQUE CITY:
PARIS

1 Rue de Rivoli   4 Grand Palais
2 Place Vendôme   5 Palais de Chaillot
3 Palais de Elysée   6 Palais Bourbon

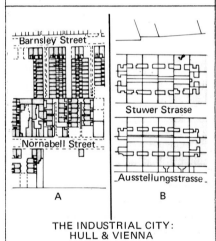

THE INDUSTRIAL CITY:
HULL & VIENNA

A Hull—old housing area now redeveloped;
   vacant space represents wartime bombing.
B Vienna—a section at the Second District;
   housing is still dense.

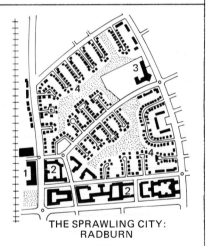

THE SPRAWLING CITY:
RADBURN

1 Shopping Center   3 School
2 Apartment groups   4 Single family homes
                     and green space.

FIGURE 2.5. The four types of cities depicted illustrate different internal patterns that reflect their history. The medieval city was highly irregular and was dominated by the focal points of castle, cathedral, city hall, and market square. Renaissance-Baroque cities, on the other hand, are best illustrated by the capital city in which early planning reflected civic projects carried out by the ruler and expressed in the pattern of buildings and boulevards. In the industrial period, regularity became characteristic of the dense residential structures housing factory workers. Finally, the period of the automobile has witnessed the centrifugal spread of cities with the super-block or subdivision an important unit of settlement. Radburn, New Jersey, was an early example of such community planning. The large amount of space within and between these new residential areas led to use of the term "sprawl" to illustrate the process. (Plan of Radburn reprinted with permission of D. Van Nostrand from A. B. Gallion and S. Eisner, *The Urban Pattern*, 1963, p. 128.)

FIGURE 2.6. The focus of medieval Bremen was the Market Square and the adjoining City Hall (Rathaus) and Cathedral (Dom). A recent addition has been the civic building on the right. (Courtesy of Landesbildstelle Bremen.)

that frequently curved to conform to the hilly defensive site. A wall surrounded the city, thus restricting the horizontal growth and causing high population densities. At times this wall had to be supplemented by additional walls. Gradually, the middle class began to make itself felt, either by establishing a market near the heart of the core or as a new commercial "suburb" outside the wall. The latter frequently originated near a city gate where there was a break-in-transport of goods and where toll or tax stations, inns, storehouses, and crafts were established. As the city expanded, this "suburb" became the "New Town." In German-speaking areas, the term "Burgher" (citizen) referred to the persons living near the "Burg," using it in times of danger. Guild hall and town hall represent capital attracted into the settlement and the autonomy granted to this group by the charter. Perhaps the most important single institution produced by the medieval culture was a new form of guild—the "universitas." Organized to prepare a person for the practice of a vocation, the university emphasized the professions—law, medicine, and theology. Starting with Bologna in 1100, and following with Paris, Cambridge, and Salamanca, most of the great European universities were created in the Middle Ages, contributing to medieval civic design through the superblock and urban precinct divorced from the old core. Other aspects of the medieval city include the location of specific functions by street (e.g., weavers, coppersmiths, etc.), the combination of work place and residence in one building, the presence of gardens, and some early separation of individual neighborhoods centered on parish churches and markets. Since the streets of medieval cities were for travel by foot or cart and for separating buildings or districts, the crooked narrow lanes were sufficient.

The medieval city, therefore, had several foci to a degree not found in the cities of antiquity. The "Burg" was a place of security but was less a focal part of community life than the cathedral and the daily market. In spite of the rise of a middle class, the church remained a vital daily force in the city, and the cathedral as a physical structure must have had a tremendous effect on the citizen, as he looked up at it from the narrow street below. Even today it is the primary landmark. Perhaps the most amazing characteristic of the medieval city is that in spite of its small size, a variety of architectural forms, from Romanesque to early and late Gothic, could fit together and reflect the collective spirit represented by urban forms as sponsored by lord, clergy, and middle class.

It is perhaps easy to exaggerate the acceptable qualities of spatial organization within the medieval city. In the early Middle Ages, green space, including gardens, was preserved and the disposal of waste was handled satisfactorily. Later, however, the degree of overcrowding within the walls became serious and the necessity for constructing multi-story tenement houses led to serious problems of sanitation and health.

In terms of external political organization, the cities that evolved during the Middle Ages reflected the fragmentation of feudalism. If a lord shared power within the city, he certainly had a reduced base for enlarging the domain of his city at the expense of other cities. The increasing economic contacts between medieval cities were disrupted frequently by wars as cities attempted to organize space politically and to control more of the profits available from trade. As a result, the external relations of medieval cities, including their relationships to large hinterlands, were generally unstable. By the sixteenth century, however, the balance of feudal power came to an end in many parts of Europe. Certain princes, who had formerly encouraged the balance-of-power within the city because of necessity, now began to expand their authority, and this power gradually came to be reflected in the cities they controlled.

The reasons for this change are difficult to pinpoint. One important cause was the Black Death during the fourteenth century which wiped out between a third and a half of the population. In the social disorganization that followed, increasing power came into the hands of the princes or dukes who controlled armies, trade routes, and great accumulations of capital. The new absolute ruler was encouraged in the development of centralized power by trading and banking interests, who found the various tolls of feudal Europe—road, bridge, river, and city—very restrictive to the flow of goods to an increasing market. For example, the number of toll stations along the Rhine increased during the Middle Ages from nineteen to sixty. Tangible benefits, therefore, came from the security and expanded hinterland of a central state, a sort of "King's peace." However, as the power of the elite group rose, the collective aspects were bound to suffer as we have seen earlier in urban history. Urban liberties gradually were lost as prince and supporting group removed the rights granted by the charter. Financial groups took over town functions, including the trade monopolies which had benefited the entire community. Medieval universities were transformed from international associations of scholars to nationalistic organizations, servile to the new despots. The church was not able to oppose the trend toward absolutism and its representatives even participated in it as prince-bishops. In short, the city was replaced by the state and lost its essential characteristics, especially the collective tradition. However, the organization of external space improved since the central state appeared to be a more convenient instrument for this purpose than a group of independent but warring cities. Perhaps, there is a lesson here from urban history which illustrates the fluctuation between elite control, which offered advantages in the organization of space, and collective control, which furthered a high degree of participation. The question one asks, even today, is whether collective participation can survive in an era when the organization of urban space in larger settlements seems to be the inevitable trend.

THE RENAISSANCE AND BAROQUE CITY OF THE NATIONAL STATE AGAIN ILLUSTRATED ELITE CONTROL OF RULERS WHO LEFT THEIR MARK THROUGH AUTHORITARIAN CIVIC DESIGN. The end of the Middle Ages is marked by the replacement of municipal power with royal or state power. Elite control replaced the attempts at collective control of the late medieval period. The strong king, duke, or oligarchy gradually reduced the power of the rising middle class and assumed control of the cities. Cities were now subordinate to a new permanent political and economic organization of space called the national state. During the sixteenth through the eighteenth centuries the ruler, supported by nobles, army, and commercial-financial interests, managed to extend his influence. The art of war was perfected as gunpowder made all but the most impregnable fortifications obsolete. The beginnings of the agricultural revolution took place as the old medieval three-field system, based on use of fallow, was replaced by rotation systems that produced both grain and fodder, thereby increasing the supply of varied food for the cities. Mining of metals increased and helped to support a new capitalistic economy. A tremendous amount of money flowed into royal coffers through monopolies on rent, taxes, tolls, patents, and booty. Industrial activities were sponsored (e.g., royal porcelain), and a network of commercial agents developed a monopoly on trade, contrasting with the operations of separate towns in medieval times. The financial and noble classes benefited through their support of the king by grants of land, monopolies, and other special privileges. Finally, the independence of the craftsman of medieval times, who carried his tools with him, came to an end as machines like the spinning wheel and draw loom increased the gulf between master and worker.

This royal power was reflected in the city, most notably in the capital city which felt the impact of ruler most strongly. Unlike the medieval period, when the rising middle class left its impact on many cities (and founded new ones, too), the effects of the Renaissance and Baroque periods were felt in only a few cities. Few new cities were established. Instead, the capital city represented the consolidation of royal and state functions, and these functions were reflected in the internal forms (see fig. 2.5). All institutions were subordinate to the king who felt secure enough to reside in a grand palace instead of a castle. The palace and grand boulevard became the focus of functions and forms which were "national" in status: office buildings for the bureaucracy, courts, factories, fortifications, barracks, arsenal, parade grounds, and theatre. The museums and galleries included not only the "sponsored" art of the court but also the accumulation of booty from conquered areas. Finally, recreation grounds, zoological gardens, and parks were "royal" or "national" in nature. Palaces built by nobles could also be called, in a sense, "national."

The organization of this national city was left to the engineer. In the Renaissance period, partial changes were made in the forms of older medieval cities, like Paris or London or Vienna, but in the Baroque era, the reconstruction became wholesale. The design was not derived from the social contents of the city as it was during the gradual evolutionary planning of medieval times, but was a sudden attempt to portray the power of the ruler. The emphasis was on grandiosity and space—large buildings separated by long continuous vistas. The presence of old buildings was no problem—they were simply razed and long avenues were laid out lined by similar forms with a horizontal roofline and numerous monuments (see fig. 2.5). A king wished to look out from his palace to an unbroken horizon or ride at the head of a triumphal procession down the avenue. The geometric form was utilized as a pattern and supplementing the straight line was the crescent (Bath), circle with radial axes (Karlsruhe), and the star (Paris) (see fig. 2.7).

The forms created in these capital cities thus were often personal as well as national, that is, they reflected the power of the ruler. This at-

FIGURE 2.7. Although not a capital city, the important social center of Bath, England became known for its examples of formal planning. The most apparent forms in the picture are the semi-circular Royal Crescent and the circular Circus. (Courtesy of the City Architect and Planning Officer, Bath, England.)

tempt to create the effect of power in architecture is seen today in some 20th Century cities like Moscow and Sofia, Bulgaria, where large monumental buildings from the Stalin period can be seen. Even a city like Tehran in Iran illustrates this spatial characteristic which was so important in the Renaissance-Baroque period.

It is interesting that the Baroque forms of European cities have made a lasting impression on planning because of the results that are visible. The tourist in Europe today is apt to seek out the Baroque portions of cities, and planners study them because the results, only possible under central power, were quick, visible, and striking. Examples of such elite civic planning are numerous: the palaces of Versailles and Schönbrunn; the Ringstrasse of Vienna; Place Vendôme of Paris; the Horse Guard barracks of London; the Opera in Milan; the Tivoli Gardens of Copenhagen; Unter den Linden in Berlin, and the royal parks of many European cities.

However, the influence of Baroque planning also had a negative effect on planning in the modern period. Its association with arbitrary power and control helped the rise of *laissez-faire* in cities and initiated distrust of any comprehensive municipal planning which might limit the free will of the individual to develop a parcel of land.

The establishment of royal or national forms in a city stands in contrast to other aspects of the city prior to the industrial revolution. There was little provision by the ruler for civic nuclei and for neighborhood development. Housing conditions were poor since the limits set by fortifications often forced the building of high tenements with inadequate sanitary facilities. An important contribution, however, to the internal forms of the city was the residential square, which is today such an important fragment of green space in the densely populated cities of Europe, especially Britain (e.g., Berkeley Square in London). Perhaps the most serious loss in the Baroque city was the communal association—the degree of municipal control and participation that accounted for so much of urban life in Greek and medieval cities.

Creativity was a sponsored part of the court life in the Baroque city and the group with time for creativity—the nobles—devoted their time to palace intrigue instead of more useful activities. One must remember, however, that the "national" city was larger than the medieval city, and the village tradition of participation became more difficult to retain than in the Middle Ages, when few cities were larger than 50,000. In the seventeenth century, London, Amsterdam, Antwerp, Paris, Lisbon, Seville, Milan, Rome, Naples, and Palermo all had 150,000-250,000 people. In the eighteenth century, as the influence of worldwide commercial contacts were felt, these cities grew even more rapidly.

ELITE CONTROL OF A DIFFERENT TYPE WAS EVIDENT IN THE LARGE INDUSTRIAL CITY WHICH BENEFITED FROM WORLD-WIDE EXTERNAL RELATIONS AND A NEW TECHNOLOGY OF PRODUCTION. Beginning with the nineteenth century, a new trend becomes visible—that of "urbanization." Up to this time we have witnessed what might be called the development of the "city," a form of settlement in which only a small proportion of the total population lived. After 1800, cities became a more significant object of rural migration and gradually included larger proportions of a state's population. This trend has accelerated since that time until today two-thirds or more of the population of advanced countries resides in cities. Such a change was impossible in the early Baroque period since only the capital and a few commercial cities generally benefited from the direct influence of kings while most of the settlements were agricultural villages or towns.

However, beginning about 1780 in England, the urban process was accelerated as industrialization became the basis for the growth of cities. The urban and industrial processes are intimately related since three of the primary factors in industrial location—labor, capital, and market—are found in cities. Urban centers became the focal points of the manufacture and exchange of goods on a much larger scale than in medieval times, and therefore were capable of extremely rapid growth. Manchester, in the heart of Lancashire, England, the birthplace of the Industrial Revolution, had only 6,000 people in 1685 but by 1801 it was 72,275 and by 1851 the population had risen to 303,382. Other industrial cities exhibited similar growth patterns (see table 2.1).

The first of two revolutions that made possible this increase in the size of cities and in the rate of urbanization was commercial in nature. Overlapping with the Baroque period, the Commercial Revolution refers to the great expansion of trade around the world. The Revolution began with the great voyages of discovery, but its effects on the settled areas of Europe were not noteworthy until permanent and regular contacts were maintained, largely through colonies. The result was a great influx of wealth and new materials into the colonial powers—England, Netherlands, France, and Spain. The effects were first felt in capital cities like London, The Hague, Paris, and Madrid. Next, port cities such as Bremen, Liverpool, Amsterdam, Antwerp, Bordeaux, Barcelona, Marseilles, and Naples expanded to handle this trade, many of them possessing commercial traditions dating from the Middle Ages or earlier. Finally, cities such as Liège, Cologne, and Strasbourg, located on the great rivers of Europe, also were accessible to the commercial stimuli.

The focus of this trade, with the exception of Spain, was the area of northwestern Europe. Here the strong rulers of the Renaissance and Baroque periods had protected and assisted the merchants and bankers in their efforts to expand international zones of commercial influence. Money in various forms began to accumulate as capital in these national states. Raw materials, upon reaching the home country, had to be handled, stored, sold, processed, and fabricated. Therefore, increased warehousing and wholesaling activities appeared at an early date, especially in the ports and other cities stimulated by the Commercial Revolution. People engaged in commercial activities began to acquire money which they wanted to spend on various goods. Therefore, the demand for goods exceeded the limited supply that had been available from the guild or cottage industrial systems. Recognizing this demand, the bankers and merchants began to utilize the capital for investments in methods, materials, and equipment that would provide quicker ways to produce goods. Thus was born the stimulus for an industrial revolution.

A revolution in the production of manufactured goods required three changes: (1) invention of machines to do the work of hand tools; (2) use of steam and other kinds of power to replace human and animal muscle; and (3) the adoption of a factory system where the various manufacturing processes could be synchronized as a line of production. The changes began in Lancashire, England, about the time of the American Revolution as machines powered by water were used to make cloth. Pro-

TABLE 2.1
The Growth of Cities in the Nineteenth Century

		Population in 1850 (00 omitted.)		
		1800	**1850**	**1890**
London		958,8	2,362,1	4,211,7
New York		62,9	660,8	2,740,6
Paris		546,9	1,053,3	2,448,0
Berlin		173,4	378,2	1,578,8
Vienna		232,0	431,1	1,341,9
Chicago		0,0	30,0	1,099,0
Philadelphia		81,0	408,8	1,047,0
St. Petersburg		270,0	490,0	1,003,3
Bombay	ca	150,0	ca 560,0	821,8
Rio de Janeiro	ca	125,0	ca 170,0	ca 800,0
Hamburg-Altona	ca	120,0	205,0	711.9
Manchester-Salford		90,4	388,5	703,5
Buenos Aires	ca	70,0	ca 120,0	677.8
Glasgow		77,1	329,1	658,2
Liverpool		82,3	376,0	518,0
Budapest	ca	61,0	156,5	491,9
Melbourne		0,0	23,1	490,9
Birmingham		70,7	232,8	478,1
Brussels		66,3	188,5	465,5
Naples	ca	400,0	ca 415,0	463,2
Boston		24,9	136,9	448,5
Amsterdam		217,0	224,0	408,1
Marseilles		111,1	195,3	403,7
Copenhagen		101,0	ca 143,0	375,7
Leeds		53,2	172,3	367,5
Leipzig		32,1	62,4	357,1
Pittsburgh-Allegheny		1,6	67,9	343,9
Breslau		62,9	110,7	335,2
Mexico	ca	137,0	ca 150,0	329,5
Sheffield		45,8	135,3	324,2
Odessa		?	101,3	313,7
Dublin	ca	160,0	261,7	311,2
Lisbon		350,0	275,0	307,7
Rome	ca	153,0	175,9	300,5
Venice	ca	150,0	? 128,0	132,8
Barcelona		111,4	183,8	272,5

Source: A. F. Weber, *The Growth of Cities in the Nineteenth Century* (1899; reprinted., Ithaca, N.Y.: Cornell University Press, 1967), p. 450.

duction rose rapidly as various inventions led to improved machines and a new source of power, i.e., the spinning jenny and power loom increased spinning and weaving production per man and steam powered those new machines. However, the steam engine required a large supply of cheap fuel, a need which was met by the use of coal. Energy derived from coal also became important to the production of increased amounts of iron for making machinery. Suddenly the location of coal became very important in the development of cities. In Britain coal could be sent by coastal ship or via canals to London or to commercial centers, but land transport by railroad was not common until the 1840s. An alternative, therefore, to moving coal was the development of new factories *on the coal field* and the growth of towns around them, generally using an old market town or village as a nucleus. A location on or near a major coal field was a primary factor in the rapid growth of such industrial cities as Manchester, Sheffield, Glasgow, Newcastle, Bradford, Nottingham, Birmingham, and Swansea.

On the European continent, the pattern of the Industrial Revolution was somewhat different because the railroad played a stronger role. The Revolution began in Belgium in the early 1800s and gradually spread to the Netherlands, France, Germany, and other countries. As in Britain, the influence of the coal fields was great and fortunately most of them, except for those in Upper Silesia, are located in a belt in northwestern Europe from northern France through Belgium and the Netherlands to Germany. Therefore, the capital and other commercial cities of this area could, with the help of the railroad, attract factories based on coal and participate in the Industrial Revolution. However, new manufacturing cities like Essen (Ruhr area), Charleroi (Sambre River), Saarbrücken (Saar area), and Kattowitz (Silesia) also developed on coal fields, often on the site of an old medieval town of some importance. At the same time, old medieval centers of metallurgy like the Siegerland and the Harz and Ore massifs declined in relative importance because of the lack of coal.

Cities in western Europe, therefore, increased in size (see fig. 2.8) owing to the influence of industry and trade (Weber, 1899). Improved accessibility provided by rail and water transport facilitated *concentration* of productive processes, not only related industries in one city but also different industries in one district of a city. Many specialized activities evolved for handling goods—viz., transport, loading and unloading, manufacturing, storing, and selling. The factory and related activities now allowed a city to attract and hold a much larger number of people than it had in the past when cottage industries had dominated. These people were fed by increasing food surpluses, some derived from overseas, while the manufactured products produced in the cities were sold to

DEVELOPMENT OF URBANISM IN THE 19TH CENTURY

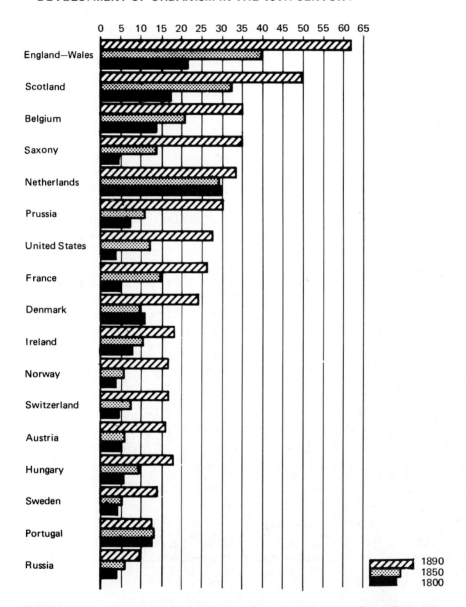

FIGURE 2.8. The graph illustrates the rapid urbanization of most European countries in the 19th Century. (Reprinted from Adna Ferrin Weber: *The Growth of Cities in the Nineteenth Century: A Study in Statistics.* Originally published in 1899 for Columbia University by the Macmillan Company, New York, as Volume XI of *Studies in History, Economics and Public Law.* First published for Cornell Reprints in Urban Studies in 1963 by Cornell University Press.)

larger market areas. Obviously, the basis for this specialized functional growth in cities was external, and the network of external relations between cities was larger than ever before in history. As the city grew larger, the local market for goods and services also increased.

Accompanying the expansion of commercial and industrial activities in the West European city were changes in agriculture that began in Britain. The countryside provided not only the food to supply the larger city but also released the labor for the factories. Innovations in agriculture (such as the reduction of fallow through crop rotation, a technique which had developed since the sixteenth century) now were improved on and supplemented by the use of machinery, fertilizer, and scientific breeding. As the Industrial Revolution developed, agricultural machinery such as the plowshare and reaper helped to increase production per man, especially in the enclosed fields of Britain and in the loess belt paralleling the coal fields in northwest Europe. The result was an increase in food surpluses for the cities and the release of surplus labor from the rural village. Entire English villages were depopulated as the rural-urban migration began. With no place to go but to the cities, this landless group found work in factories at low wages and was housed in tenement flats which lacked even the barest minimum of health standards. Thus was born the industrial tract of the Western city, where the poor urban living conditions illustrated the exploitation of labor in a newly evolving capitalist system (see fig. 2.9). The industrial worker of

FIGURE 2.9. Many British cities still include sections that reflect the crowded, unhealthy conditions of early industrialization. This view shows a portion of the Manchester conurbation in Lancashire, where the Industrial Revolution began.

the nineteenth century certainly did not share in the collective good life of the city.

The internal pattern of the industrial city reflected the technological changes. Factories and tenements were located along axes of transport—rivers, canals, and rails—where raw materials and labor could be brought together. Thus the "pedestrian city," which had characterized movement patterns of urban areas up to this time, was replaced by the "axial city." Although these axes generated congestion in the core and created barriers to internal movement, they also helped to spread the city out in a star-shaped pattern. Networks of rails—interurban, elevated, subway, and trolley—expanded to the fringe of the city and beyond, creating residential suburbs. The choice of residence was multiplied but factories for some time remained tied to the core along the "fixed" means of bringing in raw materials and shipping out products.

The most important force in this early decongestion was the trolley which Vance (1964, 50) feels was the technological development that tied suburb to central city and allowed metropolitan areas to evolve. In the United States, the streetcar era reached its height in 1900-1920 as large residential areas appeared on the edge of cities in association with these lines—indeed, the trolley was actually a tool of land speculation. The social geography of the city began to change as the elite group could now maintain control from the fringe instead of the center. Thus residences of this group appeared in streetcar suburbs on the edge of the city. As the streetcar network expanded, these residential areas became less exclusive and the longer "journey to work" of the middle classes developed. However, throughout the 1920's the centripetal forces, which focused on a single core, remained dominant. It was only after 1930 that the mobility of the automobile and truck permitted centrifugal forces of decongestion, releasing retail store and industrial factory from their ties to the fixed means of transport in the core and along the axes of the central city.

The locational forces within the commercial-industrial cities were influenced by new ideas of *laissez-faire*. In the medieval city a collective or public spirit had developed owing to the existence of a balance of power in the community and the relatively slow growth of the city. Land was viewed as something to be guarded for the community as a whole, a view that was enforced by the restrictions within the walls and by the traditional importance of "common" land. In the Baroque city, especially the capital, decisions on location were made by the ruler, and "urban renewal" in those days was no great problem. However, as the commercial and industrial influences developed in cities, various forms of land use came to depend on profit. Rather than a public institution, the city became, in Mumford's words (1961, 126), a commercial venture to be carved up. The whole concept of land changed as any part of the city was subject to sale or rent. The tendency to view land in terms of profit developed, and land uses were competitive with each other on the basis of a balance between rent and transport costs. Those sites most accessible to the largest number of people generally were the most valuable, and therefore rent was highest—conversely, transport costs were lowest. Other sites had lower rents, but transport costs for maximum purposes increased.

NB   Within such a framework of profit, it became difficult for the "public interest" to re-establish itself despite the fact that cities were chartered and as such municipal in nature (i.e., they had self government and other free institutions). Through their control of money and land, however, the bankers, merchants, and landlords came to control the development of the city and, in fact, were often responsible through politics for choosing the mayor and city council. In many cities, therefore, a subtle new form of elite control replaced the control by the king, although strangely enough this change was a reaction to the authoritarian control of the past. The predominant concept of this new commercial controlling group was that maximum freedom of the individual will produce maximum good for the community as a whole. The problem here, however, is one of contradictory freedoms. Economic freedom can conflict with political and social freedom in a community. Profit is necessary as an incentive but profit to the exclusion of other progress in the city does not always lead to a healthy organization of urban space. Economic rights generally should entail obligations for the good of the community. For example, the location of a quarry or a smoky factory adjacent to residential areas represents an economic right but may be harmful to the community as a whole.

The commercial force in capitalistic cities from 1780 to the present helps to explain the new land use pattern that evolved. The best way to describe it is *piecemeal.* Cities had now become too large to evolve slowly in an organized way as in medieval times. There was no central power to lay them out in a certain fashion as in Baroque times. Both of these periods had comprehensive planning of different types. Now, *laissez-faire* became the force that left each part of the city to develop by itself in accordance with the market factor. In such a city, real planning has no place since it is "comprehensive," and even today the world of private business is often distrustful of a municipal authority that tries to emphasize the "comprehensive plan." Under piecemeal organization of space in a city, the emphasis is often on growth or expansion at all costs, regardless of whether or not such growth fits in with other trends or characteristics of the city.

This type of *laissez-faire* organization resulted in a larger city that was gradually differentiated into commercial, industrial, and residential areas. The overall focus, however, was the Central Business District (CBD), an entirely new spatial phenomenon in urban development. Here again, the development of land for profit dominated, especially in American cities where retail trade prevailed at the expense of governmental and other public land uses. Cities are part of the economic mechanism and the CBD, as a concentration of retail and service functions, represents the point of lowest cost, from the standpoint of transportation efficiency, in the process of consumption. Since this spot is most convenient to the greatest number of people, land values reflect accessibility. The rise in American urban land values was phenomenal— e.g., Hoyt (1933, 185) states that between 1877 and 1892 land values in downtown Chicago increased 700 percent. The new core of the city became the Central Business District as the increased purchasing power generated by factory employment produced a consumer economy requiring retail outlets that were not only large but linked as corporation "chains." Such enterprises, utilizing large display windows, were located at a point of maximum accessibility so as to distribute a great variety of goods to the largest number of people. The intensity of land uses, exemplified by the vertical development of department stores, office buildings, and hotels, was made possible by the elevator and resulted in the skyscraper (see fig. 2.10) and a new profile for cities (Gottmann, 1966). It was said that the skyscraper, which was developed in Chicago in 1889 by William Jenney, "could be built as high as the elevator could go." This building illustrates the impact on the CBD of a daily movement of commuters who traveled to the core of the city by rail. In a sense the CBD replaced the market square of the medieval city and even forced the city hall to a more pheripheral position.

A major problem of this evolving commercial-industrial city in America has been the deterioration of the residential zone surrounding or flanking the Central Business District. This zone of slums and mixed land use has not been characteristic of the inner European city where, instead, the best residences are often located. However, in the American cities, as people began to escape the congestion of the center, the slum landlord bought up the vacated housing, holding it for possible commercial sale but renting it in the meantime as dense low-cost housing, which was profitable because of the demand for space and the nature of the property tax. Housing in the center often included narrow but deep lots, poor lighting, and unhealthy sanitation conditions, a contrast to the more widely spaced single-family houses or apartment buildings of the periphery (see fig. 2.5). In central areas, racial and ethnic

FIGURE 2.10. Lower Manhattan in New York City was the first urban area to exhibit a large number of skyscrapers which permitted an intensive use of vertical space. The most famous of these structures is the Empire State Building. (Courtesy of the Port of New York Authority.)

groups tended to be segregated and social disorganization was reflected in high crime rates.

The commercial-industrial city, therefore, became much more differentiated spatially than previous cities of history. Competition for land led to a valuable core known as the CBD, industrial tracts adjacent to water and rail lines, and residential areas tied to work-place by a pattern of fixed rails. This city was largely one of decisions made by private enterprise although public or semi-public utilities appeared on the scene to provide regional services of transport, sewage, electricity, and water. Some civic centers were developed. However, land use development was generally haphazard or piecemeal (being subject to economic forces), with any attempts at regulation being resisted strongly in the name of *laissez-faire*. Such resistance persisted even though mixtures of incompatible uses frequently resulted in producing an environment below minimum health and living standards.

Piecemeal development has not gone unchallenged. It became evident that a city carved up by private interests may not always benefit the

great majority of residents (Proudfoot, 1954). More than anything the
appearance of incompatible land uses, which caused both harmful physical consequences and depreciation of property values, led to demands
for some control over land use. The introduction of zoning in the United
States during the second decade of this century was a result of official
recognition of the fact that unbridled use of land by individuals sometimes reacts unfavorably upon the community as a whole. The zoning
plan of a city controls the height, area, bulk, location, and use of all
buildings and premises. The concept was fought as a transgression
against the inalienable rights of private property. However, it obtained
its legal sanction from a broadening interpretation by the courts of the
general meaning of public welfare and of the sovereign right of the state
to delegate to municipalities the right to use police power to enforce
regulations for the good of the community. According to Gallion and
Eisner (1963, 175), there was considerable acceptance of the basic
planning thesis that regulation of property use will secure to the community numerous benefits, e.g., promote greater fire safety, improved
health, additional space for recreation, and a more orderly development. Zoning was supplemented by building codes and subdivision regulations as citizens recognized that a city is actually a public environment
for all. These controls were based upon the principle that the use and
development of land constitute a right bestowed by the community upon
the individual, a right that may be withdrawn or withheld when and if
the individual violates the conditions upon which it is vested in him.
Planning departments and commissions began to appear with the goal of
developing comprehensive planning as a means of providing a milieu
for orderly private development. Large-scale building by land developers, an elite group, was thus balanced by the planning of the collective
group.

Today both builder and planner appear to be necessary to the modern city, because neither maximum freedom in building nor strong
planning is the answer to urban problems. Overall expansion of private
building in American cities is worthy of praise whereas its location and
arrangement often leaves much to be desired. The future responsibility
of planning will be to emphasize the social aspects of cities and thereby
balance the economic and political powers now wielded by private business and municipal government, respectively. The need is for planning
to provide a climate in which private building is stimulated but within a
framework set by the collective group. In theory a city should be such a
pleasant place to live that industry and other functions will be attracted
to it *because* of the control in the public interest.

It was this large commercial-industrial city that formed the basis for what Wirth called a different "way of life." This concept, which was discussed briefly in chapter 1, is a basis for the social definition of a "city" as something different from a village or small town. Patterns of social interaction tend to change in large cities owing to size, higher densities, and heterogeneity of population. A person here may be alienated from society as the bonds between individuals and groups weaken. Sociologists tend to disagree on the applicability of the Wirth concept but there seems to be little question that social interaction in a large city causes problems of spatial and social organization.

The focus in the above paragraphs has been on the commercial-industrial city as it evolved in the United States, and to a lesser extent, in Europe. However, commercial cities developed in other parts of the world, often established by Europeans or at least supported by European trade. Strong similarities were found between a port city like Liverpool in Europe and Shanghai, Yokohama, Hong Kong, Singapore, Bombay, Sydney, and Buenos Aires. Similarities also existed between a new industrial city of Europe like Birmingham, established on the coal field, and other new industrial cities like Makeyevka (Russia), Jamshedpur (India), Anshan (China), Yawata (Japan), and Monterrey (Mexico). Finally, the combination of commercial and industrial city such as Liège is also represented by Volgograd and Ahmadabad. Some of these cities may be political capitals as well and the addition of such functions may make the city predominant, or "primate" in its country, e.g., Buenos Aires.

With all of its internal defects, the commercial-industrial city was responsible for the phenomenon of urbanization around the world (see fig. 2.8). For the first time larger proportions of a state's population were living in cities, which were not only more numerous than ever before but also larger. The new commercial, industrial, and service functions of these cities attracted a steady stream of migrants from the countryside as well as immigrants from foreign areas. The "big city" offered opportunities, not only for jobs but for social contacts. At least, that was the legend that spread. In any case, 13.6 percent of the world's population in 1900 lived in cities with populations of over five thousand, as compared to only 3 percent in 1800. This change represents approximately 190 million more people living in cities in 1900 than did in 1800. In the next seventy years the rate of urbanization increased so that by 1970, 37 percent of the world's population lived in cities of over five thousand. However, these more recent changes did not take place in single cities alone but in metropolitan areas and conurbations as well.

THE COALESCING CITIES

THE MODERN METROPOLITAN AREA-CONURBATION REFLECTS IN GREAT PART CONTINUED ELITE CONTROL OF SPATIAL OR-GANIZATION ALTHOUGH THE SUBURB RETAINS ELEMENTS OF COLLECTIVE ACTIVITY. The commercial-industrial city described above represented a *first* stage in urbanization by which more and more people came to live in urban areas. This city was the first extensive attempt by man to organize space around and within a single main core. A permanent series of regional and world-wide contacts provided the basis for the growth of many cities of over one-half million persons who were engaged in a variety of specialized functions. Until the 1930s these cities were largely individual, but gradually the single-core city began to be replaced by a new phenomenon—the multi-core city. This process represents a *second* stage of urbanization—the increasing *concentration* of population around a series of nodes, especially adjacent ones. In the organization of space, there is a limit to the area that can be served adequately from one core. As the city expanded outwards, old villages were engulfed, new subcores were established, and the cities themselves coalesced.

A key element in this new expansion is the suburb or a form that is "sub-urban"—something less than urban. It is not new. Even in Greek times, the new gymnasium was often located on the fringe of the "polis" and other examples exist through history. The commercial settlement outside the gate of the walled medieval city represents a form of suburb. However, the suburban trend became significant when large numbers of people could live, and even work and shop, in the fringe areas of large cities. The trend, therefore, is tied to improvements in transport technology. As mentioned above, the commercial-industrial city possessed residential and even some industrial suburbs tied to the central city by interurban or trolley. The expanding network of urban rails permitted the first real decongestion within the city as the worker was allowed more choice in residential location. Later paragraphs develop the idea that automobile and truck led to further decongestion as gaps in residential settlement were filled, and retail trade and industry could leave the central city for the suburb. In this way the suburb became more self-contained as an urban unit.

The suburban trend began in the late nineteenth century but it did not become significant until after 1920. Residents of the central cities of the United States and Europe discovered that something was missing in the larger commercial-industrial city. Many residents longed to escape from the impersonal life of the city with its congestion and loss of individual identity. Most could only get away on weekends, perhaps taking a streetcar or walking to the rural areas that provided a retreat—a place to relax, reflect, and enjoy nature. A few could move out permanently, either to country estates or to villages located on the edge of the city. In America and Britain a few planned "garden cities" were established. Gradually others made this move as public transportation and the automobile made it possible for large numbers of people to live in a suburban village or town and still reach their job in the city. The result of these changes was the "journey to work," perhaps the most significant regular movement of people in the world today, a trend that will lead to a new organization of space represented by both a metropolitan area with a single major core and a conurbation with several major cores. The journey to work illustrates clearly the growing interdependence of activities in the modern city.

The centrifugal movement of people to the suburbs, however, represents more than just a temporary or permanent escape, but appears in part to be an attempt to recapture the advantages of the village—in the suburb there is still the chance to participate in the control and activities of community. There is a sense of participation and identity that is reflected in the suburban resistance to annexation by the central city. In addition to village traits, many suburbs possess a considerable degree of functional diversity and are capable of independent existence, in contrast to those that are merely dormitories for the central city. The total expression of suburban development around a city is the "metropolitan area."

The only thing that made the suburb possible for so many American people is mobility via the automobile. Since the 1930s owning a car has been a normal part of life for most American families and this trend is now evident in western Europe. The scale of the escape movement was bound to increase with this new mobility and, in turn, led to cities becoming ever larger in area. It became possible to live 5, 10, or 15 miles from the center of the city, depending on the access roads, and still spend less than an hour commuting. Therefore, more and more people were able to live in a single agglomerated settlement, and these settlements covered larger and larger areas, while densities of population decreased on the periphery of the city. The automobile appears to be one of the most important factors in the new trend of urbanization, i.e., it enabled increasingly larger proportions of a country's population to live in cities because it permitted a wider urban separation of work and residence. The average person participated in the escape from the core as soon as he could solve the problem of the "journey to work," and the middle-income group then supplemented the well-to-do in moving to the suburbs. This increasing mobility helps to explain why the outer rings of metropolitan areas of the United States have been increasing in population so much more rapidly than the central cities. In the 1950-60 decade, for example, the outer rings of these areas increased by 50 percent while the central cities grew by only 9 percent. In the 1960-70 decade, many central cities actually decreased in population while the outer rings included even larger proportions of the metropolitan population.

In America an entirely new form of landscape was created as a result of this permanent centrifugal movement. The old outlying cores—villages and towns—were soon engulfed in what became a spreading "suburban belt" or "ring." This ring, growing much more rapidly than the central portion of the city, possesses many kinds of suburbs. There are towns and villages, often incorporated, with specific boundaries. Between these are a variety of new residential settlements, for the most part on unincorporated county land with no traditions. Boundaries between these "suburban" settlements are vague and merge into one another without perceptible change. Names are usually assigned by a developer or subdivider. Residents have little attachment to them—in fact, frequently nothing municipal binds them together except the school and church, which may be miles apart. However, functions tend to follow the migration of people, and land use patterns in this suburban ring are dominated by major areas served by the automobile and truck—subdivision, shopping center, industrial and warehousing districts, and airport. In addition, commercial "strips" exhibit a variety of land uses oriented to the automobile including motels, gas stations, drive-in restaurants and theaters, and used car lots.

This new "suburban ring" is based on the most important new urban form of our times—the housing subdivision. In the United States this form embraces a neighborhood of single-family homes, generally isolated from main streams of traffic in the gaps between the original "tentacles" of axial trolley lines. Houses are usually of a similar type since the developer finds a uniform subdivision design the fastest and most economical means of constructing a large number of them. As a result, the suburban ring is composed of a hierarchy of these subdivisions, each containing groups having similar incomes, ages, and (perhaps) interests. Accompanying the subdivision is its sister form—the shopping center—which is located nearby and dominated by the supermarket and drug fair. Some of the more recent projects are almost self-contained neighborhood units with shopping center, school, and park. Such decentralization may go a step further in making the community completely self-contained by providing a factory for the residents, thereby eliminating the journey to work. Reston, an outlying suburb of Washington, D.C., is a "new town" of this type and others are being constructed.

Assuming the subdivision to be the major unit of this suburban ring, one may ask how these units are organized horizontally. The best answer is "sprawl," a form of irregular haphazard settlement, lacking foci and depending on the whim of the land holder, speculator, and developer (see fig. 2.5). It is facilitated by a fragmented political structure without any central control of spatial organization. Land is developed in a "leap frog" manner with projects by-passing undeveloped land being held for speculation but still prematurely committed to urban development. The city or county assists this sprawl by building trunk utilities, thereby committing the *entire area* to urban development; scattering of residences is also facilitated by the use of wells and septic tanks. Taxes on undeveloped land, even with utilities, may be relatively low and no pressure exists to sell for development. This scattered organization of space is facilitated by the use of automobile and truck and by the construction of freeways (Los Angeles) and circumferential highways (Washington, D.C.). As these routes of access are built, the degree of sprawl increases since mobility within a larger area improves. Industry and wholesaling also contribute to the suburban sprawl as space is sought for one-level plants or warehouses and accompanying parking. A special form of decentralization—the planned Industrial (or Warehouse) District—can be considered a fourth new urban form of suburbia along with the subdivision, shopping center, and freeway. Finally, a fifth form is the airport, which has placed a tremendous demand for space on the suburban ring of large cities (see fig. 2.11). All forms profit from the flexibility in transport provided by the automobile and truck, and the internal differentiation of the urban area continues as decentralization becomes predominant. The star-shaped urban area of the commercial-industrial city, based on fixed axes, is replaced by sprawl as the interstices are filled in.

In contrast to the early industrial city, where fixed transport led to *concentration* of functions in specific cities or in certain districts of cities, depending on the location of axial lines, the present industrial city exhibits a *dispersed* or sprawling pattern of functions. The degree of dispersal varies between cultural areas with the greatest being evident in the United States. In this area, the pattern is a response to the flexibility of transportation and communications. Indeed, Boal (1967) has called it a "flexible" city in contrast to the "pedestrian" and "axial" ones mentioned earlier. The ubiquitous automobile, truck, and bus permitted a freedom of location that was lacking when fixed rails dominated. The use of electricity further facilitated the re-location of factories, especially the sprawling one-floor buildings that prevail in the landscape today. Improved telecommunications contributed to this dispersal of the city functions. Whether such a dispersed, or sprawling, pattern will be the norm

FIGURE 2.11. The modern airport, especially those serving metropolitan needs and offering international connections, requires much space. Owing to its location at some distance from the core of the city, the airport has become an urban node with commercial and industrial activities. (Courtesy of the Wurgler Co., Inc., Omaha, Nebraska.)

of the future is open to question. Certainly, the freeway has helped the dispersal, acting as a new axis of development into the countryside. On the other hand, the growing energy crisis may be a factor in forcing a more compact and higher-density city. Such a pattern is certainly more evident in Europe and Socialist countries where public transportation plays a greater role than it does in the United States. It is also apparent that sprawl is not always a rational form of spatial organization as it is costly to the public in terms of utilities and it disrupts neighborhoods that are located *between* central city and urban fringe.

Sprawl in the suburbs is only one aspect of man's organization of space in the modern urban area—the *horizontal* organization. Space is also being organized *vertically* as the central core of the city is transformed through large projects. Owing to the threat of decay through the escape of stores, industry, and people to the fringe, the central portions of cities have had to change in accordance with new urban trends. With the increasing decentralization of shopping and housing, the Central Business District has become somewhat different in form and function. The means for this transformation is generally urban renewal of large tracts that include portions of the CBD and the surrounding zone of deterioration (see fig. 1.3). The primary elements of these tracts are office buildings, government centers, high-rise apartment buildings, and low-cost housing. Such a project takes cognizance of the groups that seem attached to this area—professional people, elderly and single persons, and displaced slum dwellers. The profile of the central core of American cities has risen wherever new high-rise structures, with an emphasis on use of aluminum and glass, become predominant. The most extreme examples of office skyscrapers are the World Trade Center (New York) and the Sears Tower (Chicago), both 110 stories.

The basis for the recent internal patterns of urbanization—horizontal sprawl and vertical office building—is a combination of technology and capitalism. The new *technological* developments which have permitted an increased freedom of location for residence, store, and factory (first apparent on a small scale in the commercial-industrial city), manifest themselves in the following areas: energy diversification through developments in electricity, and the transfer of oil and gas through pipelines; communications facilitated by telephone, radio, and television; mobility increased through the airplane and freeway; and building construction facilitated by utilizing light metals. As nations develop this technology, urban growth becomes almost a universal phenomenon. Supplementing this technology is the changed structure of *capitalism* as the decision-making process in industry and trade is separated from the privately-held company and factory. The corporation replaces the company, and banks and financial interests take over decisions related to policies of expansion. This expansion is no longer related primarily to the mere processes of physical production but to processes of research, education, advertising, and marketing as well—all of which depend on the interchange of ideas. The high office building is built to house this new form of capitalism, and white collar workers are necessary for handling the many forms of interdependent, specialized services which tend to group together in parts of the city: banker, stockbroker, company lawyer, consultant, university researcher, government servant, publication editor, television producer, advertising copywriter, freelance photographer, etc. Gottmann (1970, 324-5) calls this series of urban interlinkages or transactions the quaternary sector since they seem to be distinct from the normal tertiary activities. Although exchange of information has existed in the cores of all cities of history, the specialization is now much greater as the multiplicity of white collar workers indicates. The growth of such services has been a major factor in the expansion of cities upward through skyscrapers and outward through sprawl.

In contrast, then, to the era of the commercial-industrial city, when urban occupations were dominated by industry (the secondary sector), the recent growth of coalescing cities is characterized by the importance of tertiary and quaternary activities. Larger numbers of urban residents are becoming employed in retail and wholesale trade, services (professional, personal, and financial), government, transient residences, and recreation. The rise of these occupations is associated with the new technology, rising standards of living, the increasing participation of the government in national life, and the multiplicity of services required in modern industry, e.g., research, advertising, and telecommunications. All of these are related to the urban growth factor referred to by Blumenfeld (1965, 64) as the "specializing out" of functions; only the large metropolis can support the great proliferation of interdependent services of modern urbanism.

Superimposed over the economic organization of space, dominated by sprawl, is a fragmented political organization. The nature of sprawl with its disregard for distance and lack of sharp boundaries makes any overall organization difficult in American cities. The daily mobility and periodic transfers of larger numbers of people, together with the sprawl, has helped to cause a lack of cohesion within communities. Around most cities growth has spilled beyond central city limits and annexation of suburban communities is only carried out in certain cases. The result is the "metropolitan area," discussed in chapter 1, a fragmented political structure which is dominated by the cleavage between central city and suburbs.* When major metropolitan areas lie close to each other and finally coalesce, we have a conurbation or multi-centered metropolitan area. Finally, if a group of conurbations are close enough to form almost a continuous band of urban settlement, we have "megalopolis." Along the east coast of the United States from Boston to Washington, D.C. is the world's first example of such a "supercity" with 40 million people, and others are developing such as the Randstad (Holland) and Rhine-Ruhr (Germany).

These new variations in city form and in the organization of urban space in American cities are largely carried out by private interests. The actual growth is tremendous and is a tribute to American technology. However, as in the case of the commercial-industrial city, this metropolitan sprawl and high-rise development place the emphasis on the "growth" and not on the overall spatial order. Galbraith (1970, 20) states that a single minded concern for increasing production is the principal factor behind the worsening environment. He feels that the tendency of the modern economy is increasingly to serve not the public convenience but that of the more powerful producers. It is more "con-

---

*This dichotomy is discussed in chapter 9.

venient" to make automobiles that poison the air, to dump industrial waste that poisons the cities, to allow the cities to engulf the countryside in an unregulated sprawl, and to give the highways over to billboards (see fig. 2.12). Although the case may be overstated, the "growth" interests of a city, in a sense, appear to represent a continuation of the earlier form of elite control characteristic of single cities—control by a specialized group including bankers, loan and real estate personnel, contractors and builders, and major insurance companies. These construction interests, who are largely responsible for the patterns of our cities today, depend in large part upon continuous growth and expansion within a community, especially housing. When such growth lags over the country, the federal government helps to reactivate it. Frequently, such growth takes place locally at the expense of the public interest and a reaction sets in, resulting in zoning and comprehensive planning for cities; a power struggle then develops between municipal authorities and these private "growth" interests. The architect frequently finds himself in

FIGURE 2.12. The environment of most American cities is marred by the prevalence of commercial "strips," dominated by signs and enterprises served by the automobile.

the middle, for growth provides him with a milieu for activity but his training calls for respect for planning. Public participation also varies. Any improvement of the urban environment that demands sacrifices by way of higher taxes or reduced consumption may not gain support. In the suburb interest in community planning may run high, but the normal resident of a large city has little interest in the problem of effectively servicing a politically fragmented area of settlement—unless a zoning or other change affects his own piece of property.

The pattern of suburban sprawl is most characteristic of the United States, and is less evident in European cities where, until recently, mobility has been restricted. Nevertheless, since European population is often very dense, problems of urban decentralization appeared there early. The "Garden City" movement was important in England and the term "conurbation" was coined by Patrick Geddes, a British planner. Dense belts of urban settlement exist in parts of western Europe, especially along coasts, on river routes, and on the coal fields. However, private automobile ownership in Europe has lagged behind the United States, and it is only in the years since 1955 that similar centrifugal movements around cities have been possible for large numbers of people. However, the central core in European cities has remained remarkably stable owing to its continued drawing power for shopping and cultural attractions. Large park areas remain as legacies of the Renaissance-Baroque periods of royal influence. European cities generally are quite compact because of the high cost of land. Apartments dominate the housing which is served by a dense network of public transport. Sprawl is less evident, and planning is more effective owing to stronger central control, a tradition carried over from the past, and to the fact that cities are often overbounded, i.e., city limits extend beyond the built-up area. Perhaps most apparent are the regional plans around large cities like London, Paris, and Stockholm to control expansion through the use of New Towns and satellite communities. These differences between American and European cities are discussed further in a later chapter.

The decline of the single city and the development of new urban forms associated with a multi-core city have led to questions concerning the nature of planning. Many of the traditional planning principles are being challenged in the light of new discoveries in urban theory. Heyman (1965-66, 18-20) points out that cities are increasingly being viewed as centers of communication and interaction. He asks, therefore, if perhaps the emphasis on planning should not be placed on social aspects rather than on form or place, i.e., on the processes taking place rather than on the structure. For example, some planners point out that the term "land use" is imprecise in that it refers to both form and activity characteristic of space within the city. New approaches, therefore, are necessary for guiding city development. Planners have emphasized the necessity for recreating the smaller city of the past, thus avoiding the ills of the conurbation, but new voices are now raised in support of the acceptance of the universality of urban growth and planning for it. Perhaps future planning will have to take into account both the spatial and social aspects of cities in handling urban forces that are completely new in human history. Form will still be important, but the movements and interaction of people will constitute equally significant bases for city planning.

The rise of this urbanization trend in the past fifty years, and especially in those years since the end of World War II, has forced the experts to revise their thinking about the future of cities. In 1950 about 500 million more people in the world lived in cities over 5,000 than did in 1900. Between 1950 and 2000, it is estimated that over 2 billion more people will live in cities. One can imagine the problems involved in providing housing, jobs, food, and water for this number. One important aspect of the trend is that more and more people are tending to live in the big centers—metropolitan areas and conurbations. Thus London in 1800 contained only 8 percent of British population, but in 1961 it was 22 percent. The shares of Paris and New York had risen from less than 2 percent to 16.8 and 8.2 percent, respectively. In 1970, 173 cities in the world had more than 1 million inhabitants and 34 centers had over 3 million. These metropolitan areas and conurbations are the world centers of government, industry, trade and culture. The source of their urban growth is not only influx from the rural areas or smaller cities but also the birth rate increases that took place after 1945. Evidently, cities can grow larger and larger, even after a country has most of its population living in cities. The question of city growth versus urbanization, therefore, is very important.

THE CITY VERSUS URBANIZATION

In the following section the Davis hypothesis (1965, 42) to the effect that the phenomenon known as the *city* is old but that the process of *urbanization* is new, is developed. In other words, it was not until the modern period of city development that large numbers of people began to live in cities. Thus Athens, Rome, and Venice were the exceptions in their times of greatness and only a minority lived in cities. Table 2.2 illustrates the fact that worldwide urbanization is a phenomenon of the nineteenth and twentieth centuries. The percentage of world population living in cities over 5,000 has increased from 3 percent in 1800 to 37 percent in 1970. For cities over 20,000, the increase is from 2 percent

TABLE 2.2
Percentage of World Population Living in Cities

	> 5000	>20,000	>100,000
1800	3.0	2.4	1.7
1850	6.4	4.3	2.3
1900	13.6	9.2	5.5
1950	29.8	20.9	13.1
1970	37.4	32.1	23.7

Sources: Kingsley Davis, "Origin and Growth of Urbanization in the World," *American Journal of Sociology,* 60 (March 1955), 433. Emrys Jones, *Towns and Cities* (Oxford University Press, 1966), p. 32. Kingsley Davis, *World Urbanization, 1950-1970* (Univ. of California: Institute of International Studies, 1972), Vol. II, p. 40.

in 1800 to 32 percent in 1970. By the year 2000 it is estimated that 45 percent will live in cities over 20,000, and by 2050 the figure will be 90 percent. Theoretically, urbanization could *end* when the total population lives in cities, but the size of cities could *continue* to grow if birth rates exceeded death rates or if residents of smaller cities moved to larger ones.

Therefore, we truly live in an age of urban explosion. The graph (fig. 2.13) (Breese, 1969, 48-49) illustrates the increasing pace of population change and urbanization in all parts of the world for 1920, 1960, and 1980 (projected). However, great regional variations still exist. North America and Europe are the most urbanized while Asia and Africa are still largely rural. There are also vast differences between countries, e.g., England which is 80 percent urban, Bulgaria which is 33 percent, and Uganda which is only 2 percent. A few great cities in India do not make it urban (18 percent). The Communist countries are committed to rapid industrialization of society which is of course related to increasing urban possibilities for factories and housing. The Soviet Union was only 18 percent urban in 1917 when the Communist Revolution took place, but 50 years later over half the people lived in cities. The same attempt is being made in China but operating with a base of over 800 million people, the urban process is slow.

This process of urbanization is directly related to the increasing number of people that reside in large metropolitan areas and conurbations. The map-table (fig. 2.14) shows the world cities with over 2 million inhabitants in 1970. The New York Metropolitan Area alone included over 16 million people while those of Los Angeles, Chicago, Philadelphia, and Detroit ranged from 4 to 9 million. Equally large metropolitan areas existed in other countries—Tokyo-Yokohama (13 million), London (11 million), Buenos Aires (9 million), Paris (9 million), Shanghai (9 million), and Calcutta (7 million). Today it is estimated that

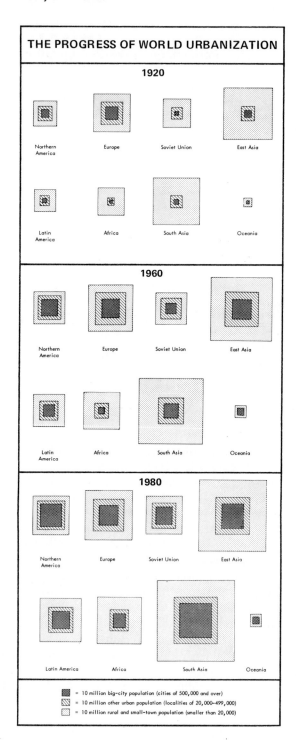

FIGURE 2.13. The graphs illustrate the changing proportions of urban centers within total populations in continental areas for (1) 1920, (2) 1960, and (3) 1980. The most significant changes are occurring in the developing areas. (Based on data contained in "The Urbanization of the Human Population" by Kingsley Davis. *Scientific American*, September 1965.)

half the total population of Great Britain lives in the conurbations while about three-fourths of the U.S. population is found in 275 metropolitan areas. Large conurbations also exist in the industrial belt of northwestern continental Europe, especially on or adjacent to the coal fields (see fig. 2.15). The Soviet Union and Japan also exhibit similar trends. These figures suggest that large cities and urbanization go together and are universal, regardless of political system.

However, this appearance of uniformity in urbanization may be deceiving. Berry (1973) has made a remarkable contribution to the understanding of urbanization by pointing out some of the cultural variations of this process and its human consequences. He feels that the Wirth model of the city as a "way of life" (discussed in Chapter 1 and mentioned again under the "commercial-industrial city"), which emphasizes the changes in social relationships brought about by the 19th Century industrial city, is not necessarily applicable to 20th Century metropolitan areas and conurbations in industrialized countries. In his view the Wirth factors of size, population density, and heterogeneity are replaced now by those of scale, interaction, and areal differentiation. In terms of scale, this new urbanization is characterized by a national urban system. The old rural-urban dichotomy has disappeared and we have what some call "urbanization without cities." Almost everyone in an industrialized country has an urban orientation, a characteristic that is helped by technological improvements in transportation and communications, e.g., jet aircraft and television. People are much more mobile, and innovations spread more rapidly than they did in the past. Increased interactional density is the result of people communicating more often on an impersonal basis—that is, face to face contacts are supplemented by others. Finally, urban society is actually becoming more differentiated rather than alike (as Wirth felt) since varying life styles emerge, e.g., ghetto versus middle class. This society is pluralistic or a mosaic of cultural groups, each with a set of values such as family, career, or localism.

According to Berry, however, the greatest consequence of urbanization, whether of a 19th Century or 20th Century type, is that it is occurring in different ways in cultural areas. These differences seem to be marked by varying degrees of public involvement in cities in order to counter the effects of *laissez-faire* urban development: this degree tends to be least in the United States and then progressively increases in the Third World, Western Europe, and socialist countries. These contrasts are discussed in later chapters.

Urban Centers of the World Over 2,000,000—1970

RANK	CITY	POPULATION IN 1970	RANK	CITY	POPULATION IN 1970
1	New York	16,077	36	Birmingham	
2	Tokyo	12,199		(U.K.)	2,981
3	London	11,544	37	Rome	2,920
4	Los Angeles	9,473	38	Harbin	
5	Buenos Aires	9,400		(Ha-erh-pin)	2,750
6	Paris	8,714	39	T'ai-yüan,	
7	Shanghai	8,500		Yü-tzu	2,725
8	São Paulo	8,405	40	Sydney	2,720
9	Peking	8,000	41	Washington,	
10	Calcutta	7,350		D.C.	2,666
11	Rio de Janeiro	7,213	42	Warsaw	2,664
12	Chicago	6,983	43	Istanbul	2,600
13	Essen-Dortmund-		44	Madras	2,600
	Duisburg	6,789	45	Boston	2,600
14	Moscow	6,750	46	Santiago	2,600
15	Cairo	5,600	47	Manchester	2,541
16	Bombay	5,100	48	Toronto	2,511
17	Seoul*	4,661	49	Bogotá*	2,500
18	Tientsin (T'ien-		50	Lima-Callao	2,500
	ching)	4,500	51	Montreal	2,437
19	Djakarta*	4,500	52	Athens	2,425
20	San Francisco-		53	Katowice-Zabrze-	
	Oakland	4,490		Bytom	2,424
21	Detroit	4,447	54	Hamburg	2,407
22	Philadelphia	4,355	55	Nagoya	2,353
23	Wu-han	4,250	56	Yokohama	2,326
24	Hong Kong	4,105	57	Canton	
25	Manila	4,100		(Kuang-chou)	2,300
26	Lü-ta; Lü-Shun (Port		58	Cleveland	2,248
	Arthur-Dairen)	4,000	59	West Berlin	2,240
27	Leningrad	3,850	60	Melbourne	2,200
28	Mukden		61	Taipei	2,150
	(Shen-yang)	3,750	62	Caracas*	2,147
29	Mexico City*	3,541	63	Singapore	2,113
30	Chungking	3,500	64	Bangkok	2,100
31	Osaka	3,307	65	Alexandria*	2,061
32	Teheran	3,250	66	Budapest*	2,060
33	Karachi	3,246	67	Glasgow	2,008
34	Delhi	3,100	68	Nanking	2,000
35	Madrid	2,990	69	Ch'eng-tu	2,000

Populations all in thousands.

*Urban center with entire population within central city.

Source: Kingsley Davis, *World Urbanization, 1959-1970* (Univ. of California: Institute of International Studies, 1969), I, Table F, Part 3, pp. 239-240.

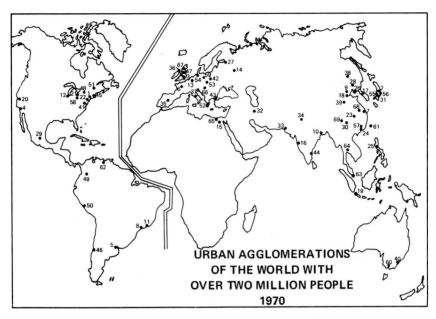

FIGURE 2.14. The number of metropolitan areas with over two million people has increased from 26 in 1950 to 43 in 1960 and 69 in 1970. These large urban areas are located in the most urbanized-industrial regions or constitute capitals, ports, or industrial cities in certain less urbanized countries. (Source: Kingsley Davis, *World Urbanization, 1950-1970,* [Univ. of California: Institute of International Studies, [1969], [I, Table F, Part 3, pp. 239-240.)

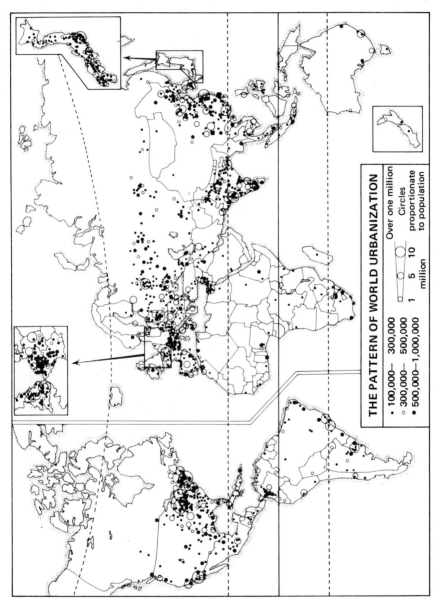

FIGURE 2.15. The map illustrates world urbanization by locating cities of over 100,000 population. Major concentrations of cities are found in the north-eastern United States and adjacent Canada, much of Europe, an eastwest belt in the Soviet Union, and portions of southeast Asia, including especially India and China. (Adapted by permission from an original map by J. Beaujeu-Garnier, *Geography of Population*, 1966, Plate 29.)

CHAPTER 3

URBANIZATION AND THE ENVIRONMENT

Everything in an urban area is related to everything else. This general principle of environmental unity expresses the basic idea behind all ecosystems that "all the elements and processes of environment are interrelated and interdependent, and that a change in one will lead to a change in the others" (Detwyler and Marcus, 1972, 10). Furthermore, such urban ecosystems are open in that they cannot function independently of the rest of the world. Finally, the primary characteristic of such an ecosystem is that feedbacks exist. Man initiates an action affecting the physical environment which eventually feeds back or affects him, often negatively (Man → Environment → Man). For example, urban man pumped oil, gas, and water from the subsurface of Long Beach, California, an action that eventually resulted in a considerable amount of subsidence in the port area of the city. Retaining walls were constructed to hold back the ocean, and treated water was pumped undergound at great expense to reduce the subsidence. Thus the feedback was apparent. In this chapter several similar processes are discussed by which urban man has affected his environment with resulting feedbacks:

Man chooses a location for a settlement that possesses site and situational attributes which will affect its later development.
Urban man changes the surface terrain.
Urban man's alteration of underground terrain affects the city above.
Urban man produces a micro-climate.
Urban man affects the patterns of vegetation and noise.

Some of the interrelationships between these processes are shown in the model (see fig. 3.1).

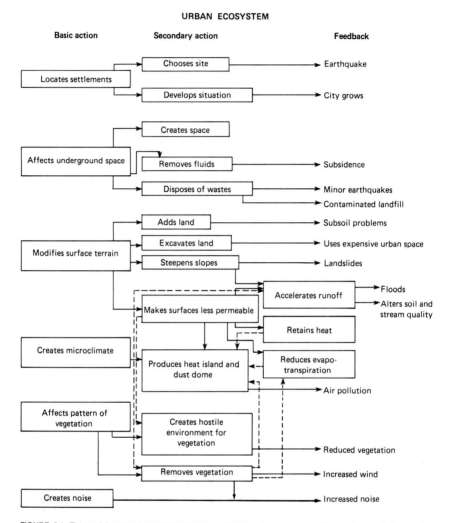

FIGURE 3.1. This model portrays those interrelationships within the urban ecosystem which are discussed in the chapter.

THE PROCESSES

MAN CHOOSES A LOCATION FOR A SETTLEMENT THAT POSSES-SES SITE AND SITUATIONAL ATTRIBUTES WHICH WILL AFFECT ITS LATER DEVELOPMENT.   The effects of terrain on urban areas are seen in the concepts of situation and site. If the situation is good, the city will generally grow economically because of good access to other cities. On the other hand, the site will influence the local possibilities of construction. These concepts warrant more detailed examination.

Historically cities are supported by their external relations with hinterlands of varying extent. Generally speaking, at a given time in the history of settlement in an area there is a need for a certain center to serve it. Within this area the actual spot at which it could be located may vary. The final selection of the spot may be based on the most advantageous location for serving the region by the prevailing mode of transportation or it may be related to a purely local aspect such as defense, water supply, or mineral deposit. Once the spot is selected, the settlement is "committed" but its ability to serve the area may vary with time. The external connections to other areas may become inadequate as forms of transport change and the size of the hinterlands vary. The way in which the center may exploit this relative location through a *long* period of time will determine its growth. One may, therefore, define situation as the location of the settlement with respect to the area it serves, i.e., its "nodality" or accessibility to other areas. Site, on the other hand, is the exact spot within the area where settlement is located.

Obviously a settlement may have different combinations of situation and site. If both are good the settlement will probably grow and if both are poor the odds are against it, especially in the long run. However, a town with good situation and poor site (New Orleans) has definite advantages in these days of technology over the town with poor situation and good site (Santa Fe). A poor site like that of New Orleans can be improved through drainage, fills, excavations, dikes, tunnels, etc., but it is much more difficult to change a poor natural location. Santa Fe's situation was fine in the early days but its subsequent growth was hindered when the transcontinental railroad bypassed it in favor of more accessible Albuquerque.

1. **Situation.** Situation then is essentially an urban attribute which leads to the greatest city growth if its location with respect to other areas is good. It is necessary to focus attention on the nodality of the spot and the possibilities of external connection and support. Relationships between a settlement and its supporting area are mutual—food, raw materials, labor, and money come into the center from the hinterland and the settlement provides the necessary jobs, goods, and services for the external areas. The situation or nodality of a settlement, therefore, is a reflection of its ability to serve as a focus and to attract people, goods, and money. This nodality is of two kinds—natural and artificial.

Natural nodality is provided by terrain and the focus of routes. For example, valleys may converge on a spot, or a gap may exist in a barrier, or the lowest bridging point of a stream may lie near an estuary. Contact between different forms of transportation—land, river, and sea—is particularly important in such nodal places. At the focus of natural routes, advantages exist for concentrating people on a permanent basis. The focus has "centrality" for a large area, but the different routes may require a change in the form of transport, i.e., there is a "break-in-transport." Accessibility is improved by technology as more efficient means of transportation—diesel trains, semi-trailer trucks, automobiles, ships, and pipelines—utilize the natural routes.

On the other hand, *artificial* nodality is important for many larger cities. This form of attraction, which can help or restrict natural nodality, is social and political in nature. The attractions provided by Salt Lake City and Mecca are social or cultural since they represent important religious centers. However, perhaps the most common type of artificial situation is related to the influence of political boundaries, thereby changing the external relations of a city. Europe provides many examples of artificial situation. The natural supporting area of Hamburg, once based in great part on the Elbe traffic and extending to Prague, is now cut off rather abruptly by the Iron Curtain. Salonika in Greece no longer is the great port for Macedonia as Yugoslavia controls much of this historical region. Vienna, situated at the crossroads of main natural routes in Central Europe and once the capital of a great empire, now dominates a small "rump" state. Political status alone may be responsible for considerable urban growth in spite of a poor natural situation. Cited as examples in such cases are those capital cities chosen as a compromise to satisfy the majority of people in divided countries—Warsaw, Madrid, Washington, and Bonn. Even the suburbs share in the artificial hinterlands created by capital cities.

One of the best current examples of artificial restrictions on nodality is West Berlin, the exclave of the Federal Republic of Germany (see fig. 3.2). Cities require an uninterrupted supporting area for continual growth, but West Berlin exists 100 miles behind the Iron Curtain in the Communist state of East Germany. Not only is the city cut off by the "Wall" from East Berlin, the capital of the Communist state (see fig. 3.3), but also its external relations with West Germany are severely limited by the restrictions placed upon rail, road, and river-canal traffic. Only the air traffic avoids Soviet control, a factor that made it possible in 1948 for the 2 million residents to receive daily supplies for 11 months by an airlift over the Russian blockade. To compensate for the restrictions placed on its economy by the lack of market for industries and by the loss of central functions for the surrounding area, West Berlin receives a large financial subsidy from the Federal Republic. These economic ties between the Republic and a portion of the former capital of prewar Germany reflect the political connections which exist because Allied forces remain in the city as a balancing force to the Russian threat. The public services also reflect the artificial situation: the subway system, for exam-

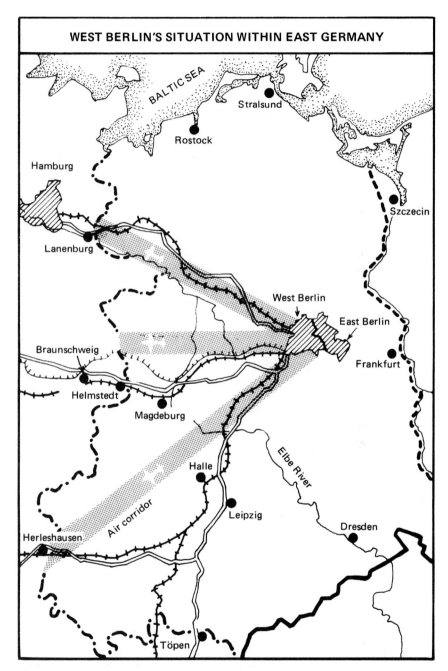

WEST BERLIN'S SITUATION WITHIN EAST GERMANY

BALTIC SEA

Stralsund

Rostock

Hamburg

Szczecin

Lanenburg

West Berlin

East Berlin

Braunschweig

Frankfurt

Helmstedt

Magdeburg

Elbe River

Halle

Air corridor

Leipzig

Dresden

Herleshausen

Töpen

FIGURE 3.2. West Berlin is located 100 miles inside the communist state of East Germany. This city has no naturaı hinterland but must depend on external support from West Germany via land, air, and water routes. (Source: Presse-und Informationsamt des Landes Berlin, 1968.)

FIGURE 3.3. The "wall" artificially separates West and East Berlin.

ple, is intersected by the "Wall" while for sewage the city pays a high fee for the use of spreading grounds in adjacent East Germany (Merritt, 1973). In recent years restrictions on the normal external relations of the city are beginning to have an effect on its economic viability (e.g., firms moving to West Germany), thereby emphasizing the importance of a good natural "situation."

2. **Site.** Although the different types of sites that cities have occupied possess considerable historical interest, the impact of site on urban development is of more immediate practical interest. Cities today are constrained to varying degrees by their sites, which in a sense are "feeding back" on man for having chosen this location. The choice of defensive sites like Athens and Edinburgh has actually worked to the benefit of these cities today, as they do not greatly disrupt urban development and actually serve as attractive landmarks for tourists and residents. On the other hand, the sites of many other cities have had extensive effects on urban growth. For example, superimposing a grid pattern over the hills of San Francisco has led to many construction and traffic problems, including "run away" cars from careless parking. The valleys which run through the cities of South Wales (Llewellyn, 1940) and western Pennsylvania are sites of smoky industries, while in Los Angeles a small creekbed—the Arroyo Seco—is the site of "linear pollution" generated along a major freeway. In New York City the marshes of New Jersey west of the

city have been barriers to residential growth and a visitor coming from this direction is confronted with one of the greatest concentrations of oil refineries and chemical industries in the United States. The feedbacks in such urban sites are obvious.

An interesting way in which terrain has affected urban growth is found in Lincoln, Nebraska. In this city of 160,000, unbalanced expansion has occurred to the south and east because of water and rail barriers to the north and west (see fig. 3.4). Consequently, city officials in their concern with the cost of providing services in the outlying areas have

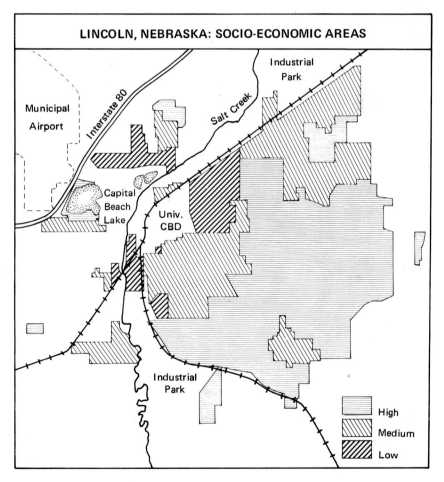

FIGURE 3.4. Lincoln, the capital of Nebraska, shows an unbalanced growth to the east and south caused in part by the barrier of Salt Creek. Socioeconomic areas illustrate some tendencies toward a concentric pattern. (Source: *Community Health Survey, 1964 and 1968*, Lincoln-Lancaster County Health Dept., Lincoln, Nebraska, 1969, p.8)

attempted to slow growth in these directions. The most apparent of these costs is sewage, which cannot be handled easily from the existing plant due to distance and terrain barriers. The city government thus set limits to eastward expansion, and in the decade 1965-75 a number of conflicts developed over this artificial restriction on "growth." Lovelace (1965) states that Lincoln is a good example of the influence of terrain on city planning.

Another way in which terrain constrains urbanism is when the foundations of buildings prove unstable and provide direct feedback. A famous example is the Leaning Tower of Pisa, which over a period of 600 years has settled unevenly owing to the presence of a layer of brackish clay (Legget, 1973, 200). One of the world's best examples, however, of the juxtaposition of two buildings that illustrate foundation engineering at its worst and at its best is found in Mexico City. This urban center is located on an old lake plain where layers of sand and clay are charged with water. The foundation of the Palace of Fine Arts rests on a thick layer of clay which has caused the building to settle over 10 feet. On the other hand, the newly constructed Latin American Tower which is built on piles driven 100 feet into a sand layer has not settled at all (Legget, 1973, 205-7).

Perhaps the supreme example of feedback from terrain is when an entire city is located on an earthquake zone. The two great zones of weakness in the earth's crust are, first, the axis that parallels the Mediterranean Sea and runs into Asia and, secondly, the mountainous rim of the Pacific Ocean. The earthquakes that occurred at Skopje, Yugoslavia (1963) and Tashkent, Russia (1966) are examples of the first belt, while those at Anchorage, Alaska (1964) and Peking, China (1976) are representative of the second. Although some progress has been made in predicting the occurrence of these hazards, the primary protection against them is two-fold: avoidance of construction in particular locations on the site and the designing of buildings to withstand the shocks, at least in part. Unfortunately, the first of these measures seemed to have been ignored at Anchorage prior to the quake in 1964. The most serious destruction resulted from landslides in areas which were underlain by silty clays with some lenses of sand. A report covering these geological conditions was available from the U.S. Geological Survey four years before, but for a number of reasons was not utilized for planning in the Anchorage area. According to Legget (1973, 408) the planning department was occupied with other tasks and lacked a geologist who might have interpreted the implications of the report.

One of the factors influencing the manner in which a cultural group responds to a hazard like an earthquake is the politics that may be involved. This factor is well illustrated by the 1963 earthquake in Skopje, Yugoslavia (United Nations, 1970; Fisher, 1964). I visited the city a day after the quake and witnessed the extensive damage in which over 2,000 people lost their lives and some 150,000 were made homeless. One reason for the high number of fatalities was a large district of poorly constructed houses occupied by minority groups. After the disaster the politics of Yugoslavia complicated the planning for a new city. The country is a federal state designed to fuse the six major groups into one nation while giving each some autonomy. One of the states is Macedonia and its capital is Skopje. Although earthquakes have occurred on this site over thousands of years, the Macedonians in 1963 felt enough historical attachment to the location to insist that the city be reconstructed in the same spot. The Yugoslav federal government in Belgrade supported this position because the seismic zone is rather extensive and any relocation would have to be some distance away. The Belgrade government also felt that if buildings were located away from the major seismic zones in the site area and if they were designed to withstand major shocks, the existing site would be acceptable. However, the federal government did insist that the Macedonians change their policy of concentrating so much of the new development (including industry) in Skopje and instead decentralize it to other cities in the area. In doing this, Belgrade was handling a political problem with delicate measures: at all costs, it wished to preserve the unity of a rather precarious multi-ethnic state. By the 1970s a rather remarkable new Skopje had grown up, designed by an international team of architects and planners who operated under the auspices of the United Nations. The city, which had 165,000 inhabitants at the time of the quake, had over 220,000 by 1970 and is projected for 350,000 in 1981. The city is also planned *around* the two linear zones of seismic weakness that project into the site, and buildings themselves are designed to withstand most earthquake shocks. Regional and local plans exist which allow for zones of industry, recreation, and agriculture. Altogether, Skopje appears to be a model for urban planning in an earthquake zone.

URBAN MAN CHANGES THE SURFACE TERRAIN.   Urban man modifies the terrain in two ways which feed back on him: he not only changes the profile of the land but also increases its impermeability. Both of these act together to increase the run off of water which may affect the quality and quantity of streams and the characteristics of soil and urban micro-climate. A quantitative assessment of man-made changes in surface terrain as a result of urbanization is almost impossible to make. However, it is estimated that in the United States over 4,000 acres of agricultural land are urbanized each day. This means that an area of rural and generally unmodified land the size of Delaware is altered in some way each year (Detwyler, 1972, 136).

Perhaps one of the most common examples of man's modification of terrain in urban areas is represented by local quarrying or mining activities. Urban construction requires building stone and gravel which are extremely low in value per unit of weight and thus expensive to ship. Consequently, most cities have stone quarries or gravel pits which compete for space with new development, e.g., residential subdivisions. In Chicago some of the most accessible areas underlain by building stone have been built over, forcing construction firms to move out to the fringe where overburdens are thicker. These additional costs of shipping and excavation added over one dollar per ton to delivered costs in the inner city (Risser and Major, 1967, in Tank, 1973, 451). This feedback is reflected in a greater degree of urban sprawl.

Even more serious are actual mining activities within or under a city. The quarry in Aberdeen, Scotland, the "granite city," is located within the built-up area. In Butte, Montana, the great open copper pit in the city is encroaching on the downtown (see fig. 3.5). The fact that this re-

FIGURE 3.5 The large open pit copper mine of Butte, Montana is encroaching on the Central Business District of the city. (Personal photo.)

source, which has formed a rather precarious economic base for the city for 100 years, continues *under* the CBD has led to plans for re-locating the *entire* District. As of the mid 1970s, the final decision had not been made because opinion in the city concerning the move was about equally divided. Here the feedback from man's mining activity in an urban area may be drastic.

The steepening of slopes in urban areas has several feedbacks, one of which involves increased runoff of water and silt, which in turn leads to floods and increased sediment and waste materials in water bodies. Reports showed, for example, that sediment from urban developments in the Potomac River Basin ran as high as 50 times that yielded from nearby agricultural lands (Detwyler, 1972, 139). This sedimentation loss is increased, of course, if vegetation has been removed, because the soil is more exposed to erosion forces and the cohesion of particles is reduced. In general, those soils most susceptible to runoff are fine sands and silts without much clay.

The increased runoff is a double-barreled process—the result of both steepened slopes and decreased permeability of these slopes. Man has created an artificial profile of slopes which retain less water now than they did in the past. An example of a creek area in Washington, D.C. before and after man's action illustrates the possibilities of feedback (see fig. 3.6). Man increasingly paves over surfaces, including especially streets and parking lots, which allow for little moisture penetration. The ratio of runoff to absorption of water in the soil is increased. Air, which is vital to the growth of soil organisms and plant roots, is also lacking. When this happens, soils tend to dry out and slump, another example of a feedback on man.

A major secondary feedback of this runoff, of course, is a flood. The chances of a 50-year flood, i.e., one that occurs once in 50 years on the average and which inundates the floodplain, are increased by the accelerated runoff in urban areas (see fig. 3.7). The diagram from Leopold (1968, 5) illustrates how the combined effects of two factors—increased storm sewers and greater impervious area—can increase the mean annual flood in a drainage area (see fig. 3.8). Values on the curves are ratios of discharge after urbanization to discharge before urbanization. An unusual climatic situation, such as a 10-inch rainfall in a few hours, will naturally have greater effect in an urban area where the runoff is rapid than in a rural one where storm sewers are absent and the soils pervious. Actual damage from such a flood may depend on human perception of the possibilities of such a hazard (see fig. 3.9). This perception, in turn, is related to the probable frequency of the event. As shown in the graph (Detwyler, 1972, 176), people make adjustments if floods occur often (Darlington), but do very little if they are infrequent (Desert

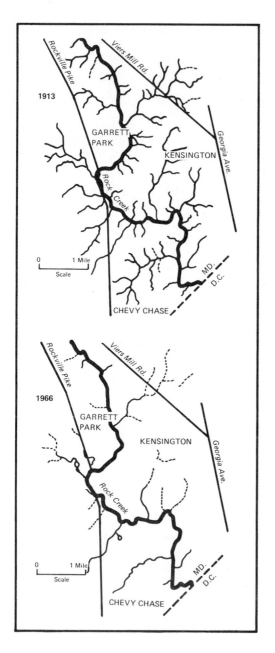

FIGURE 3.6. The alteration of a drainage pattern in a portion of Washington, D.C. as a result of urbanization. (Reproduced by permission of Unesco from *Hydrological Effects of Urbanization* © Unesco 1974.)

FIGURE 3.7. The Mississippi River in flood. Note that the entire flood plain is under water. In such a situation, restricting settlement in the plain seems more logical than building expensive protective devices. (Photo courtesy of Stan Dart.)

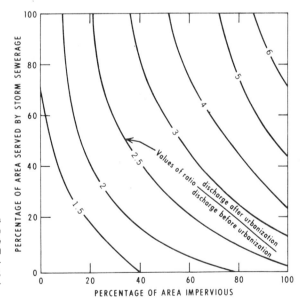

FIGURE 3.8. The combined effects of paving and storm sewers on mean annual flood for a one-square mile drainage area in a city. (Reprinted with permission of the U.S. Geological Survey from Luna Leopold, "Hydrology for Urban Land Planning," *USGS Circular* 554, 1968.)

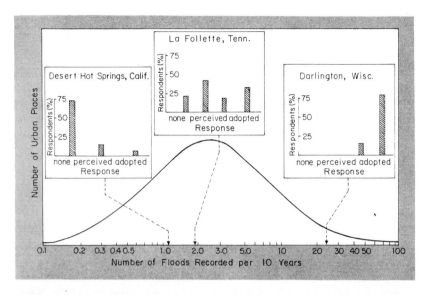

FIGURE 3.9. Flood frequencies for 496 urban places in the United States. Insets show response to flood in three communities, each experiencing different frequencies. Counter-measures appear to increase with frequency, although uncertainty is evident among a large number of communities. (From *Urbanization and Environment* by Thomas R. Detwyler and Melvin G. Marcus and Contributors. © 1972 by Wadsworth Publishing Co., Inc., Belmont, CA 94002. Reprinted by permission of the publisher, Duxbury Press.)

Hot Springs). Most places, however, exhibit no consistent frequency and it is in these sites that people are uncertain as to whether to adjust to the hazard or not (LaFollette).

Areas subject to flood are generally protected in two ways—through physical measures or by zoning. Physical protection, the more expensive approach, consists of a watershed project of ponds, levees, and reservoirs often constructed by the Corps of Engineers after a cost-benefit analysis. Agricultural practices of terracing and contour plowing are also encouraged. The aim is to "keep the flood away from the people." In recent years, however, the costs of disaster relief from floods has increased, in great part due to settlement taking place in flood plains faster than protective works can be built. Therefore, a second and less expensive approach—flood plain management—is gaining favor. Under this approach "people are kept away from the flood." Those portions of flood plains apt to be struck by the more serious floods (e.g., 100-year) are delineated on maps and zoned for those land uses that minimize settlement and damage from floods. The U.S. Government has encouraged such an approach in urban areas by underwriting flood plain insurance for those cities that have such zoning and by withholding federal aid if communities do not participate.

The quality of streams and other water bodies in urban areas is also changed by the sediment derived from accelerated runoff and by the dumping of waste products. Urban water bodies can become so overloaded with inorganic nutrients that their character is completely changed. Plant life increases and the number of fish may be reduced from the loss of customary food. This process by which lakes and streams are enriched by nutrients is called eutrophication.

Still another feedback of man's alteration of the surface terrain within cities is a landslide. Perhaps the best examples of such phenomena occur in Los Angeles where builders try to create flat residential sites in hilly terrain (Schoustra and Lake, 1969). Until 1963 they were required by grading ordinance to maintain a 1.5 to 1 horizontal to vertical ratio in slopes but this apparently was insufficient for soil stability so it was modified to 2:1. The soils in the outer portions of such slopes are generally less compact and more permeable than the main body of the hill. This condition is the result of exposure to the elements, lack of vegetation in the Mediterranean (dry summer) climate, or, in the case of fill, inadequate compaction. When *heavy* rains occur, these upper soils become saturated and seepage develops in planes parallel to the slope with the increased pressure causing liquefaction, or compaction, of the uncemented particles. This process causes loss of shear strength, or binding quality, in the soils resulting in mud flows. The situation apparently is exaggerated if the soils are of silty texture, because they are less resistant than clays to the penetration of moisture. With this kind of process, the steepness of the slope is obviously a factor in the mud slides that often occur in Los Angeles during periods of heavy winter rainfall. In some cases, whole rows of houses down slope have been buried. In addition to increasing the horizontal-vertical slope ratio, other planning measures for slopes include improved drainage devises, planting of vegetation, setback requirements for buildings above slopes, and subsurface investigations prior to development.

Still another feedback of man's modification of surface terrain occurs from waste disposal. Only a fraction of the nation's 90,000 waste-disposal sites meet the minimum requirements of sanitary landfills: daily cover, no open burning, and no water pollution problems. Instead, urban refuse is disposed of in areas where environmental problems can exist. For example, dumping on flood plains leads to contamination of the water because of the high water table and possibilities of runoff of the refuse. On the urban fringe, new subdivisions frequently have to rely on septic tanks, which may contaminate wells, especially as the residential density increases. In one suburb of Minneapolis, one-half of the wells were at one time infected from septic tanks. The nature of the soil is critical in septic tank location. Detwyler states that soils through which water percolates more slowly than one inch per hour are inadequate absorbers (Detwyler, 1972, 145). On the other hand, soils that permit percolation faster than 12 inches per hour commonly allow groundwater contamination. Generally, seepage sites should be at least 100 feet from any water supply well, 50 feet from surface waters such as streams, and 25 feet from the foundations of buildings.

In some cities located on water bodies man has altered the site by adding land to it. For example, the port area of Toronto, Canada, has been enlarged by building out into Lake Ontario using fill from excavations in the central part of the city (Legget, 1973, 378-9). Being artificially created, such terrain is susceptible to feedbacks on man, i.e., sewage contamination, if land use controls are not developed and enforced.

URBAN MAN'S ALTERATION OF THE UNDERGROUND TERRAIN AFFECTS THE CITY ABOVE.   The activities of man in cities have affected also the terrain below ground producing in some cases feedbacks of significance. Mentioned here are three different cases.

The first of these cases involves the use of underground space. Some cities have found that the terrain below ground is suitable for caves which can be used for light industry, storage, and even offices. Locationally, such caves are very convenient because they may be much closer to the center of the city than sites located in the suburbs. The costs in this case involve overcoming vertical rather than horizontal distance and the renovation of the interiors. One of the best examples of such use of underground space is Kansas City, Missouri, which is located on limestone topography. Natural caves have existed below the city for a long time, but were only used for quarrying until 1955 when a manufacturer of precision optical instruments built his plant underground to avoid vibrations from passing cars and trucks. Since that time such developments have been expanded until Kansas City has become a world leader in use of underground space for purposes such as warehousing, freezer storage, manufacturing, and office and laboratory space. The limestone, which is over 20 feet thick and dips less than one foot per mile, is covered by a dense shale layer that protects it from downward seepage of water. The natural subsurface temperature is about 50° year around, making it feasible to adjust to different uses.

A second case of man's effect on underground terrain which has had strong feedbacks is land subsidence from withdrawal of fluids underground. One of the most publicized examples of such subsidence is the port area of Long Beach, California (Poland and Davis, 1969 in McKenzie and Utgard, 1972, 79-82). Over a period of 50 years an area of 25 square miles was affected, leaving a basin-like depression amounting to

29 feet in the center; horizontal movements of nearly 10 feet were associated with the vertical movement (see fig. 3.10). The cause is primarily
decrease in fluid pressure in the oil field from removal of oil, gas, and
water, thereby increasing the grain-to-grain load and causing compaction. The process, which seems to be unique to this oil field, has been
going on since drilling started in the 1930s, and the general opinion is
that compaction has occurred in the relatively impermeable beds of silt,
clay, and shale that confine the permeable reservoir beds. Early remedial
measures consisted of levees, retaining walls, and earth filling—in
total, very expensive. More positive measures included repressuring
in the oil zones by water injection, a process that could only be carried
out after unitization of the 117 producers. This seawater was treated
chemically to inhibit corrosion and prevent bacterial growth. By 1978
the subsidence had been halted, and even exhibited some rebound,
while many effects on the landscape had been erased by a $20 million
program of earth filling.

Subsidence has also been a characteristic of the historic city of Venice, Italy (Berghinz, 1971). Built on a number of islands in the upper
Adriatic Sea, this famous medieval city with its numerous canals has felt
the impact of modern technology. Mestre, an industrial city on the main-
land, had pumped large amounts of water from aquifers in the vicinity,

FIGURE 3.10. Subsidence of land in the port area of Long Beach, California. Withdrawal of oil, gas, and water from the
ground had led, in the 1960s, to a maximum subsidence of 29 feet. (Photo courtesy of Civil Engineering Division, Port
of Long Beach.)

and this exploitation is believed to have caused an average subsidence of one inch every four years. Air pollution from the refineries and smelters of this city have also led to deterioration of the marble and bronze ornaments of Venice, thereby adding a second feedback to man's impact on this historic site. Finally, the alteration of the lagoon's topography, which is necessary for industrial expansion and to allow large ships into the port, apparently has contributed to greater frequency of high water ("acqua alta") in St. Mark's Square; at numerous times each year wooden planks are laid down for pedestrians to avoid the high water. Altogether, Venice is an excellent example of a delicate urban ecosystem that has been disturbed by man. Here the industrial "growth" interests of Italy are arrayed against those advocating the historic preservation of the city.

A third case involving man's effects on urban underground terrain is the series of Denver earthquakes in which the correlation between man's action and the feedback has been well established. In the 1960s contaminated waste water from the Army Arsenal north of the city was disposed of in a 12,000 foot well drilled for this purpose. Following the first injection of fluid wastes down this well in 1962, small earthquakes began to occur in the Denver area and continued over a period of several years until injection ceased in January of 1966. During this period some 710 quakes were recorded with 75 of them severe enough to be felt. The epicenters of most of them were within five miles of the well. Correlation between fluid injection and earthquakes is shown in the diagram and the effects of the period of no injection (September 1963-September 1964) on the reduction of quakes is clearly evident (see fig. 3.11). Evans (1966 in Tank, 1973, 76-87) hypothesized that the waste water increased fluid pressure in the well reducing frictional resistance to movement of rock masses along fault planes. The elastic wave energy released by the movement was recorded as an earthquake. This hypothesis seems to have been justified, for although the quakes continued for a year or two after injection ceased, possibly as a result of lag, no real disturbances have occurred in recent years.

URBAN MAN PRODUCES A MICRO-CLIMATE.   Many authorities have identified an urban climate that differs from the rural surroundings. The fact that this phenomenon is man-made is supported by evidence that shows it not only occurs in cities of varied topography but also that the changes are greater in larger cities and on weekdays when man is more active. The most serious aspect of this micro-climate is that it feeds back on man through the process of air pollution, but other feedbacks occur in terms of fog, growing season, etc.

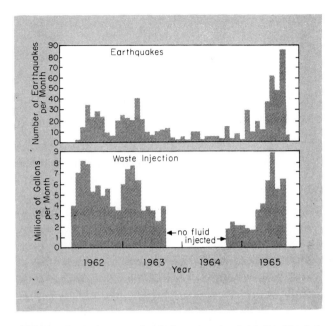

FIGURE 3.11 Relation between earthquake frequency and waste injection at the Rocky Mountain Arsenal near Denver, Colorado. (Reprinted with permission of American Geological Institute from *Geotimes*, "Man-made Earthquakes in Denver," by D. M. Evans, No. 9, 1966, fig. 3, p. 13.)

Perhaps the major aspect of urban climate is the increase in average temperatures. Daily weather forecasts generally predict lower temperatures in the suburbs than in the central city and the averages in the rural areas are even lower. Generally, these differences amount to only a few degrees in terms of averages; London climatic records for a period of 30 years, for example, show that average maximum temperatures in the city, the suburbs, and the surrounding countryside were, respectively, 58.3, 57.6, and 57.2 degrees and the average minimums 45.2, 43.1, and 41.8 degrees. These contrasts in temperatures between city and country are normally greatest in winter and during the work days of the week. The primary factor in the development of city temperatures is the presence of an *urban environment* which stores and traps not only solar energy but also the heat produced by the city itself.

Temperatures are raised in the city as large volumes of air near the surface are heated by the artificial environment. Lowry describes the various elements in this environment.[1] The rocklike surface materials of

1. William P. Lowry, "The Climate of Cities," *Scientific American* 217 (August 1967), 15-23. Many of the ideas in this section are drawn from this source.

the city's buildings, streets, and parking lots absorb more solar energy in less time than soils and, therefore, by the end of a day have stored up large amounts of heat (see fig. 3.12). This acceptance of heat in a city is magnified by the orientation of surfaces which reflect and absorb heat energy; for example, the effect of tall buildings is to increase the total amount of absorbing surface per unit of ground space. More energy is also available for heating the surface air in a city because evaporation, a process that requires heat energy, is reduced when standing water is removed quickly via drainpipes, gutters, and sewers. Finally, the dust particles in the air over a city, although reflecting sunlight and thereby reducing the amount of solar heat reaching ground surfaces, also retard

FIGURE 3.12. The large amount of concrete surface in a CBD is illustrated by St. Louis, Missouri.

the outflow of heat—thus serving to further increase the temperatures near the surface. In summary, therefore, large volumes of surface air in a city are heated by the artificial environment as the hard surface areas store heat and reduce evaporation while the dust particles retard heat loss.

Man not only creates an urban environment for trapping heat energy but also supplements the sun in producing this energy himself. The city has many sources of heat which the countryside lacks or has in far smaller numbers. Among them are factories, vehicles, and even air conditioners, which of course must pump out hot air in order to produce their cooling effect. In winter, when heating systems are in operation, the production of heat is further increased.

The city, therefore, builds up heat, cumulatively each day, producing a so-called urban "heat island" surrounded by a cooler rural countryside. During daylight hours the city builds up a lead on the country in the absorption of heat because the sun's rays in the early morning and late afternoon are more effective in heating the many vertical surfaces, while in the countryside these rays are reflected from the ground. At night the cooling of higher urban surfaces by radiation creates a cool layer of air which traps below it warm pockets of air that are still being warmed by heat stored in the hard surfaces; on the other hand, the rural areas cool rapidly by unobstructed radiation and through the action of wind. By dawn, the city is likely to be a few degrees warmer than its surroundings. During work days of the week, this process is intensified by the heat produced in factories, vehicles, and heating systems. Tall chimneys, quiet during weekends, now send out heated air at high levels and add numerous particles of dust and smoke to the surface air retarding the outflow of heat. The overall result of this process of producing and trapping heat in a city over a weekly period is to build up a surplus "island of heat" that is confirmed by isotherms. Associated with the "heat island" is a second phenomenon known as the "dust dome," which is related to the introduction of particles into the air by combustion processes— burning of coal, oil, gasoline, and refuse—creating a phenomenon over the city known as the "dust dome." The larger particles remain suspended over the city all day while the smaller are carried upwards and outwards over the suburbs. This dome-shaped layer of dust and haze is visible over most large cities.

The concepts of "heat island" and "dust dome" reveal conditions characteristic of large cities and metropolitan areas. In most cases the normal circulation of air between town and country serves to break up the concentration of particles that leads to air pollution. Furthermore,

natural mixing of upper and lower air, which also reduces concentrations, is facilitated by the *unstable* conditions found in most cities, i.e.,
heavy cooler air overrides warm air. However, if a *stable* condition develops, i.e., a temperature inversion, in which the lapse rate is reversed
and cool air rests below warmer air, concentrations of pollutants build
up because of lack of circulation. These inversions are especially bad if
they develop in a valley or basin where horizontal winds are blocked and
prevented from upsetting the stable condition. Three types of temperature inversion or stable conditions exist—radiation, topographic, and
subsidence.

The radiation inversion develops from rapid radiation or loss of heat
from the ground or from the top of the dust dome. In both cases clear
skies are essential. When the ground loses heat to the sky quickly, a cool
layer of air develops which in humid conditions becomes a ground fog.
If the loss of heat occurs from the top of the dust dome, the particles cool
and become nuclei on which the moisture in the air condenses as fog.
This fog develops first in the clear air near the top of the dome and
becomes thicker by downward growth. In both cases of a radiation inversion, the "stable" situation is generally temporary and breaks up during
the day with normal solar heating. However, it can persist if the dust
dome and climatic conditions prevent solar heating.

A topographic inversion develops in a valley situation where cold air
drainage and lack of horizontal winds prevent its dispersion. In the famous episode at Donora, Pennsylvania in 1948, pollutants from steel,
zinc, and sulphuric acid plants became concentrated in the valley long
enough to cause over 6,000 persons to become ill, some of them seri-
ously.

A more permanent and serious condition, however, is the subsidence
inversion which is responsible for the smog of Los Angeles (see
fig. 3.13). A semi-permanent high pressure cell exists off the Pacific
Coast during the summer and is characterized by descending air which
warms the upper layers. On the surface, easterly moving air is cooled as
it travels toward the land over cold water, thereby setting up a stable
climatic condition of cooler air underlying the warmed upper air. Below
the inversion layer, the particles from oil refineries and millions of car
exhausts build up as a concentration of photochemical air pollutants.
This concentration increases daily until some weather change allows the
inversion layer to rise and be dispersed. Los Angeles is unique because it
is the only large industrial city with millions of vehicles located in a dry
subtropical region on a west coast where climatic conditions of this type
can develop on a regular basis.

FIGURE 3.13. Three views of the Los Angeles Civic Center skyline: (1) on a clear day, (2) on a smoggy day with a temperature inversion at 100 feet, and (3) on a day when the base of the inversion lies at 1500 feet. (Courtesy Los Angeles County Air Pollution Control District.)

A subsidence inversion was also responsible for the famous London fog of 1952 when a high pressure cell lingered for several days, causing a concentration of coal pollutants from the millions of heating flues.

The air over our cities is sometimes referred to as a "sewer." In 1970 combustion processes poured 264 million tons of pollutants into the air over the American landscape. Only 10 percent of polluted air consists of the particulates—tiny pieces of carbon, ash, oil, grease, and microscopic pieces of metal released in the form of smoke from chimneys, smoke-stacks, incinerators, and garbage dumps. The other 90 percent of American urban pollution consists largely of invisible but potentially deadly gases. More than one-half of the contamination in the air, for example, is made up of colorless, odorless carbon monoxide, most of it issuing from the exhaust pipes of automobiles, trucks, and buses. Other gas pollutants consist of sulphur and nitrogen oxides, hydrocarbons, and ozone; a peculiar combination of these pollutants, characterized by brownish color and producing eye irritation and coughing, is found in the Los Angeles area.

Such pollution causes property damage, cleaning bills, vegetation deterioration, and, most serious, health injuries. For example, air pollution causes property damage of $11 billion a year in the United States through abrading, corroding, tarnishing, cracking, weakening, and discoloring of materials of all varieties. Some scientists feel that ozone and other substances have caused a decline in citrus and salad crops in the Los Angeles basin. Finally, air pollution is believed to be directly related to lung diseases including bronchitis and cancer. With the recognition of dangers from air pollution, control measures have improved with one example being emissions from motor vehicles. Under the Clean Air Act, The Environmental Protection Agency sets pollutant emission standards that may not be exceeded, and it is then illegal to sell a new car that does not meet them. By 1977 these standards were being enforced with the costs passed on to the consumer. On stationary sources of pollution, air quality standards are also established and implemented through state plans backed by EPA authority. However, the energy crisis has posed a roadblock to much of the progress on pollution control and the question of energy vs. environment remains a critical one.

The two major aspects of urban climate—a heat island and a dust dome—are directly related to other characteristics of this micro-climate. Climatological records show increased cloudiness and fog over cities: for example, warm air rising over a city provides the conditions for cloud formation on many days when clear skies prevail in the country; furthermore, in winter the higher consumption of fuel produces more particulant pollutants and more warm water vapor, thus providing nuclei for vapor condensation as fog in stable air conditions following the arrival of a cold wave. The same conditions which lead to increased winter fog—presence of nuclei and increased water vapor—may also cause greater amounts of precipitation, especially in the downwind section of cities. Both the cloudiness and precipitation of city areas may also be related to increased convection and turbulence over the rough man-made townscape. At the same time, the city's many structures, while increasing wind turbulence, have a braking effect on wind speeds and cause a greater frequency of calms. In summary, Landsberg's figures (1956 and quoted in Lowry, 1967, 20) show that the city, compared with the countryside, has 5-10 percent more cloudiness, 30 percent more fog in summer and 100 percent more in winter, 10 percent more precipitation, and 20-30 percent lower mean annual wind speed.

Overall, urban climate offers several advantages over country climate, the most important ones being lower heating bills, fewer days with snow, and a longer gardening season. Landsberg has estimated that the city has about 14 percent fewer days with snow than the countryside. Lowry mentions that the season between the last freeze in the spring and the first freeze in the fall may be three or four weeks longer in the city than in rural areas. In spite of these advantages of urban climate, however, there is little doubt that through air pollution man has caused a city's micro-climate to deteriorate.

URBAN MAN AFFECTS THE PATTERNS OF VEGETATION AND NOISE. Man's effects on vegetation and noise in the city have been irregular. In the days before streets were widely used for automobiles and trucks, housing was constructed gradually and accompanied by an interstitial forest along these arteries. As man's mobility increased, the pace of construction was stepped up and large areas for subdivisions and shopping centers were developed; in such projects, the bulldozer and vegetation were incompatible. At the same time, noise from these projects and from greater traffic began to be noticeable. An air view of a large American city today, therefore, often reveals an interstitial forest in the older residential areas but fewer trees in the core and newer suburbs. Parks and green zones are also lacking in many areas because of the difficulties that public authorities have in competing for land on the open market. For example, it is recommended that 10 percent of space in a city be allocated for parks, but it seldom exceeds five percent on the average.

Trees in the older parts of American cities tend to be of similar species. In early days the tendency was to plant the same type of tree along many streets because little was known about the possibilities of diseases affecting them. With the deforestation of American cities by Dutch elm disease, foresters in urban areas have made conscious attempts to develop a tree plan incorporating a variety of species.

What has been the feedback from man's neglect of vegetation in a city? Smith (1970) has outlined some of these. In the first place, noise is more apparent when vegetative cover has been reduced. Conifers are more effective in this regard than deciduous species which lose their leaves. Secondly, the filtering effects of vegetation on aerosols and gases is reduced. Trees possess the ability to intercept and hold certain aerosols, especially if the particulates are less than 40 microns in size, e.g., ragweed pollen. The ability of trees to asorb gases is not clearly defined, but leaves exposed to *low* levels of sulphur dioxide, for example, may transform the gas into sulphate, which is less injurious to the plant. A third feedback of a lack of vegetation in the urban environment is greater extremes of temperature. Trees again, through the process of transpiration, provide moisture for evaporation which is a process taking heat out of the air. The absence of trees, therefore, helps increase summer temperatures. At the same time the winter temperatures are lowered if trees are absent because the air, heated by convection from the surface, is dissipated more rapidly. Finally, the absence of vegetation in the city allows for less absorption of precipitation, thereby contributing to greater runoff which may affect stream quality. It is obvious from the above statements that vegetation in the urban ecosystem is related closely to climate, terrain, soils, and surface-ground water.

On the other hand, man makes the urban environment more hostile to existing or new vegetation. The main effects are dryness, mineral deficiency or contamination, and air pollution. Our tendency is to waterproof surfaces or compact them, reducing access to supplies of moisture and air, and causing the slumping mentioned earlier. Our raking of leaves, etc., interrupts the normal cycle of decay of materials by micro-organisms, thereby causing a lack of certain minerals. The use of salt for de-icing roads, on the other hand, actually kills adjacent vegetation, while the increased use of weed killers on grasses makes its conversion to gardens difficult. Finally, air pollutants like ethylene (CH_2), which are emitted by vehicle exhausts, cause leaf fall and flower dropping.

The American city has become increasingly noisy. Any noise over 90 decibels may be harmful if endured for a long time, while one over 70 dB may be bothersome. Table 3.1 shows that primary sources of noise are linear in pattern along streets and include emergency vehicle sirens, pneumatic drills, motorcycles, trucks, and autos. Other important sources of noise are trains, jet aircraft, and outboard motors. Long-term effects of noise on humans are illustrated by

TABLE 3.1

Typical overall sound levels. Measurement in parentheses indicate distance from the sound source. (After Committee on Environmental Quality 1968.)

Noise Source	Decibels
Threshold of pain	140
Large pneumatic riveter (4')	130
Overhead jet aircraft—4 engine (500')	120
Unmuffled motorcycle Construction noise (compressors and hammers) (10')	110
Loud power mower Rock and roll band Subway train (20') Heavy trucks (20')	100
10-HP outboard (50') Small trucks accelerating (30')	90
Heavy traffic (25' to 50') Office with tabulating machines	80
Autos (20')	70
Dishwashers	
Conversational speech (3')	60
Private business office	50

taxi drivers who have experienced "threshold shift" in their hearing, i.e., they can no longer distinguish low sounds. The greatest "spot" sources of noise are airports, whose growth have had tremendous effects on adjacent land use. Most large metropolitan airports have had to project Noise Exposure Forecasts for the next few decades in order to determine the areal effects of such expansion on the city. Such forecasts involve a detailed correlation of projected traffic, types of aircraft involved, and frequency and pattern of operations throughout each 24-hour period. The solution of problems related to jet noise around airports will come about through a combination of land use controls, including greenbelt buffers, and technology related to reducing engine noise. However, the recent controversy regarding the high level of noise found in new jets like the Concorde illustrates the difficulties inherent in this problem.

THE MODEL

In this chapter several processes by which man has affected the urban environment with consequent feedbacks have been discussed. As noted in the model (fig. 3.1), these processes are interrelated. In paving the surfaces of cities, man is affecting not only urban climate but also the amount of runoff and thereby the quality and quantity of water in streams. He is also making the soil more hostile to vegetative growth. Indirectly, noise is increased as paved surfaces involve construction and traffic. These interrelationships illustrate the fact that the urban area is an ecosystem in which "everything is related to everything else." As the size of these areas increases, man must be even more aware of the consequences of altering the environment.

EXTERNAL RELATIONS
OF CITIES

Having examined historical and ecological foundations of urban spatial organization, it is now necessary to probe more deeply into the external relations of cities. Man organizes space around a series of nodes for the purpose of carrying out political, economic, and social activities. For example, he must form governments, exchange goods, and establish social institutions. Since spatial interaction between people forms the basis of these activities, this topic, covered in chapter 4, serves as a useful introduction to the external relations of cities. The result of this interaction is a system of cities but the problem is one of breaking down this system for analysis. This writer chooses to do it on the basis of types of spatial interaction. The more *regular* movement forms the spatial foundation for a *central-place* system, the subject of chapter 5, in which the locational pattern of settlements providing ubiquitous goods and services is analyzed. Finally, the more *sporadic* movements, such as manufacturing, when superimposed on the central-place system, lead to an *urban* system, the focus of chapter 6. In all three chapters, the contrast between theory and reality is stressed.

CHAPTER 4

THE CITY AS A FOCUS FOR SPATIAL INTERACTION

All settlements represent a means of spatially *concentrating* labor at certain nodal points to carry out functions for a society. For example, goods are manufactured and exchanged at certain places where the tasks can be divided among specialists. Political and social functions also can be carried out at these focal points. However, the basis for such concentration, regardless of size, is the movement and interaction of people, goods, and ideas.

One of the most impressive indicators of potential interaction is the way technology has reduced the world in terms of time-distance for movement and communications. A map of the "shrinking" United States from 1912 to 1970 illustrates that in terms of transcontinental travel time a person can cross the country now by jet in the same time that it took by rail to traverse Massachusetts in 1912 (see fig. 4.1). In the field of telecommunications, Abler (1971,1) shows that the time necessary to establish a transcontinental phone call has been reduced from 14 minutes in 1920 to 30 seconds in 1970. These revolutions in physical movement and in communications have had considerable effect on the growth of certain urban areas because the friction of distance for goods, people, and information has been reduced for any given nodal point. We notice, for example, decreases in the size of lower level centers in central place hierarchies and increases in the higher levels. The larger cities benefit most from rapid increases in tertiary or service activities which in turn depend on quaternary functions or transactions of information between people. However, these increases in spatial interaction are not shared equally by all communities since rail service, interstate roads, air service, and communications bypass many of them.

Spatial interaction, then, serves as a useful introduction to an analysis of the external relations of cities. It is necessary to look first at the general basis for movement of people and goods. Secondly, two different types of interaction are examined in terms of models that express spatial relationships between (1) two or more major settlements (gravity) and

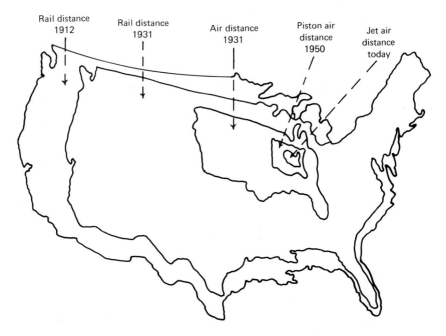

FIGURE 4.1. The United States has shrunk in the sense of time-space convergence. Coast-to-coast travel, which required four days by rail in 1912, is now possible in five hours by jet plane. (From Marion Clawson, *America's Land and Its Uses*, published for Resources for the Future, Inc., by The Johns Hopkins University Press, 1972.)

(2) a settlement and its surrounding area (breaking-point). Thirdly, three spatial patterns derived from interaction are discussed.

THE BASES FOR INTERACTION

Ullman (1956) identified three bases for these types of interaction.

COMPLEMENTARITY. A first base for interaction is that two places complement each other, i.e., that one requires something the other has. For example, a city provides medical services for the surrounding countryside (see fig. 4.2) or a regional specialty, like California wine, is shipped to various parts of the United States. Consequently, it appears that one essential characteristic of complementarity is a *difference* between the areas of origin and destination of interaction. When two areas have different levels of economic development, raw materials may be shipped long distances from Developing Countries to industrial market areas. Interaction even occurs between what appear to be similar areas when certain industrial products come to the United States from Japan as a result of differences in labor costs. Finally, rural to urban migration movements occur all over the world as people seek the opportunities that are not available in the countryside.

INTERVENING OPPORTUNITY.   Still another base for interaction is an intervening opportunity between points of origin and destination. Ullman argues that much interaction over long distances is in part affected by the shorter interactions that exist between. For example, the American transcontinental railroad obviously was stimulated by the complementarity of California and the Atlantic Seaboard; the evolution of this linkage, however, was facilitated by the way-business in between, a phenomenon that may not be important in a trans-Sahara rail connection! A more local example is the establishment of a gasoline service station closer to a person's residence than the one he has been using, thereby providing an intervening opportunity. In this case people are substituting a nearby place for one further away, a process by which some of the normal interaction with the distant center is filtered away.

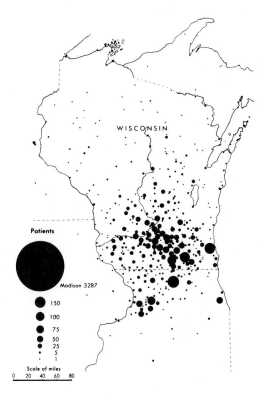

**HOMETOWNS OF PATIENTS
AT JACKSON CLINIC**
Madison, Wisconsin

WISCONSIN

Patients

Madison 3287

150
100
75
50
25
5
1

Scale of miles
0   20   40   60   80

FIGURE 4.2. The service area of a medical clinic in Madison, Wisconsin, includes large sections of southern Wisconsin and northern Illinois. The number of patients declines with distance and quantitative measures of this characteristic can be used for indicating precisely the basis of support. (Source: John W. Alexander, Economic Geography. © 1963, Prentice-Hall, Inc., Englewood Cliffs, New Jersey, fig. 29-10. p. 557. Reprinted by permission of the author and publisher.)

TRANSFERABILITY.   A third factor influencing interaction is the transferability of the product. Obviously, distance affects the movement of goods or people and this movement decreases or "decays" with distance from the point of origin. This inverse relationship between interaction and distance is often called the "friction of distance," an effect which depends on the specific value of the good or the goal of a person. In both of these cases, an important factor is the ratio of transport costs of good or person to total value of product or trip. These transport costs in turn are related to the frequency of movement—for example, ubiquitous stone or gravel is generally quarried close to cities for it requires frequent movement of low value products for which transport costs are proportionately large. Daily newspapers also exhibit low specific value because of high transport costs, while a weekly newsmagazine has higher value and can move farther. In the case of people moving, transferability in length of trip is held back for *daily* shopping trips because of the increase in transport costs while vacation trips, made infrequently, involve greater value and, therefore, distance.

Transferability, however, does not always reflect the friction of distance. The subsidized mass transit systems of Europe, for example, illustrate attempts to provide transport for large numbers of people at prices that do not cover the cost, especially during night hours.

These bases for interaction are economic and are based on the assumption that man's spatial behavior is rational. This assumption has been enforced by Zipf's principle of least effort (1949), which states that people tend to minimize the costs of overcoming the friction of distance. There is little question regarding the importance of this factor but one may argue as to whether or not it is always the controlling force in spatial relationships. Perhaps the best example is provided by Americans who locate in the suburbs: these residents seemingly do not behave rationally in trading off high transport costs for a large lot (low rent). Such a choice seems to be related to a value system that places an emphasis on possession of green space. This idea is similar to that of Firey (1945, 140-142; 1947, 87-135), who emphasized that the exclusive residential area of Beacon Hill in central Boston survived because of cultural relics of sentiment rather than through economic factors of convenience to the center of the city. In his view, space can possess certain *social qualities* which form the basis of locational decisions. Apparently, human beings are not entirely rational in their spatial behavior, although the principle of least effort probably should be considered as a model against which reality can be measured.

THE INTERACTION MODEL

THEORY. It seems logical to discuss first the theory that has been developed for spatial interaction as a basis for later comparison with reality as revealed by empirical studies. Davis (1973, 133) feels that interaction theory differs from central place theory in that it is "less formally constituted in abstract terms and mainly comprises a series of empirically-derived structural equations linked together by the single concept of gravity." This concept, which is analagous to Newton's law of physical gravitation, is based on a model which states that movement or exchange between two places is directly proportionate to the product of the populations (or some other measure of volume) and inversely proportionate to the distances (or distance to some exponent) between the two places. The formula, which was expressed by Carey in 1858-59, is as follows.*

$$I = \frac{P_1 P_2}{D}$$

where: I is the measure of movement or interaction between two places (P_1 and P_2)

P_1 is the population of the larger of two places

P_2 is the population of the smaller of two places

and D is the distance (generally in miles) between the two places P_1 and P_2

An example of the application of this formula is given (see fig. 4.3). The two key variables in this equation are obviously population and distance, factors which require further definition.

The population in this case actually represents the *mass* or attractive force. Other means of indicating this attraction in a place could be used such as employment, income, or volume of sales, but population is normally the most convenient one. However, some writers advocate multiplying the populations by "weights" or figures indicating differences that may exist—such as sex, income, or education—within a given culture (Lowe and Moryadas, 191). If cross-cultural comparisons of interaction are being made, some indication of these differences may be necessary.

The distance variable also may change depending on conditions. Reilly (1959, 49-50), for example, in testing the effects of distance in 255 cases of marketing, found that the exponent of 2 was most applicable. Thus,

*For details on the various concepts of interaction see Converse (1949) and Carrothers (1956).

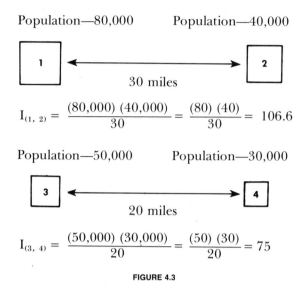

Population—80,000   Population—40,000

$$I_{(1,\ 2)} = \frac{(80{,}000)\ (40{,}000)}{30} = \frac{(80)\ (40)}{30} = 106.6$$

Population—50,000   Population—30,000

$$I_{(3,\ 4)} = \frac{(50{,}000)\ (30{,}000)}{20} = \frac{(50)\ (30)}{20} = 75$$

FIGURE 4.3

the friction of distance is probably less for a daily journey to work than for shopping trips in a city. Similarly, 20 miles is not far to an American, but it may be the lifetime limit to the resident of a small peasant town in China.

REALITY.   According to the theory of interaction as represented in the model, one would expect the volume of flows to reflect directly the size of the cities and indirectly the distance between them. For example, large cities like New York and Chicago supposedly would generate more interaction than Kansas City or Phoenix. To test this hypothesis, Taaffe (1956) compared numbers of air passengers generated in major cities with their populations. He found in general that there is a relationship between size of city and amount of air-traffic generated per capita. However, certain differences existed between reality and what might have been expected on the basis of size, and four factors were isolated to explain these: dominance of larger centers; traffic shadow (location within 120 miles of a larger city); function; and length of haul. Thus, the unshaded circles on the map represent cities that have fewer air passengers than might be expected from their population totals (see fig. 4.4). Note that many of these are located within the traffic shadow of a larger center which tends to be "the airport" for a cluster of cities. Philadelphia and Baltimore lie within the traffic shadows of New York and Washington, respectively, although more recently an international airport has been shared by the two southerly cities. Cities with resort and commercial functions, like Miami and Atlanta, respectively, generate

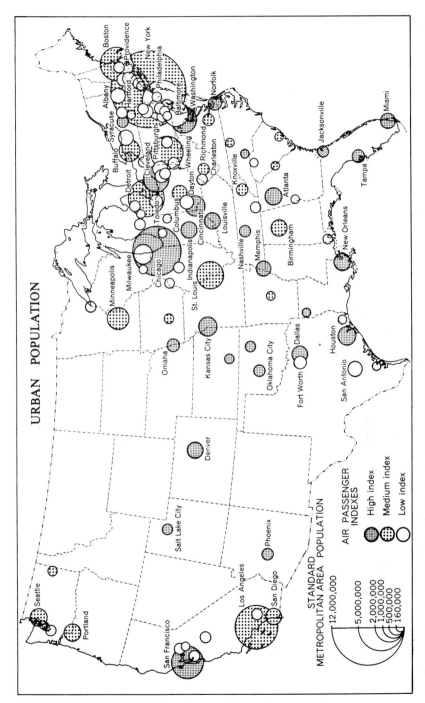

FIGURE 4.4. The map illustrates the relationship between urban population and air traffic in the United States for 1950. Size of circles indicates urban population while the index represents degree of importance of the city as an air traffic center. Note that many cities close to large cities have low indices. (From Edward Taaffe: Air Transportation and United States Urban Distribution, *Geographical Review*, vol. 46, p. 221, fig. 2.)

more air traffic than the larger manufacturing cities such as Pittsburgh or Detroit. Finally, cities located some distance from major population clusters like Salt Lake City possess higher indices of air traffic than their size would seem to justify. Taaffe's work provides a basis for giving weights to the population figures in any interaction model based on airline traffic.

A separate factor that strongly affects the volume of spatial interaction is the presence of a political boundary. In this case Mackay (1958) has found that such a barrier results in strong variance from what could be expected on the basis of size and distance. In a study of telephone interaction within Ontario, across the Quebec-Ontario line, and across the Canadian-American line, he found that size of city and distance apart were factors influencing interaction, but that the provincial and international boundaries reduced expected linkages. Therefore, the number of calls between cities of similar size and distance apart was 5 to 10 times less for cities in different provinces than for those within the province. Similarly, the number of calls across the international frontier was 50 times less than expected on the basis of size and distance.

An extension of the gravity concept is the potential model. Whereas the former describes the interactions themselves among all points in a system, the latter considers places one at a time with respect to interaction potential with all other places in a system. The potential model, therefore, represents the sum of different interactions. It has been applied most frequently to population but can be used for other phenomena. Harris (1954) was successful in illustrating marketing potential for cities of the United States.

THE REGIONAL MODEL

A fundamental aspect of the external relations of any large settlement is its region or zone of influence. Although geographers deal with both uniform and nodal regions, urban spheres of influence are nodal in that they serve as nodes or foci of interaction. As distance outward from the settlement increases, the domination of the center tends to weaken, and eventually the influence of some competing settlement becomes greater. Actually, this area of dominance includes a number of single *service areas* which focus on the settlement—commuting, newspaper circulation, retail and wholesale trade, education, etc. Each service, such as a newspaper or physician, has a minimum *threshold* of population support which is included within a given distance or *range*. The patients who utilize the medical clinic in Madison, Wisconsin, referred to earlier, may be considered to comprise one type of service area for this nodal center (see fig. 4.2). Notice how the threshold of support decays with distance, but that this decay is much sharper to the south where patients in parts of northeastern Illinois can find *intervening opportunities* (or clinics) in Chicago or other cities. Such boundaries are distorted.

Any city will include a number of these service or nodal areas with differing thresholds and ranges. The most ubiquitous of these services are contiguous in terms of threshold, i.e., they are *central* services and the thresholds are derived from the neighboring area for which they are *central* in terms of accessibility. The number and extent of these services represent the keys to a settlement's place in a hierarchy of settlement, a basic principle discussed in the next chapter. However, many more specialized services such as a manufacturing plant or a university are not ubiquitous and draw their support from larger areas which are not necessarily contiguous. Many firms possess national or international markets for their products as shown in the map for Cushman Motors of Lincoln, Nebraska (see fig. 4.5).

When separate and contiguous service areas for a settlement are combined, the total zone of influence is called a *city region* or *urban field.* Some writers use the terms *tributary* or *supporting* areas, the first one rep-

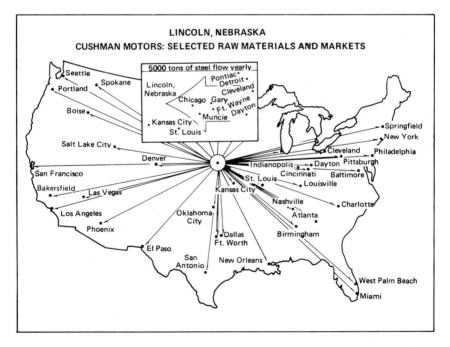

FIGURE 4.5. Cushman Motors of Lincoln, Nebraska has a national market for small vehicles. The external relations of this firm include not only the various markets but also the supply of raw materials. (Courtesy Cushman Motors, Division Outboard Marine Corp.)

resenting an area *to which* the city sends its goods and services while the latter is the region that sends goods, people, and monies *to* the city. Actually, this relationship between urban and rural area should be considered interdependent since movement or interaction is in both directions. In any case, these terms all refer to the same phenomenon—the zone of interaction around a settlement.

THEORY. A primary geographical problem involved in any city region is determining its limits. Administrative limits to a city are *discrete* as are physical breaks like a water body. However, most city regions are *continuous* since the service areas comprising them include thresholds which fall off rapidly close to the city and more slowly farther away. Drawing a boundary for the service area, therefore, is subjective in that a choice must be made, e.g., 50 percent of the threshold. Trying to combine a series of such lines into one city region boundary becomes complex and, as a result, attempts to delimit such regions have been theoretical and empirical. The first of these is represented by the breaking-point formula, which represents an adaptation of the gravity model.* In this case, a "breaking point" or line of division is made between two cities based on their populations and the distance between them. The formula is derived from the gravity model as shown below.

$$D_2 = \frac{D_{1-2}}{1 + \sqrt{\dfrac{P_1}{P_2}}}$$

when D_2 = breaking point P_1 = population of larger place
    (miles from P_2) P_2 = population of smaller place
and D_{1-2} = distance from P_1 to P_2

The method provides an objective way of determining one *type* of city region or service area which, although based on population, is assumed to correspond to that of retail trade. If the breaking-point were established between a given city and a number of other surrounding and competing cities, it would be possible to delimit the theoretical trade area.

*This adaptation was by P. D. Converse, *Journal of Marketing*, 1949. An earlier one is

$$\left[\frac{B_1}{B_2} = \left(\frac{P_1}{P_2} \right)^x \left(\frac{D^2}{D_1} \right)^n \right]$$

Reilly's "law of retail gravitation" which represents the volume of retail trade patronage that a city's residents will give to other cities.

REALITY. To what extent does such a method correspond to reality? Here empirical studies are necessary. Reilly's breaking-point represents only one service area—retail trade—out of many that make up a city region. A comparison of the various service areas which Ullman (1943) delimited around Mobile, Alabama with the breaking-points between Mobile and other cities allows the measurement of reality against theory (see fig. 4.6). Only one of the points is close to the retail service boundary. The points for both New Orleans and Birmingham are closest to the line delimiting 50 percent or more of out-of-town newspaper cir-

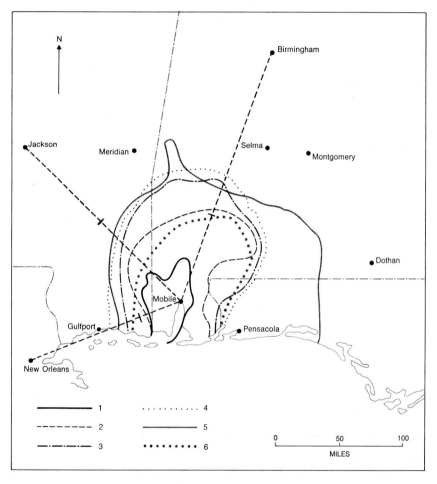

FIGURE 4.6. Selected service areas of Mobile, Alabama. The lines indicate areas from which the city secures 50 per cent of the business related to 1) retail trade, 2) wholesale grocery, 3) wholesale meat, 4) wholesale produce, 5) wholesale drugs, and 6) newspaper circulation. (Adapted with permission of the Department of Geography from Edward Ullman, "Mobile: Industrial Seaport and Trade Center," 1943, figure 7.)

culation from Mobile but this is not true for Jackson, Mississippi. It is apparent that while the breaking-point may represent a rather realistic boundary between two cities in terms of competition, a service line only tells *part* of the story regarding the make-up of a city region. The map illustrates very well the transferability effect of interaction mentioned above. In the first place, the distortion or elongation of boundaries around a nodal center is evident here as distances to competing centers, which represent intervening opportunities to people in the urban field, vary. Secondly, the lines of separate functions like retail and wholesale trade reflect varying frequencies of movement, i.e., the more frequent travel for shopping restricts transferability of people more than it does movement for wholesaling purposes.

Chapin's delimitation of city regions in North Carolina (1965, 142) provides another example where urban spatial theory is compared to reality. The boundaries of retail trade areas as defined by newspaper circulation data do not correspond to the theoretical regions of influence based on Reilly's law (see fig. 4.7). The real regions follow existing county boundaries which leads one to ask if this represents the actual situation or if circulation data is compiled by counties. The newspaper, however, generally is a good indicator of regional influence around a

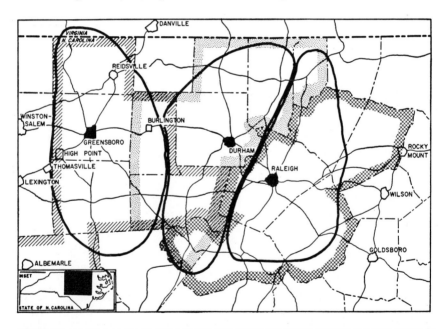

FIGURE 4.7. Retail trade areas in three North Carolina cities. Shaded boundaries identify trade areas as in 1950 by the Credit Bureau of Circulation for local newspapers. The solid heavy lines identify the theoretical trade areas determined by applying Reilly's law of retail gravitation. (Reprinted with permission of University of Illinois Press from F. Stuart Chapin, *Urban Land Use Planning*, 1965 [2nd edition].)

settlement since it reflects the day-to-day focus of activity by most people—commuting, retail trade, and specialized services. More than anything, perhaps, it builds up a community of interest by giving people a means of identifying themselves with certain aspects of the settlement such as a job, school, athletic team, concert orchestra, or political party. The newspaper can do much through its editorials, human interest, and even advertising to create a "city of the mind."

In terms of their shape, urban regions are distorted, fragmented, or truncated, types emphasized by Haggett (1966, 44). The theoretical area derived from the breaking-point may include *general* distortion like elongation in one direction if enough measurements are made but *details* between these measurements are only interpolated. As mentioned above, distortion of city regions in the real world often reflects the presence of intervening opportunities in certain directions which shortens the zone of influence. Fragmented regions, of course, are exemplified best by overseas markets. Truncation, on the other hand, illustrates the effect of a major boundary. For example, Lösch showed in 1954 that the Mexican portion of the El Paso metropolitan region, as based on the presence of Federal Reserve bank branches, is considerably reduced in size as compared with the American side (see fig. 4.8).

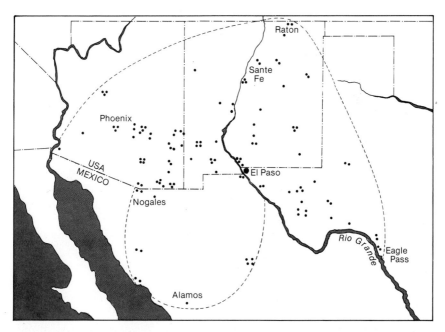

FIGURE 4.8. The effects of an international boundary on a metropolitan region. El Paso's region, as defined by banks having accounts in the city, is much reduced in Mexico. (Redrawn from "Location of Reserve Districts in the United States," 63rd Congress, Second Session, Senate Document 485, 1914, p. 140.)

A comparison of theoretical and actual urban regions can be further exemplified by the competing hinterlands of two major metropolitan areas. In this case we are comparing the breaking-point between the two centers with a zone that is a composite of several service areas. In 1955 Howard Green used seven specialized indicators to depict the zones of influence in New England exerted by New York City and Boston.

—Railroad ticket purchasers
—Truck freight movement
—Newspaper circulation
—Long-distance phone calls
—Origin of vacationers
—Business address of major industrial firms
—Metropolitan correspondents of banks

The map portrays the median of the seven boundaries together with the breaking-point (see fig. 4.9). A close correspondence between the two is obvious, but distortions are also present among the service areas. For example, state political boundaries are a factor in helping Boston to have an inordinate proportion of bank correspondents. Nevertheless, the map clearly illustrates the modern tendency for large metropolitan areas to disregard political boundaries in organizing urban space economically. In this case the historic region of New England in a realistic sense has been broken up by the influence of New York City which now has close functional ties with much of Connecticut.

PATTERNS DERIVED FROM SPATIAL INTERACTION

As seen from the discussion above, *total* interaction between urban centers is based on population and distance. However, the spatial *pattern* of this interaction is related to the frequencies of movements between settlements of different size. As stated earlier, these settlements represent a means of spatially concentrating labor at certain points for carrying out functions for society. It appears that the spatial interaction or movement between settlements is of two kinds—regular and sporadic. The regular movement is carried on systematically to provide goods and services that are required frequently (see fig. 4.10-1). The most logical pattern that results is one of central places which are distributed uniformly over the landscape to maximize the distribution of such goods and services. We call such a uniform pattern a *central-place system* and its regularity is, in part, based on the regular frequencies of movement. The other type of movement is sporadic because it is more irregular in providing specialized goods and services. This irregularity may be either clustered,

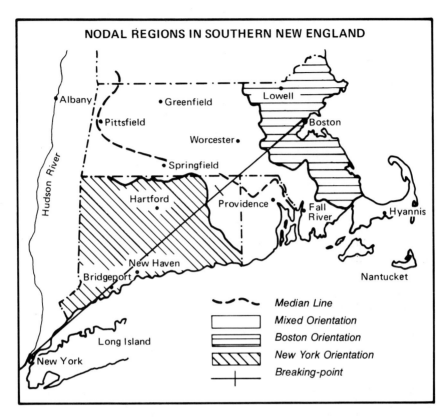

FIGURE 4.9. The organization of space by large metropolitan centers is illustrated by New England where New York and Boston have split what was once an historical regional unit. (Source: Howard L. Green, "Hinterland Boundaries of New York City and Boston in Southern New England," *Economic Geography,* 31 [1955], after fig. 9. Reprinted with permission.)

because of the distribution of resources or industries, or it may be linear from the influence of transportation (see fig. 4.10-2,3). When the regular and sporadic patterns are combined an *urban system* is present (see fig. 4.10-4). These three patterns—uniform, clustered, and linear—were identified by Harris and Ullman (1945, 7-12). In the next two chapters, the central-place and urban systems are examined in detail. However, first it should be useful to look more closely at the basis for this separation of interaction into three patterns which correspond to three types of functions. Most cities are supported externally by a combination of these since they represent different ways in which people interact and organize space.

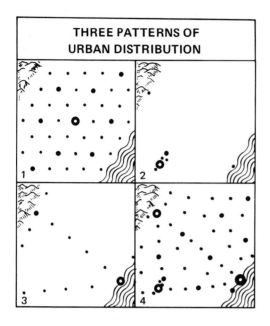

THREE PATTERNS OF
URBAN DISTRIBUTION

FIGURE 4.10. No. 1 illustrates that central places are distributed in a uniform manner to supply ubiquitous goods and services regularly to surrounding areas. On the other hand, No. 2 exhibits specialized functions, which tend to cluster owing to site characteristics (e.g., mines) or complementary activities (e.g., manufacturing). Finally, in No. 3 transport centers are aligned in a linear fashion with the greatest activity found where physical, commercial, or political "breaks" in transport occur. No. 4 combines the others. (Source: Chauncy D. Harris and Edward L. Ullman, "The Nature of Cities," *Annals of the American Academy of Political and Social Science*, 242 [1945]: 8.)

CENTRAL-PLACE FUNCTIONS. The most ubiquitous functions carried out by a city for external areas are referred to as central-place functions because they must be carried out *regularly* for a large number of people in the surrounding area. All settlements derive support from the income obtained from the supply of such goods and services. Examples of such functions include:

Type	Example
retail	grocery
service	garage
wholesale	soft drinks
manufacturing	baking
education	grade school
government	county offices
recreation	bowling

People from the surrounding area come into a central place to utilize these enterprises on a regular basis. The key word is "regular" for the frequency of use requires that the location be central in order to reduce the friction of space. The most important "regular" functions are those of retail trade and various services (personal, business, repair, and recreational), but other functions are also important. Each rank of the settlement hierarchy may possess a certain number of these central-place activities.

Hamlet	Village	Town	City
general store	grocery	supermarket	supermarket
service station -garage	service station	service station	service station
tavern- restaurant	restaurant	restaurant	restaurant
	drug store	drug store	drug store
	elementary school	elementary school	elementary school
	church	church	church
		physician	physician
		appliance store	appliance store
		county court house	county court house
			motel
			department store

As shown, goods and services tend to be more diversified at each stage of the urban hierarchy. Not only are certain services generally obtainable in a city that are unobtainable in town, but the choice within each type of service is also greater. Centers of the same class tend to compete for hinterland support; for example, a farmer will decide in which hamlet to buy supplies or the village inhabitant in which town to see a physician. On the other hand, competition also exists between different levels. The village inhabitant again must decide whether to drive to the town or to drive further to the city for a better choice of physicians; he may also wish to shop at the department store, something he cannot do in the town.

The hierarchy of settlement, therefore, is first of all established by the provision of different levels of ubiquitous goods and services on a regular basis. At the higher levels, these goods and services become less ubiquitous as the frequency of need is reduced. Retail services are common to all central places while wholesaling is not; the latter, however, requires centrality and in many ways this function is an excellent indicator of the hierarchy. Owing to this need for centrality, the pattern of central places tends to be even although distorted by terrain and transportation. The relative size of each center may change with time as accessibility varies. In recent years the large centers in the United States have become even larger at the expense of the smaller centers owing to the influence of the automobile and to other factors. In some states it is, therefore, common to hear references to the "dying" village and small town.

SPECIAL FUNCTIONS.   In contrast to the rather ubiquitous functions that most cities provide for their surrounding areas are the special functions provided by cities for extensive areas. Such cities are referred to as special-function cities, and their pattern of distribution is much more irregular than that of central places. For example, a particular mineral deposit will give rise to a mining city, or special advantages with respect to raw materials, labor supply, market, and transportation may enable a center to become an important manufacturing city. A city dominated by a university will be an education center, or one heavily influenced by federal or state employees will be a governmental center. Note, however, that these functions are *also* present in most of the central places but are more ubiquitous in nature. For example, a central place may have a sand quarry, bakery, elementary school, and court house which represent ubiquitous mining, manufacturing, education, and governmental activities, respectively. However, these functions are not regionally specialized as in cities like Hibbing, Minnesota (mining), Akron, Ohio (manufacturing), Ann Arbor, Michigan (education), and Washington, D.C. (government).

The locational pattern of specialized function cities then is often highly irregular since such cities may be fixed by site characteristics that are nonrepetitive. Furthermore, their supporting areas are large and not necessarily continuous since a manufacturing firm, for example, may draw on widely scattered resources and sell its products to diverse markets. Support of a university may also vary widely. Therefore, centrality within a local area is not as important for a special function center as it is for a central place. This irregularity of location may involve clustering of several special function cities, a pattern which often derives from similar resources (mining) or complementary activities (manufacturing). The manufacturing belt of the United States illustrates a concentration of cities supported by regional, national, and international markets and facilitated by a host of interdependent activities such as transportation (e.g., Great Lakes), interlocking industries (e.g., component parts), banking and research facilities, marketing channels, and skilled labor.

It is apparent that special functions bring much "basic" or external income into a city and, therefore, attempts are made by planners and chambers of commerce to expand these functions for their city.

BREAK-IN-TRANSPORT FUNCTIONS.   A third type of external support for a city is provided by "breaks" along routes of transport. These "breaks" can be of three kinds. Most common, perhaps, is the physical transfer of goods from one form of transport to another, e.g., ship to rail. The commercial "break" involves a change in ownership.

Finally, the crossing of a frontier implies a political "break," since customs procedures are introduced. Ports are the most common BIT points as all three types of "breaks" may be involved. Here in-coming ships contact other ships, pipelines, railroads and trucks. In port areas opportunities also exist during the physical "break" for selling, storing, processing, or exchanging of goods. Such activities provide much employment and attract considerable wealth into the city. Ports like New York provide banks, warehouses, industries of various kinds including refineries, and a variety of transport services. The increasing use of "containers," however, has modified break-in-transport activities.

The distribution of BIT centers, like that of special function cities, is generally irregular. In addition to ports, there are railway hubs like Chicago and cities located between contrasting regions, such as Denver. Many cities tend to be aligned along different transport routes, while settlements away from the route may be less frequent. Relief may affect the pattern of routes. Therefore, the distribution of BIT centers is irregular and hinterlands may be of considerable size.

These three types of activities are not mutually exclusive among cities. Although many smaller- and medium-size cities of the world exhibit a predominance of one type, the larger cities possess all three in varying proportions. The port of New York, for example, is a break-in-transport point; as a principal center of wholesaling and retailing it possesses central-place functions; and as a major American center of manufacturing it is a specialized city. According to one urban classification New York is predominantly BIT, but in an absolute sense its central-place functions are greater than those of Denver, which is *first* of all a central-place city.

The breakdown of urban functions into three types serves to illustrate that some are more evenly distributed than others. The ubiquitous central-place functions are quite uniform in distribution while the specialized and transport functions exhibit more irregular patterns. When combined on a map, however, the regularities tend to be obscured by the irregularities (see fig. 4.10-4). The next chapter focuses on the *central-place* system, for certain generalizations can be made about these ubiquitous activities. A key aspect of regular movement is its frequency and the manner in which a hierarchy of movement between settlements of different size is established. Following the central-place discussion, a chapter on the total *urban* system includes an interpretation of the processes by which specialized and transport functions supplement and distort the central-place ones. The distortion will be greater in areas like Pennsylvania, where coal and industry are present, than in an agricultural area like Nebraska, where the central-place pattern is more apparent.

SUMMARY

The first part of this chapter illustrated spatial interaction theory using two models derived from the gravity concept of physics, i.e., interaction between two places is affected directly by their populations and inversely by the distance between them. The general interaction model represents a means of measuring movement between two or more centers, while the breaking-point model allows one to determine the point of equilibrium between two centers, thus facilitating regional delimitation. Contrasts between theory and reality are presented for both cases.

Carrothers (1956, 99) states that the interaction model illustrates the predictability of spatial behavior in the aggregate, something not usually possible for individuals. However, he warns that such a concept cannot be applied rigidly to all situations but that the threshold where the power of individual decision-making critically affects the results should be determined before the concept can be broadly applied in practice.

The second part of the chapter included a brief discussion of the *patterns* derived from spatial interaction. Regular and frequent movements lead to more uniform *central-place* systems while sporadic movements are related to specialized functions that, when added to the central-place patterns, result in *urban* systems. The next two chapters deal with these two systems in terms of theory and reality.

CHAPTER 5

THE CITY AS PART OF A CENTRAL-PLACE SYSTEM

Central-place theory is an attempt to explain the locational pattern of settlements providing ubiquitous goods and services. The size and spacing of these settlements seem to be directly related to number and types of functions provided. Since these particular settlements are *central* to given populations, we call them "central places." Although the Christaller model is the generic base and most important statement of this theory, it was preceded by other work, especially that carried out by American rural sociologists. It must be kept in mind that such theory applies *only* to central places, i.e., those settlements performing central-place functions within a landscape and not the more specialized functions of manufacturing and transport. The location of central-place settlements exhibit *repetitive* patterns and the hypotheses explaining their existence can be more easily formulated and tested than can those for settlements with specialized functions, such as manufacturing, which tend to be more *sporadic* in location. In this chapter, two statements of central-place theory are discussed and both are compared with reality: following a brief summary of the Kolb model of 1923, the Christaller model of 1933 is analyzed and tested in four different situations which, in a sense, reflect certain changes in geographic methodology during the past 40 years. This approach logically leads into chapter 6, which incorporates the specialized functions in an analysis of the *total* urban system.

THE KOLB MODEL AND REALITY

One of the first models to depict the theoretical pattern of location for service centers was Kolb's in 1923. His research reflects the long tradition of the American rural sociologist, who focused very early on service relations between town and country. A large number of early studies were carried out in Wisconsin, especially Dane County (which includes Madison), and published in the Bulletin of the Agricultural Experiment Station. Later these articles were assembled and published as separate volumes which have become classics in rural trade-area literature (Kolb and Brunner, 1946).

The interest of urban geographers today has centered on Kolb's descriptive model of 1923, not only because it preceded the work of Christaller by ten years but also because it predicts a somewhat different locational pattern. Kolb isolated several levels of trade centers, four of which are shown in the diagram (see fig. 5.1). The major centers (A, B, C) possess three zones of influence—primary (P), secondary (Sc), and specialized (Sp). Unlike Christaller, no consistent geometrical or mathematical relationship is drawn between the locations of the different centers and their zones of influence. The various zones of influence increase at each level of the hierarchy because of the greater size of cities (A: 5,000) and towns (B: 1,200-5,000) as compared to large villages (C: 400-1,200) and small villages (D: 100-400). Consequently, the dominant characteristic of the pattern is one of *clustering* of smaller centers away from bigger ones. Distances between each level of center (i.e., D to C versus C to B versus B to A) increase in miles, according to Kolb, along the scale of 4, 15, and 36.

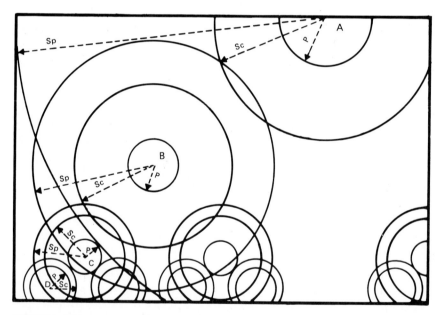

FIGURE 5.1. Kolb's model of service centers emphasizes the clustering of lower order centers away from the large ones. Note the relative importance of the different zones of influence for centers A, B, C and D: 1) Primary (P), 2) Secondary (Sc), 3) Specialized (Sp). (Source: J. H. Kolb, "Service Relations of Town and Country," *Research Bulletin*, University of Wisconsin, Agricultural Experiment Station, 58, Dec. 1923.)

The zones of influence change in relative importance within the hierarchy (see fig. 5.1). The primary zone is significant at all levels, but its *relative* size is much greater around the smaller centers. Notice that the smaller villages (D) in the diagram have a large primary zone and a smaller secondary one, while the specialized ring is absent. The secondary zone —characterized as one of "general trade, banking, and high school influence"—is relatively great around the towns (B) and large villages (C). Finally, the specialized zone—exemplified by functions like quality clothing and furniture stores and medical and recreational services—becomes steadily more important with rank. At the city level (A) this zone is relatively larger than the same zone at the town level (B) and includes almost all three zones of the town.

The value of a model like Kolb's is that reality can be measured against it, and the factors causing the discrepancies isolated. A good example of "reality" is provided by the isolines of influence for different goods and services around Madison in Dane County (see fig. 5.2). The primary distortion in these lines is the "resistance" provided by the town of Stoughton to the influence of Madison. Stoughton's size (5,101), in relation to other towns nearby like Cottage Grove, Deerfield, and Cambridge (200 to 594), helps to explain this resistance and its greater variety of services. Although all three are "towns" in terms of their areas of influence, Stoughton for historical reasons is much larger. A primary reason given by residents of the other three centers for purchasing clothing at Madison is because the "best goods" are found there. The people of Stoughton, on the other hand, are more mixed in their reasons with "nearest" source being almost as important as "best goods," while "unspecified" reasons are more frequent as well. The implications of these differences is that Stoughton's selection of goods is competitive with Madison's while the other's are not. Stoughton, therefore, *does not* lie within the specialized trade zone of Madison as Kolb's model would predict while the other three towns do. Reality does not always agree with theory.

THE CHRISTALLER MODEL

The first person to develop a theoretical base for central-place location was Walter Christaller in 1933. Essentially, he concluded that the various relationships in the central-place hierarchy can be theoretically expressed through a hexagon pattern that reflects geometrical and mathematical regularities. Owing to the important effect that Christaller's work has had on the development of geographic methodology, it is necessary to look at his model of the urban hierarchy as established in

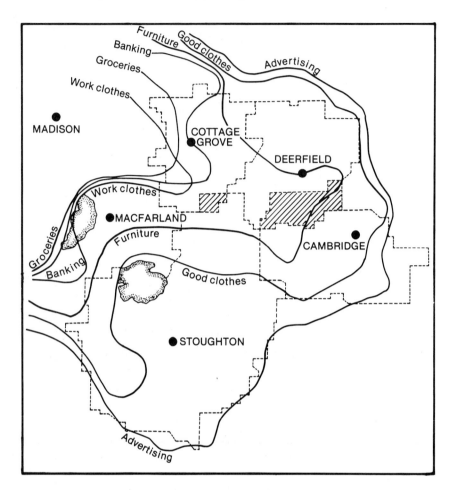

FIGURE 5.2. Kolb's model in the real world: zones of influence around Madison, Wisconsin. Note the "resistence" of Stoughton. Dashed lines represent trade areas of centers. (Source: J. H. Kolb, "Service Relations of Town and Country," *Research Bulletin,* University of Wisconsin, Agricultural Experiment Station, 58, Dec. 1923.)

south Germany of the 1930s. Although this model is based on small trade areas which reflect the transportation of the time and place, the location principles of Christaller's central places can be applied in any settlement situation. Assuming uniformity of physical conditions, purchasing power, and transportation in the area, Christaller concludes that the locational pattern of trade centers is controlled by the radial movement of traffic, which creates circular trade areas and causes centers with equivalent functions to be spaced at approximately equal distances from one another (see fig. 5.3). He further believes that the hierarchy of places, i.e., ranks, is based on marketing principles which differentiate

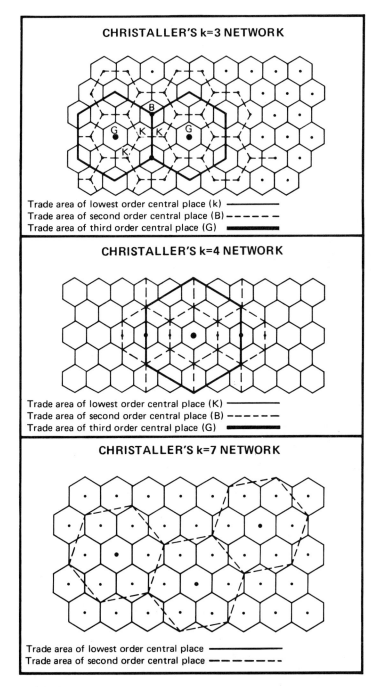

CHRISTALLER'S k=3 NETWORK

Trade area of lowest order central place (k) ──────
Trade area of second order central place (B) ──────
Trade area of third order central place (G) ████████

CHRISTALLER'S k=4 NETWORK

Trade area of lowest order central place (K) ──────
Trade area of second order central place (B) ──────
Trade area of third order central place (G) ████████

CHRISTALLER'S k=7 NETWORK

Trade area of lowest order central place ──────────
Trade area of second order central place ──────────

FIGURE 5.3. The three basic principles of central-place theory as developed by Walter Christaller: marketing (k = 3), transportation (k = 4), and administration (k = 7).

those central functions possessed by each order. The most essential principle is the range of a good, or the distance the dispersed population will travel to buy an article or service offered at a central place. The various limits to this range are the main factors in the competition between central places and in the support of different ranks. The limits to the range of a good are defined as follows (see fig. 5.4) (Getis, 1966, 221):

> Lower limit—the line enclosing the number of consumers necessary to provide the minimum sales volume required for the good to be produced and distributed profitably from the central place. It is called the *threshold level* of the good.
>
> Real limit—the line marking the proximity of an alternate center which can offer a good for a lower price at a certain distance from the first center.
>
> Ideal limit—the maximum radius of sales beyond which the price of the good is too high for consumption. Although the ideal can also be a real limit it is normally found when no competition exists from another center.

Obviously, the ranges of different goods will vary. The area of support for a given number of these goods is referred to as the complementary region to the central place. If a large region is to be served by a network of these complementary regions, the hexagon is the geometric figure that most efficiently organizes space without overlap (unlike the circle). Therefore, Christaller assumes that the basic pattern of central place regions would be that of hexagons.

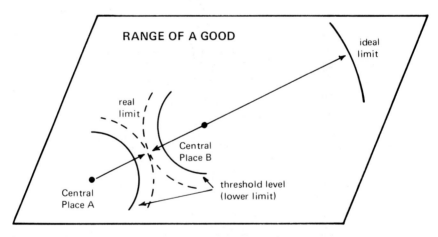

FIGURE 5.4. The range of a good, say radio, offered at both A and B. Since the threshold level is less than the real limit, both central places will produce it. The real limit, halfway between the two central places, shows the trade area for radios for each place. Those customers living beyond the ideal limit must either do without radios or establish a new central place to supply the good. (Source: Arthur and Judith Getis, "Christaller's Central Place Theory," *Journal of Geography, 65* [1966], Fig. 1.)

The next step is to depict how the levels of the hierarchy emerge and where they are located. As Getis (1966) explains, the basic marketing principle involved is known as the k=3 network, which assumes a mathematical relationship between the complementary regions of central places of different ranks.*

Starting at the top of the hierarchy, one assumes two adjacent central places, called G centers, which offer all of the goods and services from order 1 (with the highest threshold) to order 100 (with the lowest threshold) (see fig. 5.5). The "real" limit of the highest order good demanded (that of order 1) defines the boundary between the two G centers and their hexagon-shaped complementary regions. Since the range of the highest good sets the border, ranges will decline with goods 2, 3, 4, etc., and larger and larger numbers of consumers are left between the two G centers.

G: $1, 2, 3, \ldots, 29, 30, 31, \ldots, 49, 50, 51, \ldots, 100$
B: $30, 31, \ldots, 49, 50, 51, \ldots, 100$
K: $50, 51, \ldots, 100$

With some good, perhaps good of order 30, enough "surplus" customers exist over and above the thresholds of these 30 goods for G centers to allow the development of alternate centers (B).

In turn, the B centers supply goods 30, 31, 32, . . ., 100 *at lower prices* than the G centers in the areas between the threshold ranges of those goods from the G centers; G itself will also provide these goods for its own immediate area. B centers are located at the maximum economic distance from the G centers, i.e., on the outermost edges of the G complementary regions (the "real" limits). B centers in turn leave progressively larger numbers of "surplus" customers outside the threshold limits and with some good, perhaps good of order 50, these are large enough to permit the existence of a third rank of center (K). K centers provide goods 50, 51, 52, . . ., 100 at *lower prices* than the B centers in the areas outside the thresholds. The existence of four other types of centers is accounted for in the same manner. Obviously, the goods become more ubiquitous farther down the hierarchy, i.e., from good 1 to 100.

In building up the hierarchy, each level supplies all the goods and services that the centers below it will provide plus some additional ones, e.g., G centers provide goods 1, 2, 3, 4, . . ., 100 while B centers provide goods 30, 31, 32, . . ., 100, etc. (see fig. 4.12). This further implies an *interdependency* between ranks in that all centers except the smallest have

*Getis, "Christaller's Central Place Theory," pp. 220-26. The description of the k=3 network is from this source.

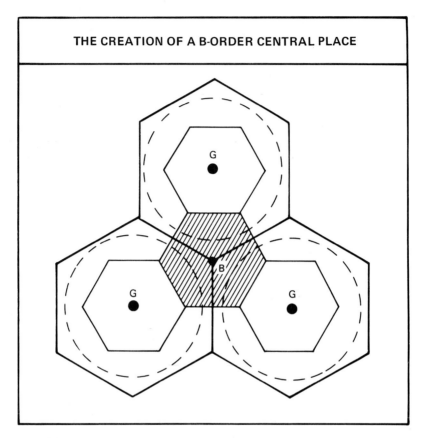

THE CREATION OF A B-ORDER CENTRAL PLACE

FIGURE 5.5. The creation of a B Order central place.

——— Each G center serves good or service 1 to its entire complementary region. All goods, from 1, 2, . . .,n, are supplied by G centers.

- - - - - - Threshold of good or service 15. It encloses areas less than the real limit. However, the area between the thresholds of the three G centers is too small to allow the establishment of new central places able to supply good or service 15.

——— Threshold level of good or service 30. It encloses areas with enough consumers for certain goods to allow the establishment of a new central place between the G centers.

The real limit of good or service 30 supplied by a new order central place, B. B centers supply goods 30, 31, . . ., n. G centers also supply these goods and services, as well as those of higher order.

(Source: Arthur and Judith Getis, "Christaller's Central Place Theory," *Journal of Geography*, 65 [1966], fig. 4.)

other centers dependent on them for the supply of certain goods. Thus B centers have K centers and their complementary regions, and all centers of a lower rank than K, dependent upon them for the supply of goods 30, 31, 32, . . ., 49. In turn, B centers and their complementary regions depend on G centers for the supply of goods 1, 2, 3, . . ., 29. Each complementary region of a B place is serviced with those goods by three G centers, and Christaller assumes that one-third of B's trade goes to each. Each G center thus serves its own region for the supply of goods 1,

2, 3, ..., 29 as well as one-third of the complementary regions of the six B centers. In all a G center serves three total B-type regions. This is called a k=3 network where k equals the total number of complementary regions of next lowest order served by the central place of next highest order. Likewise, three complete K-type regions are served with goods 30, 31, 32, ..., 49 by a B center, and so on.

The explanation above shows that the urban hierarchy of central places is derived from the unique series of functions and supporting areas which each level possesses. Since the population of a town depends on income derived from the number and types of functions which it performs for its supporting areas, then centers performing similar functions will have similar populations and a hierarchy will develop.

Christaller's original hierarchy as established in southern Germany in the 1930s included seven orders. Utilizing the principles outlined above, especially the concept that centers performing similar functions will have similar populations, he was able to establish figures for each level of the hierarchy to include distances apart, populations of the centers, and populations and areas of the hinterlands (see table 5.1). The hamlet is the basic trade area, its size being based on the distance a farmer can walk with his cart in an hour (about 2-3 miles). Thus, hamlets would be spaced 4.5 miles apart. In such a geometric network of hexagons, where higher ranking centers serve three times the area of the next level, distances increase consistently by $\sqrt{3}$, e.g., $\sqrt{3} \times 4.5$. Similarly, the area of the hinterlands at the next level of specialization would again be three times larger. The systematic ratios of the various orders of the hierarchy to each other are apparent in the table, the k=3 principle being predominant.

TABLE 5.1
Some Data for the Various Sizes of Urban Centers
According to Christaller's Hierarchy

Grades of urban centers	Towns Population	Towns Distance apart (mi.)	Tributary areas Population	Tributary areas Sq. mi.
I Market town	1,000	4.5	3,500	17
II Township center	2,000	7.5	11,000	51
III County seat	4,000	13.0	35,000	154
IV District city	10,000	22.5	100,000	463
V Small state capital	30,000	39.0	350,000	1,390
VI Provincial head city	100,000	67.5	1,000,000	4,170
VII Regional capital city	500,000	116.0	3,500,000	12,500

Adapted from: Walter Christaller, *Die zentralen Orte in Süddeutschland* (Jena, Germany: Gustav Fischer Verlag, 1933). Trans. C. W. Baskin (Englewood Cliffs, N.J.: Prentice-Hall, Inc., 1966), table on p. 67.

The k=3 relationship is called the marketing principle because every customer is as close as possible to a center at every level of the hierarchy. However, a transport system to serve such an arrangement is not efficient for the important links between larger places do not pass through intermediate ones. Under a revised arrangement of hexagons (rotation of network through 90 degrees), where the complementary region of a place is served with higher level goods by two (instead of three) higher level centers, the transport routes between larger centers connect a maximum number of important places of lower order (see fig. 5.3). Thus, for example, the complementary areas of K centers are provided with goods 30-49 from two B centers (one of which might be a G in rank), and direct transport routes connect a G with B centers and some K centers. As a result, the trade area of each larger place would be four times as large as the next smaller one, i.e., one B serves itself and one half of six adjacent K-size regions. This series of relationships is referred to as the k=4 or transport principle. A third principle based on administration was also proposed by Christaller in which the division of smaller areas between larger areas is not convenient. Obviously, if smaller ones are not to be divided, the only logical arrangement is for the larger place (B) to serve the entire market area of the six surrounding places (K). Under this ideal arrangement, called the administration principle (k=7), each larger market area is seven times as large as the one smaller (see fig. 5.3). Nesting, which refers to the capture of the intermediate center by the higher one, is automatic here whereas it is only implied in the other two models. Transportation in the k=7 arrangement is not too efficient and customers travel farther than in the other two arrangements.

In contrast to the interaction models discussed in the preceding chapter, central-place theory is more formally abstract in attempting to derive an optimum arrangement of settlement based on the provision of goods and services. The Christaller model tends to be deterministic and allows for little variability in terms of place or time. In spite of this, however, it does isolate a *regular* spatial pattern within an urban system and thus provides a basis for testing generalizations about settlement processes and for making comparisons between different systems.

KOLB, CHRISTALLER, AND REALITY

Perhaps most fundamental to the Christaller model is a spatial organization in hierarchal form in which differences in population size are related to the number of goods and services provided. A village has all the central functions and establishments that the hamlet has plus more of these and some additional functions that set it apart. Since the threshold or support for these increased number and variety of functions must be larger, the population of villages should be larger and they should be spaced farther apart. The early studies of central places tended to focus on the *hierarchy* and especially on how it is reflected in the functions found in the settlement and in the *spacing* between centers of different rank. Several phases are recognized. The first one is based on subjective identification of ranks and is represented here through work by Smailes in England and Wales. The second phase, illustrated by the work of Brush, actually includes the empirical testing of aspects of Christaller in the real world of southwestern Wisconsin. Third and fourth phases, stimulated in part by Brush's work, are evident in the more sophisticated statistical testing of central-place hierarchies in Snohomish County, Washington, and southwestern Iowa.

ENGLAND AND WALES. The earliest attempts at the empirical classification of the hierarchy of settlement hypothesized by Christaller were based on the *a priori* assumption that such a distinctive classification could be found (Carter, 1972, 91). Thus, such studies were aimed not so much at testing the *existence* of a hierarchy but at identifying the *basis* for ranks that were assumed to exist. Consequently, there was little attempt to compare an area with the Christaller model. The pioneer attempt to use an existing hierarchy for establishing ranks was Smailes' work on the urban hierarchy of England and Wales (1944). One interesting aspect of this approach is that it was carried out again in 1965, thereby providing a time dimension to the analysis.

Smailes, apparently using a base year of 1938, decided that functions *in* an urban center actually reflect its horizontal range of influence and therefore its rank in the hierarchy.* Intuitively, he felt that the "town" was a basic unit in the ranking. Once he decided which functional attributes mark a town, he could build upward to various classes of the city and downward to the village. On the basis of empirical studies, he decided that a town is represented by the trait-complex ABCD as follows:

A—Economic status as represented by a Woolworth store and three banks
B—Secondary school and hospital
C—More than one cinema
D—A weekly newspaper

*Several authors contrast two early approaches to the study of urban hierarchies characteristic of central-place systems. The first, used by Smailes, focuses on functions *in* the settlement that reflect the hierarchy. A second one, exemplified by the work of F.W.H. Green on English bus hinterlands (1950; 1966), emphasizes the varying urban *fields* that illustrate the hierarchy. The latter work is based on defining spheres of influence within a hierarchy of centers by the pattern of bus movements. This concept in turn was a precursor of work in graph theory in which hierarchical structure was derived from a matrix of flows and linkages between centers (Davies and Lewis, 1970).

Since all of these are not always present in what he felt was a "town," Smailes provided for certain alternate possibilities in order to include those towns lacking one or two of the necessary functions. Therefore, he also provided for the following supplementary indicators:

A'—Equivalent economic status—three banks but no Woolworth store
A"—Lesser economic status—two banks
B'—Secondary school *or* hospital
C'—One cinema

As a result of empirical investigation, Smailes concluded that the minimum qualifications for town ranking are indicated by the symbols A'B'C'D or A'BC'. He was, therefore, able to systematically determine which settlements in England and Wales can be considered towns and to map them. He also recognized that British towns normally include such other characteristics as a range of professional people, branch insurance offices, specialized retail businesses, certain governmental offices, and a head post office. In fact, he found that the latter was probably the most satisfactory single criterion for town status. However, he did not include any of these features as minimum qualifications for town status.

Smailes' purpose was to find the basic indicators for a British town and then subtract or add to these in order to identify the other ranks in the urban hierarchy. He recognized that the urban scale is continuous and therefore didn't expect sharp breaks in the hierarchy. Eventually he came up with the following urban hierarchy: major cities; cities; minor cities or major towns; towns; sub-towns; and urban villages (see fig. 5.6).

The levels below a town are based on the original ABCD indicators. Smailes felt that sub-towns generally lack one or more of these attributes and decided that A"B'C' was the minimum necessary for such status. Sub-towns, therefore, possess at least two banks, a secondary school or hospital, and a cinema; in general, they are also either suburbs of larger cities or independent settlements in rural areas. Below the sub-town level is the urban village which has less than three of the minimum features.

In building upward from the town, Smailes' criteria for the higher levels of the urban hierarchy are less clear. He states that the city as opposed to the town, offers services of greater range as well as of more specialized character, and the inhabitants of urban village, sub-town, and town must look to it for such things as higher education, special medical treatment, and many types of entertainment.

Heading the hierarchy are the fifteen "major cities" which represent the accepted culminating points of regional organization for governmental agencies and private enterprises in England and Wales. In-

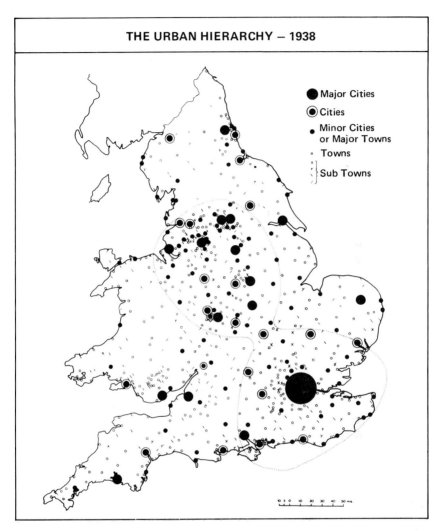

FIGURE 5.6. The urban hierarchy of England and Wales as defined by Smailes, who utilized functions evident in the center as a basis for his analysis. (Source: Arthur E. Smailes, "The Urban Hierarchy in England and Wales," *Geography* Volume 29, 1944, p. 43. Reprinted by permission of the author and The Geographical Association.)

cluded, for example, are the great ports, provincial stock exchanges, branches of the Bank of England, major newspapers and universities, and centers of specialized medicine.

The class known as "cities" fills the next layer in the urban hierarchy, and is chiefly distinguished from "major cities" by absence of elements promoting greater regional influence—certain features of regional importance like stock exchanges and universities being lacking. The difference is characterized by the contrasts between Newcastle, a "major city" for northeast England, and Middlesborough, an industrial "city" in the same area, or Norwich, the regional "major city" for East Anglia, as compared to Ipswich, a "city" of Suffolk county. The "cities" are large market centers with department stores, some importance in wholesale distribution, and limited regional importance in services, e.g., telephone and health care.

The final place in the urban hierarchy is occupied by those settlements which are intermediate between cities and towns. Smailes calls them minor cities or major towns. In general, they possess a greater range of services than the ABCD complex of towns because of specialized functions in industry (Stockport), county administration (Guilford), and recreation (Torquay). The minimum populations of these centers range from 10,000 to 30,000 and owing to their size they have numerous banks, several large cinemas and hospitals, evening newspapers, and a considerable choice of shopping facilities.

In summary the six classes of settlements refined by Smailes comprise an illustration of the urban hierarchy by means of functions *in* the city. Although he does not measure hinterlands, the horizontal implications in Smailes' method are evident, for each class possesses an urban field based on the service areas of the defined functions. The spacing and gradations are clearly evident on the map (see fig. 5.6). A total of 470 places appear as towns and cities and another 250 as sub-towns. Owing to wide divergence within each class, no attempt is made to establish population levels for the hierarchy. Smailes noted that each successive class, e.g., city, major town, and town, increases roughly in *number* in the ratio 1:3:9. The determination of such regularity in the urban hierarchy is a major result of empirical research.

The conceptual value of Smailes' method of establishing an urban hierarchy is illustrated by its use in 1965 for comparative purposes after some twenty-five years. Utilizing a much larger number of criteria R. D. P. Smith (1968) subdivided Smailes' top four categories into eight suborders. A chief assumption is that the diversity of the central-place activities is more important than the intensity of those included in separating the various ranks. The hierarchy within the metropolitan area (an internal characteristic of cities) is not portrayed but it is noted that although shopping intensity in some suburbs may exceed that of rural service centers, the range of activities is generally less. In spite of the many factors that might lead to a change in the 1965 pattern over that of 1938 (e.g., decline of railways, increasing mobility, the war, drift to the south, and innumerable economic changes), the two patterns are remarkably similar (see fig. 5.7). In general, about twice as many centers gained in status as lost. For example, certain regional centers began to emerge in former areas of small units. Perhaps a dominant trend, however, is the increasing strength of small centers in the areas of economic growth as activities decentralize (e.g., London and the Midlands). This

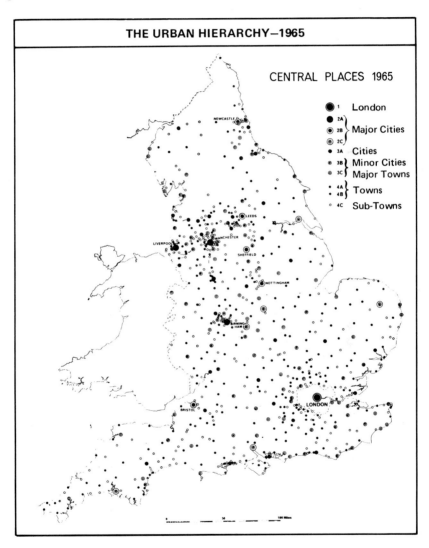

FIGURE 5.7. A detailed delimitation of the urban hierarchy of England for 1965 was developed by R. D. P. Smith. Although more criteria were utilized and a larger number of urban categories was developed, the similarity to Smailes' pattern is apparent. (Source: R. D. P. Smith, "The Changing Urban Hierarchy," *Regional Studies,* [1968]: 6, fig. 1.)

change contrasts with areas of decline where people either move to larger centers or migrate elsewhere. In the East Pennines and Northumberland, certain centers of all levels have declined and subsidies given to these "development areas" seem to have been less effective than in Lancashire, at least as reflected in the hierarchy. However, it must be kept in mind that industry normally is not a central-place activity, and therefore the effects of its decline may not truly reflect impact on a *central-place* hierarchy.

Although this empirical approach to an analysis of the urban hierarchy has theoretical implications, it is obvious that studies of changes in the hierarchy through time are useful to planning. This is illustrated in England where regional planning is facilitated, especially in the "development areas" located on the old coal fields. Here overspecialization has been characteristic of economic activity in the past and analysis of the hierarchy helps planners make decisions as to the location of government inputs.

Smailes' work illustrates the problem common to studies of this type in that no real theory is presented. No theoretical model exists against which the settlement hierarchy of England and Wales is measured but instead general statements are obtained by methods of induction. This type of generalization has no explanatory power of itself. The only real model is the use of two trait complexes—A'B'C'D or A'BC'—to represent a town, but these complexes bear no systematic relationship to the other ranks. Real-world exceptions to the trait complex model are noted, e.g., several places given town rank that are not Urban Districts and vice versa. The Smailes' approach thus suffers from the weaknesses of a subjective approach. Precise definition of *all* the ranks are not given and the basis for selection of criteria, e.g., a Woolworth store, is not clear. Perhaps most apparent is the lack of systematic relationships between centers of different ranks, e.g., the nesting of functions. Consequently, checking on the results would be difficult as would applying it in another area for purposes of comparison. Nevertheless, the Smailes' approach was an important seed study in central-place research because it focused on certain regularities connected with central places. Finally, it also represented a contribution to the regional geography of Great Britain.

SOUTHWESTERN WISCONSIN.   In 1953 Brush attempted a classification of settlements in much the same way as Smailes had but for a smaller area—Southwestern Wisconsin (see fig. 5.8). He found 235 settlements ranging in size between 20 and 7,217 inhabitants. On the basis of map analysis, he found a three-step hierarchy of 142 hamlets, 73 villages, and 20 towns. The minimum requirements were as follows:

Hamlet: At least five functional structures (residential, commercial, etc.) clustered within one-quarter of a mile.

One to nine central functions.

Village: More than 10 central functions.

At least four of the following: automobile sales, farm implement dealers, appliance and hardware stores, lumberyards, and livestock feed agents.

Three other essential services such as a bank, telephone exchange, or automobile repair shop.

Town: At least 50 retail establishments of which 30 had to be types other than grocery stores, taverns, and service stations.

Banks and weekly newspapers.

High schools.

Four professional services, either physicians, dentists, veterinarians, or lawyers.

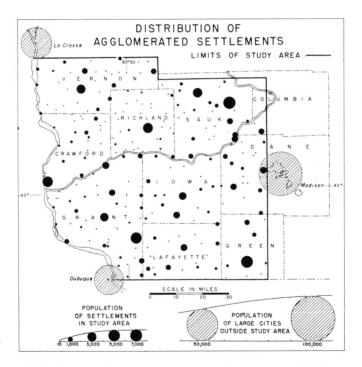

FIGURE 5.8. The central-place hierarchy of southwestern Wisconsin based on 1950 Census data. (From John Brush: The Hierarchy of Central Places in Southwestern Wisconsin, *Geographical Review*, vol. 43, pp. 381 and 396, figs. 1 and 7.)

This classification, therefore, was based on the relative frequency of different functions found in the three levels which were identified in the field. One could argue, as Berry and Garrison (April 1958, 146) did, that Brush proved what he assumed to exist but this does not appear to be the case. The classification actually *emerges* from the locational data and not from any presumed grouping of central functions. Brush's work helped to stimulate a new approach—developed by Berry and Garrison and discussed in the next section—which represents further sophistication in central-place analysis.

A primary objective of Brush's work was to *compare* Wisconsin with the theoretical model of Christaller and in this sense his work makes a contribution beyond that of Smailes. The overall conclusion is that although southwestern Wisconsin bears a superficial resemblance to the Christaller pattern, it also has strong clustering tendencies similar to the pattern hypothesized by Kolb. The big factor seems to be the effect of varied transportation in Wisconsin in comparison to the horse-and-cart movement assumed by Christaller for Bavaria. Variations of reality from theory in Wisconsin are found in three categories:

1. **Population of centers.** Whereas Christaller believed that the population means of three successive classes would be 1:2:4, Brush found that in Wisconsin they were 1:8:55.* He states, for example, that the mean population of villages was 486, while that of towns was 3,373. Projecting the ratios backward, the hamlet mean populations would be 61.

2. **Spacing.** Although *mean* actual distances between centers of the same class did not differ greatly from the distances found within a theoretical hexagon system, the *actual* effects of clustering are obscured. In fact, Brush found a tendency for centers to group themselves in rows or clusters away from larger centers, a pattern that would seem to be more similar to Kolb's model than to Christaller's (see fig. 5.9). A primary characteristic of the latter model is that hamlets are as close to villages and some towns as they are to each other, a pattern that seems unrealistic to many scholars. Brush found that, measured as clusters, hamlets were only 4.8 miles apart instead of 5.8 in a theoretical hexagon pattern and that distances from hamlets to villages increased to 5.6 miles and from hamlets to towns to 6.9 miles. The same increase is found in the distances between villages and between villages and towns. Evidently smaller centers in Wisconsin tended to cluster closer together away from the influence of larger centers, a pattern that Kolb noticed first in 1923.

3. **Shape, size, and population of tributary areas.** A third aspect of deviation from hexagon theory discovered by Brush was that tributary

---

*Brush's article used ratios of 1:8:50. The corrected ratios resulted from personal correspondence.

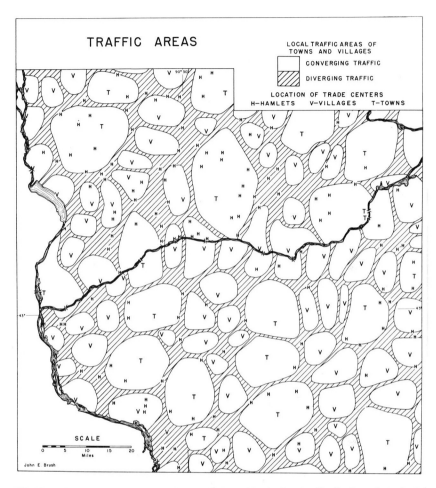

FIGURE 5.9. The pattern of traffic areas in southwestern Wisconsin. Note the clustering of hamlets, linear effects of routes, and large zones of towns. (From John Brush: The Hierarchy of Central Places in Southwestern Wisconsin, *Geographical Review,* vol. 43, pp. 381 and 396, figs. 1 and 7.)

areas, or complementary regions in Christaller's terminology, deviate in shape, size, and population from the theory (see fig. 5.9). In the first place, they are not circular (hexagons), but elongated in one or more directions, generally away from a row or cluster of centers. This is particularly evident near railroads or roads, where competition has existed along the route but not away from it. Secondly, the sizes and populations of tributary areas have been affected by the increasing influence of the towns. For example, village areas of influence should be 82.5 square miles (three times the 27.5 square miles of hamlets). In fact, they are only 47.5 square miles, not only because of competition along axes but also because of the encroachment of town areas; the latter is largely a function of increasing mobility of the population. Even the town's *local* area, which theoretically should be the same size as that of the village because the same local services are provided, is four times larger than it should be. Furthermore, both the population of the town and its local area were increasing at the expense of villages and hamlets; however, the town populations apparently were increasing faster than area populations were. Brush found, for example, that the town populations were greater than the population of their local-areas while village populations were not. Thus, towns are disproportionately large in population in relation to the population of their *local* areas. At the same time, however, town populations are disproportionately small in relation to the total population of the *regional* hinterland they control because these areas have increased even faster. For example, the town region will include peripheral areas and four dependent villages with respective village territory.

In comparing, then, theory and reality in settlement patterns of Southwestern Wisconsin, Brush found that the actual populations of centers, their distances apart, and the characteristics of their tributary areas varied from the hexagon pattern. Populations increase more rapidly with rank, as do distances apart, while tributary areas exhibit varying patterns.

Brush attributed much of the difference between theory and reality in Wisconsin to transportation developments that were not characteristic of the Christaller marketing model (k=3). Thus, he feels that Christaller's transport model (k=4) is more applicable although he doesn't actually test it. The original regular pattern of centers was disturbed in the middle of the 19th Century by rail lines which tended to follow terrain ridges. The improved accessibility allowed centers on these axes to grow into villages and, especially, towns. The later development of more flexible automobile and truck traffic caused distance to decay so that towns tended to increase their range of influence and size at the expense of hamlets and villages. Consequently, the more isolated hamlet disappeared or shrank in size, and the regular Christaller pattern was altered. People located in the smaller places increasingly used the larger towns for satisfying a variety of needs, thus reducing the importance of nearby smaller centers. These influences from transportation would help to explain the increase in *local* town tributary area and in town population relative to this tributary area, a pattern that was not apparent for villages.

Brush suggests that cross-cultural laws of central places may be difficult to derive. For example, he found in densely populated sections of Europe that lower-order centers seemed to have a greater variety of services than American counterparts (1953, 402). Primary reasons for this difference appeared to be higher rural population densities and smaller *range* of the thresholds, which in Europe are due to lower transport mobility. Furthermore, comparisons are affected because the United States is rather unique in its dispersed rural settlement while farmers in most European countries live in villages. Such differences affect thresholds of service functions.

SNOHOMISH COUNTY, WASHINGTON.   In the late 1950s the directions of central-place research began to shift. By then a considerable and recognizable body of theory regarding central-place systems existed, derived in great part from Christaller and supplemented by empirical work. Evidence showed that the *size* and *location* of a village were related to its central functions, i.e., the provision of goods and services, and that this village was linked to the hamlets below it and to the towns above it in an interdependent system. However, real *proof* that a central-place hierarchy actually existed was lacking. In 1955, Vining (1955, 167-9), for example, stated that Brush's division into hamlet, village, and town was arbitrarily based on differentiation along a continuum of population. He felt that such classifications were not *independently* derived from the data utilized. Apparently stimulated by Vining's statement, Berry and Garrison (April, 1958) derived statistically from real world data a system of central places which are differentiated in a class system rather than along a continuum. A main advantage of this approach is that it facilitates *comparisons* with other areas, something that had not been easily possible in the studies by Smailes and Brush.

Berry and Garrison tested the existence of the central-place hierarchy in Snohomish County, Washington, a rural area immediately east of the city of Everett.* The primary problem was to determine whether or not central functions fell into groups of classes and, if so, whether these classes were associated with classes of central places, as theory suggests they ought to be. In the analysis four steps were followed:

1. Ranking the functions.
2. Grouping the functions.
3. Ranking and grouping the central places.
4. Relating functions to central places.

1. **Ranking the functions.** A basic hypothesis in Christaller's model is that the population of a center is a function of the number of goods and services provided. This relationship is best seen through the differ-

---

*The analysis below is extracted and summarized from the original articles by Berry and Garrison (April and October, 1958). The primary example is taken from Garner and Yeates (1971).

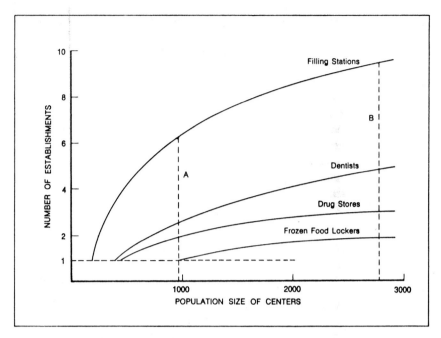

FIGURE 5.10. Differing thresholds for selected central functions in Snohomish County, Washington. When the population of a center is 938, one frozen food locker is present, and 1.9 drug stores, 2.7 dentists, and 6.3 filling stations may occur. (Reprinted with permission of *Economic Geography*, from Brian Berry and William Garrison, "A Note on Central-Place Theory and the Range of a Good," Oct. 1958.)

ing *thresholds* of population necessary to support given functions. Functions that depend on lower thresholds are based on greater frequency of demand and thus are related to the degree of centrality which they possess. Such lower threshold functions will enter the central-place system more easily and will occur more frequently than higher threshold functions, i.e., they will be more ubiquitous. Consequently, a first step in the analysis of the Snohomish County system was to rank the functions on the basis of their thresholds which were in turn derived from their relationships with the populations in 33 centers of the county.* These relationships were shown in scatter diagrams for each of the 52 variate functions with population (P) and number of establishments (N) as parameters to determine the relationship between P and N for each function. Best-fitting curves of the exponential growth series $P = A(B^W)$ were fitted to each of the scatter diagrams using standard least-squares techniques, after logarithmic conversion. The graph (see fig. 5.10) showing the relationship between number of filling stations and population for the 33

*Carter (1972, 95) states that the approach is weakened because the thresholds do not include the populations of rural areas surrounding the centers.

places is shown. The best-fitting curve indicates an exponential relationship between the two variables, i.e., as places become larger they add fewer establishments than would be expected.

The primary purpose of the scatter diagrams was to use the equations of the best-fitting curves for each of the 52 central functions to estimate the *threshold* population needed to support the first complete establishment. This threshold was obtained by calculating the value of P in the equation when $N = 1$. The ranking of selected functions by their threshold size is given in the table (see table 5.2). They range from 196 for service stations to 1,424 for health practitioners. One notices, for example, that the first dentist requires 426 people, the first drug store 458, and the first frozen food locker 938. However, since the population-functional relationship is exponential, each additional establishment of any function requires a greater threshold than the previous one, i.e., the fifth service station requires more than the fourth. Furthermore, this amount of increase is greater at the higher levels than the lower ones. The graph shows how this works (see fig. 5.10): a threshold of 938 supports 6.3 service stations while 2,800 is required for 9.9; however, 938 people support one frozen food locker and 2,800 support only two of them. Consequently, each additional service station and locker require more threshold than the preceding one but the increase is greater for the locker. A primary factor in this increasing threshold increment apparently is economies of scale: as the size of central place increases, the existing establishments can spread their costs over more people thus cutting cost of unit production or service and permitting larger establishments to be added, which in turn require a larger threshold. Another factor in the delay of entry of additional establishments may be the ability of existing ones to continue to provide goods and services to a larger but *denser* population from the same location.

The implications of this first stage of the Snohomish County study are important. The type of functions that a central place can support are related to its population or threshold. Larger centers can support higher functions and many establishments of the lower functions. Smaller centers occur more frequently in the landscape but support fewer functions and fewer establishments of the lower functions.

In contrast to the variates, where the number of establishments varied for each function, the attributes included only one of each (e.g., a post office). The 15 attributes were related to population by calculating the point-biserial coefficient of correlation between each of the activities and the population of the centers. The activities were then ranked on the basis of these coefficients, r_{pb}, since it was observed that higher correlations were associated with occurrence in larger centers.

TABLE 5.2
Threshold Populations for Forty Urban-Based Activities

Class 1_1		Furniture stores, etc.	546
Filling stations	196	Variety stores, "5 & 10"	549
Food stores	254	Apparel stores	590
Churches	265	Lumberyards	598
Restaurants and snack bars	276	Banks	610
Taverns	282	Farm implement dealers	650
Elementary schools	322	High schools	732
Class 2_1		Dry cleaners	754
Physicians	380	Billiard halls and bowling alleys	789
Real estate agencies	384	Jewelry stores	827
Appliance stores	385	Hotels	846
Barber shops	386	Shoe repair shops	896
Auto dealers	398	Frozen food lockers	938
Dentists	426	Class 3_1	
Motels	430	Sheet metal works	1,076
Hardware stores	431	Department stores	1,083
Auto repair shops	435	Hospitals and clinics	1,159
Drug stores	458	Undertakers	1,214
Auto parts dealers	488	Photographers	1,243
Meeting halls	525	Laundries and laundromats	1,307
Feed stores	526	Health practitioners	1,424
Lawyers	528		

From "A Note on Central Place Theory and the Range of a Good" by William Garrison and Brian J. L. Berry, *Economic Geography*, 34, October 1958. Reprinted by permission.

2. **Grouping the functions.** The second step was to test the rankings of variates and attributes for grouping tendencies, i.e., to determine if every member of a group should be closer to some other member of the group than to any other.

In the case of variates, the distribution of population thresholds was tested for randomness using a X^2 (Chi-square) test for significant differences between expected and observed reflexive relationships. The reflexive relationships are those determined by nearest-neighbor analysis as developed by the ecologists, Clark and Evans (1954). The test showed that the observed distribution of thresholds was non-random at the 0.05 level of significance, and that this distribution was non-random in a grouped rather than a "more even than random" manner. Thus, three groups of central functions (1_1, 2_1, and 3_1) were found to be present.

The attributes were also found to fall into three groupings (1_2, 2_2, and 3_2) with a special class for general stores. The test involved standard techniques for determining significant differences between the r_{pb}'s at the 0.05 level of significance.

3. **Ranking and grouping the central places.** A third step was to rank and group the central places. The ranking was based on the number of functions each possessed. The Clark and Evans' test of randomness was then applied to this distribution and a Chi-square test showed that groupings occurred. Three groups of central places—A, B, and C—were isolated.

4. **Relating functions to central places.** A final step related the grouping of functions (both variates and attributes) to groups of central places. The result was a table giving the number of enterprises per function per central place. An analysis of variance between the cells in this table resulted in support for the existence of significant differences between functions and between centers at the 0.95 level of significance. These results confirmed the fact that a hierarchy of central places exists in a statistical sense.

The Snohomish County study apparently supports Christaller's original idea that population-size groupings in a central place hierarchy arise as a result of income derived from activities providing goods and services for differential thresholds. In other words, discrete groups of activities—in which differences between groups are greater than those within groups—lead to discrete population levels. However, *reality* departs from *theory* in Snohomish County in the case of several cities which possess larger populations than would be expected on the basis of their central functions. Four of these are suburbs for either Seattle or Everett, and population growth is based more on the nearness of large cities than on serving as a central place for the surrounding area. Snohomish itself is a county seat and supports extra population with this function.

The statistical approach utilized by Berry and Garrison represents an advance over earlier methods discussed in this chapter. Not only does it allow the determination of exactly how the results were obtained but it also permits a comparison of different central-place systems. For example, King (1961) applied the method to New Zealand and found similar groupings of functions although the thresholds differed. However, he points out that the grouping technique includes an element of subjectivity which raises questions as to whether or not the method demonstrates conclusively that a central-place hierarchy exists in a statistical sense. Marshall (1969, 66) believes that Skinner (1964-65) comes closest to this goal in his analysis of Chinese centers because he shows discrete stratification between groups in three ways: first, by clear differences in the inventories of goods offered by market centers at different levels; secondly, by equally clear breaks in the population sizes of the centers; and thirdly, by the fact that official market days in successively higher orders occurred with increasing frequency.

SOUTHWESTERN IOWA.   Another classic study which illustrates even more sophistication in terms of central-place analysis was carried out in southwestern Iowa by Berry and his colleagues (1962). In this case an agricultural area just east of Council Bluffs was analyzed in depth at aggregate and elemental levels. At the former level, factor analysis was utilized while at the latter consumer behavior was introduced.

1. **Aggregate analysis: entry and grouping of functions.** In this analysis the occurrence of central functions in the study area was summarized by preparing an incidence matrix in which the rows were central places and the columns were central functions. Cells in this matrix were coded one if a function was present in a center and zero otherwise. The matrix was then subjected to direct factor analysis, from which it was concluded that the study area contained three orders of central places and three orders of central functions associated with them. These three orders were then shown as points on a graph in which the abscissa was the number of central functions in places, and the ordinate was the logarithm of the number of functional units in places. This graph (figure 5.11) shows a smooth continuum of centers from the smallest "village" to the largest "city," yet it has been divided into three orders. Berry states that there are "breaks" in functional complexity between these orders, and that each order forms a "regime" with its own distinctive slope on the graph. This approach, while it permits a hierarchical classification of centers from factor analysis, does not explicitly incorporate a consideration of the locational disposition of the centers.

2. **Elemental analysis: consumer behavior.** The above analysis of city-size relationships and entry-grouping of functions was carried out at the aggregative level of inquiry. Berry, et al. also supplemented this analysis with a more elemental or microscopic one focused on consumer travel behavior as derived from interviews with central-place and rural residents. Contrasts between patterns for food and clothing illustrate how the central-place hierarchy is reflected in distances travelled.

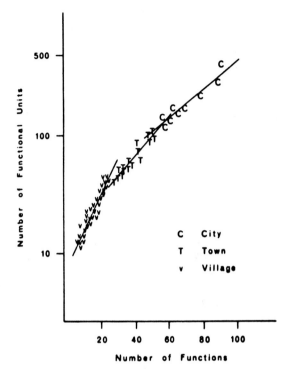

FIGURE 5.11. The relationship between functional units and number of functions by rank in the hierarchy. (Reprinted with permission of the Regional Science Association from B. Berry, H. G. Barnum, and R. J. Tennant, "Retail Location and Consumer Behavior," *Papers and Proceedings,* 9, 1962.)

Food is one of the most ubiquitous services because of a high frequency of demand (see fig. 5.12). People dislike traveling far for groceries because they must do it often. Consumer travel for urban dwellers in southwest Iowa is confined to the centers themselves while farm families generally travel to the nearest center. Thus, distance traveled relates to size of center and reality seems to agree with theory. The main exceptions apparently are the people who, for unknown reasons, travel a considerable distance to buy food in Council Bluffs or those within the trade area of Griswold who go to Red Oak.

Clothing provides a contrast with food since it is a much less ubiquitous good which is purchased infrequently (see fig. 5.13). Its threshold, therefore, is much larger than that of food. Moreover, people like to compare shop for quality clothing, a factor which may attract them to the center with the most clothing stores. Urban travel behavior for clothing in southwestern Iowa, therefore, illustrates a pattern of movement to larger centers, i.e., from Oakland (a town) to the city of Atlantic. Rural dwellers also travel to the larger centers. A primary departure of reality from theory is the "capture" of Griswold by Atlantic. Actually, the former lies in the overlapping trade areas of both Atlantic and Red Oak;

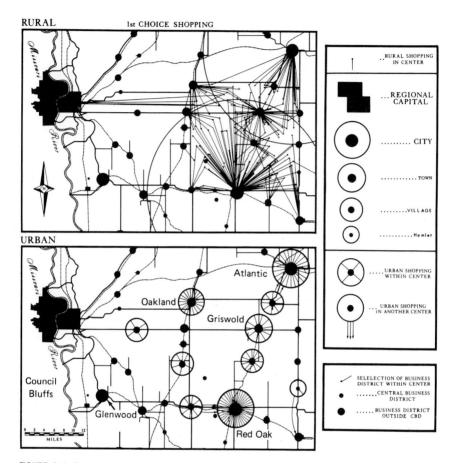

FIGURE 5.12. Rural and urban shopping patterns for food in southwest Iowa reflect low thresholds. (Reprinted with permission of the Regional Science Association from B. Berry, H. G. Barnum, and R. J. Tennant, "Retail Location and Consumer Behavior," *Papers and Proceedings*, 9, 1962.)

however, for certain reasons, again not specified, all consumers interviewed traveled to the former for clothing.

One of Christaller's original assumptions was that perfect competition existed and that consumers would not cross the boundary lines of the market areas. Although the two maps show this to be generally true, some travel lines extend into other market areas and illustrate that consumer travel decisions are based on other criteria besides physical distance between consumer and producer.

Although consumer behavior theory as discussed above for central places would indicate that distance traveled varies with level of center and availability of goods, reality may vary considerably when a different

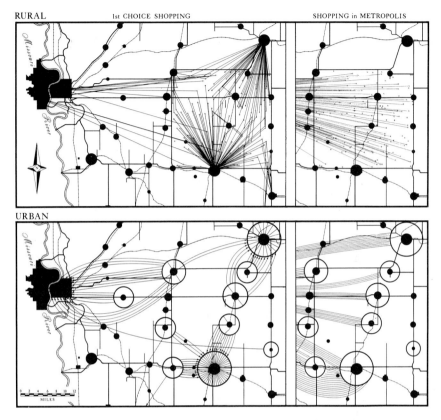

RURAL   1st CHOICE SHOPPING   SHOPPING in METROPOLIS

URBAN

FIGURE 5.13. Rural and urban shopping patterns for clothing in southwest Iowa reflect large thresholds and some interpenetration of trade areas. (Reprinted with permission of the Regional Science Association from B. Berry, H. G. Barnum, and R. J. Tennant, "Retail Location and Consumer Behavior," *Papers and Proceedings*, 9, 1962.)

culture is involved. For example, the Mennonites of southwestern Ontario (Murdie, 1965) have different patterns of consumer behavior, especially for the more specialized goods. This group, in retaining the old traditions, has a reduced demand for goods, uses horse and buggy for transportation, and has a low level of information regarding the modern world due to reduced utilization of mass media communications. As a result, their travel patterns for clothing purchases are quite different from those of modern Canadians. Since their dress is plain with most clothes made at home from yard goods, style and comparative shopping are unimportant. Consequently, they travel to the nearest place regardless of size (see fig. 5.14). On the other hand, their travel patterns for banks are rather normal because this service is more specialized and less closely related to the personal traditions of this cul-

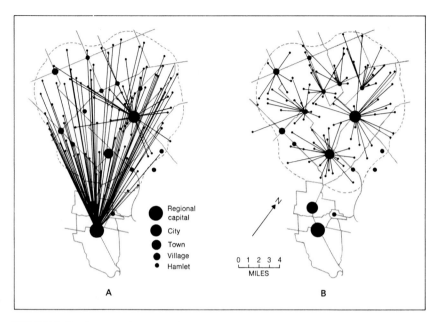

Regional capital

City

Town

Village

Hamlet

0 1 2 3 4
MILES

A   B

FIGURE 5.14. Shopping patterns for clothing differ between "modern" Canadians (A) and old order Mennonites (B). (Reprinted with permission of *Economic Geography* from R. A. Murdie, "Cultural Differences in Consumer Travel," *Economic Geography,* July, 1965.)

tural group. This contrast in travel patterns illustrates that, in the case of cross-cultural comparisons, size of center as a factor in consumer travel must be supplemented by that of perceived behavior space.

3. **Spacing.** An analysis of central places generally includes not only a discussion of the hierarchy but also the spacing between centers. The study of central places in southwestern Iowa concludes by stating that the pattern may resemble a k=4 network more than that of either a k=3 or k=7. However, because of the influence of the rectangular land survey system, the overall arrangement is quite dissimilar from the hexagon pattern of Christaller. Berry, et al. emphasize that *nesting* or capture of complete complementary regions of lower centers takes place in a k=5 network. In other words, the city now has captured additional villages from the town areas so that its complementary region is five times that of the town while the latter is reduced to k=1, or one village area. The sketch illustrates what may happen in southwestern Iowa when settlement is adapting to a linear-rectangular survey and road system instead of the radial one more common to Europe (see fig. 5.15). Morrill (1974, 80) has also suggested rectilinear central place patterns, but his k=4 pattern differs from that of Berry. Evidently more attention should be de-

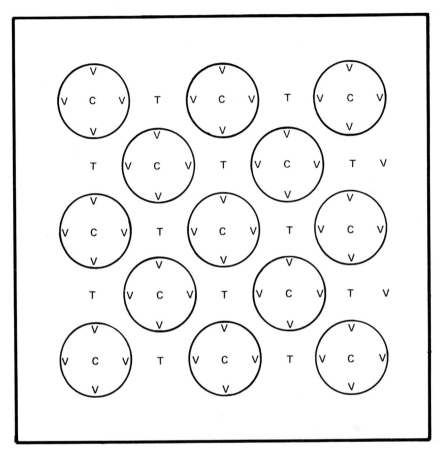

FIGURE 5.15. A hypothetical k=5 network of central places in southwest Iowa that reflects the rectangular land survey system. (Reprinted with permission of the Regional Science Association from B. Berry, H. G. Barnum, and R. J. Tennant, "Retail Location and Consumer Behavior," *Papers and Proceedings*, 9, 1962.)

voted to the effects of cultural traits, such as a survey system, on central-place theory.

Isard (1956) and others also have illustrated how the effects of population density might affect a spacing pattern of hexagons. If populations are dense, as around a city, the ranges of goods and services are smaller and the pattern of hexagons is small. On the other hand, as population density decreases, the threshold necessary to support a good may be spread over a larger area, spreading out the hexagon pattern. Kolars and Nystren (1974, 101) have shown how such a pattern changes from east to west in the real world of the Upper Midwest (see fig. 5.16).

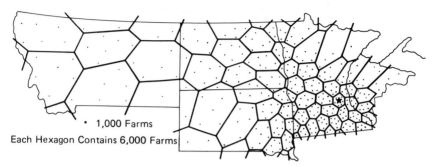

FIGURE 5.16. Changes in the central place pattern over the Upper Midwest as population density decreases from east to west. Each hexagon contains 6,000 farms and each dot represents 1,000 farms. (From *Human Geography* by John Kolars and John Nystuen, Copyright © 1974 by McGraw-Hill Book Company. Used with permission of McGraw-Hill Book Company.)

OTHER APPROACHES. The four approaches used in the latter part of this chapter—developed respectively by Smailes, Brush, Berry and Garrison, and Berry, et al.—illustrate not only different ways of testing the central-place hypothesis but also methodological changes in the discipline. However, these approaches represent only a portion of the literature on this important topic. Although many geographers accepted the Christaller thesis and merely tested it in the real world, others were more critical and did not even accept the uniformity of the pattern. For example, Dacey (1962) and King (1962) found that when central-place patterns are subjected to nearest-neighbor analysis, the distribution is random rather than uniform, a direct conflict with the Christaller concept. Furthermore, this problem of pattern, and the related one of whether or not hierarchies are universal, seem to be tied in with the separation of central-place systems from urban systems. The latter system is the subject of the next chapter.

Supplementing the criticism of uniform patterns in central-place theory was a second one based on perception of the consumer. Golledge, et al. (1966) found in Iowa that the grouping of central-place functions on the basis of travel behavior produces a different ordering of functions into ranks than grouping on the basis of occurrence of function. Such a finding illustrates the early tendency to derive spatial structures on the basis of assumptions regarding rational "economic man" rather than deriving them from a firm base of research on spatial behavior.

SUMMARY

In this chapter, the central-place system has been discussed as a preliminary to understanding the overall urban system. The former system provides goods and services that are required regularly but at different frequencies by a population. Consequently, a hierarchy of central places, designed to provide these goods and services, emerges which possesses a degree of regularity in structure suitable for theory building. The Christaller theory of central places stands as the most important spatial foundation for explaining the location of settlements around and within cities, and much of the geographical research on this topic since his statement of 1933 has been aimed at testing his ideas. However, as Morrill (1974, 81) points out, the real contribution of central-place theory has not been the observation of strict geometric regularities but rather the isolation of spatial behavior which suggests *reasons* for the regularities. Thus, for example, behavior may help to explain why consumers do not always minimize distance traveled to satisfy their desires.

Examples have been given of different approaches to the analysis of central places. Smailes derived an urban hierarchy in England and Wales without reference to Christaller. Brush, on the other hand, compared the settlement pattern of southwestern Wisconsin with Christaller. Stimulated by Brush's arbitrary classification, Berry and Garrison utilized statistical methods to derive the hierarchy from the data of one area, Snohomish County, Washington. They showed that settlements do tend to group themselves into population classes based on the goods and services they provided. A few years later Berry and his colleagues supplemented this work by a rather sophisticated analysis of the central places of southwestern Iowa. In this study, analysis was carried out at aggregate scale by factor analysis and at elemental scale by interviews, the latter permitting interpretation of consumer travel behavior. Although the studies summarized above represent only a fraction of central-place work, they do provide examples of the progress of geographic research in this field. The use of statistical methodology in the recent studies has facilitated more realistic comparative studies of central place-systems than did the earlier subjective approaches.

Evidently progress in defining and explaining the *ranks* in the urban hierarchy has been greater than in interpreting the actual *locational* patterns of settlements in this hierarchy. Most geographers, for example, find that Christaller's theory is closer to reality in connection with these ranks than in the spacing of these centers. A reason may be the rigid hexagon model which forces smaller centers as close to large centers as to each other, a pattern that Kolb did not find. Nevertheless, the mathematical consistency of the Christaller model has made it a useful starting point for testing central-place systems in the real world.

The regularity of the central-place patterns, of course, provides a firm base for further analysis of the urban system. The urban system includes not only the central-place components but also the more sporadic specialized functions which exhibit far fewer regularities. Consequently, theory is less adequately developed here. Nevertheless, some generalizations regarding the total system can be made as is evident in the next chapter.

CHAPTER 6

HE CITY AS PART
OF A URBAN SYSTEM

In the preceding chapter, the central-place model was tested as a basis for explaining the reality of providing ary services for a system of cities. This comparison of theory with rea apparently reveals that although regularities exist in the distribution oods and services to a population, distortions are also present to a considerable degree. However, if *specialized* functions are superimposed the central-place activities, the problem of finding regularity in hierarchy and location is even more difficult. The contrast between central place and specialized functions is evident in fig. 4.10. As Morrill states (4, 84-5), "central-place theory explicitly excludes other town-building activities that produce goods for export," rather than serving the n itself and its immediate surroundings. This difference—local ve external support—may provide us with one key to interpreting th tal urban system. The sections below illustrate different approaches plaining this system, and in all of them external support is a signi nt factor in urban growth.

RANK-SIZE VS. PRIMACY: THEORY AND REALITY

In most urban systems the regularity of location that was so apparent in central-place systems begins to be distorted. However, the regularity of hierarchy seems to maintain itself to some degree so for this reason much research on urban systems has been focused on this approach. No real theory in the sense of Christaller has been established, but instead two empirical statements have served as the basis for testing such systems in reality. The first of these is known as the rank-size rule and the second as the concept of the primate city.

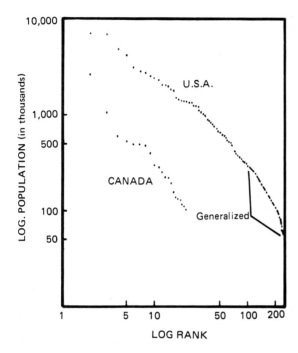

FIGURE 6.1. Rank-size relationships for the 243 SMSA's in the United States and the 22 CMA's in Canada, 1971. (Fig. 2.10 [p. 53] from *The North American City* by Maurice H. Yeates and Barry J. Garner. Reprinted by permission of Harper & Row, Publishers, Inc.)

In 1949 Zipf postulated the rank-size rule which states that the population of a particular city in an area is equal to the population of the largest city in the area divided by the rank of that particular city. In other words:

$$P_r = \frac{P_1}{r} \text{ or } P_1 = P_r \times r$$

where P_r = population of a city of rank r
      P_1 = population of the largest city
      r   = rank of a given city

In some cases, a constant is added to the population figure in order to weigh it for comparative purposes. The diagram illustrates the 1970 SMSAs of the United States in rank-size on a double log graph, a pattern that resembles a continuous rather than a stepped hierarchy (see fig. 6.1). The intriguing relationship between size and rank is apparent. Yet when this rule is actually applied, deviations are found to occur. For example, examine the five largest American SMSAs:

SMSA	Rank	Population (1970)	Rank-size rule
New York	1	11,571,899	
Los Angeles	2	7,042,075	5,785,949
Chicago	3	6,978,947	3,857,300
Philadelphia	4	4,817,914	2,892,975
Detroit	5	4,199,931	2,314,380

It can be seen that a relationship exists between population and rank, yet the expected figures derived from the rank-size rule are lower than actual figures. Since this may in part be due to the rather artificial size of SMSAs, data for Urbanized Areas are used, figures which correspond perhaps more to actual "cities" as such:

Urbanized Area	Rank	Population	Rank-size rule
New York	1	16,206,841	
Los Angeles	2	8,351,266	8,103,420
Chicago	3	6,714,578	5,402,280
Philadelphia	4	4,021,066	4,051,710
Detroit	5	3,970,584	3,241,368

In this case the correspondence between theory and reality is much closer. In any use of the rank-size rule, obviously the size of the largest city is crucial. In the case of New York, the Urbanized Area population (16,206,841) is larger than that of the SMSA (11,571,899) since the metropolitan area actually includes four SMSAs which together make up the Standard Consolidated Area. Use of the Urbanized Area figure is preferable because it more truly represents the total metropolitan population.

The above test of the rank-size rule was limited to only five cities, and a real test should include all cities in the system. The rank-size relationships shown in fig. 6.1 are more apparent for the United States than for Canada where distortions occur, most notably in the nearly equal rank of Montreal and Toronto.

Granted that the rank-size rule applies in the United States, what can be said about its application in other parts of the world? Berry has made a rather extensive study of rank-size, and concludes that it is inseparable from the concept of primacy (Berry, 1961, 573-588). This "law," first mentioned by Mark Jefferson in 1939, refers to the tendency for each country to have one dominant city that reflects the characteristics of that culture (Jefferson, 1939, 226-232). As such, it tends to maintain itself, attracting economic, political, and cultural functions. Therefore, the primate city is generally several times larger than the second city in rank. The concept of primacy stands at the other extreme from the rank-size rule because the regularity of population rank is distorted in the former case. Berry has tested both of these concepts in a world cultural context using city-size graphs for 38 countries. The graphs, of log type so that the distribution appears as a straight line, show cumulative percentages of cities over 20,000 population measured against city size. A sample of the results are shown and indicate that correlations of either rank-size or primacy with degree of economic development are difficult (see fig. 6.2). For example, the graphs of rank-size distribution include industrial

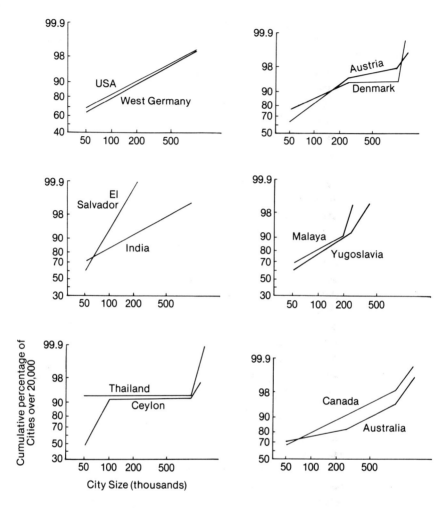

FIGURE 6.2. Selected primate and rank-size distributions for different countries. (Reprinted with the permission of University of Chicago Press and *Economic Development and Cultural Change* from Brian Berry, "City Size Distributions and Economic Development," July 1961.)

countries like the United States and Italy as well as developing countries like India and El Salvador. The same is true of the graph for primacy where Denmark and Thailand exhibit similarities. Distributions intermediate between rank-size and primacy include countries as divergent as Australia and Yugoslavia.

Although these two concepts of rank-size and primacy do not constitute theory in a true sense, they can be used to illustrate certain regularities of spatial organization. Why, for example, do different countries approximate one or the other patterns or a combination of both? Berry finds no consistent correlation between any of the three distributions and the degree of urbanization in a country, thus challenging a concept that had existed for some time. An explanation of the divergences of individual countries from the patterns apparently relates to the historical development of these areas, and Berry offers certain generalizations concerning this factor:

1. A primacy pattern seems to be present in those countries that were colonies, i.e., dependent on some outside country, with recent development focused into one center that has long served as capital and cultural center, e.g., Uruguay. Small countries that once had extensive empires also seem to exhibit primacy, e.g., Portugal, Spain, and Austria, while others which are small but without this background may not require intermediate level centers owing to economies of scale with respect to the largest city.

2. A pattern of city distribution intermediate between primacy and rank size seems to reflect some degree of regionalism. For example, Yugoslavia has long been a state characterized by several strong ethnic groups. These groups are now reflected in a federal structure that is modified toward primacy because of artificial attempts at centralization from Belgrade, both in the past and in the present.

3. A rank-size pattern seems to include many countries that are considerably industrialized or with a long history of urbanization. Here again, however, a long history of separate regional development may, even if industrialization is not present in all areas, lead to a rank-size distribution, e.g., Italy.

Berry concludes his comparison of city-size distribution by proposing a hypothesis: Increasing entropy is accompanied by a closer approximation of rank-size rule. This hypothesis suggests that such a distribution occurs when the forces affecting this distribution are many and act randomly within the context of growth proportionate to size of city (Berry and Garrison, March 1958, 90). Such conditions are apt to be present in industrial countries. Primacy, on the other hand, is simpler because it is affected by fewer forces, especially since it often occurs in countries that are small, possess a shorter history of urbanization, and have a less complex political and economic structure.

The rank-size rule and the concept of primacy illustrate that systems of cities have different growth patterns. In some countries growth occurs at many levels of size while in others it is concentrated at certain levels, often the top. The previous chapter demonstrated that the central-place functions tend to create a hierarchal pattern of regularity, but this pattern must be supplemented so as to examine why some cities grow and others do not. Urban authorities agree that growth in an urban system is from *external* support—from functions like trade, industry, and others that attract income to the city from outside. Four concepts or models are used below to illustrate how external sources change the sizes and locational pattern of members of an urban system. First, a mercantile model is examined to illustrate the effects of wholesaling. Secondly, industrial models are introduced to show how manufacturing supplements the overall pattern. Thirdly, the economic base concept is employed to depict how urban growth takes place, especially through a factor known as the multiplier effect. Finally, a circular and cumulative process model is utilized to clarify why certain metropolitan areas, especially older ones, have exhibited rather persistent patterns of growth.

THE MERCANTILE MODEL: THEORY AND REALITY

Vance is one of the few urban geographers to offer a model supplementing that of central places (Vance, 1970). He feels that the Christaller model represents a closed system based on the resources of its immediate area. This type of urban system is endogenous in that growth can come only through enhanced demands on the part of local consumers. In other words, relating external inputs to a central-place system is difficult. These external inputs are very important in "new" lands where a system of trade may develop *before* a central-place system does. Consequently, Vance feels that an open-system model is necessary to take into account external influences, and to explain observable similarity among cities located in contrasting regions. Thus, for example, Boston and Philadelphia possessed early similarities based on trade. He calls this exogenic concept the "mercantile model" because it is based on wholesaling, a form of activity he believes must be considered in accounting for growth in a system of cities, particularly those in pioneer lands of settlement. Such a model, therefore, helps to explain the urban systems of many "new" lands, such as Canada, the United States, and Australia. In the United States, the Mississippi and Missouri River towns "grew out of trade, not out of the agriculture of the corn belt" (Vance, 1970, 164-5). In other words, this trading process operated *before* the central-place process in a pioneer landscape. In this sense, these cities bear resemblance to Burghardt's "gateway cities," which "set up" the countrysides that in turn "set up" central places (Burghardt, 1971, 285).

The mercantile model is shown on the accompanying map as it applies to the settlement of the United States (see fig. 6.3). After initial periods of searching and testing for productivity in a new land, points of attachment were formed on the coast for the introduction of settlement and trade. In its early stages this trade developed a broad "seed bed" of

The Mercantile Model   The Central-place Model

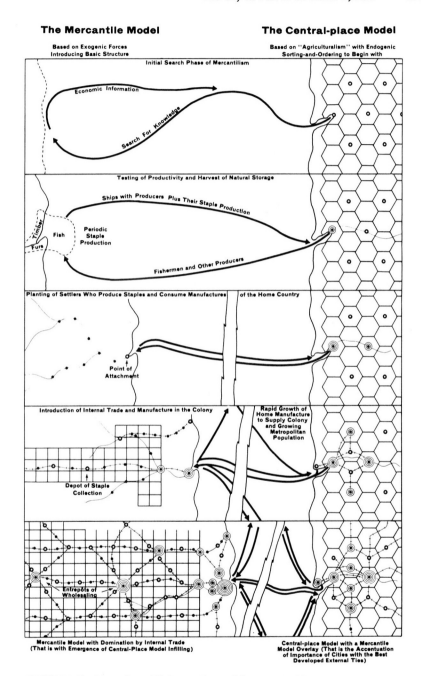

FIGURE 6.3. The "mercantile model" of James Vance which stresses the initial development of aligned trade centers prior to central-place infilling. (Reprinted with the permission of James Vance from *The Merchant's World,* 1970.)

activity that led to later specialization. As Vance states, "Boston was born of fish and naval stores but grew up as a wholesaling city on wool, leather, and electronic parts" (Vance, 1970, 152). These multiple points of attachment on the east coast of North America competed with each other to carve out hinterlands linked to them by rivers, canals, and railroads. This competition marked the economic history of 19th Century America. New York's exploitation of the Hudson-Mohawk Valleys for canal and railroad enabled it to capture the Middle West hinterland ahead of Boston, Philadelphia, and Baltimore. As the interior of the United States opened up, *entrepots,* or transportation cities, developed at accessible points to stand as receptacles of the exogenic forces of wholesale trade. At first these receptacles were the river towns because of the importance of this transportation form, and later railroads actually reinforced this pattern rather than changing it radically.

These entrepots or exchange points served first as collecting points and the distribution function developed later. The river and coastal ports shipped to Europe the staples of the region (e.g., furs) and received the manufactured items and tropical staples that made up the return flow. A vast intelligence regarding the conditions of marketing in the region was gradually developed in these centers. Ultimately, this knowledge helped certain entrepots to become wholesaling centers equipped to distribute products according to the demand in the region. This, in turn, would lead to what Vance calls the "internalization" of wholesale trade—the process by which commercial centers supplement external trade with local or regional activities. Finally, these same centers became locations for manufacturing because of the external flows of collection and the internal flows of distribution. In this way, Vance believes that functions of retailing and industry were implanted on top of the original commercial pattern. He thus provides links between spatial patterns of commerce and those of central place and manufacturing.

The spatial pattern of settlement that evolves from the mercantile model is *linear* and therefore stands in contrast to the classical Christaller pattern. Vance explains this pattern in terms of a series of "alignments" of *entrepots.* The first of these alignments is the series of "points of attachment" or footholds on the east coast, all derived from external stimuli. Although in part wholesaling centers today, they remain as ports of foreign trade. A second series of alignments marks the routes between the ports and staple-producing interior, e.g., Great Lakes alignment, starting from the Hudson-Mohawk Valleys and extending through Cleveland, Detroit, Chicago, and Milwaukee. This alignment, which predates the railroad, is supplemented by later alignments that reflect not only external trade but also domestic commerce and the development of railroads and manufacturing: Ohio-Missouri, Appalachian-

Piedmont, Great Plains, Rocky Mountain Piedmont, and Pacific Coast. According to Vance, these alignments include cities which were established by history and today maintain wholesaling functions by tradition. The mercantile model helps to interpret some similarities in urban systems that are not explained by central-place theory. Vance believes that when settlement and economic development were introduced from outside—as in much of the Western Hemisphere and Australia—the mercantile process operated before the central-place one did. In Europe, where feudalism existed for so long, he seems to feel the central-place pattern preceded one derived from external trade and wholesaling. The mercantile model is an evolutionary one rather than spatial, and its application to various cases is perhaps less satisfactory for a geographer than the central-place concept. Nevertheless, it does provide us with a link between central-place and specialized functions in an urban system, and in this way assists in explaining growth patterns.

Johnston (1973, 32) feels that the Vance model explains spatial aspects of urban systems. The model suggests to him that the rank size and primate distributions are not mutually exclusive. A country, therefore, may have a combination of the two. Primacy has been related to dependence on external trade in terms of the rise of a large port city. At the same time, rank-size has been related to the degree of industrialization. Thus, a trade-dependent, highly industrialized system would have a rank-size distribution topped by a primate city. However, these ideas are very tentative and much research remains to be done on models that reflect external and internal components to urban systems.

INDUSTRIAL LOCATION AND THE URBAN SYSTEM

Most industry is located in urban areas of some kind. However, some enterprises are more ubiquitous than others and thus bear resemblance to a central-place pattern. The regularity in the distribution of such industries is related to accessibility to local markets. On the other hand, irregularity in industrial location, and therefore distortions in the overall urban system, are often a function of accessibility to resources, labor, regional markets, or breaks in transport. Each of these types of accessibility is treated below.*

ACCESSIBILITY TO LOCAL MARKETS. A first major type of manufacturing found in *most* communities is one that is based on a local market. Such industries have a low threshold of population support and,

*The theoretical approach used here which is focused on different types of accessibility, was developed by the author from a variety of sources.

therefore, are located in both small and large urban areas with the number of establishments increasing by size of center. A key factor is the *frequency* of use, e.g., baked goods or soft drinks which are produced near the customer. These types of industries are called ubiquitous, because they are found everywhere, and city-serving or non-basic, because the threshold is provided by the local rather than the external market. Since their location is central to a local threshold, their pattern of distribution tends to be regular and similar to that of a central-place hierarchy.

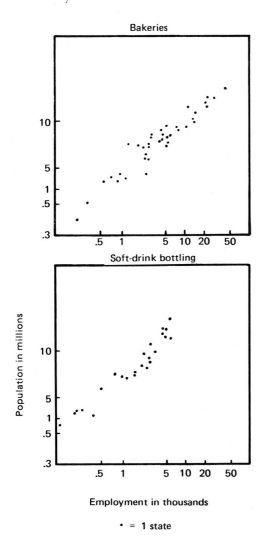

FIGURE 6.4. Two ubiquitous urban industries which show a high correlation of population and employment are bakeries and softdrink bottling. (John W. Alexander, *Economic Geography,* © 1963, pp. 298. Reprinted by permission of Prentice-Hall, Inc., Englewood Cliffs, New Jersey.)

Those industries based on local markets generally are located in the nearest center because their transport costs are a high percentage of the total delivered costs. These costs are high because the products: (1) age quickly—bakery products and newspapers; (2) increase in bulk—bottling and brewing; (3) are of low value—printing. Scatter diagrams of bottling and baking (see fig. 6.4), for example, show a high degree of correlation between population and employment, thereby confirming their ubiquitous characteristic (Alexander, 1963, 298). In addition, Alexandersson (1956, 82-92) found that all American cities over 10,000 population included the above industries plus that of construction materials.

ACCESSIBILITY TO RESOURCES.   A second type of industrial location associated with urban areas is related to resources, the most common being construction materials. Most communities require sand and gravel plus building stone, materials which are fairly ubiquitous in nature. Thus, most urban centers will have enterprises of this type with the pattern again resembling that of central places because of high transport costs relative to the value of the product.

More significant in terms of resource-oriented industries are those related to a regional location, e.g., coal mining, oil drilling, or timber producing areas. Many urban centers, either dispersed or clustered depending on the particular raw material, are located in these areas. For example, a large part of the petro-chemical industry is situated in eastern Texas to take advantage of huge regional reserves of petroleum and gas. The location of these industries in urban areas *near* the resource is based on their particular raw materials which either *lose weight* in the processing or are *perishable*. Most smelting or wood industries involve a loss of weight so that locating away from the source of raw material would not be practical. The copper mining towns of Butte and Anaconda, Montana, for example, possess concentrating and smelting plants, respectively, because of the great weight losses in both of these processes. Factories of the Great Western Sugar Company are located in many larger settlements of the irrigated region of northeast Colorado where sugar beets are a regional resource and the weight loss in processing is great. The fruit products utilized in canneries like those of towns in Sacramento County, California, are perishable, and, therefore, must be handled quickly near the source of raw materials. These resource-based towns generally never become large in size and, in the case of mining, often decline if the raw material is depleted. Old mining-smelting towns are a feature of the landscape of parts of the American West.

ACCESSIBILITY TO LABOR.   Labor costs in a manufacturing process can be critical to location in at least two ways. First of all, accessibility to *low cost* labor can be significant if labor represents a large proportion of total costs. The best example is the cotton textile industry which is now heavily concentrated in the Piedmont region of the South, often in small towns, where the low wage-scale, largely a result of the absence of labor unions, was a main factor in the relocation of firms from New England. Furniture factories in the same area also take advantage of low wages because of the large percentage of handwork involved. A second way that labor acts as a locational factor for industry is in *special skills* that may be present. Many large firms like those producing steel or machine tools locate in areas of high population density because the regional market possesses a by-product of skilled labor that can be tapped.

ACCESSIBILITY TO REGIONAL MARKETS.   A location in a regional market area is becoming more and more a characteristic of certain manufacturing. In the early days of automobile production, for example, Henry Ford was able to show that large-scale operations (economies of scale) in large assembly plants reduced costs per unit of production and *offset* costs of moving cars to a wide market. Thus, the early automobile industry exhibited a concentrated pattern in southeastern Michigan, serving essentially a national market. Later on, as the American population expanded, the industry began to concentrate in certain metropolitan regions which possessed the threshold of demand necessary to support large-scale operations. Consequently, a number of assembly plants became possible in different parts of the country (e.g., Kansas City) and it was possible to *combine* scale economies with reduced transport costs to customers.

New York City illustrates a location which minimizes transport costs to a large regional market represented by the eastern portion of the manufacturing belt. The thresholds supported by this population, which includes the city itself, contributes to the great diversity of manufacturing there. Furthermore, external economies, or benefits from a location near other firms or services, become possible as exemplified by steel or component parts for machinery being produced in the same region. In a sense, the manufacturing belt is both a source of raw materials and market for machinery factories, which help to explain their location there. Finally, as transport technology improves, the thresholds accessible to a location are increased even more, and certain products with a relatively high value like hardware can even serve a *national* market from a location such as Rockford, Illinois.

ACCESSIBILITY TO BREAKS-IN-TRANSPORT. Break-in-transport points, especially port cities, generally enjoy a favorable location for industry. Normally, freight rates taper, i.e., they increase at a decreasing rate with distance, and thereby favor industrial locations at either the source of raw materials or at markets. An intermediate location along a 1,000 mile land route, for example, would include two 500-mile transfers which would be more expensive than the one longer haul of 1,000 miles. However, if a breaking-point exists along this route which *necessitates* a transfer of goods such as at a port, the advantages of the longer haul are lost for the other two locations. A factory located in a port, for example, would be competitive because of the equalizing of haul and terminal costs. This factor helps to explain the increasing attraction of port locations for manufacturing. For example, raw materials from overseas can be easily assembled at coast sites after low-cost shipment. Iron and steel plants especially profit from this arrangement and, indeed, a coastal location of most new steel plants is a geographic phenomenon of Western Europe since the end of World War II. Oil refineries are also located in large port cities, primarily because it is economical to ship in raw material by tanker and distill it centrally into many different products for subsequent distribution to inland consumers; a related factor is the higher costs of shipping refined products.

This brief summary of industrial location illustrates certain selected factors that influence the overall development of an urban system. Manufacturing, like wholesaling, is a special function that *supplements* the central-place functions discussed in the last chapter. Unlike these functions, however, predicting the locations of industry is difficult because of the varying factors involved. Only in certain industries that are ubiquitous, either because of accessibility to local markets or to certain resources, is a regular predictable pattern present which resembles that of central places.

It is obvious that factors other than those mentioned above can affect industrial location and urban growth. Technological innovations like the invention of the automobile in a suburb of Detroit can be important. The presence of an ideal climate can affect some industry such as aircraft production. However, in the long run it is felt that resources, labor, markets, and transportation have the greatest impact on manufacturing location and thus on urban growth.

ECONOMIC BASE: THEORY AND REALITY

A summary of the attempt to explain the geography of urban systems is now necessary. In chapter 5, it was explained that regularity in size and location of urban centers is related to the process of providing goods and services for a population from central places. The central-place hierarchy that emerges, therefore, derives its growth from its own area and in this sense is endogenic. When the exogenic or external forces of growth are added in the form of wholesaling or manufacturing, the locational pattern is distorted, and the steps in the hierarchy may be evened out so that more of a continuum emerges unless factors leading to primacy are present. However, these endogenic and exogenic forces have been analyzed in largely static situations, a condition that necessitates an examination of the dynamic or growth aspects of the urban system. Why are certain size cities in the system growing faster than others? One pattern that seems important in highly developed urban systems is increasing concentration of population in metropolitan areas. If this is true, understanding the reasons for this type of urban change is important.

A major concept that helps to clarify the processes of urban growth is the economic base. This concept is founded on the idea that a city's growth is dependent on a combination of basic and nonbasic sources of income. The basic sources are derived from *external* markets, e.g., a new factory. However, the 1,000 new basic employees of the factory require services which in theory are not available in the city. Therefore, perhaps 1,000 *internal* or nonbasic people are necessarily added to the city's population to provide gasoline, food, pharmaceutical goods, etc., for them. The basic-nonbasic ratio is the ratio between these two populations that exists in a given city, and the multiplier effect is the automatic growth of nonbasic functions generated by basic functions. In the example given above, the 1,000 basic to 1,000 nonbasic population ratio is 1:1, and the second 1,000 is the multiplier effect.

Obviously the identification of this basic support would be useful in understanding a city and in projecting its future possibilities for growth. However, this separation of basic from nonbasic activity is not easy. For instance, sale of manufactured products to an external market is "basic" as is the sale of groceries to the farmer. The barber in a resort hotel who serves only tourists is performing a basic activity in contrast to the barber who handles only local residents and is thereby nonbasic. Of course, most barbers do both, an illustration of the problem involved in attempting to separate basic-nonbasic activities. Through various methods a ratio can be computed which gives the relative percentages of basic and nonbasic activities in a city, i.e., the degree to which it depends on external activities for support. The distinction between two types of spatial relationships—in this case, external and internal—is fundamental to geographic analysis.

What are the geographic qualities of the economic base concept? All cities have a specific employment structure, but it is not certain how much of this employment is related to external support. For example, if a factory produces all of its products for sale outside the city, the entire plant employment is basic. But it would be helpful to know for all activities in the city the extent to which the goods and services are sold outside or inside the city since locational aspects of markets are fundamental in urban growth. Alexander (1954, 250) illustrates these geographic qualities of the concept by showing total and basic employment in Oshkosh and Madison, Wisconsin (see fig. 6.5). The patterns of basic employment in these cities are completely different from those of total employment because the respective functions of these two cities, manufacturing and government, largely basic activities, are isolated from activities like retail trade and services, which are both basic and nonbasic. Therefore, separation of the basic-nonbasic elements in a city provides a view of economic ties which bind a city to other areas. Manufacturing and government are the essential functions which tie Oshkosh and

URBAN ECONOMIC STRUCTURE

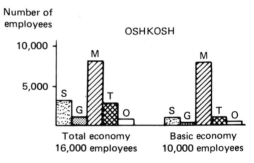

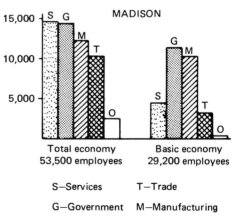

FIGURE 6.5. The graphs illustrate how certain functions are basic in supporting a city. In Oshkosh, Wisconsin, manufacturing is a basic function while in Madison, government and manufacturing are basic. In both cases, the basic elements are obscured when only the total economy is considered. (Reprinted with permission of *Economic Geography* from John Alexander, "The Basic-Nonbasic Concept of Urban Economic Functions," *Economic Geography,* July 1954.)

S—Services   T—Trade

G—Government   M—Manufacturing

O—Others

Madison, respectively, to other areas and bring money to the cities. If we were to extend this classification to other cities, we would have the basis for a more realistic classification of cities in terms of external support. In many functional classifications the nonbasic activities "cloud the picture," for it is the basic activities which express a city's service to its region.

A primary problem in dealing with the economic base concept is the difficulty in determining the ratio for individual cities. Any approach must deal with the difficulties of measuring cities versus metropolitan areas as well as the fact that most employees engage in both basic and nonbasic activities. Three common methods of determining the ratio rely on employment data which are used for a detailed survey, an approximation method, or establishing minimum requirements. A fourth method—input-output analysis—employs money flows and, owing to lack of space, is not included here.

The detailed survey is time-consuming and expensive. Interviews and questionnaires are used to cover all or a large proportion of the enterprises in a city to determine the percentages of goods and service that each firm sells externally. These percentages are then applied to total employment figures in each enterprise to determine the percentage of workers that can be considered basic. The total number of "basic employees" in the city will provide the final ratio. Such a method is only practical for a small or medium-sized city as in the cases of Oshkosh and Madison.

The second method of determining the economic base is an approximation technique. Developed by Homer Hoyt for large cities, it employs census data to compare the proportions of city to national employment in various activities with the proportion of city population to national population. The assumption is that the population of a particular urban area consumes its proportionate share of the national totals of goods and services, and, therefore, that this amount is nonbasic; production beyond this amount is basic. For each specific activity in which the city's proportion of national employment in that activity exceeds its comparative proportion of population to national population, the activity is considered basic to that degree. These excessive proportions are totalled for all lines of activity to give the total basic employment for the city. This method, of course, is subject to criticism, especially as regards the assumption that city and national performances can be compared in terms of output per employee.

A third method of discovering the basic-nonbasic ratio in a particular city is that of establishing minimum requirements. Originated by Ullman and Dacey (1962), census data for given industries are used to determine the American city with the lowest proportion of its labor force employed in that industry.* The assumption is that this labor force is the minimum required by any community to satisfy its *own* needs and that all employment in *excess* of this amount in any other community is basic or export employment. Repeating this process for other industries would yield a basic total for each industry in each community and by combining these the total basic employment of any particular city could be determined.

The minimum-requirements approach provides one of the best shortcuts to determining the economic base. Ullman and Dacey have prepared a graph that depicts the best-fitting regression lines joining the minimum requirements for metropolitan areas of different population classes (see fig. 6.6). For example, these requirements for three activities in three different size classes of metropolitan areas for 1950 were as follows:

	100,000-150,000	300,000-800,000	over 1,000,000
Retail trade	12.1	13.3	14.8
Wholesale trade	1.4	2.3	2.1
Nondurable manufacturing	4.2	3.7	4.9

*Ullman and Dacey argue that taking the actual minimum is most consistent. Tests they conducted revealed that "oddball" cases were few in number.

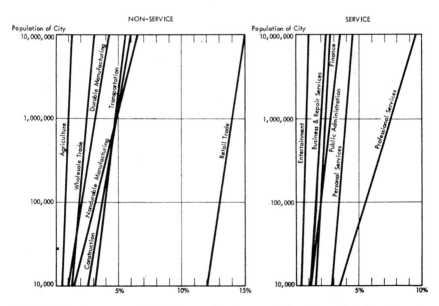

FIGURE 6.6. Minimum requirements for 14 industry types, based on regression lines. The x-axis indicates employment as per cent of total city employment. (Reprinted with permission of Department of Geography, Royal University of Lund, Sweden from *The IGU Symposium on Urban Geography-Proceedings,* 1962.)

The graph and table distinctly show that regularities exist in the minimum requirements that a city must have to sustain itself. These requirements, which are nonbasic in nature, increase with the size of the city, a characteristic that is examined below.

The minima vary depending on the function. The highest minima are for retail trade because all cities have a certain amount which is generally greater than 12 percent. Wholesale trade, on the other hand, is much less ubiquitous and the minima are lower. Finally, the shape of lines may vary with function; for example, professional services especially seem to be related to cities of larger size, perhaps because such activities may require larger thresholds.

The application of the minimum requirements approach to a real world situation shows that the approach is valid. For example, when it is applied to Madison, Wisconsin a test of its validity is possible because Alexander used the detailed survey approach in this city. The similarity of results is seen in the table which gives percentages of basic or *export* employment ascertained by the two methods:

Madison, Wisconsin

	Survey method	Minimum requirements method
Manufacturing	19	18
Retail trade	6	4
Services	9	12
Government	21	26

The application of minimum requirements to a large city is very revealing. For example, when applied to St. Louis (see table 6.1), the greatest excess, or basic employment, over the minimum requirements as taken from the regression lines is found in manufacturing (Ullman and Dacey, 1962, 132). About 33 percent of the total employment in the city is in this category and it represents almost 60 percent of excess or export employment. Transportation and wholesaling persist as traditional functions with a certain amount of basic employment, but other categories are mostly average. When applied to any city, therefore, such a test can illustrate aspects of urban growth that are obscured by regular employment figures. A primary virtue of the approach is that it provides a realistic basis for comparing cities.

A chief value of the economic base concept is that the multiplier effect provides a clue concerning urban growth. One of the most revealing characteristics of this effect is that it seems to bear a fairly direct relationship to the size of the center. In 1950, for example, shortly before Alexander made his analysis of Oshkosh, this city had a basic-nonbasic ratio

TABLE 6.1
Estimates of Export-Minimum Components.
St. Louis Metropolitan Area, 1950.
(All figures are in percents)

Activity	St. Louis Employment	Minimum Requirement for City of St. Louis Size	Basic or Export Employment	
			Excess (Col. 1 − Col. 2)	% of Total Excess
	(1)	(2)	(3)	(4)
Agriculture	2.0	1.1	0.9	2.1
Mining	0.4	0.0	0.4	1.0
Construction	5.2	5.1	0.1	0.2
Mfg.: Durable	16.6	5.2	11.4	27.1
Mfg.: Nondurable	16.9	3.3	13.6	32.3
Transport, etc.	10.1	5.0	5.1	12.1
Wholesale Trade	4.7	2.5	2.2	5.2
Retail Trade	15.8	14.3	1.5	3.6
Finance, Insurance	4.1	2.3	1.8	4.3
Business, Repairs Services	2.4	2.1	0.3	0.7
Personal Services	6.0	4.1	1.9	4.5
Entertainment	0.9	0.8	0.1	0.2
Professional Serv.	7.9	8.0	−0.1	—
Pub. Administration	5.0	3.0	2.0	4.8
Other	2.0	1.2	0.8	1.9
Total	100.0	58.0	42.0	100.0

Ratio Internal or Nonbasic 1.4: Basic or Export 1.
Total Population: 1,681,281, 1950.

Reprinted with permission of Department of Geography, Royal University of Lund, Sweden from Ullman, Edward and Dacey, Michael, "The Minimum Requirements Approach to the Urban Economic Base," in Norborg, K., ed., *Proceedings of the IGN Symposium in Urban Geography*, Lund, 1962, p. 132.

of 1:0.6. New York City, on the other hand, had an estimated ratio of 1:2.4. The implication of this pattern is that if a new factory employing 1,000 people is added to both New York City and Oshkosh, for example, the latter city would automatically require 2,400 nonbasic employees to service them while Oshkosh would only require 600. This relationship, therefore, illustrates that although cities require export or basic functions to grow, the effects of these functions will vary depending on size. The larger cities will automatically gain more growth, through the multiplier effect, of nonbasic activities than will the smaller cities. These nonbasic activities are the minimum requirements that we examined earlier. An understanding of the factors behind the relationship between size of city and economic base ratio serves then to clarify the process of metropolitan growth.

Ullman, Dacey, and Brodsky (1969, 7) provide figures which support this generalization concerning size and importance of nonbasic functions. Using this minimum requirements approach, they find the following percentages of *basic* employment for cities of different size:

> 10,000—68 percent
> 270,000—50 percent (Davenport, Iowa SMSA)
> 1,700,000—40 percent (Newark, New Jersey SMSA)
> 15,000,000—28 percent (New York SCA)

A main reason for this relationship, they state, is that the larger cities are more self-contained than the smaller ones. In a larger city, apparently, thresholds for a variety of specialized services are available. Consequently, a new factory, for example, might be able to take advantage of other activities such as component parts, banking, advertising, and university research. Since these activities serve local enterprises, they are largely nonbasic, and this portion of the ratio increases. Other advantages in the larger city might be the training of a labor force, selection of houses, and availability of recreational amenities. In other words, the larger city stands by itself better than the smaller city does because there may be less need to go elsewhere for services. Such a variety of nonbasic or service activities seems to support certain geographers' contentions that a city's activities prosper in proportion to the number of similar as well as complementary activities that are located near one another (Abler, Adams, and Gould, 1971, 360). The cost savings that accrue when several activities operate at the same place are called *external economies.* These economies, up to a certain point, help explain metropolitan growth. A map (see fig. 6.7), prepared by Northam (1975, 155) using data provided by Ullman, Dacey, and Brodsky, illustrates the pattern of high nonbasic components in larger metropolitan areas, a pattern which in part illustrates external economies.

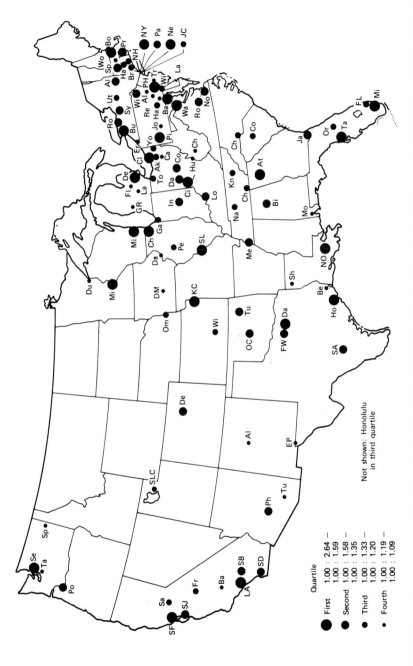

FIGURE 6.7. Basic-nonbasic ratios for 101 SMSA's with populations over 25,000 (1960) by quartile. Based on data in E. Ullman, et al., *The Economic Base of American Cities*, 1969. (Reprinted with permission of John Wiley and Sons from Ray Northam, *Urban Geography*, 1975.)

Another aspect of self-containment is greater diversity in function with size, a characteristic which seems to add stability to the city. For example, Detroit in 1960 had a high nonbasic component (65 percent) and yet it also had a high index of specialization, i.e., lack of variety in its basic functions (Ullman, Dacey, and Brodsky, 1969, 62, 69). In a situation like this, the high proportion of population in nonbasic services can provide a "cushion" if the overspecialized automobile component gets in trouble through a slump in the economy. Although it is true that many of these services are themselves dependent on a healthy automobile situation, it would appear that in a large city other alternatives for specialist employment exist while the variety of services itself can add elements of diversity. Indeed, Blumenfeld argues that it is the nonbasic activities that are most important for stability in a large metropolis while the basic or "export" functions can be replaced (Blumenfeld, 1967, 368). Such a statement may be misleading for realistically both basic and nonbasic activities are important in a city, and the two seem to complement each other. One doesn't work without the other. A good example is provided by Lincoln, Nebraska. Although this city of 160,000 is helped by basic activities of state government and a large university, such a situation may not always be stable. From 1945 to 1961, only one factory employing over 10 persons was added to the city. When the Lincoln Air Force Base closed in the early 1960s, a lack of diversity in this capital city was evident. Fortunately, a strong program of industrial development led by the Chamber of Commerce was initiated. Before 1962, not a single ready industrial site of more than 10 acres existed but by the end of that year four tracts complete with utilities and totalling 900 acres had been completed. In the next five years, an estimated 2,000 employees were added to the city's industrial payroll, a pattern that has continued into the 1970s. The impact of this increased basic employment on Lincoln was also evident in the nonbasic services that were added as a multiplier effect. This effect was most evident in the continued expansion of Gateway, the major regional shopping center that serves the eastern portion of the city.

A MODEL OF METROPOLITAN DEVELOPMENT

From the preceding section, it is apparent that larger cities have greater diversity of function and thus are more self-contained than smaller cities. But not all larger cities grow at the same rate. An analysis of the urban growth process should include some reference to the factors of differential metropolitan growth. Fortunately, a stimulating model has been provided by Pred (1965), who links urban growth to industrialization through the factor of *initial advantage* by pointing out the persistence of older cities in the industrial growth of the United States (see fig. 6.8). For example, the ten most important industrial cities in 1961, which accounted for 37.5 percent of the nation's manufacturing value, were, with the exception of Los Angeles, among the most important cities during the early industrial growth period of 1860-1910 (see table 6.2). According to Madden (1956), these cities showed remarkable stability of population in the censuses of 1870-1950. In 1973 these same ten cities, except for San Francisco, were in the top 15 in the United States in both population and manufacturing (see table 6.3). Even the older cities of New Orleans, Cincinnati, and Buffalo, which were among the top ten in population in 1860, but which are not now in the top 15, have exhibited remarkable staying power in commercial influence. Apparently these early cities had something going for them, something Pred associates with an early start, which established *inertia* against change in location and which provided certain advantages of growth that are self-perpetuating. How does this process, which results in increasing concentration of population and industry in certain early cities, work?

Pred calls the model which illustrates this process of concentration the "circular and cumulative process of industrial and urban-size

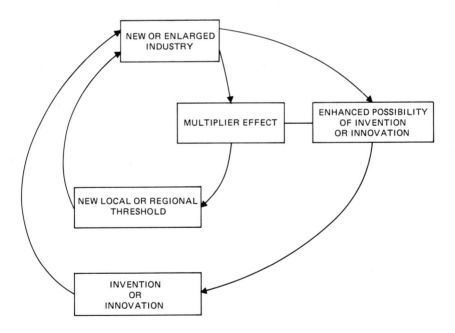

FIGURE 6.8. The circular and cumulative process of industralization and urban-size growth. (From Allan Pred: Industriali- zation, Initial Advantage, and American Metropolitan Growth, *Geographical Review*, vol. 55, pp. 165 and 181, Figs. 1 and 3.)

TABLE 6.2
Population Growth in Ten United States Cities, 1860-1910

	Population, 1860	Population, 1910
New York	1,174,799	4,766,883
Chicago	112,172	2,185,283
Philadelphia	565,529	1,549,008
St. Louis	160,773	687,029
Boston	177,840	670,585
Cleveland	43,417	560,663
Pittsburgh	49,221	533,905
Detroit	45,619	465,766
San Francisco	56,802	416,912
Los Angeles	4,385	319,198

Source: Pred (1965)

TABLE 6.3
Population and Manufacturing in the Fifteen Largest
United States Cities, 1973[x]

	Population[a]	Manufacturing[b]
New York	14,853	24,464
Los Angeles	8,941	18,279
Chicago	7,643	19,734
Philadelphia	4,806	9,239
Detroit	4,446	11,792
San Francisco-Oakland	3,143	2,896
Washington	3,020	1,068
Boston	2,898	6,257
Dallas-Ft. Worth	2,464	4,094
St. Louis	2,391	5,190
Pittsburgh	2,365	4,157
Houston	2,168	4,180
Baltimore	2,128	3,469
Cleveland	2,006	5,213
Minneapolis-St. Paul	2,000	3,731

[x]City figures are for SMSAs except for New York and Chicago (SCAs) and Los Angeles (3 SMSAs)
[a]In thousands
[b]Value added in millions of dollars
Souce: Statistical Abstract of the United States, 1975, pp. 21-2, 886-939.

growth," a term derived from Myrdal's principle of "circular and cumulative causation." This model focuses on two circular chains of reaction which together were responsible for much of American metropolitan growth in the period after the Civil War. One of these was a multiplier effect which was generated by new basic and nonbasic manufacturing functions in cities to produce a series of supporting services and population increases that in turn generated the thresholds necessary for even more factories. The other effect was one of innovations which were in part derived from interaction among immigrants attracted to America by employment opportunities in the existing centers. Both of these effects, working together, act in a "snowballing" fashion as illustrated below.

The functional links between innovations during industrialization led to persistent growth in certain urban areas. Since the productive processes in most industries were broadly similar, they could easily be converted through new innovations from the manufacture of one commodity to that of another. Pred uses the Cadillac Automobile Company of Detroit to illustrate how linkage of innovations is reflected in a historical sequence of production—machine tools, bicycle gears, gasoline engines for motor boats, and automobile engines. In such a situation footloose industries like machine tools, which are high in value, can help the growth of existing centers since they can locate at a source of innovation like Detroit and ship from there. This random location of footloose industries is one factor helping to explain why industrial structures may differ between metropolitan areas of similar size.

One of the most important factors in this period of industrial concentration in larger cities was *external economies* which increased functionally (rather than arithmetically) with size. These economies included not only interfirm linkages and sharing of facilities in large urban centers but also increasing specialization of manufacturing processes. In other words, each successive stage of production in the manufacturing process became more interdependent as the complexity of inputs of raw materials and semifinished products increased and the importance of any one decreased. Such interdependence between the stages favored urban locations where many of the stages could be in closer proximity. These urban sites were further enhanced by the establishment of higher freight rates on manufactured goods than on raw materials and by the development of cheap, easily transmitted electrical energy. All of these factors worked together to favor a location in certain larger centers.

Although the Pred model illustrates the general processes of metropolitan growth, it is particularly useful in accounting for the persistence of the leading industrial centers, and thus helps answer the question as to why *some* large cities grow more than others. Pred states, for example, that "in an interacting system of cities in an expanding space economy, the circular and cumulative growth process does not persist indefinitely for all places" (Pred, 1965, 173). Many forces may act to introduce selectivity into the growth process with one of the most conspicuous being geographical expressions of *initial advantage*. For example, the innovations associated with railroad technology in the latter part of the 19th Century reduced freight charges per ton mile and thereby favored the growth of *existing* centers by raising the thresholds of some industries which in turn increased these minimum optimal *scales of operation*. In other words, firms in existing centers had their market areas enlarged by cheaper transport inputs, allowing them further divisions of labor and mass-production economies, thereby increasing the practicability of satisfying regional and national demands from a limited number of cities. The cheaper transport inputs in this period are illustrated by the increase in average length of railroad hauls from less than 110 miles per ton in 1882 to about 250 miles per ton in 1910. These scale economies were continued when innovations in machinery permitted reduced per unit production costs and the substitution of transport outlays for labor and other costs, thus extending even further the market areas.

Pred emphasizes, therefore, that external and scale economies were *selective* in metropolitan growth, favoring the growth of certain centers which had an early start. These tendencies were facilitated even more by the greater relative accessibility of the early urban centers. A map of accessibility to population in 1900, which represent *potentials of interaction* between people, illustrates the persistence of those cities located in the New York-Chicago axis (see fig. 6.9). Finally, other selective factors favoring the existing metropolitan centers were horizontal-vertical integration of firms and the availability of labor and capital.

Another factor that may cause inertia or persistence of early centers, in the urban system, is the hierarchy of services that exists among metropolitan areas. McNee (1971, 107-124) points out that these areas seem to be linked together in a national hierarchical system. Thus New York has persisted as a supranational center while Chicago, Cleveland, Pittsburgh, and Dayton reflect reduced degrees of regional influence, as exemplified by services like banking, insurance, advertising, publishing, and the theater. People tend to possess mental maps regarding the rank of such areas which may cause them to persist despite other locational forces working for change. Thus the central-place concept, which was discussed largely for smaller places in the last chapter, may help to explain the resistance of an urban system to change at any level.

The evolution of the American urban system, therefore, is clarified by a simple model emphasizing the interrelations of the multiplier effect and innovations in centers having an early start. Although the diseconomies existing in such centers cannot be ignored, the overall effects of external and scale economies in such a system provide a rather stable growth pattern of concentration and inertia. At the present time, how-

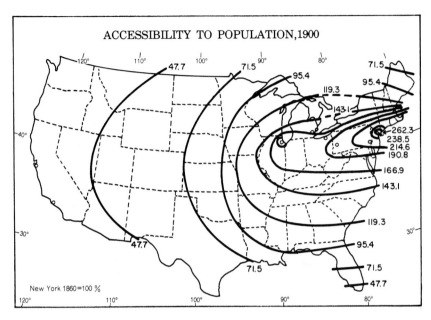

FIGURE 6.9. A map of population potential for the United States in 1900. Note the importance of the northeast, especially New York City. (From Allan Pred: Industrialization, Initial Advantage, and American Metropolitan Growth, *Geographical Review*, vol. 55, pp. 165 and 181, Figs. 1 and 3.)

ever, a new trend in urban growth is evident and may eventually offset or even reverse the persistent growth of the centers emphasized in the Pred model. This trend is the rapid expansion of population in the "sun-belt" states of the south and southwest. Between 1970 and 1975 the population of this belt, and the western mountain states, increased by nine percent as compared with a one percent growth rate in the northeast and Great Lakes regions. For example, population increased 25 percent in Florida and Arizona, 15 percent in Colorado, and nine percent in Texas. Several factors explain the migration of population to these areas: attractive climate; growth industries like electronics; presence of inexpensive labor, land, and construction; easily available and relatively inexpensive energy; and lower state and local taxes. The largest cities that have shared in this growth are Los Angeles, Dallas-Fort Worth, Houston, and Atlanta—all now in the top 16 in population for the country. Many observers feel that a national growth policy may be necessary to cope with the differences in regional balance that are evolving. The advantages that Pred associated with an early start may possibly be less important in the future just as they eventually declined in Great Britain.

SUMMARY

In this chapter, several models have been employed to isolate certain processes that are operative in an urban system. The rank-size and primate concepts were used to illustrate the existence of distortions in a central-place hierarchial system. Mercantile and industrial models were then used to gain insight into factors that cause the urban system to be altered from a central-place system. The economic base concept was introduced to indicate the complementarity of basic and nonbasic elements of growth in an urban system. Finally, the Pred model illustrated how initial advantage was linked to innovation and the multiplier effect to provide a certain amount of concentration and inertia among older metropolitan areas in an urban system. Madden's documentation of the stability of these areas between 1870 and 1950 seems to indicate that individual cities do not develop independently of the urban system of which they are a part. However, the nature of the future urban system remains in doubt. Is the recent expansion in the "sunbelt" states going to alter the persistence of the old pattern? In Great Britain, for example, the old pattern of regional dispersion of metropolitan growth on the coal fields, which was characterized by over-specialization of industry in most of them, was stable for a long time. However, many factors, including linkages to the European continent, have led to a new pattern of concentration in southeast Britain with accompanying diversification of industrial types. Thus, factors associated with initial advantage in an industrial region may disappear with time.

THE INTERNAL RELATIONS
OF CITIES

The preceding three chapters have dealt with the *external* relations of urban areas. Man tends to organize space around a series of nodes in order to carry out certain political, economic, and social activities. However, these nodes also possess an *internal* organization that is important and which, in great part, reflects the external relations. For example, Smailes derived his urban hierarchy in England and Wales by using the internal forms that reflected a certain degree of external influence, e.g., a Woolworth store. So external and internal relations are closely related and the preceding chapters have provided some insight into an understanding of these connections. Nevertheless, we must now analyze some of the ways in which man has organized space *within* cities. The method chosen is three-pronged. Chapter 7 deals with "intraurban movement" employing the assumption, as I did for external relations, that the spatial patterns of urban areas are based on interactions between people. In chapter 8, the focus is on the "growth" of cities in order to introduce the historical factor as it affected urban evolution in the American cultural area. Finally, chapter 9 deals more specifically with why things are "located" where they are in cities. In this chapter the emphasis is more on individual uses of land while in chapter 8 the focus is on the larger overall patterns. In all three chapters, models are employed and tested against real-world situations.

CHAPTER 7

INTRAURBAN MOVEMENT

LESLIE DIENES
Department of Geography

Land use patterns as they exist in American urban areas are derived from interaction between people. This interaction has two components, physical mobility and communications. The first of these may involve a physical move while the second relates to the flow of information between people that influences movement. Physical movement, in turn, may be broken down into two types, permanent, such as a change in residence, and temporary, exemplified by the journeys to work or shop. It is the spatial dislocations of temporary urban movement, for example, that contribute so much to the fundamental urban problem of traffic congestion. Intraurban movement provides a dynamic spatial foundation for understanding both land use and traffic patterns in urban areas. Furthermore, this movement illustrates quite well the combination of macro and micro approaches in geography. Recent developments in the field have been characterized by a focus on both aggregate spatial structure (macro) and individual behavior (micro). The two are related through the complementarity of structure and process. For example, a blighted residential neighborhood exhibits a certain structure in the aggregate sense that is the result of the process of decision-making about residential location by many individuals. Although the aggregate pattern may be explained in part by a given theory, a complete explanation generally requires some interpretation of individual behavior.

What types of movements take place in cities? A metropolitan study of Toronto in 1964 indicated that the average daily trip volume was about four million—a truly staggering figure. The home was either the origin or destination of most trips (see fig. 7.1). The single most important trip is the journey to work which is involved in almost half of the moves. These work trips are also longer than non-work trips and more concentrated in time. The two peak periods of travel to and from work, of course, involve automobiles but also are the times when public transit is most important. Certain other trips—shopping, personal business, and

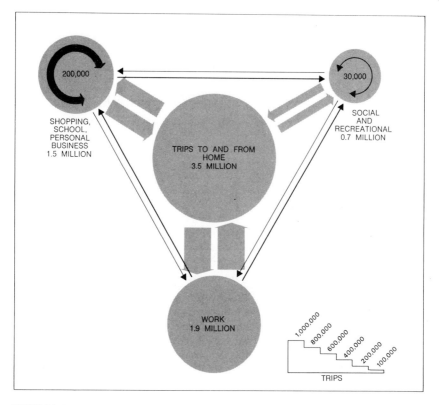

FIGURE 7.1. As an example of intraurban movement, Toronto reflects the importance of home-based trips. Of those trips made in a vehicle, the journey to work dominates. (Source: *Metropolitan Toronto and Region Transportation Study*, The Queen's Printer, 1966. Used with permission.)

social-recreational—are more completely automobile-served and less concentrated in time. For example, shopping is important in mid-day while social-recreational trips concentrate in late afternoon and evening.

BASIC FORCES BEHIND MOVEMENT

Centripetal and centrifugal forces, identified by Colby (1933), seem to be basic to all movement in cities. The former is directed to the center and was important in early urban development focused on a strong Central Business District. The latter is evident today in the outward movement of people to the suburbs facilitated by the automobile. Centrifugal forces actually are related to uprooting forces in the cores of large cities and result from the increasing lack of site possibilities (e.g., water frontage), traffic congestion, high rents and taxes, nuisance complaints (e.g., air pollution), and legal restrictions. In a sense, such centrifugal forces are "push" factors which are complemented by the opposite "pull" factors in each case, e.g., an industrial park on the fringe of the city includes factories that were "pushed" out to gain space and avoid congestion. These forces gradually overcome the centripetal forces that had pulled enterprises into the core of cities for so long, viz., central accessibility to the entire city, functional linkages to certain other enterprises, and prestige locations like Fifth Avenue in New York City. Some functions such as offices which depend on regular linkages between worker and worker, such as lawyer and banker, still rely on basic centripetal forces, but the increasing mobility and possibilities for communications make the centrifugal forces more apparent today.

Centrifugal forces help to explain the outward movement of people, stores, and firms to the outer rings of metropolitan areas during the post-World War II period. For example, the population of the suburbs of American metropolitan areas increased between 1950 and 1970 by 35 million people as compared with only ten million in the central cities. The percentage of increase in retail trade in the suburbs of the 37 largest SMSAs during the period 1958-1968 was 45 percent, while it was only five percent in the central cities. Finally, employment in manufacturing for the same cities during the same period increased 16 percent in the suburbs but *declined* by six percent in the central cities. Truly, the centrifugal forces seem predominant, a situation that has contributed to an increasing dichotomy between central city and suburb. However, it should be kept in mind that the basic component in this outward movement is White population. By 1985, it is estimated that 58 percent of the U.S. Black population will live in the central cities of the SMSAs while only 16 percent will live in the suburbs. So the centrifugal forces do not apply to all components of the American population.

PERMANENT MOVEMENT: RESIDENTIAL LOCATION

Separating permanent and temporary movements within the city is obviously impossible as a permanent change of residence may be greatly affected by a regular temporary movement like the journey to work. However, for purposes of analysis the two are separated here but interrelated where necessary.

Bureau of the Census figures show that one-fifth of the American population changes residence every year, a rate that apparently has been remarkably uniform since 1947. This population mobility is further illustrated by the fact that, on the average, 50 percent of the population changes its place of residence every five years. Some have gone further and generalized that the average person will move eight or nine times in a lifetime.

A sample study by Boyce (1969) of residential mobility in Seattle provides useful supplementary data as a case study. He found that 26 percent of all housing changes occupancy each year, but that in the low-value Black areas this percentage rises to 38, while high value areas showed a turnover rate one-third of this. It appears, then, that those who can least afford to move may do most of the moving. Furthermore, they do not move as far. In the lowest housing-value category, almost 60 percent of the Black moves were within this type of housing while only 24 percent of the White moves were. This tendency of Blacks to move to another low-value house perhaps accounts for the average distance of only 1.2 miles. On the other hand, the major type of move by low-value White and by middle value groups was farther, generally to the next higher housing value with the pattern, according to Boyce, resembling that of a star-burst. Finally, high-value housing moves were directed to other high-value areas which are quite separated in Seattle. Moves to the suburbs, on the other hand, never amount to more than 16 percent for any group and are almost negligible by low-value Black groups who face barriers of "fiscal zoning" related to minimum size of residence.

THE PROCESS OF RESIDENTIAL CHANGE: THEORY AND REALITY.   One conceptual approach to intraurban migration was developed by Brown and Moore (1970) and is expressed in a model of individual decision-making (see fig. 7.2). This approach reveals that residential change actually involves a sequence of decisions which are often made within a spatial and environmental context. Furthermore, an understanding of individual responses to environmental conditions may not only provide a better basis for prediction of aggregate residential relocation but also supplement the planning process in urban areas. The authors state that a fundamental idea in the model is Wolpert's (1965) *place utility* or the individual's level of satisfaction or dissatisfaction with respect to a given location. Intraurban migration is viewed as a process of adjustment whereby one location is exchanged for another in order to satisfy the needs and desires of the migrant. Place utility will vary between groups as seen in the ease with which younger people move as against many older residents who have formed particular attachments to places.

The Brown-Moore decision model begins with a household subjected to stress from two sources: (1) internal changes in family structure and (2) external changes in the immediate environment which make the present location unsuitable (see fig. 7.2). Stress, which reflects the place utility of that location, is derived from the difference between the collective needs of the family and the characteristics of its environment. For

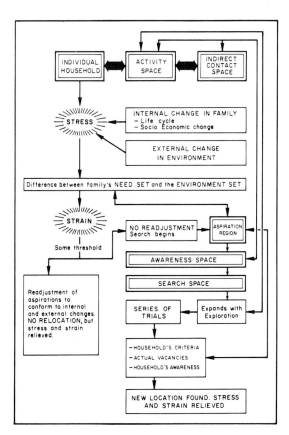

FIGURE 7.2. The conceptual pattern of the Brown-Moore model of urban residential location. (From *Transportation Geography* by Elliot Hurst. Copyright © 1974 by McGraw-Hill Book Company. Used with permission of McGraw-Hill Book Company.)

example, a person who busses to work may be given a better job in an area without public transportation—a case where the monetary needs of the family are at variance with the environment as regards transportation. The person has three alternatives: adjust family needs by rejecting the job, restructure the environment by purchasing a car, or relocate the household nearer the job.

"Push" factors appear to be more important than "pull" factors in the development of the stress resulting in divergence between family needs and environment. Rossi's model (1955) of life-cycle changes, for example, shows that at least five of the eight or nine moves a person makes in a lifetime are related to the cycle. Specifically, changes in residence generally will occur as a person grows up and leaves home, marries, has children, and retires. Three of these occur in the 15-25 age bracket. Most of these changes reflect push factors and can establish the stress mentioned above.

However, the environment can also change, thereby diverging from the family situation. Examples of such environmental change include the spread of residential blight, encroachment by an ethnic group, and construction of commercial or industrial sites in the area.

The actual decision to relocate, according to the Brown-Moore model, comes when the difference between residential need and environment becomes so great that the "stress" becomes a "strain." At this point the person either changes his evaluation of need or environment to relieve the strain so that he is satisfied in the same location, or he makes the decision to move. At this time, certain aspects of search behavior emerge. The average person has a mental map of the city which includes an "awareness space," or an area with which he is familiar owing to both direct contact ("activity space") and indirect contact through mass media and advertising (see fig. 7.3). The nature of this space, of course, will vary among individuals of social groups. Within this "awareness space," a person develops a "search space" which is enlarged and begins to exceed awareness space on the basis of exploration. This search space may not agree exactly with the "aspiration region" because the latter includes many parts of the city that fit his needs but in which he will never search. Actually, the aspiration region includes upper and lower limits for three sets of factors: residential criteria, existence of vacancies, and awareness of these vacancies. The actual search consists of a series of trials which modify both the search space and the aspiration region. For example, the individual or family may aspire to a fine new house in the suburbs, but search may reveal that a location in an older section, originally not contemplated, may be suitable.

It should be pointed out that the decision to change residence is not entirely up to the mover. Here reality departs from theory as a real estate agent may suggest a location completely away from the "search space" of the individual contemplating a change. For example, development of new housing in a city takes place in areas in which builders perceive that residents wish to buy. In Lincoln, Nebraska, for instance, most new subdivisions have been constructed to the south and east rather than north and west. The latter directions include not only the flood plain barrier of Salt Creek but also the major railroad lines and the airport (see fig. 3.4). However, this barrier is narrow and the airport noise pattern is limited. Consequently, much excellent residential land exists on the north and west sides of Lincoln but is undeveloped because of a perception which builders hold.

Individual perception also provides a useful explanation for reality in residential change when it varies from what is expected on the basis of theory. Rossi (1955), for example, could predict 87 percent of the rea-

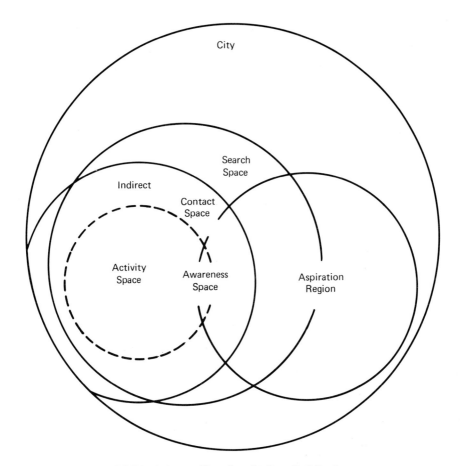

FIGURE 7.3. Aspects of "space" as related to residential location.

sons for people moving, many of which were related to the life cycle. However, these reasons did not cover certain people who behave differently than expected. Some urban specialists allow for such variation by recognizing "movers" and "stayers." Unexpected "movers" cited windfalls or other unforeseen events for a change in decision while the unexpected "stayers" found themselves unable to sell their house or obtain a mortgage.

TEMPORARY MOVEMENTS

In contrast to more permanent movements like the change in residence are the temporary ones that dominate the traffic patterns of cities. These movements include two components: first, miscellaneous ones such as school, shopping, social, professional, and recreation trips which are spread out over 24 hours; secondly, superimposed on this pattern, the journey to work which is concentrated into a few hours each day. As shown on the two maps, both patterns are random and dispersed (see fig. 7.4). However, the journey to work volume is much greater and be-

(a)

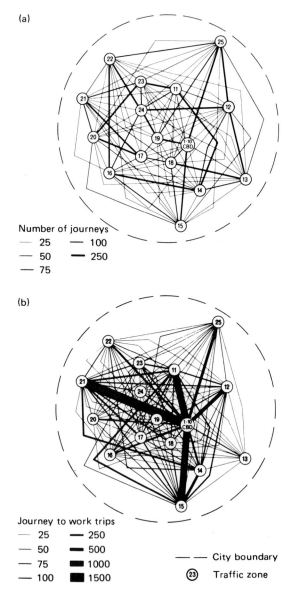

Number of journeys
- — 25   — 100
- — 50   — 250
- — 75

(b)

FIGURE 7.4. Components or urban movement: (a) dispersed journeys occurring throughout the day; and (b) work journeys occurring at peak hours. (Michael E. Eliot Hurst, ed., *I Came to the City*. Copyright © 1975 by Houghton Mifflin Company. Reprinted by permission.)

Journey to work trips
- — 25   — 250
- — 50   — 500
- — 75   — 1000
- — 100   — 1500

– – – City boundary

(23) Traffic zone

comes concentrated around fewer nodes. Since most trips are by automobile, congestion develops around these nodes or focal points. An approach to understanding these temporary movements is to examine their direction, types, and behavioral characteristics.

SOME DIRECTIONAL IDEAS.   These temporary movements seem to be random, but actually some directional forces are operating. Basic centripetal and centrifugal forces mentioned above apparently are important in the journey to work. For example, people move out to the edge of the metropolitan area, but their jobs do not follow them, so a centripetal commuting pattern is set up. In the case of minorities, especially Blacks, the jobs move while discrimination and low income prevent their place of residence from following: as a result, the journey to work for these people may be centrifugal. Note in the map how the centroids for Whites and Blacks in Detroit are reversed with time (see fig. 7.5). White jobs follow White residents, but Black residents lag behind Black jobs. These basic centripetal and centrifugal forces seem to be less important in multidirectional movements like shopping and social contacts. However, the CBD may still serve as a focus for some centripetal movement such as specialty shopping or recreation-cultural attractions.

Adams (1969) has pinpointed a sectoral bias in intracity movements which has the advantage of placing the centripetal-centrifugal forces in a behavioral framework. He feels that because of duplication of services in different sectors of the city, a person will focus temporary intraurban movements within the sector where he lives. Not only is he most familiar with this sector over others, but he also finds the necessary variety of services, e.g., shopping, recreation, which satisfy his needs. In other words, his "activity space," a concept mentioned above in connection with residential location, tends to be biased within this sector. This bias reduces visits to other sectors of the city, especially if they require a trip across town or near the center.

JOURNEY TO WORK.   The journey to work for many Americans seems to involve a sacrifice. They *appear* to be willing to trade off the transport costs of long trips for the reduced rents of suburban locations which often permit larger lots. Such a generalization seems to be supported by Getis' hypothesis (1969) of a frictionless zone within which the number of travelers does not vary systematically with distance (see fig. 7.6). Beyond this zone, which he feels is three to five miles in most large cities, distance does play a role. Getis infers that perhaps individuals are indifferent to distance up to a point, but he is not able to prove this conclusively. In Toronto, trips to work averaged about one-half

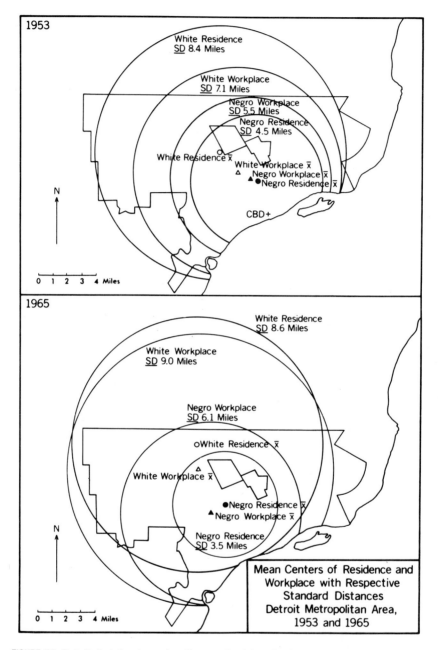

FIGURE 7.5. Centroids illustrating changes in residences and workplaces for whites and blacks in Detroit. Note that for whites workplace tends to follow residence in time while for blacks this is reversed. (Reprinted with permission of the Department of Geography, Northwestern University from Donald Deskins, Jr., *Interaction Patterns and the Spatial Form of the Ghetto*, Special Publication No. 3, 1969.)

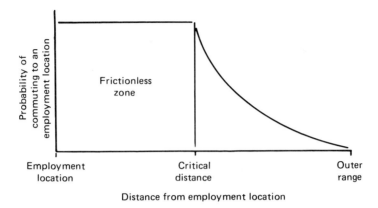

FIGURE 7.6. The concept of "frictionless space" within an urban area. (Reproduced by permission from the Annals of the American Geographers Association, Vol. 1, 1969, by Arthur Getis.)

hour, indicating that people are willing to spend at least an hour a day in this manner.

The hypothesis that Americans commuting to work trade off high transport costs for lower rents may be too simple. Such an assumption should be supported by data showing that those groups best able to afford high transport costs will travel farthest. Yet, that is not always the case. For example, Halvorson (1973) found in Charleston, West Virginia that the middle income groups reported the greatest separation of residence from work. He also found that only a small proportion of the individuals surveyed reported that work access played a role in their choice of residence. Consequently, it appears that the location of a residence in the city is not necessarily related to the location of a job. Such a conclusion would still provide for the "frictionless zone" that Getis found for intraurban movement, but it would not emphasize the ability to pay transport costs as a factor in residential location. Apparently, a variety of factors affect where a person lives and only one of these may be where he works. In many cases a person will pay high transport costs to get to work, and yet not necessarily be able to afford them, simply because he wants a residence on the edge of the city. The conclusion is that what might be expected in terms of the journey to work is not always found in reality.

JOURNEY TO SHOP. The above sections reveal that residential location and the journey to work are *in part* explained through the way that individuals behave spatially. However, shopping trips are the result of consumer decision processes and, therefore, behavior is more explicit in explaining these movements. These trips are made more often in comparison to those involving residential change, and they involve a greater variety of destinations than the journey to work. Consequently, explaining the pattern of shopping trips can be quite difficult. One concept that is useful in this context is that of the "mental map." A consumer possesses a spatial perception of the total urban area which is imperfect with respect to knowledge of the city's commercial structure because it is based on a particular "activity space." According to Huff (1960) the perception of opportunities for shopping is based on the images an individual has of the contents of this space and the ease of movement within it (see fig. 7.7). For example, his content imagery is based on things like

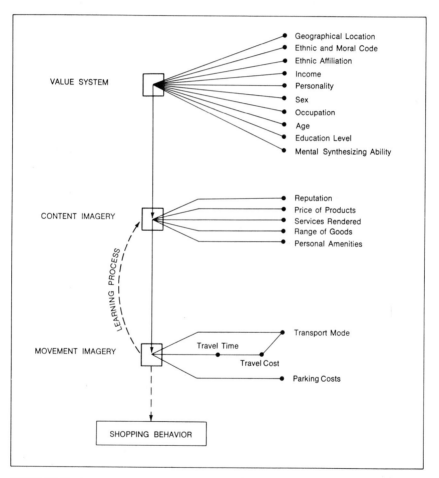

FIGURE 7.7. The conceptual framework explaining factors influencing consumer shopping behavior. (From *Regional Science Association Papers and Proceedings:* "Typographic Model of Consumer Behavior" by Huff, 1960. 6: 159-173, fig. 6. Reprinted by permission.)

reputation of the firm, prices, service, range of goods, and personal amenities—factors that might send him to the CBD instead of a shopping center. On the other hand, his movement imagery, which relates to mode and costs of transport including parking, might push him toward the shopping center. Both sets of images are influenced by his value system, which includes such factors as ethnic background, income, sex, age, occupation, and educational level.

Huff's model helps to clarify the irregularities that show up in shopping behavior. People do not always travel the shortest distance and in fact may behave rather irrationally in this respect. One of the most useful concepts for uniting the images of content and movement is that of "trip utility." This concept is defined as the *difference* between the reward from the trip and the costs that one accepts in making it. A person may be prepared, for example, to travel a considerable distance to purchase a needed insecticide if his lawn condition warrants it. Such a case may be quite specialized and require an addition to his "activity" space since it may not be found within the shopping facilities with which he is familiar. If he has several objectives in shopping, he has different options open to him. He might visit four different enterprises in succession (as a traveling salesman would), or he can travel farther to a large shopping center where all items can be purchased. The shopping center represents a higher level in the hierarchy than the individual places, and the person's decision will be based on overall "trip utility." At the same time, it is well to recognize that trip utility will change with time as his image of content and movement changes. These changes may occur either as a result of enlargement of his activity space or from changes in the city itself. In the latter case, new shopping facilities may have been added or access to older ones improved.

The preceding discussion illustrates that consumer shopping behavior is quite different from spatial behavior associated with residential location and with other temporary urban travel. In the first place, shopping trips seem to be less frequent than expected as data reveal that only about eight percent of total person trips by destination were for this purpose. Journeys to work and for social-recreational purposes are much more fixed in terms of destinations, and the movement decision is less complex. Secondly, shopping trips are more sensitive to the frictional effects of distance, a fact that leads to the more regular spread of facilities in contrast to work and recreational places, e.g., golf courses. Thus, this type of trip is shorter in a time and distance sense. It was found that such trips in Chicago, for example, averaged only 2.8 miles as compared to 4.3 miles for social-recreational trips and 5.3 miles for journeys to work (CATS, 1959, 38). Finally, shopping travel patterns are less regular in time and space since they do not fit into the rush hour pattern and have a variety of nodes as goals. As a result, they are much more dispersed timewise during the day and spatially throughout the urban area. In some cases, they are single trips and in others multi-purpose ones. In short, they are much harder to predict.

Given this difficulty of predicting shopping patterns, what methods are available to marketing firms for recommending the location and construction of a shopping center? Huff (1963) feels that one approach is to apply the gravity model within a probabilistic framework to determine a shopping center trade area. Although this approach ignores many factors affecting the decision to build a shopping center, including the political ones, it does illustrate the possibilities of determining the trade area for such a center on the basis of its size and its distance from aggregate potential customers. The focus in such an approach is on the consumer and his choice process that gives rise to observable spatial behavior. Huff believes that since the average customer does not have perfect information about the stores he intends to visit, he will make the choice of an alternative in a probabilistic fashion. Thus Huff makes three basic assumptions about the customer: 1) he will be attracted to a store in direct proportion to its size because his chances of finding a given item are increased in proportion to this factor; 2) he will want to minimize the time he spends on a shopping trip; 3) finally, his willingness to travel will vary with the type of product. Thus the gravity model can be applied here for the customer will be attracted to a given center in direct proportion to the number of items sold (reflected in selling space) and indirectly according to distance. A formal expression of Huff's model is as follows:

$$P(C_{ij}) = \frac{\dfrac{S_j}{T_{ij}^{\lambda}}}{\displaystyle\sum_{j=1}^{n} \left(\dfrac{S_j}{T_{ij}^{\lambda}} \right)}$$

where $P(C_{ij})$ the probability of a consumer at a given point of origin i traveling to a given shopping center j;

S_j the square footage of selling space in shopping center j;

T_{ij} the travel time involved in getting from a consumer's travel base i to shopping center j; and

λ the time exponent

A case study of the application of the Huff model is the portrayal of shopping probability contours for two adjacent shopping centers in Las Vegas (see fig. 7.8)*. At the time of the study, Center A existed as the largest one in the city with a retail area of 1,000,000 square feet. A marketing firm was asked to compute the effective trading area for a planned shopping center of equal size (B) to be located at a site on the northern margin of A's market area. Driving time from the center of each city census tract to the two centers was obtained by measuring distances between major intersections and dividing by average speeds for those distances. The lambda figure for travel willingness was set at 3 which reflects the wide range of goods available in a shopping center. Arrays of shopping probability for each tract were then computed for the two centers and plotted as equi-probability contours. Note that competition from centers to the west and east of B restricted the contours in these directions. On the south, the large trade area of A overlaps B's in its largest extension, thereby restricting its potential even further. As a result of this study, the firm recommended that site B was not an optimum location for development of a major-sized shopping center although a smaller one might have been successful. However, the size of the tract dictated the decision to plan a major one. Another drawback was the lack of potential for future shopping growth since the center would have to draw heavily on the downtown and immediate surrounding area rather than the expanding suburbs. Furthermore, expansion plans of some adjacent competitors would put the new site at a further disadvantage.

Zanarini (1973) states that consumer behavior is much more complicated than the gravity model assumes, but he does feel that it provides a simple picture of the relative impacts of size of center and driving distance. Additionally, Huff shows that other factors can be built into the model. For example, instead of assuming that the statistical units are uniform in terms of socio-economic characteristics, differences among them such as number of households, income, and shopping habits can be included. In summary, the Huff model seems to be a logical basis for initial prediction of consumer shopping behavior around a potential shopping center. The success of any such center, however, rests on additional factors such as the size of the parcel, income level of the shoppers, and the politics involved.

MACHINE SPACE IN THE CITY

One might reasonably conclude a chapter on movement in the city with the concept of "machine space." In other words, after examining per-

*The author is indebted to Roger Zanarini of Upland Industries, Omaha, Nebraska, for assistance on this portion of the chapter.

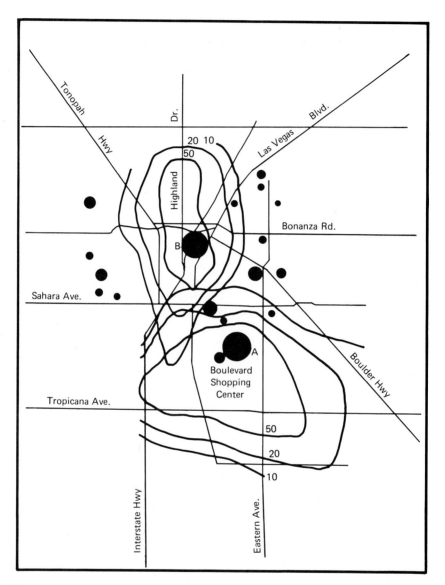

FIGURE 7.8. The application of the gravity model within a probabilistic framework to determine the feasibility of locating a shopping center in a particular area of Las Vegas, Nevada. Areas of circles correspond to sizes of shopping centers in square feet. Equiprobability contours of 10, 20, and 50 are shown. (Adapted from 1973 data provided by Roger Zanarini, Upland Industries, Omaha, Nebraska.)

manent and temporary movements in urban areas from behavioral viewpoints, it seems logical to ask what is the *result* of all these movements. The answer in the American city, at least, is an environment in which priority has been given to machines for making these movements.

Horvath (1974) documents this concept of "machine space" with respect to the automobile as he feels this machine—whose U.S. registrations number over 100 million—may prove to be the most significant innovation in 20th Century American culture. However, the rail has had an equally strong influence on urban space and although the automobile dominates today, the persistent barrier effects of railroads in cities is evident to most people. In any case, machine space in a city appears to be the spatial manifestation of American urban technology.

Horvath defines machine space as any area that is devoted to movement, storage, and servicing of automobiles, and has delimited such space in a study of East Lansing, Michigan (see fig. 7.9). Total machine space ranges from 65 percent in the CBD to 25 percent in the low-density area of owner-occupied middle-class homes. A correlation appears between age of the block and the amount of machine space, and indeed Horvath likens the expansion of automobile territory to the cycle of erosion from youth, when driveways and garages exist, to old age, where practically an entire block is converted.

The process of land conversion to uses connected with the automobile seems to be related to the planning process where the typical approach is to keep the stream of machines flowing. The automobile is given first priority based on the fact that people want it that way. As a result, more access roads are created which in turn lead to new land uses attracting more traffic leading to demands for more access roads. The dilemma is illustrated by an exchange of letters between a traffic engineer and Lewis Mumford (Wolfe and Mumford, 1961). In response to the engineer's pleas that he is only giving the people what they want, Mumford asked if perhaps his job was rather to recommend what is best for the city in the long term rather than utilize the market-place approach to planning.

Horvath feels that machine space constitutes territory that is alienated from people. The automobile gets first priority on urban space, one reason being that so many land uses depend on access to people who arrive by automobile, e.g., motels and "drive in" restaurants, banks, and movies. Efforts to close off space to machines are met with resistance, largely on the basis of keeping open access to private property. Even the increase of traffic accidents and the growing correlation between autos and air pollution seem to make little difference. However, a beginning is being made, especially in Europe, to create automobile-free zones in cities and to develop alternate sources of transport. The most interesting development is the construction of a mass-transit system in San Francisco. This sytem, called BART for Bay Area Rapid Transit, is the first of its kind constructed in an American metropolitan area in 50 years. A network of electric trains, which operates on the surface as well as un-

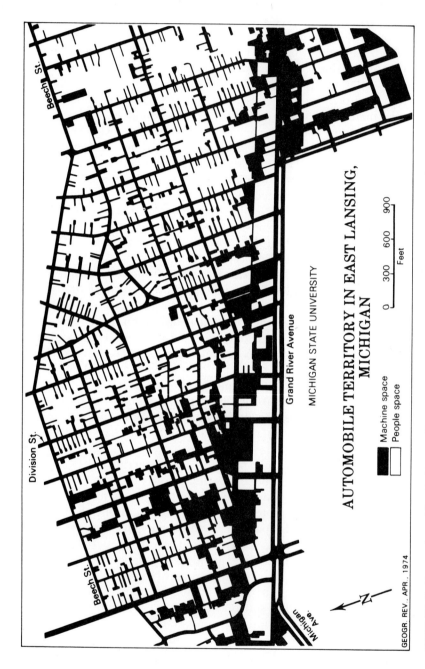

FIGURE 7.9. Machine space (automobile territory) in a part of East Lansing, Michigan, spring 1970, at ground level only. (From Ronald J. Horvath: Machine Space, *Geographical Review,* vol. 64, p. 170, fig. 1.)

derground and elevated, covers the Bay Area at average speeds of 40-50 miles per hour. A primary problem here, as in most rapid transit systems, is that many passengers at the end of the trip still find themselves some distance from their destination; thus, a second trip by bus may be necessary. Such a rigid system of transportation also ties future planning to a pattern with little flexibility, a situation that may not be realistic in an urban environment that is changing so rapidly. Furthermore, mass transit only adds to machine space.

The basic problem connected with machine space is congestion. Most American cities involve a 19th Century layout that is incompatible with 20th Century dispersal trends. The rectangular pattern was largely introduced to facilitate a division of land and not to channel movement of vehicles. A tremendous number of urban streets are not really used while the remaining ones are overloaded. In addition, many barriers to movement exist—especially rivers and railroad lines that served as locational attractions for the early wholesaling warehouses and industrial factories. When a pattern of mobile automobiles, trucks, and buses is superimposed on this old pattern of streets and axial barriers, congestion is bound to occur. The problem is magnified because the vehicles require parking space. This contrast between old and new patterns is illustrated by the CBD, where parking is lacking and streets cause congestion, and the suburban shopping center, where parking areas are included. The American city, then, is characterized by a spatial behavior that gives priority to machines within a pattern established in great part during the last century.

SUMMARY

This chapter has considered movement within the American city as a basis for the land use patterns that develop there. Commercial, residential, and other patterns originate as a result of intraurban interaction. In the past the basic forces in this interaction were centripetal around a dominant CBD but more recently they have been centrifugal as man's mobility has increased. However, as the nodes of interaction have expanded, these movements have become quite diverse as cross-town directions are introduced. Two types of movement were considered—permanent and temporary. Several models and concepts were introduced to analyze the processes of residential location and the journeys to work and shop. Finally, the concept of machine space is used to emphasize the priority given to the automobile in American society.

Remarks made in this chapter are most applicable to American cities or at least to cities of industrialized countries. Other cultures depend more on public transport or on walking, and their patterns of movement may be different. Some of these patterns are mentioned in the chapters on comparative urban development.

Before turning to that topic, however, examining some of the locational processes in American cities is advisable. A chapter on growth patterns in the American city serves as a basis for a second chapter devoted to the analysis of why people locate where they do in urban areas.

CHAPTER 8

GROWTH OF THE METROPOLITAN AREA

MODELS OF URBAN LAND USE EVOLUTION

One way to continue the analysis of internal spatial organization of the city is to approach it historically. This method involves applying general models of urban spatial development to the actual growth of American midwestern cities. Such a historical overview provides a spatial foundation for more detailed analysis of location of land uses in the next chapter. The three models of urban growth described below reflect different eras of transportation, and when used together can illustrate the historical factors in land use differentiation. In 1925, an ecologist, Ernest Burgess, developed a model stressing the importance of growth by concentric rings. A decade or so later, Homer Hoyt, an economist, tried to account for differential growth within the rings by sectors. The two approaches were similar in that they both emphasized residential land use at the expense of other uses. Largely to correct this deficiency, Chauncy Harris and Edward Ullman, geographers, suggested that urban areas tend to grow around a series of nuclei. These three models will be examined in terms of generalization versus reality (see fig. 8.1).

THE CONCENTRIC ZONE MODEL.   In the 1920's, Burgess was a member of a group of sociologists at the University of Chicago who concentrated on processes of human ecology involving man as an organism adapting to his environment. Burgess, specifically, focused on the processes of urban growth. He felt that as cities expand a process of distribution occurs which sifts and sorts and relocates individuals and groups by residences and occupations. This sifting and sorting takes place concentrically by rings as follows:

Central Business District (Loop)
Zone-in-transition
Residential zone of industrial workers
Higher class residential areas
Commuters' zone

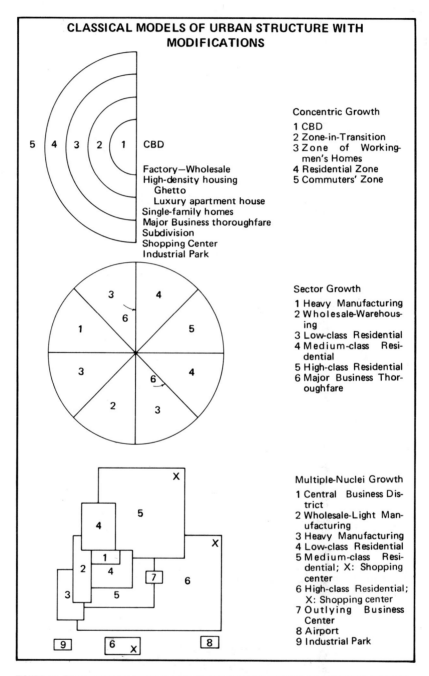

CLASSICAL MODELS OF URBAN STRUCTURE WITH MODIFICATIONS

5 | 4 | 3 | 2 | 1 CBD

Factory—Wholesale
High-density housing
 Ghetto
 Luxury apartment house
Single-family homes
Major Business thoroughfare
Subdivision
Shopping Center
Industrial Park

Concentric Growth

1 CBD
2 Zone-in-Transition
3 Zone of Working-
 men's Homes
4 Residential Zone
5 Commuters' Zone

Sector Growth

1 Heavy Manufacturing
2 Wholesale-Warehous-
 ing
3 Low-class Residential
4 Medium-class Resi-
 dential
5 High-class Residential
6 Major Business Thor-
 oughfare

Multiple-Nuclei Growth

1 Central Business Dis-
 trict
2 Wholesale-Light Man-
 ufacturing
3 Heavy Manufacturing
4 Low-class Residential
5 Medium-class Resi-
 dential; X: Shopping
 center
6 High-class Residential;
 X: Shopping center
7 Outlying Business
 Center
8 Airport
9 Industrial Park

FIGURE 8.1. The three classical models of urban structure emphasize concentric and radial growth around one nucleus or expansion within a system of several nuclei.

These five belts include different forms of land use, but the emphasis is on residential districts which seem to develop concentrically from the center. Although he recognized that a variety of factors may affect this pattern, his primary emphasis was *ecological,* that is, how the physical processes of urban expansion match up with the social processes of human organization. A basic aspect of ecological expansion is the tendency of each inner zone to expand its area by invading the next outer zone. This process is called succession and is fundamental to the Burgess model of historical urban growth around a single nucleus.

The Burgess model is developed around a process that went on in the past and, with modifications, is going on today. The origin of change in all the rings is the invasion or movement into and out of the *zone-in-transition* which sets up similar movements into and out of the outer rings. A major characteristic of this zone-in-transition is an instability of land use which results from the possibilities for change. Prongs of commercial use may invade the area and the possibility of further change serves to induce landlords of the residential areas to neglect the maintenance and improvement of their housing, many hopeful that a greater profit will result from sale of the land for a commercial site. This housing, therefore, deteriorates through age and neglect but is still in demand by the city's lowest income groups. In the zone-in-transition are ghettos similar to those described by Burgess—the "Black Belt," "Little Sicily," "Germantown"—where immigrants from overseas or rural Negroes from the South are (and were) forced to settle because it is the only place where housing is (and was) available, often through relatives or members of their own economic class (see fig. 8.2). According to

FIGURE 8.2. Segregated areas of American cities are of ethnic or racial types. In recent years several such areas have been the sites of urban disorders, some violent in nature.

Burgess, they "succeed" other people of the same class who then invade the adjacent "zone of industrial workers homes." The human environment in the zone-in-transition (or deterioration) is thoroughly disorganized, with poor housing, lack of educational and health facilities, split families, unemployment, and racial conflicts the end results. Besides residential slums, this zone of mixed land use includes parking lots, used-car sales areas, low-grade bars and restaurants, pawnshops, warehouses, wholesale facilities, and small industry. Although it may encircle the CBD, more often it is accentuated on one side, the so-called "zone of discard"—districts where social unrest is great, civil-rights disorders have erupted, and overcrowding and segregation are prevalent. Preston and Griffin (1966) and Preston (1966) have refined this concept.

Burgess viewed the zone-in-transition as a key to understanding certain urban social phenomena. In this zone blighted housing represents the physical erosion associated with social phenomena like crime, race, low income, disease and disorganization. This belt constitutes a major problem area of American metropolitan areas as it is invaded by low-income groups, especially Blacks, and deserted by others, especially Whites. One factor in the perpetuation of this belt, therefore, is the restriction placed by society on outward movement of low-income groups. Housing for these groups is generally profitable in the zone-in-transition because of the pecularities of the tax structure, a factor discussed in the next chapter.

Burgess himself recognized the distortions that exist in such an idealized pattern of growth and land use. Complications are introduced by terrain features, climate, transport axes, and older cores that were absorbed during the processes of historical growth. The five zones are not sharply demarcated from each other but represent ecological gradients. A grid-pattern of layout common in American cities also cuts across the concentric rings. Many people have criticized the theory on the basis of these distortions from reality. However, Burgess' most severe critic was Davie (1937) who felt that most cities include radial and other patterns of commercial land, industrial areas located near transportation by water or rail, low-grade housing situated near industrial and transportation areas, and higher-class housing scattered in a haphazard fashion. In short, the concentric rings are not complete but are broken into segments. For example, the zone-in-transition or the nearby wholesale area often develop on only one side of the CBD. Davie concluded that there was no universal pattern, in fact not even an "ideal" type. It would appear that Burgess' emphasis on residential land uses tended to subject his concept to criticism that it was not broad enough to comprise all forms of land use; furthermore, including non-residential uses as distorting factors is not sufficient if the theory is to be a comprehensive framework for understanding the areal differentiation of the city. Most authorities, however, agree that in spite of irregularities, the Burgess pattern is recognizable in parts of most cities, especially in the zones near the Central Business District.

THE SECTOR MODEL.   Homer Hoyt saw the concentric-zone theory as a useful starting point for explaining internal differences within cities, but he felt that various modifications are necessary. In studying the pattern of change in residential areas of American cities over a number of years prior to 1939, he concluded that urban growth is axial (Hoyt, 1939). In each city, residential characteristics such as age, degree of ownership, race, condition, and facilities were found to correlate with three levels of rent—high, medium, and low. From a historical point of view, the high rent areas, apparently, tend to influence the growth of the entire city. Generally, starting on the more pretentious side of the Central Business District, these areas grow outwards as sectors, generally unable to move sideways because of parallel wedge growth by middle income groups (see fig. 8.1). In other parts of the city, low income sectors or wedges also develop. In each sector lateral growth generally is not feasible owing to competition or to incompatibility, and therefore expansion outward to the open land is almost necessary.

Hoyt believed that the high rent areas lead the growth and affect the development of the other sectors. Here money is available to develop residential land on the edges of the city and the prestige of such districts tends to pull middle income groups in this direction as parallel wedges. The low-rent areas are left to follow the sectors least desired by the others. Hoyt stated that certain principles seemed to characterize the pattern of high rent expansion as follows:

Along established routes or toward another nucleus
Toward high ground, where flood danger is lacking, or along waterfronts
Toward free open country, avoiding deadends or barriers
Along the fastest existing transport lines
Toward homes of community leaders

Hoyt noticed that these trends were persistent during the period of study and that high-class business establishments in the CBD seemed to follow in the wake of the high-rent residential areas.

Although Hoyt emphasized the residential areas within the city, other types of land use exhibit axial patterns. Americans can recognize certain arteries of retail business which extend out in striplike patterns from the core. Similarly, heavy manufacturing and transport facilities, especially railroads, are often found along low-lying land running through the city (fig. 8.3).

FIGURE 8.3. An older industrial area of Omaha, Nebraska. A primary locational factor is the railroad from which spurs lead off to separate firms. Marginal to the area are commercial and residential districts. (Courtesy Gate City Steel, Omaha, Nebraska.)

The sector concept, however, is not to be thought of as a rigid model. Hoyt admitted that exceptions exist. One example is the construction of high-rise luxury apartment houses in densely populated areas near the center of the city in order to supply apartments for people (e.g., single or retired) who wish to be near shopping and cultural-recreational activities. Real estate promoters, therefore, have the power to influence the direction of high-rent growth under certain conditions. Criticism of the sector theory, however, still came from Firey (1947, 49, 77-86), who concluded that Hoyt did not give sufficient weight to the effects of cultural factors in land use, e.g., sentiment and symbolism. For example, Firey stated that a peculiar residential area such as Beacon Hill in Boston can be explained only in non-rational terms like "social value." Some years later, Hoyt (1964) reexamined the sector theory in view of the changes since 1940 and found it still applicable, although he stated that widespread use of the automobile had introduced a greater element of flexibility in urban growth.

THE MULTIPLE-NUCLEI MODEL.   In accounting for the distribution of activities in an urban area, the concentric-zone and sector theories utilize only one nucleus. However, urban residents realize that actually several nuclei exist around which growth takes place, especially in metropolitan areas. Therefore, Harris and Ullman (1945) added a third theory—that of multiple nuclei—to the group of empirical models for internal expansion and differentiation of cities (see fig. 8.1).

These nuclei can arise as a result of a city's historical evolution. For example, urban growth from one nucleus may engulf older villages which then act as new nuclei within the urban area. On the other hand, new shopping centers or industrial districts may be established as new nuclei within the city. Whether these nuclei arise over a long time or are established quickly, their development reflects four principles of geographic association:

Special facilities. Certain functions within the city require special facilities: the Central Business District demands accessibility; a port area needs deep water frontage; manufacturing cannot operate without transport facilities and land; and finally, residential areas generally require protection from floods. Special facilities, therefore, help to account for poly-nucleation in the urban area.

Attraction. Similar activities have a tendency to group together because they profit from mutual association. Examples of this type of association include department stores for comparative shopping, financial and office functions, wholesaling activities, and a series of industrial areas which use the same transport facilities. In many cities, a series of used-car lots line "automobile row."

Repulsion. Dissimilar activities will often repel each other as exemplified by residential vs. heavy industrial areas and retail vs. wholesaling districts.

High rent. Certain enterprises cannot profit from central locations and therefore avoid high rents of these sites. For this reason, wholesaling and warehousing districts are generally located in undesirable sites, often on low land near railroads.

What do these four principles illustrate regarding the origin of nuclei within urban areas? Figure 8.1 shows a generalized pattern of nuclei within a city. Prominent among these nuclei are the business districts. The Central Business District and Outlying Business Districts each possess accessibility, the former for the entire city and the latter for a neighborhood area. Enterprises within these districts profit from centrality and therefore pay higher rents characteristic of such locations.

Within these business districts there is also a segregation of activities owing to attraction of similar activities or repulsion of dissimilar ones. For example, department stores may be attracted by clothing stores but repelled by the wholesale district.

Newly organized industrial districts also illustrate these four principles. The factories here require special transport facilities and are attracted by the lower rents and similar enterprises that may also locate there. On the other hand, they may be repelled by an adjacent older factory which is outside the tract but which still gives off much smoke.

A third example of the multiple-nuclei theory is provided by the hierarchy of residential areas that exist in any city. High-rise apartments develop near the CBD because people living there want the special facilities of this location and can afford the higher rents. On the other hand, poor residences exist not far away in the zone-in-transition and repel improved commercial uses while attracting the "seedy" stores and other uses typical of margins of the Central Business District. In other parts of the city, new neighborhoods develop, especially in recent years with the rise of large subdivisions. These developments are often uniform, since they are designed for particular income groups; the higher ones possess special sites that are well drained with good views, while the poorer ones may evolve in low areas and are destined to become future slums.

The prototype of the multiple-nuclei city is Los Angeles with four metropolitan subsystems located in a basin 100 miles across that encompasses nearly 10 million people and 122 incorporated cities (Preston, 1970). These nuclei are held together by 1,000 miles of freeway (fig. 8.4). As a relatively new conurbation, Los Angeles was created by the very forces of dispersal and sprawl that are tearing other American cities apart. Economic opportunities offered in the second largest regional economy in the country helped to attract some 200,000 new residents each year since 1940. One primary factor in the continuous pattern of sprawl has been the cheaper housing in the vacant areas between the nuclei but in recent years higher costs of land have forced greater densities through the use of smaller lots and construction of multi-family housing. The sprawl of housing has been accompanied by decentralization of commercial and employment activities to a degree unmatched in any other American urban area (see fig. 8.5). Finally, the lack of any real political-cultural focus in the area has led to urban renewal in the old central core where a new government civic center has emerged (see fig. 1.3).

FIGURE 8.4. The freeway, in providing accessibility within the major urban areas, requires a tremendous amount of space. In the Los Angeles area, over 500 miles of freeway are necessary to accommodate the nearly six million automobiles and trucks that are the prime means of intra-urban transport. (Courtesy Division of Highways, Department of Public Works, State of California.)

APPLYING THE THREE MODELS TO AMERICAN URBAN GROWTH

Adams' (1970) examination of residential structure in American Midwestern cities forms one of the most intriguing attempts to use growth models in a real-world context.* He developed a concentric model of growth based on nonfarm housing construction data for the United States between 1890 and 1960. During this period the graph of building

*Adams, John S., "Residential Structure of Midwestern Cities," *Annals of the Association of American Geographers*, 60 (March 1970), 37-62. This portion of the chapter draws heavily on this source.

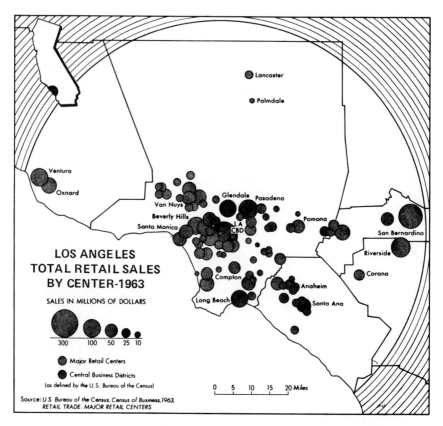

FIGURE 8.5. The decentralization of commercial activities within a large metropolitan area or conurbation is illustrated by the pattern in Los Angeles for 1963. (Source: R. E. Preston, "Recent Changes in the Size and Form of the Southern California Metropolis," *California: 1970, Problems and Prospects*, Association of American Geographers, 1970, fig. 9.)

activity shows a boom or bust pattern of fluctuation (see fig. 8.6). In terms of economic expansion, the movement of foreign immigrants and rural farm workers into cities set up a process of residential relocation that culminated in the addition of new housing on the margins of the built-up area. The process involved invasion and succession of concentric zones in a manner analogous to that described by Burgess. When a business recession occurred, unemployment rose, the demand for housing slackened, and immigration and construction diminished. Thus, new houses existed but there were fewer buyers. Chicago, for example, shows this pattern of boom and bust that is reflected in wide and narrow rings of housing constructed in the respective periods. The city's population rose from 2.6 million in 1919 to 3.4 million in 1927 before falling between 1927 and 1932; the early period of increasing population contributed to a building boom with annual permit values of new housing that rose from $35 million in 1918 to $367 in 1926. The housing ring, therefore, is wide. After 1927, the annual volume of new construction fell to $4 million in 1932, a period that is represented by a narrow ring.

The model Midwestern city developed by Adams is assumed to be average for the United States. Cities of this region, he feels, illustrate the most representative proportions of four transport eras that have dominated American urban development. These eras, in turn, he correlates with the cycles of residential construction for the nation:
—the pedestrian-horsecar era: up through the 1880s
—the electric streetcar era: 1880s to World War I
—the recreational auto era: 1920s to 1941
—the freeway era: post World War II
Adams feels that the circular pattern of growth is most apparent during the first and third eras while a star-shaped sector pattern is more evident in the second and fourth. A problem exists today in differentiating these eras as they are submerged in the overall built-up area. However, the age of housing and its type (single- or multiple-family) and style provide keys to the eras.

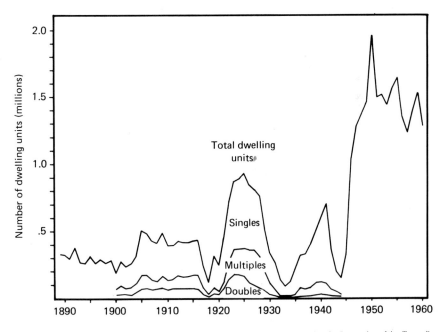

FIGURE 8.6. Cycles of housing construction in the United States as based on Census data for the number of dwelling units started each year, 1889-1960. Types of dwelling-unit are available only from 1900-1944. (Reproduced by permission from the *Annals* of the Association of American Geographers, Volume 60, 1970, J. S. Adams.)

THE OLD CORE AND THE PEDESTRIAN-HORSECAR ERA. In this period, which ends in the late 1880s, the city was relatively small and compact since the means of moving large numbers of people horizontally (electric streetcar) and vertically (elevator) were not developed until the 1880s. Most residents were able to walk to work and to shop, thereby influencing a considerable mixture of land uses. Growth of the city, therefore, led to higher densities within the existing built-up area. Housing constructed in this era was usually of multiple family (including tenement) types with the highest densities approaching a thousand people per acre for low-income groups. Adams (1970, 49) states that four- and five-story walkup apartment buildings, visible for mile after mile in places like south Chicago and north St. Louis, represent the landscape of this era. Horsecar lines were used in this period but did little to change the urban form. Primary exceptions to compact growth were estates of the rich in the countryside and commuter towns located along rails out of the city. In 1893 the Illinois Central Railroad, for example, delivered 14,000 daily commuters to south Chicago. Industrial areas began to align themselves along these lines as they had along river fronts.

THE ELECTRIC STREETCAR ERA. The electric streetcar era began in the 1890s and extended to the end of World War I, a period that is clearly evident in the "plateau" of housing construction in the graph (see fig. 8.6). Transportation costs were reduced for large members of middle class people who could now move to the suburbs and still get to work (Warner, 1962). As a result, a star-shaped pattern was superimposed on the previous compact urban layout with tenacles of lines extending out into undeveloped areas permitting some decongestion of the core. Adams thus provides for sectoral development (Hoyt's model) to supplement the concentric growth. The change in means of transport was rapid: in 1890, 70 percent of street railways were still horse-drawn while by 1902 almost all were electrically operated. The process of expansion was in a sense "directed" by the transit companies who often cooperated with the land developer. The speculation in land was based on increasing prices along the lines so that more intensive commercial or industrial uses replaced housing. The overall price of land made lots relatively small and led to considerable multiple-family housing. In certain large cities the streetcar was supplemented by rapid transit, a pattern most evident in the subway of New York and the "El" of Chicago; by-products of this transit were discrete nodes of commercial activity which sprang up near the "stops" along these lines. Here, it is possible to see the beginnings of multiple-nuclei development (the Harris-Ullman model). In the cores themselves, the skyscrapers reflected a technology that supported a more intensive use of land and facilitated personal contacts between office workers in a way never possible before.

Perhaps the single most apparent result of this urban era of rail expansion was the increasing social stratification of groups by spatial areas. In the previous compact city, different social groups were located near each other, and neighborhoods thus contained a mixture of groups. With the "liberation" of the rich classes to the rural exurbs by railroad and the middle classes to suburb by streetcar lines, the separation of work and residence was made possible, and neighborhoods tended to become more uniform in their economic characteristics and sense of values. Thus, social stratification was increasingly reflected in the physical spread of the city. Vance (1964, 50) goes so far as to say that the transformation of most American cities from the stage of simple urbanism to complex metropolitanism can be dated from the first or second decade following the introduction of trolleys. This new metropolitan development was accompanied by an improvement in the public environment including especially utilities like electricity, water, and gas.

THE RECREATIONAL AUTO ERA.   Adams calls the next period the era of the recreational auto because the automobile, bus, and truck provided a new flexibility to location in a city. Although the streetcar remained important in the United States until 1945, automobile registration increased from 500,000 in 1910 to 32,000,000 in 1940 and the number of passengers using motor buses rose from 1.5 billion in 1925 to almost 10 billion in 1945. This increased accessibility to the fringes of the city was a factor in altering the old star-like pattern of the previous era. Residential construction was now possible in the interstices between the streetcar axes, thereby once again evening out the expansion of the city as a whole. The model reflects, then, a shift from sector growth back to concentric again. The graph of construction actually shows two building booms during the era—the first in the 1920s and, following the Depression, a second one at the close of the 1930s prior to World War II (see fig. 8.6). Although some similarities exist between the two in terms of house style, the number of multiple-family dwellings was much less in the late 1930s as higher income was reflected in greater construction of single-family homes. Owing to the auto orientation of new neighborhoods and possibly to material shortages in the Depression and in World War II, many urban landscapes of these periods are marked by the absence of sidewalks or curbings. The residential land use pattern was supplemented by outlying business centers developing around an earlier village or neighborhood nodal point which were, in many cases, annexed to the city. Widespread commuting commenced and the garage became a part of most dwellings. Finally, the automobile-oriented shopping center began to make its appearance. The multiple-nuclei model, therefore, became more evident in urban structure.

THE FREEWAY AUTO ERA. The fourth period in the development of the American Midwestern city is differentiated from the previous one by the impact of freeways. In this case Adams feels that the freeway acted in a manner similar to that of the electric streetcar in encouraging residential development in areas opened up by the new arteries of transport. Around the Midwestern city, an irregular ring of suburbs developed, often dominated by uniform ranch-style homes. Because of speculation and other quirks in the land development process, these subdivisions sprawled out in a leap-frog pattern. The residents were mostly commuters and their commercial requirements led to the construction of nearby shopping centers. Thus, elements of sectoral and multiple-nuclei growth again became evident. The graph illustrates the tremendous boom in residential construction after 1945, when each year saw the addition of a million dwelling units (see fig. 8.6). The increasing flexibility of location extended to industries as commercial trucking permitted the decentralization of this activity to the suburbs, often in industrial parks. A greater number of traffic-generating modes now existed within the metropolis so that the pattern of movement departed further and further from a radial one centering on the CBD.

A MODEL OF THE MIDWESTERN CITY AND ITS DISTORTIONS. The purpose of Adams' work on the cycles of growth in the Midwestern city was to derive an average or typical pattern. By combining the national construction data into groups corresponding to the cycles of growth identified he developed a model that represents the average pattern for each cycle (see fig. 8.7). The width of the rings, which is based on the amount of housing, reflects average national rates of economic expansion and urban population increase from the late 19th Century to the 1960s. The model also agrees with and partially explains empirically derived distance-decay models of urban population density. For example, he states that transport technologies *determined* densities and spatial arrangements in each of the growth rings. Thus, in general, the housing and population densities of the rings decreased outwardly as mobility of people increased. At the same time, however, distortions from these rings occurred in spatial arrangements owing to the axial growth of the second and fourth eras. These distortions are shown in a second model that supplements the first one (see fig. 8.8). Adams states that streetcar

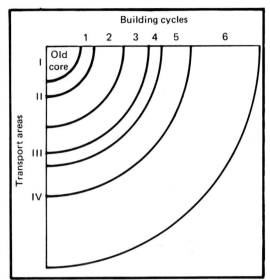

FIGURE 8.7. Spatial structure of a quadrant of the model city. The six building cycles of the 1890's, 1900-1919, 1920's, 1930's, 1940's, and 1950-1960's are apparent in Fig. 8.6. The width of the rings is based on the relative amount of housing construction and on density levels prevailing in each period. (Reproduced by permission from the *Annals* of the Association of American Geographers, Volume 60, 1970, J. S. Adams.)

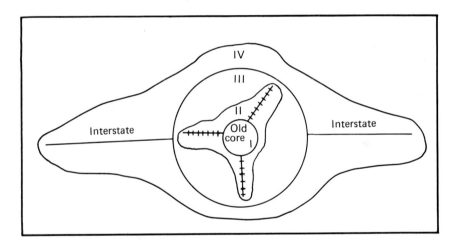

FIGURE 8.8. Expected distortions from concentric growth patterns. Transport eras I (foot travel) and III (recreational auto) promoted compact and circular urban patterns while eras II (streetcar lines) and IV (freeways) led to star-shaped deviations from a concentric form. (Reproduced by permission of the *Annals* of the Association of American Geographers, Volume 60, 1970, J. S. Adams.)

and freeway often *directed* residential development as against the other two eras when people on foot or automobiles *followed* it. Consequently, the transport systems of the first and third eras provided a movement surface in which concentric growth was predominant because expansion was theoretically possible in all directions. By contrast, the systems of the second and fourth eras exhibit the channels and nodes of high-speed movement. In these eras axial and nodal growth departed from concentricity.

Adams' last step was to actually test his model of residential construction in the midwestern city of Minneapolis. Using census data he obtained the median age of housing in all census tracts and then plotted isolines to correspond with the periods used in his model. Strong similarities between the model and the map are apparent (see fig. 8.9). Perhaps most obvious are the lobes of cycles that correspond to streetcar and freeway development. On the other hand, the cycles between these exhibit a more even or circular development. A second similarity between map and graph is found in the width of the rings, e.g., the narrow belt of housing built in the 1930s. Adams also ran two traverses through Minneapolis from core to suburbs and found that the growth rings were clearly identifiable, thereby confirming that the model can serve to predict variance in age of housing from what might be expected.

THE THREE MODELS IN RETROSPECT

Adams' work represents one of the few attempts to test the three urban growth models in a real-world situation, not only in the Midwest but also in a specific city. He has found that concentric and axial growth seemed to alternate in the Midwest city as transport technology changed. The star-shaped axes of the streetcar and freeway alternated with periods of even growth when pedestrian and automobile were dominant. Consequently, his work confirms the rather strong persistence of these early models developed by Burgess and Hoyt.

However, both of these latter models focused on residential land use and assumed the dominance of one commercial core—the CBD. So movement of people in both of these models was presumed to be radial both in a daily sense and over a period of time. The multiple-nuclei concept, on the other hand, was designed by Harris and Ullman to allow for the new nodal points that were supplementing and even replacing the CBD. In this model, axial movement is still important but *crosstown* traffic becomes equally significant. Adams' model thus emphasizes the affects of radial movement along streets and freeways, but although nuclei are mentioned does not give attention to the effects of movement between sectors and nodes. The multiple-nuclei model needs to be tested in a way similar to that of Adams' work on the other two models. For example, what have been the growth patterns through time of the various nodes and what factors have affected differences in their sizes?

Attempts to combine the three models of urban growth have been rare. One of the most interesting ones is by Murdie (1969, 169) who pointed

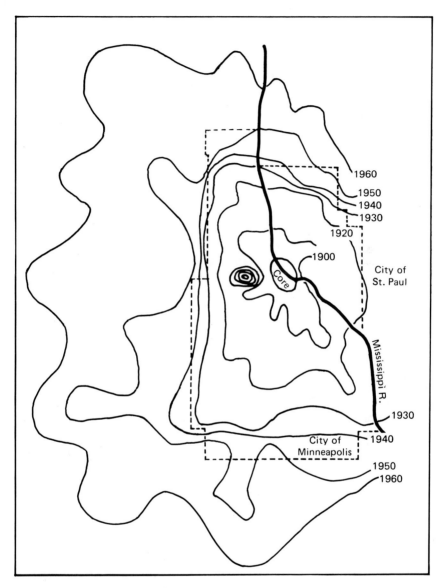

FIGURE 8.9. A test of the growth model in Minneapolis. Note the similarities between the rings here and those in Fig. 8.7 (widths overall) and Fig. 8.8 (lobes present in eras II and IV). (Reproduced by permission of the *Annals* of the Association of American Geographers, Volume 60, 1970, J. S. Adams.)

out how the models illustrate social patterns in Toronto, Canada. Following leads provided by Shevky and Bell (1955), he found that urban populations tend to sort themselves out spatially on the basis of certain economic and social characteristics. When aggregate data of these characteristics were subjected to factor analysis within a framework of subareas in the city, it was discovered that these data tended to group into three spatial dimensions: 1) economic status, such as family income and education, varied by sectors; 2) family status, such as age and size, varied by concentric rings; while 3) ethnic status varied by cluster or nuclei. The process by which these three factors differentiate urban populations apparently is related to fundamental changes that a society undergoes as it industrializes and urbanizes. The sorting by economic sectors agrees not only with Hoyt's concept of three different grades of residential value but also with Adams' ideas of directional bias. On the other hand, family sorting by rings takes place in all sectors as improved economic status and changes in the life cycle permit a residential change to better housing in the outer belts. Finally, owing to reasons of voluntary or involuntary segregation, ethnic groups cluster in nodes or in a manner resembling multiple-nuclei. The map shows how these three spatial dimensions are responsible for "social areas" in Toronto (see fig. 8.10). Such areas have been identified in other North American cities, and they show a remarkable persistence through time. This method of analysis is called factorial ecology because it is based on the inter-relationship of a number of socio-economic factors in given subareas of a city. According to Berry (1965, 115-116), the series of such analytic studies make it possible to state definitely that the three models are independent, additive contributors to the total socio-economic structuring of city neighborhoods. In other words, if the concentric and axial schemes are overlaid on a city, the resulting cells will contain neighborhoods that are remarkably uniform in their social and economic characteristics. Johnston (1970, 365-366), on the other hand, feels such patterns are not necessarily repetitive, especially in the fact that the highest status groups are not always located on the periphery. Apparently, more research is necessary in relating the three models to the residential structure of cities. At the present time, they only partially explain why people locate where they do.

Morrill (1974, 191-8) also made tentative efforts to combine the three models of urban growth. He feels that the concentric pattern resembles a gradient of land use around the core with competition for land resulting in an outward ordering of land use from commercial, to multi-family, to single-family residential. The different sectors, on the other hand, not only reflect variations in land use, e.g., wedges of residences or industry,

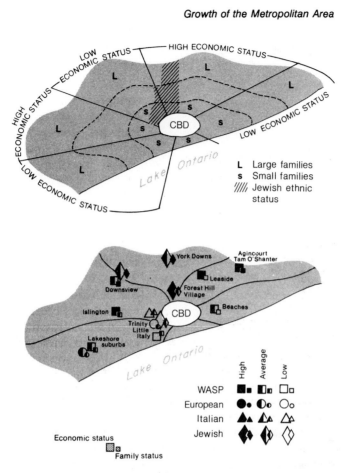

FIGURE 8.10. An attempt by Murdie in Toronto to combine the concentric, sector, and multiple-nuclei patterns of urban growth. Family size (social) varies by rings while economic status changes by sector; ethnic groups tend to cluster. (Reprinted with permission of Department of Geography, University of Chicago from R. A. Murdie, *Factorial Ecology of Metropolitan Toronto, 1951-1961,* Research Paper 116, 1969.)

but also social class differences which most cities possess. Finally, Morrill would superimpose a central place structure over the gradient and sectors to explain nodes of commercial activity that all large cities require. Owing to decreasing densities of population outward from the core, these nodes will be farther apart on the edges and competition for land around them will create minor gradients which modify the original one for the city as a whole. This hypothetical pattern is illustrated by the "tent" model which actually is an urban density surface (see fig. 8.11). Further research is necessary to work out the processes behind the growth patterns implied in such a model.

THE URBAN DENSITY SURFACE

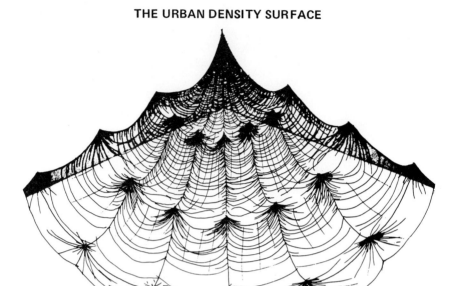

FIGURE 8.11. The urban density surface. Land values and intensities of use are greatest at the nodes of greater accessibility on major arterials. (Reprinted with permission from Berry, et al, *Commercial Structure and Commercial Blight,* Univ. of Chicago, Dept. of Geography Research Paper No. 85, 1963, fig. 3.)

SUMMARY

In this chapter the subject of spatial organization *within* urban areas is continued by examining three historical growth models that have prevailed in the United States. Early growth was both concentric and axial around one core area—the CBD—while more recent expansion has been taking place around a series of nodes facilitated by the greater mobility of the population. Population densities have decreased outward accordingly. Adams' interesting attempt to apply the concentric and sectoral models to the real world of the Midwestern city supports these growth patterns and isolates four eras—pedestrian, streetcar, automobile, and freeway—in which these patterns alternate. These four eras correspond rather closely to the housing construction cycles that prevailed between 1880 and 1960. Adams further tested his model in some detail in Minneapolis. This work represents a start in developing a model that realistically portrays the growth patterns of cities. It is particularly important that the multiple-nuclei model, which is so significant today, be combined with the other models. Finally, these models should be tested in the cities of other countries to see if they have cross-cultural applicability.

CHAPTER 9

LOCATION OF LAND USES
IN THE METROPOLITAN AREA

In the previous chapter the *growth* of the American metropolitan area was interpreted in terms of theory versus reality. Three models of urban growth were described and applied to the reality of American conditions. Apparent from this analysis is that the large American city was affected *historically* by changing accessibility—first toward one core, secondly along several axes, and finally around a variety of nuclei. These patterns are macro in nature, however, and should be supplemented by an interpretation of locations of land use at the micro scale. Consequently, it is necessary to look at certain factors that explain the location of individual uses like the department store, shopping center, apartment house, single-family house, industrial plant, and school. These various uses of land exhibit degrees of regularity that can be explained in theory so that exceptions to the pattern are more meaningful. In the first section of this chapter, some of the theoretical considerations affecting land use location are examined. This section leads into a discussion of individual land uses in which the models are examined against reality. Finally, commercial land use is discussed using the Murphy model of Central Business District structure. No attempt is made to cover all land uses but examples are given to illustrate the *processes* involved.

URBAN LAND USE LOCATION: THEORY AND REALITY

HAIG AND LAND USE THEORY. In 1926 Robert Murray Haig set forth some propositions that remain basic to urban land economics and to the explanation of land use location in cities. He realized that cities are established because of the advantages of agglomeration, and that location in the city is basically a matter of overcoming movement costs. These costs are social as well as economic in nature and the most efficient city minimizes them in the aggregate for all residents. The costs of movement, or "costs of friction" as he termed them, have two dimensions—transportation costs and site rentals—which are inversely related to each other (see fig. 9.1). Transportation costs are incurred by moving people

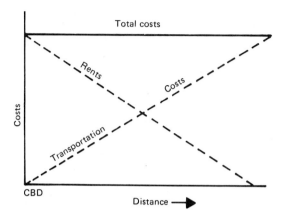

FIGURE 9.1. The costs of friction represent the reciprocal costs of rent and transport costs. Low transport costs reflect good accessibility to a site, thereby increasing its rent-producing possibilities.

or goods around the city. Site rentals, on the other hand, are charges made for sites where accessibility may be obtained with comparatively low transportation costs.* The pattern of site rentals is really equivalent to the pattern of land values. Thus, an enterprise will pay in rent an amount that corresponds to the transportation costs saved by reason of the accessibility of the site. Transportation costs and site rentals, therefore, are complementary and in total represent the costs of friction (Haig, 1926, 421-2).

How does this inverse relationship between the two costs of friction work? The situation is analogous to the agricultural zones of von Thünen in that urban enterprises differ in their ability to turn accessibility into profit. Those establishments that benefit from the maximum accessibility or interaction with other places in terms of time-distance will occupy the sites of highest rent. These sites will be expensive because of the savings on transport costs to people patronizing them. Consequently, they must be utilized intensively, that is, a high return per unit of land must be realized in order to pay for such sites. In other words, low transport costs are traded for high rent. The department store, which depends on mass sales, must minimize its transportation costs for the most people and, therefore, locates at a point of maximum

*The term site rental should not be confused with the term economic rent that is used by economists. The latter expression was first developed by Ricardo who defined it as the difference between net return from investment in fertile land and land that is marginal in terms of fertility. Von Thünen, a German farmer of the 19th Century, defined it·in terms of net return from location and made it the basis of his theory of agricultural regionalization. Haig, on the other hand, used the more conventional term of site rental or contract rent, the amount paid by a tenant to a landlord for use of his property. Site rental and economic rent on a location may be the same, but more often they are different. A strong landlord can make the site rental equal the economic rent, while a weak landlord may not.

accessibility; at the same time, to pay the rental at this location it must capitalize the site intensively by expanding its commercial space vertically. Department stores have traditionally located in the Central Business District which has been the optimum point of accessibility to both private and public transportation. More recently, however, these stores form anchors to large shopping centers which are also accessible, at least to large numbers of people using automobiles.

Other locations in the urban area also represent trade-offs between site rental and transport costs. High-rise apartment buildings near the CBD can command high rent in return for low transport costs because the tenants, often young couples without children or older people, desire access to the CBD where they can work and shop with limited need of an automobile. On the other hand, the suburban resident, who often possesses superior purchasing power, may trade off low rent for higher transport costs because he desires a sizable lot and is willing to increase his total transport costs to get it. These costs include not only greater distances but also maintenance of two cars because of the varied pattern of trips to job, shop, school, and social activities. Although this resident is not following Zipf's principle of minimizing the costs of overcoming distance, he has minimized his *total* costs of friction in terms of his value system. The willingness of Americans to trade-off high transport costs for low rent in the suburbs reflects then perhaps irrational behavior from an economic point of view and in the aggregate does not result in minimizing the total costs of friction in the city (Haig's ideal). In fact, Alonso (1964, 5-11, 101-5) believes that such a case illustrates the weakness of using Haig's costs of friction as a basis for measuring location in a city. He feels that three factors—quantity of land, quantity of goods and services, and distance—must be set against a pattern of individual preferences in order to explain the equilibrium of a land use. Variations in preferences permit possibilities of substitution amongst the three variables in order to reach maximum satisfaction.

Although Alonso's model permits greater sophistication in explanation of urban location, this writer prefers to stick with the costs of friction in testing reality against theory. Recognizing that rent is not related in a simple way to transport costs, the trade-off between these two variables is easy to grasp by the normal person and other factors, like preference in the quantity of land, can be built into the case—as was done with the suburban resident above.

The influences of rent and transport costs seem to change with time and between cultures. For example, American rent curves around a node seem to have steepened, in part through inflation, while transport curves have become more shallow as the automobile and better roads have reduced the effects of distance. Therefore, rent around the CBD or other nodes may fall off more rapidly than it did in the past while transport costs may increase more slowly. Thus, total costs of friction may vary over time in any urban location. In addition, the curves will differ between cultures, e.g., the transport curve will tend to be shallower in America than in other cultures where the automobile is less apparent. Cities in such countries will tend to be more compact, and strip or sprawl patterns of land use will be less evident.

This theoretical trade-off of rent and transport costs around a CBD is normally shown as a series of rent gradients or bid-rent curves which reflect urban land use zones (see fig. 9.2). The basis for this zonation is a competitive bidding for accessible sites among the various urban activities. Again, the analogy to von Thünen is evident. Commercial activities are generally the highest bidders for accessible land, whether in the CBD or at other optimum nodes of accessibility. Industrial users seem to rank next while residential uses are third. In the diagram, commercial uses would be profitable out to "a" but actually superior to industrial uses only to "x." Industrial uses, in turn, are profitable to "b," but residential uses become of greater importance at "z." The main factors here again are the differing abilities of these three functions to turn accessibility into profit. At a given distance, for example, industry can outbid commercial activities for a site because access is reduced for the large numbers of people that retail business relies on for shopping thresholds. A major factor is the increasing transport costs for the commercial activities versus those for the industrial ones, i.e., the curve for

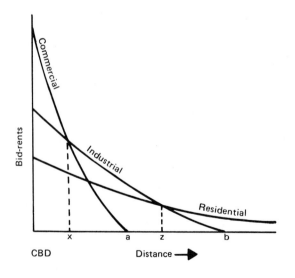

FIGURE 9.2. The slopes of bid-rent curves vary by land use with distance from the CBD. Commercial uses outcompete industrial and residential uses at the accessible CBD where lowered aggregate transport costs offset the higher rents. Accessibility is also more important to industry than it is to residences.

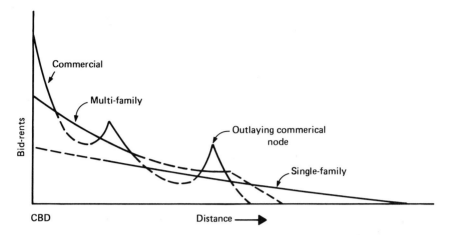

FIGURE 9.3. Hypothetical bid-rent curves in an urban area. Commercial uses outcompete different residential uses at the accessible nodes where lowered transport costs offset the higher rents. Multifamily residences can also outcompete single-family homes for the same reason.

transport costs is steeper for the former than for the latter. At the same time, the commercial activities must use the inner site intensively in order to take advantage of the lower transport costs and to pay the higher rent.

The above models relating to rent and transport costs, however, are designed for a hypothetical city with one major node—the CBD. In actual fact there are many of these nodes, each with bid-rent curves representing a tradeoff of rent and transport costs. As in the rural areas, the commercial nodes can be ranked in terms of accessibility and, therefore, exhibit central-place regularities. However, other nodes also exist such as industry, education, and recreation. At the same time, rent curves for multi-family and single-family residential uses differ. Thus a more realistic profile of rents in a city is shown in models in which both concentric zone and multiple nuclei appear (see figures 9.3 and 8.11). The costs of friction concept, therefore, not only facilitates predictions concerning land use in the city but also can be related to the three models of urban growth mentioned in the last chapter.

THEORY VERSUS REALITY. It is obvious that distortions exist in a theoretical urban system of land use zones based on complementarity between site rentals and transport costs. Indeed, these distortions motivated Haig to develop his concept of the costs of friction. He felt that the ideal city is one in which the *aggregate* costs of friction for the most people are at a minimum. Although this hypothesis assumes that land users all have the same preferences—something Alonso (1964) shows is not necessarily true—it still offers a useful way of establishing a model city against which distortions in costs of friction can be measured. Thus, one inappropriately located enterprise will create additional transportation costs for all other enterprises because the minimum pattern of costs has been distorted. Haig believed that zoning control, which would prevent such a misplacement, serves to insure a fair allocation of costs in which each enterprise bears its share. Unfortunately, many urban enterprises do not carry their fair share of the costs of friction. This situation is called an externality because costs are born by an external source. The concept represents an attempt to illustrate the interdependency among urban land uses, i.e., that the value and use of a parcel depend as much on its locational characteristics as on its degree of improvement. Externalities are the basis of many of the deviations in land use reality from theory. Let us now examine some examples of these deviations.

1. **Relic land uses.** Perhaps one of the most evident examples of a land-use location that is inappropriate from the standpoint of the costs of friction is an older or relic land use that was established when these costs were different. Haig uses the example of the garment industry in central Manhattan but the argument could be applied to many industries located in the cores of cities (Haig, 1926, 424; see also Kenyon, 1964). He points out that most business enterprises consist of a packet of functions which combine to affect location. In the case of clothing, manufacturing and wholesaling were both important in fixing the original location of this industry in downtown Manhattan. Labor makes up a high percentage of the total costs of the garment industry, and the fact that large numbers of workers could be assembled by subway and railroad was important. In wholesaling, New York City's position as a fashion center and its nearness to competitors were advantages since the concentration of showrooms permitted maximum comparison by buyers. Land use in this district was intense with high buildings near 34th Street combining retail and wholesale activities on lower floors with manufacturing on upper ones. Haig points out that even in the 1920s this industry did not bear its share of the costs of friction since its presence spoiled the character of the choice shopping district, blocked streets into the area, and pre-empted transit facilities. Consequently, the aggregate of the costs of friction was increased and an externality was created which was born by the rest of the city. Today, the garment industry and others like it, in many cases, linger on through inertia but the disruption is even greater in terms of cost. More often these labor-intensive industries have moved to the suburbs where labor is still gathered by automobile and other costs like land are reduced. Developments in communication have overcome the need for nearness to competitors in terms of styles.

Another example of relic land uses that distort the cost of friction is the persistence of older prestige areas in the central portions of cities. Firey (1945, 140-142 and 1947, 87-135) has pointed out that culturally rooted values such as sentiment exert a causative influence on land-use patterns that may override economic ones related to rent and transport costs. Such values help to explain the distinctive character of places like Beacon Hill in Boston and Georgetown in Washington, D.C. They also seem to be related to Wolpert's concept of place-utility, i.e., the level of satisfaction or dissatisfaction with respect to a given location (Travis, 1972, 30-31). Finally, these values support Alonso's (1964) hypothesis that the preferences of land users will not always be based on minimizing the costs of friction.

2. **Underuse of land.** One of the most apparent anomalies of land use in American cities is that much land is underused, i.e., it could be used more intensively. Again, in an ideal city where the aggregate costs of friction are minimal, intensive land use in the most accessible locations should be expected. Yet, asphalt-paved parking lots exist in commercial districts (see fig. 3.12) while slums are located on land nearby. Large vacant parcels occur in places within the builtup area. All of these represent externalities in that accessible land is not being used intensively. None of these uses is bearing its share of the aggregate costs of friction in a city.

The location of blighted areas seems to be an anomaly in the American city. Haig, for example, stated that "some of the poorest people live in conveniently located slums on high-priced land" (Haig, 1926, 403). According to a city's rental gradient of land, those sites located on the margin of the CBD should be relatively high in value, yet in a previous chapter we have seen that this "zone of transition" is the focal point of deterioration. Burgess showed that immigrants and later racial groups first located here, creating ghettos of high residential densities (see fig. 8.2). These groups replaced residents who had moved to the outer sections of the city. Gradually, this housing deteriorated and was not replaced by better housing or more intensive uses largely because growth in this zone ceased. The reasons for this are complex, but two seem to be paramount: (a) commercial and other uses lagged in the area not only because of the deteriorating environment but also because better mobility was facilitating decentralization of activities to the suburbs; (b) maintenance of the area for residential purposes was discouraged by the tax system. The latter factor requires some clarification.

A paradox exists because land in a slum is relatively high in value but the structures there do not reflect this. Actually, this is not as much of a paradox as it appears. The slum is profitable because of the total rent from large numbers of people, housed at high densities. However, if the

land is redeveloped, it must be used more intensively in order to amortize it, i.e., as a high-rise apartment house or as a commercial site. Such
development is rare and so the predominant land use in these areas is
dilapidated or deteriorating housing.* This area becomes fertile ground
for the slum landlord who benefits from the irrationality of our property
tax system. Hall (1967) states that the property tax was instrumental in
creating the slums and has been a chief reason why they have been perpetuated—this tax makes dilapidation and neglect profitable. The demand
for low-income housing, especially housing that is "open," is so great that
any given slum landlord does not need to compete for tenants. Maintenance of his building adds to his expenses but not to his income from it.
Moreover, thanks to the property tax, he pays twice for any noticeble
improvement on his premises since plumbing, fire escapes and garbage
disposals, safe stairways, etc., not only cost money initially but also carry
a tax penalty (i.e., larger tax payment) because they increase the assessed
valuation of the property. Therefore, a landlord who can count on full
occupancy without making improvements has every reason not to make
them. Furthermore, he can subdivide the building into a large number
of dwelling units, thereby preserving gross income while offering indi-
vidually low rents.

The solution seems to be reform of the tax system including the separation of taxes on land and property, which now constitute "realty" and,
therefore, bear the same rate. Land should be taxed at a high rate because location may increase its value; then the owner would be obliged to
develop it for a more productive use. On the other hand, property
should be taxed a a lower rate which would place no penalty on erecting
quality structures and then maintaining them properly. In such situations, land owners would be induced to recover the high tax on land by
putting it to effective use in an intensive manner with the additional
incentive that doing so would not add much to their pre-existing taxes.
According to an article in *Fortune* (Prentice, 1965, 190), the more intensive development of the central city area would help to drain the demand that is now stimulating urban sprawl. One line of attack on the
blighted condition of our cities, therefore, is reform of the tax structure.
However, such reform may be difficult not only because of the tradition
behind the venerable property tax but also because of the power of slum
landlords in the community.

---

*The 1960 Housing Census defined substandard housing in two classes: (1) dilapidated,
which does not provide safe and adequate shelter and which endangers the health and
safety of the occupant, and (2) deteriorating, which possesses certain intermediate defects
that must be corrected to provide safe and adequate shelter. Deteriorating housing includes dwellings that are not yet considered dilapidated. Owing to the subjective nature of
these categories, they are not used in the 1970 Census.

The hypothesis that the tax structure is a major factor in perpetrating *underuse* of land in American cities is supported by Robert Hutchins and several land economists in a film entitled "One Way to Better Cities." Of course, slums are just one example of such underuse. Mahoney (1975) in a study of a portion of the CBD of Lincoln, Nebraska, found that the most underused land was assessed the lowest taxes. One of the most notable examples of this underuse appeared to be parking lots. Some lots were located within 100 yards of the peak value intersection and yet taxes were quite low. Apparently, the tax is computed on the improvement (asphalt) rather than on site-location. Seemingly, the taxes were not enough to force the owner to capitalize his location. Large tracts of vacant land elsewhere in the city also emphasize this pattern of underuse. In many cases these parcels were being held either for speculative purposes or as a reserve for future expansion by businesses or institutions. The tax on such "undeveloped" land is generally insufficient to force development. Other vacant parcels are considered "dead land," or land unavailable for use, because of tax delinquency. Evidence seems to show, therefore, that underuse of land in a city, whether it be slum, parking lot, or vacant parcel, is encouraged by the tax system and increases the *aggregate* costs of friction. As a result, externalities are created which are born by other members of the community.

3. Land use contrasts between central city and suburb. Still another distortion in land uses from a pattern that reflects minimum aggregate costs of friction within a metropolitan area is the dichotomy that exists between central city and suburbs. This dichotomy reflects the political fragmentation that is particularly evident in the United States where the tradition of local option for small governments has been a chief factor in the creation of a ring of suburbs around central cities. The amount of resistance to change toward greater regional control surprises many foreign visitors. Indeed, Peter Hall, a British geographer and planner, states that one of the most persistent features of 20th Century life in America is the apparent failure to reorganize metropolitan *government* in line with metropolitan *development* (Hall, 1966, 203; my italics). By this he meant the growing cleavage between central city and suburbs and the inequities resulting from this dual pattern. This cleavage is shown in the model and table (fig. 9.4 and table 9.1). Economically, the suburbs are much better off than the central city because of the influx of affluent white population, retail enterprises, and manufacturing (quadrant 1). These residents continue to use the services of the central city but pay no taxes there, leaving it to be supported by lower-income groups, especially Blacks, who are, in turn, "zoned out" of the suburbs by economic and discrimination barriers on housing (quadrant 2). The condition of the central city progressively worsens and revenue becomes unavailable

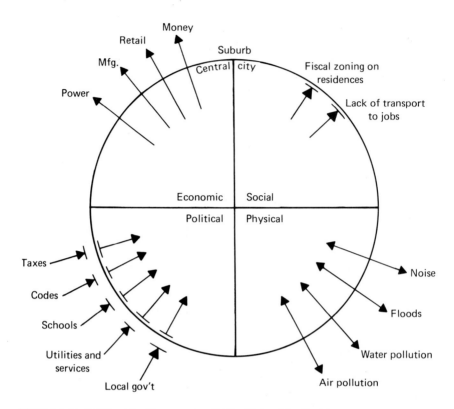

FIGURE 9.4. A model of the metropolitan area system. Note the differing relationships between central city and suburb in the four quadrants. For example, economic activity leaves the central city while low income groups cannot. Physical problems override all boundaries. A fragmented political system makes the solving of such spatial dislocation difficult.

to improve it. Finally, physical problems, like air pollution, which are regional in nature, are difficult to solve owing to governmental fragmentation, i.e., city, county, state, and numerous other overlapping jurisdictions (quadrants 3 and 4). In such a fragmented system, minimum aggregate costs of friction are particularly distorted for intraurban movement. "Machine space," dominated by facilities created for the automobile, truck, and bus, is superimposed on the 19th Century pattern of street grid and fixed barriers that originally served a pedestrian or rail-oriented populace. Central-city congestion has recently been exacerbated by the busing decisions which have caused new patterns of movement within these areas; at the same time, the suburbs are facing the problem of housing and providing services for an unusual number of whites hoping to escape busing.

The central city-suburb dichotomy present in most American metropolitan areas represents a type of spatial organization in which politi-

TABLE 9.1
American Metropolitan Areas:
Examples of Socio-Economic Contrasts
Between Central City and Suburbs

	Central City	Suburb
Percentage of metropolitan population, 1960	51	49
Percentage of metropolitan population, 1985 (projected)	37	63
Population growth in percent, 1967-1985	13	106
Population density, 1970 (p. sq. m.)	4,463	2,627
Median family income, 1968	$8,648	$10,114
Substandard housing (percent of U.S.), 1960	21	15
Median value of owned housing, 1970	$16,500	$20,800
Median contract rent, 1970 (per mo.)	$91	$113
Crowding (percent with 1-3 rooms), 1970	25	12
Employment in manufacturing (percent of change, 37 large SMSAs), 1958-1968	−6	16
Taxes (weighted per capita averages), 1964-1965	$199	$152
Services (municipal expenditures per capita in 37 large SMSAs), 1965	$232	$132
Retail trade (percent increase in 37 large SMSAs), 1958-1968	5	45
Nonwhite population (as percent of U.S. nonwhite population) 1985	58	16
Nonwhite poor (as percent of U.S. poor), 1966	44	10
Nonwhites as per cent of total unemployed, 1967	40	NA

Sources: *Building the American City,* 1968, pp. 3, 42-3, 47, 50-1, 74, 413-4.
Current Population Reports, Series P-23, No. 33, 1970, pp. 2, 25.
General Demographic Trends for Metropolitan Areas, 1960 to 1970, PHC(2)-1, 1971, pp. 15-17.
Urban American and the Federal System, 1969, p. 10
The Economic Future of City and Suburb, 1970, p. 25.

cal barriers prevent the aggregate costs of friction from being minimized (see fig. 9.5). However, resistance to regional government, in which these barriers could be reduced, remains great, primarily because of the local-option tradition in American life. Ratcliff (1955, 133), building on Haig's ideas, feels that this local option is evident when each urban unit, acting on what is presumed to be its own interests, may control the assignment of activities within its boundaries in such a fashion as to exclude developments that would be appropriately located from the metropolitan standpoint. Such dislocations have contributed to the feeling—sometimes expressed regarding the largest metropolitan areas like New York City—that they may be ungovernable.

Another aspect of inefficiency of the costs of friction in metropolitan areas is urban sprawl. This process of metropolitan growth occurs generally on unincorporated county land where any real zoning has been

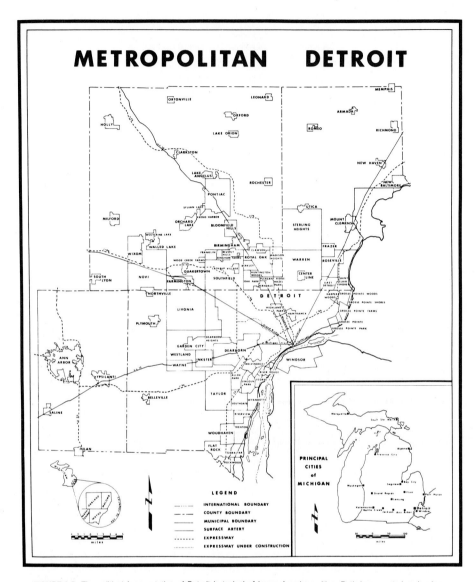

FIGURE 9.5. The political fragmentation of Detroit is typical of larger American cities. Both incorporated and unincorporated urban centers exist. Hamtramck is an enclave in the heart of the metropolitan area. (Source: R. Sinclair, *The Face of Detroit*, National Council for Geographic Education, 1970, fig. 14.)

slow to develop. Consequently, land speculation occurs and considerable land is held, waiting for the density of population to increase in order to allow it to be sold for intensive development (see fig. 9.6). In the meantime, low-intensity subdivisions of single family homes "leapfrog" beyond the open land. Scofield (1963, 70) points out that speculative practices have created an "artificial" scarcity of land that is reflected in the gaps in settlement within and around the metropolitan area. Here an externality is created because speculators are not bearing their share of the cost of friction. They benefit especially from the tax system that permits them to hold land out of use until the population density is high enough for their parcels to rise in value. Sprawl is expensive to the taxpayer, especially in a cultural system that organizes space in a rectangular system as America does. Not only does it increase expenses for services and utilities in terms of dispersive tendencies but it also may be unhealthy if septic tanks and wells become too dense. Furthermore, the pattern of spatial organization is often haphazard or piecemeal. Subdivisions are followed some years later by shopping centers and other services. The resulting suburbs are not cities in the true sense of the word but "urban tissue" lacking any real sense of community. Nevertheless, they are defended with some justification owing to advantages of local control. Future possibilities of increased energy costs, including gasoline, however, make the question of sprawl of great importance to present-day planning.

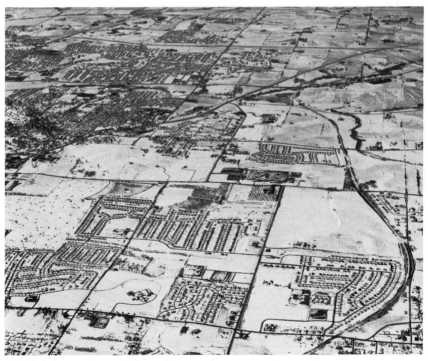

FIGURE 9.6. Urban sprawl on the outskirts of American cities frequently features "leapfrog" growth—large subdivisions separated by farmland or vacant areas held for speculation. The entire region is committed to ultimate urban development. (Courtesy of the Wurgler Co., Inc., Omaha, Nebraska.)

What are the cures for this fragmentation? As stated above, the American city is underbounded, i.e., the legal boundaries lag behind the built up area, and regional control of the outer areas is lacking. The European tendency to develop within a commune framework, where legal boundaries often permit "overbounding," is not easy to apply where minor civil divisions like communes are not utilized and all land that is not incorporated or annexed belongs to a county.* Annexation is one solution, but is a slow and costly process, often creating bitter feelings among people who see their taxes go up, even if utilities are improved. A second solution is city-county consolidation which is being tried in some places in the United States. In many cases, the city taxes actually help to subsidize the poorer counties and a combination makes economic sense. The third approach is federation.

The experience of Toronto, Canada with federation is examined with interest by other large metropolitan areas. In this case, a two-tiered structure was created in 1954 by the province of Ontario following a petition by the city, and no approval by the electorate was required. A metropolitan government handles the regional or area-wide tasks like sewage disposal, water supply, housing, property assessment, and transportation. On the second level, six units exist (formerly 13) which carry out functions not assigned to the metropolitan government such as local planning and fire protection. The approach has the advantage of retaining some local control while, at the same time, making regional decisions for the greater whole. Progress on most regional tasks has been apparent, especially in supporting public works projects and in establishing greater equality of school financing. However, less success is evident on social goals involving the dispersal of low-income housing within resistant neighborhoods. Fizer (1962, 118) feels that although the federation probably would never have been approved originally by the voters in the 1950s it would have been overwhelmingly supported by them eight years later.

4. **Government input on land use.** Some land economists feel that government influence has been the greatest single factor to distort the economic factors that Haig identified 50 years ago. Actually, his attempt to point out the importance of rent and transport costs was really a justification for more government input in the form of zoning. He believed the role of zoning is to complement the economic forces bearing on location of land uses and to prevent *individual* exploitation at the expense of the group.

One example of such zoning would be early allocation of land at uniform intervals for future schools, fire stations, and hospitals, whose uses

*Except in New England where "towns" resemble communes.

are of a central-place nature and must be located close to the people for frequent travel. Elementary schools, for example, normally should be within one mile of all students for walking purposes. However, public authorities generally cannot compete for land in the market place in the same way that private developers can. Therefore, zoning is employed to insure this pattern. If the schools or fire stations were inappropriately located, the aggregate costs of friction would be increased.

Perhaps the most apparent example of government input in urban land use is renewal of portions of the central core which has been declining in importance owing to dispersive economic forces. Such attempts to renovate large portions of inner cities have been subsidized by federal money and in the process have dislocated large numbers of low-income people. One argument against renewal is that the CBD was a product of a different era and it should decline by natural means. A counter argument is that the CBD is the heart of the metropolitan area and remains the most accessible place to the most people. To have it in a state of decline, with stores boarded up and crime rampant, is to increase the aggregate costs of friction, not only for the entire area but especially for the people who live around it. Writing off the core of a city, therefore, without making some effort to revitalize it to play a role in the metropolitan scheme of things seems illogical. So a new role, undoubtedly different from the dominant one it played in the past, is emerging. One only has to look at the changing core areas of American cities in the 1970s to see that the CBD is playing this new role, especially as an office center. New skyscrapers for this purpose are the mark of skylines all over the United States, and have become new symbols of corporate power just as the castle and cathedral were symbols of power in the past (see fig. 9.7).

COMMERCIAL LAND USES IN THE URBAN AREA

Commercial nodes tend to dominate the pattern of spatial organization in a large city or metropolitan area. Many of the journeys to work and shop focus on a business node while extensive areas of commercial uses front on major and minor arterials. The Central Business District (CBD) has long been predominant among these nodes and is still recognizable by its profile, greater traffic, and bright lights (see fig. 9.8). In recent years, however, the other commercial areas, including the planned shopping center, have been increasing in importance at the expense of the CBD. Even as early as 1958, 85 percent of the retail sales in Chicago were made outside the CBD (Loop) as the links between "worker" and "nonworker" (shopper) have decentralized. Vance (1962, 488-499) states that most CBDs lost many of the mass-selling outlets (department, variety, clothing, and drug stores) while retaining the specialty ones (e.g.,

FIGURE 9.7. The downtown of Atlanta reflects the changing structure of the Central Business District with an emphasis on office buildings, both private and public. New hotels like the Hyatt Regency are also evident.

FIGURE 9.8. A busy street intersection in a Central Business District. As suburban shopping centers become relatively more important, such scenes may become less common.

jewelry) that require larger thresholds. They tried to counteract this loss by constructing office buildings where links between "workers" and other "workers" can be facilitated. Public buildings are also rising in the cores of cities. With these locational changes has come a need for models to interpret and explain them.

Prior to World War II most retail development was unplanned and consisted of a hierarchy that Proudfoot (1937) classified as (1) CBD, (2) outlying business center, (3) principal business thoroughfare, (4) neighborhood business street, and (5) isolated store cluster. In most large cities today the Proudfoot hierarchy of unplanned commercial areas can still be recognized. For example, the outlying business center was often a small town on the outskirts of the city that had been annexed in the course of growth, while the principal business thoroughfare was a strip of commercial uses along a major arterial. In the early days both depended on the streetcar for bringing customers.

After 1940, however, most new commercial centers were planned and built quickly on one site to service the large numbers of people who were moving to the outer rings of the city. Although the most important types of new shopping centers are nucleations of different size, examples of planned ribbons and specialized areas are also numerous. Any classification of shopping areas in a large city, therefore, should include both unplanned and planned types. Table 9.2 represents a modification of Berry (1963, table 2) with the Proudfoot categories shown in parentheses.

The outstanding feature of the organization of commercial space in large metropolitan areas is the order that seems to exist. As in the case of rural central places, a hierarchial pattern exists that reflects access to different thresholds of population. An example of such a hierarchy is shown for Chicago (fig. 9.9). The nucleations are clusters of retail and service functions located at major access points within the urban area. The CBD, of course, is generally accessible to the most people, particu-

TABLE 9.2
Major Types of American Metropolitan Commercial Areas
(unplanned and planned)

Centers	Ribbons	Specialized Areas
Central Business District (1) —unplanned	Traditional shopping street (3)—unplanned	Automobile row
Regional (2)	Highway oriented ribbon or urban arterial (4)—	Entertainment district
Community (2)	unplanned	Medical centers
Neighborhood	New suburban ribbon	Etc.

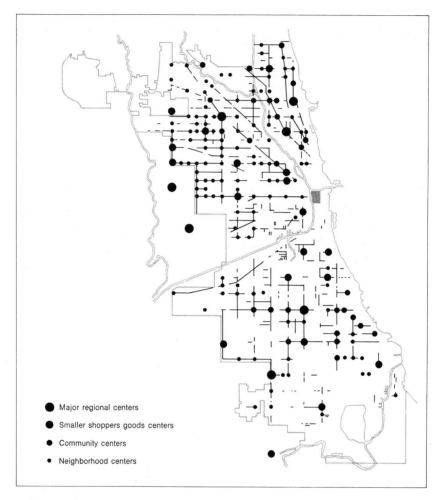

FIGURE 9.9. The hierarchy of shopping centers in the city of Chicago. (Reprinted with permission from Berry, et al, *Commercial Structure and Commercial Blight,* Univ. of Chicago, Dept. of Geography Research Paper No. 85, 1963, fig. 10.)

larly if all forms of transport are included, but the large regional shopping center is often even more accessible considering time of travel and cost spent on parking (see fig. 9.10).

Ribbons of commercial use generally are located along major arterials rather than at major intersections and thus are less accessible. Consequently, the functions that locate in these commercial strips are oriented to people who make one stop, either by traveling the arterial or by visiting it from an adjacent neighborhood. Unlike the nucleation, there is little functional interlinkage between the enterprises that locate

FIGURE 9.10. The planned shopping center now serves as a focus of commercial activity in American suburban areas. Note the large space provided for parking around the center which, unlike the CBD, features easy pedestrian access between stores. (Courtesy of the Wurgler Co., Inc., Omaha, Nebraska.)

there, such as department and clothing stores. Strip types themselves vary somewhat in that the highway-oriented ribbons serve the automobile for drive-in or repair functions whereas urban arterials often include space-users like a furniture store or lumber yard. New suburban ribbons and traditional shopping streets, on the other hand, cater to the daily needs of nearby residents, e.g., a drive-in bank or a supermarket, and more linkage between functions may exist. The skid-row areas are a form of traditional shopping street located on the deteriorating side of the CBD.

Specialized areas differ from nucleations and ribbons in that they are clusters of one type of use and their location depends on the services provided. For example, automobile rows tend to develop on certain urban arterials while a medical complex may be at a major intersection; a group of large discount stores often locate on arterials between the CBD and major shopping centers. In some cases, a cluster of household enterprises, including large space-using furniture stores, may exist some distance away from shopping centers in order to avoid high rent. Theater and financial districts are examples of specialized areas often located in the CBD. Perhaps the outstanding feature of specialized areas, and the reason for their emergence, are the linkages between them: they generate savings by making comparative shopping possible and by sharing facilities and advertising.

*CLARK UNIVERSITY MODEL OF THE CBD DISTRICT—AN AT-
TEMPT AT THEORY.*   The most commonly cited spatial model of the
Central Business District was developed in the 1950's by R. E. Murphy
and his colleagues at Clark University. Their work consisted of a detailed
study of nine sample CBDs in the medium size category—100,000 to
250,000. Although the model may suffer from its date, it still provides
perhaps the best generalization of the land use in a CBD and, therefore,
is a measuring rod against which changes in time and place may be
made. In the following section, the model is described and then one
aspect of it is tested in a real-world situation.

The first aspect of the model is delimitation of the CBD, which is
often difficult to do on a map. Stores and other office and governmental
buildings of this District gradually merge into residential uses, frequently poor dwellings interspersed with run-down commercial and
wholesaling activities. Is there any precise way of delimiting the edge of
the CBD? Several methods have been developed based on population
densities, employment data, traffic counts, land values, and land uses.
Murphy and Vance (July 1954) found that land values and land uses
provide the best basis for understanding the marginal areas of this
District.

Urban *land values* in the CBD drop off sharply from their peak near
the maximum point of accessibility, generally an intersection marked by
department stores and other intensive uses. Murphy and Vance found
that in selected cities of 150,000-250,000 inhabitants, the land values
drop 40 percent in the first 100 yards. Such a decline points to the ability
of certain enterprises to turn accessibility into profit since the high cost
of land near the peak value intersection can only be paid by large concerns that benefit from access to many customers. The decline in land
values continues until a point where residential uses become important,
generally coinciding with the inner margin of a zone of deterioration.
Here land values amount to only 5 percent of the peak value. Although
this 5 percent line represents a fairly realistic means of uniformly delimiting the CBD, certain weaknesses present problems in application: difficulty of securing land value data; existence of tax-free property; and
vertical varieties in land use. Perhaps the biggest disadvantage to the use
of land values, however, is that non-CBD uses may be included, e.g., as a
result of the rise in land values that accompanies the construction of
high-rise apartments in zones of CBD expansion.

Efforts at delimiting the Central Business District and understanding
its structure seem to yield the best results if based on *land use.* Detailed
mapping of land use in nine cities (150,000-250,000 population) by
Clark University geographers resulted in the development of three

categories for the model as follows (Murphy, Vance, and Epstein, 1955, 26):

Retail Business (RB)	*Service-Financial-Office* (SFO)	*Non-CBD* (NCBD)
Food	General Offices	Public and Organizational
Clothing	Headquarters Offices	Wholesale and Storage
Household	Finance	Manufacturing
Auto	Service	Vacant
Variety	Transportation	Residential
Miscellaneous	Transit Residences	
	Parking	

These different uses were found to vary spatially by distance from the peak value intersection. From the point of view of *total space,* horizontally and vertically, the relative importances of the three groups change in the following manner from the center outwards (see fig. 9.11):

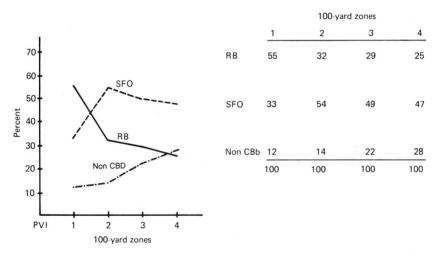

	100-yard zones			
	1	2	3	4
RB	55	32	29	25
SFO	33	54	49	47
Non CBb	12	14	22	28
	100	100	100	100

FIGURE 9.11. A graphic and numerical portrayal of land use changes by zones in the CBD as derived from the Murphy-Vance model. Figures include total space (all floors).

The graphs with table constitute the Murphy model. A second graph (fig. 9.12) portrays the various land uses in each of the three groups for all nine cities upon which the model was based plus the average of these. The important factors that help to explain the changes in uses by zone are mentioned briefly.

—The RB uses, which decline away from the Peak Value Intersection (PVI), depend upon contact with the maximum number of people and

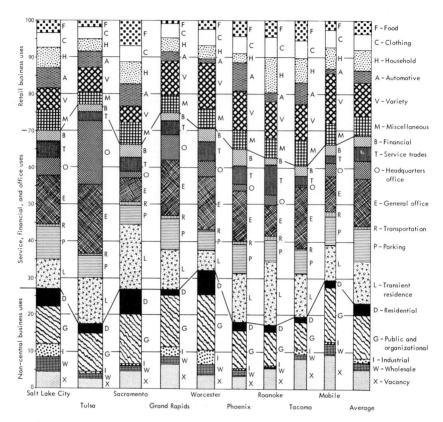

FIGURE 9.12. The pattern of land uses in the CBD's of nine American cities shows certain regularities. These uses can be conveniently grouped into three classes: retail, service-financial-office, and non-CBD. (Reprinted with the permission of *Economic Geography* from "A Comparative Study of Nine Central Business Districts," *Economic Geography*, Oct. 1954.)

therefore utilize profitably the high-priced but accessible land in zone 1 (see figures 9.11 and 9.12). Such land uses are of two types, either those depending on frequent purchases from a large selection of goods at different prices (e.g., department stores) or infrequent purchases of specialty items (e.g., jewelry). In both cases, the enterprises are accessible to the entire city. Furthermore, mutual association of certain stores—department, clothing, and drug—seems to be a characteristic of a location which takes advantage of complementary and comparative shopping practices of Americans.

—On the other hand, the SFO uses do not require maximum accessibility to customers so the more expensive locations are unnecessary. Normally, office buildings, banks, hotels, railway-bus stations, parking lots, and personal services reach a maximum in intensity a short distance out from the center, i.e., in this case, the second 100-yard zone; from this zone, such uses again decline in importance outwards (see figures 9.11 and 9.12). Like the inner zone of RB uses, this zone exhibits an intensity of land use on high-priced land that is reflected in high buildings serviced by elevators.* For office buildings, this location is central for work force, clients, and ancillary services, while the opportunities for personal contact represent white-collar linkages that make these buildings a stable part of most CBDs. Public buildings such as city hall or court house, which may have been near the point of maximum accessibility at one time, now are generally in zone 2 or 3. Again, mutual associations of certain SFO uses, such as offices located near banks and YMCA or hotels near to transport terminals, are frequently characteristic of this zone.

—The third category of land use—non-CBD—naturally exhibits a minimum importance in the core and increases steadily in relative importance as one travels toward the fringe of the District. These uses vary considerably from RB and SFO uses and even from each other. In fact, the incompatibility of these uses gives rise to problems of instability and deterioration.

It is perhaps necessary to emphasize that political and social factors supplement the economic factors in marking the differentiation of the city cores. For example, a recent urban trend is the development of civic centers comprising public buildings and open space that yield no tax return.

In a dynamic sense the fringes of the CBD are advancing and retreating. In one direction, referred to as the zone of assimilation, luxury stores, offices, financial organizations, and hotels tend to expand into residential areas—most often those of good quality. In the other direction, referred to as the zone of discard, the admixture of uses—commercial, wholesale, manufacturing, and residential—leads to stagnation and development of "skid row" characteristics—run-down bars, hotels, cinemas, and restaurants. Used-car and parking lots are important and many vacant structures exist.

The structure of the CBD as given here is highly generalized. Overall spatial differentiation of RB, SFO, and Non-CBD uses by zones is rather consistent in most cities, but the sizes of the zones will vary according to size of city. The vertical variation outward from the peak value intersection must also be considered. Upper floors will not show the same pattern of change as ground floors do. However, mapping of total CBD

---

*In New York there are over 30,000 elevators, which every day carry passengers a total of 125,000 miles. Rents often decrease vertically, although "pent-house" apartments or restaurants may yield high returns.

space permits one to utilize ratios of CBD and Non-CBD uses to de-limit the edge of the District; Murphy and Vance (July 1954, 209) de-cided that a block should be included in the District if (1) at least half the total floor space, and (2) the area of at least one entire floor, are made up of central business uses. These ratios also can be used to delimit the so-called "hard core" of the CBD, i.e., that area where the commer-cial intensity is greatest; Davies (1960) suggests that 80 percent of the total floor space and four entire floors in a block should be commercial in nature to warrant inclusion in this area; in addition, the land unit values should be at least 30 percent of the peak land unit value. Delimita-tion of a hard core within the CBD corresponds somewhat to the attempt by Horwood and Boyce (1959, 19-26) to differentiate between intensive "core" and semi-intensive "frame" in such Districts. The outer frame contrasts with the core through its characteristics of partial development, dissimilar buildings, external business linkages, and intercity transporta-tion foci.

THE CBD MODEL VERSUS REALITY.   Since the Clark University model was based on medium-sized cities, testing it in larger metropolitan areas may not be realistic. Therefore, a test of the model was made in the 1970s in Lincoln, Nebraska, a city of 165,000, and the results illustrate some of the similarities and differences that can emerge by comparing reality with a model. Lincoln possesses a linear CBD aligned along "O" Street and, as Murphy states (1955, 24), in such a pattern "the rate of decline is much lower along the axis of the District than at right angles to the axis." Consequently, the test utilized a cross-section of blocks aligned at right angles to "O" Street and employing the four 100-yard zones as in the Clark model. The PVI was assumed to lie on the axis at 12th Street. Because of the difficulty of mapping upper floors, only *first floors* in both cases were used in the comparison. Moreover, Clark University indices developed to determine the limits of a CBD made it clear that certain outlying blocks in the Lincoln cross-section were not properly part of the District. It should be remembered that because a cross-section was used, generalizations made about the comparison are tentative.

A comparison of graphs for the Clark University model and the *cross-section* of Lincoln reveals some strong similarities in the pattern of land uses in addition to certain differences that can be partially ex-plained (see fig. 9.13). In general, a land use map shows that retail uses decline in area away from the PVI in both cases, but in Lincoln this decline is interrupted by an increase in the 300-yard zone (see fig. 9.14). A main reason for this is the presence of the University of Nebraska adjacent to the CBD, causing an increase in the number of retail outlets

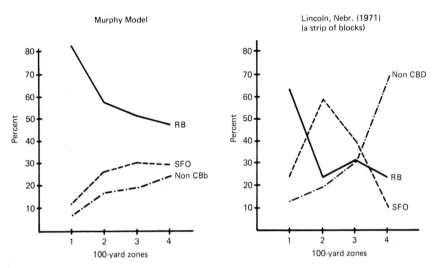

FIGURE 9.13. A graphic portrayal of land use changes by zones in the CBD for the Murphy-Vance model and for a sample of Lincoln, Nebraska. Data are for first floor space only.

catering to students. Such a situation is unusual and represents one of the strongest factors behind the distortion of theory from reality in the Lincoln area. For example, the area near the University includes a major bookstore, fast-food stores, a clothing enterprise, and a gas station.

The graph lines for service-financial-organizational uses differ somewhat. The Lincoln pattern shows a larger number of these uses in the first three zones because of a high concentration of offices and parking garages there. These uses seem to be closer to the PVI in Lincoln than in the Clark model because of the linear nature of the former's CBD, i.e., the decline of intensive uses is most rapid away from the "O" Street axis. Furthermore, the presence of the University and state government buildings seems to be a factor in the overall healthy condition of the CBD, which in turn has affected SFO categories, e.g., business services. Still another service that is unusually high in the second zone is theaters, which have concentrated in a belt on the side of the CBD near the University.

Non-CBD uses increase in both graphs, but more abruptly in Lincoln. As mentioned, the University accounts for part of this while a large, old church, a fraternal order building, and the headquarters of a religious organization all add to the total. Finally, the linear nature of the CBD again is responsible for the persistence of considerable residential land within the fourth 100-yard zone.

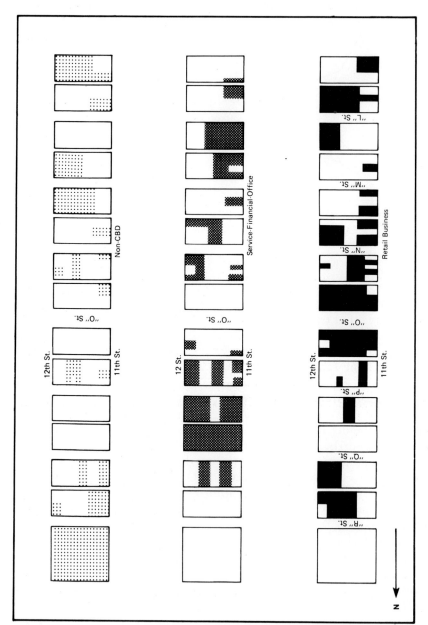

FIGURE 9.14. Land uses by three groups within a section of the CBD of Lincoln, Nebraska. Data are for first floors in 1971.

Although the above test of the Clark model against reality in Lincoln is brief, it serves to indicate some of the ways the individual CBD may vary from a general model. The Clark model, of course, is now somewhat old and a revised one might show considerable change. Certainly, these changes are evident in the Lincoln cross-section. Perhaps the most significant influence is public input in land use, a factor land economists have been emphasizing. The city of Lincoln has purchased a square block facing on "O" Street and within the framework of the Urban Redevelopment Act, is rebuilding it into a "Centrum" complex featuring retail uses and parking for 1,000 vehicles.

HIERARCHY OF SHOPPING CENTERS—COMPARISONS WITH RURAL PATTERNS. Geographers recognized quite early that a great deal of similarity existed between the pattern of central places in rural and in urban areas. This similarity is to be expected because the distribution of goods and services must take place in a hierarchical fashion in cities just as in the countryside. The same principles of threshold and range would apply. Therefore, it became logical to use the Christaller model of central places as a theoretical base and to measure *metropolitan reality* against it. We are indebted to Berry for much of the work on the hierarchical pattern of outlying shopping centers in which Chicago is used as the test case (Berry, 1963; 1967).

Although a hierarchy of shopping centers is apparent to any observer in a large city like Chicago (see fig. 9.9), the nature of the threshold support is quite naturally different in urban areas than in rural ones. Obviously, the density of population is much higher in the city, a fact which leads to smaller ranges for given central-function thresholds and allows different business types to enter the hierarchy at lower levels than in rural areas. This characteristic was tested by Berry (1967 32-4) and the results are shown in a graph that illustrates the differences between the two hierarchies (see fig. 9.15). If the slope of the lines separating hierarchical levels in urban and rural areas were vertical, the central place hierarchy in both areas would be similar, i.e., a regular relationship would exist between area served and density, while population served would stay constant. Instead, the "lines separating levels slope backward to the left, indicating that trade areas increase in size as densities drop, but not as fast as the densities decline, so that the sizes of populations served fall (Berry, 1967, 33)." This means that a function which can enter the urban hierarchy at the convenience shop level could only do the same in a rural area at a higher level.

It is possible to generalize further that the higher population densities present in urban areas as against rural ones permit not only lower

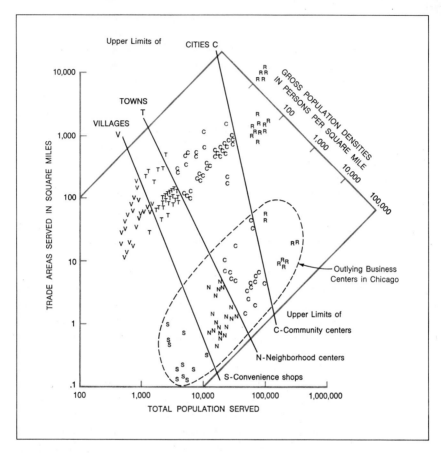

FIGURE 9.15. Some systematic variations between the hierarchies of urban shopping centers and those of rural central places. (Brian J. L. Berry, *Geography of Market Centers and Retail Distribution*, © 1967, pp. 33. Reprinted by permission of Prentice-Hall, Inc., Englewood Cliffs, New Jersey.)

entry of functions but also greater functional specialization. These higher densities permit thresholds to increase very rapidly so that the gradient between functional levels may be very steep. Both of these qualities of urban commercial centers—lower order of entry and greater functional specialization—are supported by data compiled by Berry (1963, tables 19 and 35) for unplanned centers in Chicago and by Berry, et al. (1962, tables 4-6) for southwestern Iowa. The neighborhood centers, for example, although at the lowest level, include clothing, drugs, jewelry, and other functions that are only found in towns in the countryside. Not only is functional specialization high but it is also strong within types, e.g., types of clothing. The regularity of this dense pattern of commercial areas in Chicago is shown in figure 9.9.

Another important difference between the rural and urban hierarchies of central places is the effect of socio-economic variations which are much more apparent in the urban areas. In spite of higher population densities, thresholds generally are less in urban lower-income areas because of lower purchasing power. Berry (1963, table 44) found that low-income neighborhoods in Chicago lacked both the highest level of major regional centers and to some extent the community-level centers. Instead, they tended to possess a higher proportion of low-level neighborhood centers. As a result, the commercial hierarchy in such areas tended to be simple, consisting of two levels—smaller shopping-goods centers that supplied more specialized items (e.g., hardware) and a larger number of neighborhood centers that provided basic necessities (e.g., food). As might be expected, structural differences also exist between the functions represented in these levels in low- and high-income areas. The shopping-good centers in the former areas tend to be fewer in number and in variety of function, while the neighborhood centers are just the opposite. Because they are so basic to low-income areas, neighborhood centers are larger in terms of number of stores, total ground-floor space, and variety of function represented. Furthermore, individual establishments tend to be larger owing to lower rents for land and practicality of combining specialized and convenience goods in one store.

Still another contrast between rural and urban shopping facilities is the greater importance of specialized areas in urban areas. Clusters of common uses like automobile "rows" and theater districts are less apparent in rural settlement hierarchies because of the low thresholds present.

A final contrast between the rural model of shopping and urban commercial reality is the greater importance of the *planned* center in the latter. Rural shopping facilities tend to resemble unplanned urban centers in terms of number and structure and, therefore, some of the contrasts between rural and urban can be seen by comparing unplanned and planned centers *within* an urban area. The planned centers are generally smaller in overall size and have fewer types and establishments while individual establishments are larger. These differences are to be expected because of the costs of laying out a planned shopping center in comparison with the gradual evolving of unplanned ones. The former tend to concentrate on core functions, and peripheral enterprises like furniture, liquor, insurance, and movie theaters may be ignored. One-story structures in planned centers may help to reduce the functional diversity there as well, e.g., space for offices is lacking. These differences are more evident at upper-level shopping centers than at the neighborhood level. The lack of duplication of similar enterprises in a planned shopping center is often a result of attempts to restrict competition between stores within the center, thereby maintaining a healthy economic situation. Also, the larger enterprises, a function of today's technology, help to counteract the lack of duplication.

SUMMARY

In this chapter, Haig's model of the "costs of friction" in urban areas is used as a basis for testing the location of land uses in theory against reality. Although this model tends to simplify the spatial structure of cities, it does provide a spatial foundation for measuring distortions from the pattern one might expect when the aggregate costs of friction are minimized. Four types of distortion are examined—relics from the past, underuse of land, contrasts between central city and suburb, and governmental input on land use locations. Although these four examples do not cover the options possible in any large urban area, they do illustrate the reasons why many land uses are located where they are. Furthermore, this approach seems to offer greater explanatory possibilities than a straight description of individual land use types.

The second major portion of the chapter includes an analysis of commercial land uses in the urban area. Again, a well-known model for the CBD, developed at Clark University, is discussed and tested in a real-world situation. Finally, the hierarchy of shopping centers, so evident in any large city, is examined in connection with central-place ideas.

The overall conclusion that emerges from the three-chapter analysis of internal relations of cities is that considerable order exists in urban areas and that, although reality differs often from theory, explanation is facilitated by such an approach. However, when one deals with cities in different cultural areas, the distortions from theory become greater, especially because much of the theory is based on the North American city. Nevertheless, this geographer, who has spent considerable time in other cultural regions, feels that a book on the *Spatial Foundations of Urbanism* should include reference to cities in other areas. The next three chapters, therefore, deal with three examples of cultural variations in urbanism.

COMPARATIVE SPATIAL ASPECTS OF URBANISM

The preceding chapters have included an evaluation of certain patterns of spatial organization which exist between and within cities. The emphasis in these chapters has been on the American city although some non-American examples have been used. However, cities in other parts of the world exhibit unique characteristics peculiar to their special cultural area. In most cases the historical background and site characteristics of these cities are different from those of America. Patterns of external relations and internal characteristics of such cities also differ. The greatest contrasts exist between cities in culture areas that possess industrialized societies, and those in areas dominated by preindustrial groups. Geographers and other specialists have only recently emphasized the comparative aspects of urban study since the process of contrasting cities from different cultural realms is very difficult: data including statistics vary, and field work may be restricted owing to language and security problems. A surprising amount of work has been done, however, as indicated in chapters of *The Study of Urbanization,* edited by Philip Hauser and Leo Schnore (1965). Certain cross-cultural concepts useful in comparative urbanism are beginning to emerge. Still, any generalizations regarding the characteristics of cities around the world may be considered as tentative and somewhat subjective in nature.

The author does feel strongly, however, that a book emphasizing geographic aspects of urbanism should include reference to spatial characteristics of cities in parts of the world other than the United States. Having lived in Western Europe for eight years and having carried out urban research there, he feels qualified to make certain statements concerning the cities of this area. Frequent travel to the Communist states of Eastern Europe and the Soviet Union permits description and limited interpretation of the "socialist" city. Visits to other parts of the world have been much briefer, but written documents permit the development of certain ideas concerning a third type—the "preindustrial" city. The cities of the world may certainly be grouped in other ways, but based on personal experience, the author has restricted himself to these three types. Obviously the three types of cities are not parallel. The Western European city and the "socialist" city are largely industrial in terms of technology and bear many similarities to American cities; however, they do differ, particularly in the degree of control through planning. Finally, completely different concepts in terms of technology and social structure mark the preindustrial city, although many of the leading cities of this category have "Western" characteristics, derived either from the "colonial" period or from recent changes since independence.

These three types of cities are also identified by Berry (1973), who has attempted to show that urbanization is not a universal process. After illustrating the contrasts between the 19th Century industrial city and 20th Century metropolitan growth (see chapter 2 above), he analyzes the different paths taken by cities in the Third World, Western Europe, and the Socialist countries. The basis for this cross-cultural differentiation is a model based on degrees of *public intervention* used to counter the human consequences of laissez-faire industrial urbanization. These cultural areas have used various public means such as civic design, housing policies (especially for low-income groups), financial aids, and New Towns to correct the problems that arose in early industrial cities. The greatest amount of intervention has been in the Socialist or communist countries. This general cross-cultural concept of Berry's model, i.e., public intervention, is utilized below but the author also develops separate models of his own to explain the processes involved in the three cultural areas.

CHAPTER 10

THE WEST EUROPEAN
CITY

THE WEST EUROPEAN CITY

PERIODS OF GROWTH. Certain difficulties arise when generalizations are attempted concerning a "West European" city. In the first place, all European cities are not alike since the continent represents one of the greatest mixtures of cultural groups of any area of equal size in the world. The British, French, Finns, Hungarians, Italians, etc., have each developed certain specific attributes of cities. Moreover, present technological and economic changes in Europe are affecting the patterns of their cities, making them more alike and even similar to American cities in some ways. We find such phenomena as retail concentration and decentralization, modern office buildings and apartments, traffic problems, and industrial parks. Yet, in spite of individual differences between European cultural areas and recognition of certain "Western" trends of urban uniformity, certain spatial aspects of European cities distinguish them from American, "socialist," and "preindustrial" cities. These European cities have evolved during a long era of urban development which can be divided into several important periods.

Dickinson (1951) believes that there were four such historical periods of West European city development: Roman, Medieval, Renaissance-Baroque, and modern. These were discussed in chapter 2 from an historical point of view. Emphasis was on the importance of Europe in the general evolution of agricultural, commercial, and industrial developments which contributed to urbanism, especially the enlargement of external support for cities. Some mention was also made, however, of the internal characteristics of European cities during these periods.

In the following section a model of the West European city is developed as shown, using the three major periods of medieval, Renaissance-Baroque, and industrial (see fig. 10.1). It is apparent that the model is most applicable to the larger cities of medieval regions and of later national states. In such cities the three periods together have pro-

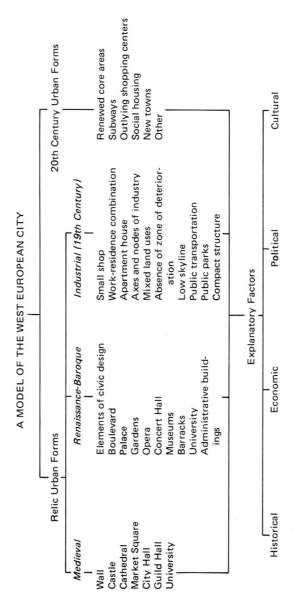

FIGURE 10.1. A model of the West European city incorporating relationships between urban forms from different eras and explanatory factors.

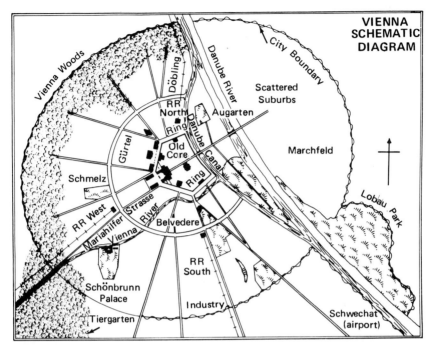

FIGURE 10.2. A generalized scheme of Vienna as visualized by the planner. The layout is radial with the old core encircled by the famous "Ringstrasse." An outer boulevard—the Gürtel—and the Vienna Woods are partially concentric with the Danube River dominating the landscape to the east.

duced an assemblage of spatial forms—a model against which individual cities can be tested. In this case, the city tested is Vienna, a former imperial capital city (see fig. 10.2).* Following a description of the effects of historical periods on the spatial organization of this city, general 19th Century relic forms of West European cities are identified and major explanatory factors discussed. Supplementing this discussion is an analysis of certain 20th Century urban forms that have emerged in part from the increasing importance of tertiary functions. The newer forms are particularly apparent in Western Europe since 1960 and reflect the strong degree of public intervention in the spatial organization of these cities, thus supporting Berry's cross-cultural model. The final portion of the chapter is a summary of urbanization in West Europe.

*The writer spent the academic year 1967-68 in Vienna as a Fulbright Research Scholar, attached to the Institute of Regional and Urban Planning in the Technische Hochschule. An outstanding source on the city is *Wien*, written by two geographers, H. Bobek and E. Lichtenberger (1966).

THE CITY OF VIENNA. A notable characteristic of older European cities is the *medieval core.* In Vienna the "old city" is delimited and encircled by the "Ring," a series of wide, park-like boulevards that are comparable to other great European avenues such as Champs Elysées of Paris. During the course of history in Austria, the focus of activity within the old city shifted several times and, therefore, the four common elements of a medieval core—Burg, cathedral, town hall, and market place—are not contiguous (see fig. 10.3). An early Roman town called Vindobona was located at the present Hoher Markt. Early medieval elements of the core of Vienna were created during the Babenberg period of 1150 to 1273, when this dynasty ruled the Duchy of Austria from a castle located at Am Hof. However, the primary rulers associated with the development of Vienna as an imperial capital were the Habsburgs, who ruled Austria—both as a Duchy and as an Empire—from 1273 to 1918. During most of this period, both Hoher Markt and Am Hof apparently served as market squares. The Guildhall, used by the town council, is still present, located between the two squares, while the Gothic cathedral, St. Stephens, is south of Hoher Markt. Finally, the early Babenberg castle was replaced by the Hofburg (castle) of the Habsburgs, but in a western portion of the old city. Therefore, several focal points—two squares, a city hall, a cathedral, and two castles—served as nuclei around which the old medieval city developed. These focal points, which can be seen today, reflect the three groups important in the Middle Ages—emperor and nobles, clergy, and merchants. Little else remains from the medieval period except a few churches and the irregular and narrow street pattern which attracts the tourist but hampers modern traffic.

In other parts of Europe this medieval core exists, more or less, depending on the situation. Wars, especially World War II, have destroyed many of those cores, but very often they have been restored. In many cities, modern commercial activities have had to shift outside the old city producing two cores as in Frankfurt—the old, focused on the City Hall (where John Kennedy spoke in 1963), and the new, focused on the "Zeil" shopping street.

Not all of the medieval cities of Europe evolved slowly around an irregular core as described above. In parts of central Europe, planned towns were established with regular streets as part of settlement projects. Perhaps the best examples are the Germanic settlements in Slav areas, e.g., Greifswald, Pilsen, and Königsberg.

Elements of civic design were added to the old town of Vienna during the *Renaissance-Baroque* periods (see fig. 10.3), when the Habsburgs, like other authoritarian rulers throughout Europe, influ-

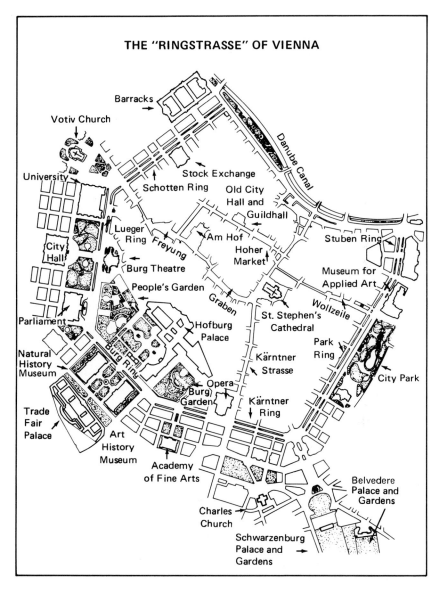

FIGURE 10.3. The "Ringstrasse" of Vienna comprises a series of grand boulevards that enclose the old core of the city. Within the old city are medieval market places and cathedral while situated along the "Ring" are the city hall and buildings from the Baroque period of civic planning.

enced the capital cities by constructing personal and public buildings that reflected the growth of the nation-state. The imperial capital of Vienna developed relatively late and, like much of Austria, is dominated by Baroque architecture, though Italian and French influences are apparent. Many of the great buildings of Vienna, including the Charles Church, Schönbrunn Palace, Hofburg Palace, National Library, and the Belvedere Palace were designed, entirely or in part, by the great Austrian architects, Johann Fischer von Erlach and Johann Lucas von Hildebrandt. These men lived at the time of the victory over the Turks in 1683, when jubilation set the tone of the picturesque Baroque style. According to Rickett, "Baroque is still part and parcel of Austrian life, as well as the outstanding feature of the Austrian landscape; it is more than a form of art; it is a way of life."* Architecturally, Baroque is the visible sign of confidence in the future as expressed in the facade.

In Vienna, the influence of royal power continued past the Baroque period and overlapped the uncontrolled developments of the commercial-industrial era. In other words, Franz Joseph, emperor of Austria, had great influence on the pattern of Vienna while at the same time factories and worker apartments were being constructed. Many of the public buildings of Vienna's central core were designed in the nineteenth century and supplemented the older medieval and Baroque structures. The greatest project was the "Ring," a series of boulevards flanked by public buildings and parks, which was laid out after 1857 on the site of the old town walls (see fig. 10.3). In its conception, this project parallels Haussmann's reconstruction of central Paris. Today one recognizes an impressive but questionable architectural mixture of Neo-Gothic and Neo-Classic structures along the Ring including the Stock Exchange, University, City Hall, Burgtheatre, Parliament, Natural History and Art History Museums, Hofburg, and State Opera House (see fig. 10.4). Large palaces or town houses of the nobility were concentrated throughout the central area and a variety of shops and specialized industries reflected Vienna's position as an imperial capital. Large park areas, including the Vienna Woods, further illustrate the royal power of this period. In other parts of Europe, this same power of royalty resulted in the grandeur of buildings and parks in cities like London, Paris, Copenhagen, The Hague, Amsterdam, Rome, Karlsruhe, Florence, Berlin, and Budapest. Most of these cities were national capitals at the time, while Karlsruhe and Florence represent centers of historic regions in Germany and Italy, respectively.

*Richard Rickett, *A Brief Survey of Austrian History* (Vienna: Georg Prachner, 1966), p. 53.

FIGURE 10.4. Vienna from the air. The "Ringstrasse" and associated public buildings and parks are clearly visible. The Danube River and Canal are evident in the background. Note the high density of buildings and the low skyline. (Source: Landesbildstelle Wien-Burgenland, Vienna, 1960.)

The third historical period influencing the development of Vienna and other European cities was the *industrial era*. The agricultural, commercial, and industrial revolutions spread from west to east over Europe stimulating production and trade. Agriculture supported more urban residents and the expansion of industry called for employees in factories, transportation, and finance. Such developments were bound to affect the forms of European cities as they began to evolve toward present-day patterns. With the rise of commercial-industrial forces in city building the royal power declined. In Vienna, however, royal power collaborated with private interests in city building to develop shopping facilities, railroad lines and terminals, industrial tracts, and apartment houses (see fig. 10.2). The public tradition, therefore, remained strong, and governmental authorities continued in the construction and reconstruction of buildings which reflect Vienna's position as a cultural center for central Europe.

Whereas medieval and Baroque forms of Vienna are associated with the inner core and its surrounding Ringstrasse, industrial forms developed in the outer areas on both sides of the Gürtel ring. The sketch (fig. 10.2) shows how railroads, which led to Germany and parts of the Empire, penetrated into the city from different directions although in no case reaching the inner core. (A similar pattern is found in London and Paris.) Large factories and tenements were constructed along these axes and along the Danube River and Canal. In addition, light industry was developed as a part of housing tracts with the apartment buildings often surrounding the factory. Commercial areas, consisting mostly of small shops, emerged along major arteries (e.g., Mariahilferstrasse) and in the old cores which represented former towns or villages absorbed by the expanding *Reichstadt* (e.g., Döbling).

19TH CENTURY RELICS OF URBANISM

Today the West European city possesses a variety of relic forms from the past (see fig. 10.1). Those forms developed during the medieval and Renaissance-Baroque periods are clearly observable and contribute to the unique "sense of place" so important in European cities. Although important for the tourist, these early forms actually are small in area. It is the 19th Century forms associated with industrialization which today are more significant as relic forms over which 20th Century ones are superimposed:

THE SMALL SHOP.   Small, specialized shops are certainly one of the most important characteristics of European cities (Hoyt, 1959). The tradition of the small shop goes back to the medieval period when streets were lined by numerous stalls of craftsmen and merchants. Shops today line the main arteries and serve adjacent neighborhoods of densely populated apartment blocks (see fig. 10.5). Department stores and supermarkets exist in the big cities, but many individuals still prefer to patronize the small shops specializing in such things as meat, milk, vegetables, fish, confectionery, leather, toys, children's clothing, hats, etc. These shops also follow the custom of closing for several hours during the noon period so that the proprietor can return home for the "big meal" of the day. Retail concentration in large stores is developing, but the pattern remains in part similar to that of the 1920-40 period in the United States when the personal touch at the "corner grocery store" was the rule rather than the exception. In Vienna this pattern is perpetuated by laws which discourage the consolidation of various retail enterprises. Changes are occurring very slowly due to tradition and also because local planners wish to avoid abrupt economic dislocations in Viennese neighborhoods. Furthermore, Europeans are only now beginning to acquire the automobile-mobility that permits shopping in more distant, consolidated stores, and the large refrigerators necessary to reduce fre-

FIGURE 10.5. A main shopping street in Vienna—Mariahilfer Strasse—is lined by small shops. The floors above include apartments. Note the stone construction and ornate facade.

quent shopping trips. Even in outlying shopping areas, the small shops predominate because retail centers represent old villages or towns that have been engulfed in metropolitan expansion. Transformation is taking place slowly as larger stores replace the older shops, not only in the center but also in the suburbs.

COMBINATION OF WORK AND RESIDENCE. Related in part to the continued existence of a small shop is the phenomenon of the residence used as a place of work. Normally this is most apparent in retail sales, but it is also true for services and even small handicraft industries (e.g., cabinetmaking). Small-scale operation and specialization makes this combination possible, enabling the owner to save on overhead. Professional people like doctors and lawyers also combine workplace and residence because office buildings, either in the Central

Business District or in the residential neighborhoods, are less prevalent than in the United States.

DOMINANCE OF THE APARTMENT. Although the apartment represents a relic form from the 19th Century in West European cities, it has continued as the predominant residential dwelling unit since it provides the most economical way of constructing living space in an area where dense population makes urban land expensive. Public authorities have been involved in this housing, either in terms of financing or direct ownership, especially in the persistent development of low-income dwelling units as a supplement to most projects. Tradition also is a factor in the European preference of apartment over house; only in Britain, where semi-detached dwellings abound, is the continental trend not as prevalent. The old apartment buildings in a city center contain shops on the street level, but at intervals large doors lead to inner stairways and provide access to individual apartments (see fig. 10.6). Therefore, the older residential areas, which are built flush to the streets with a courtyard in the center, contrast with the newer postwar apartment buildings which are freestanding and resemble American styles (see fig. 10.7). Be-

FIGURE 10.6. A view of one of the older residential areas of Vienna characterized by high building and population densities. Minimum conditions of air, light, and sanitation in this housing are low. (Source: Landesbildstelle Wien-Burgenland, Vienna, 1959.)

FIGURE 10.7. Recent postwar apartment houses in Vienna are of the high-rise type but are spaced for reducing overall density and often include some **shopping** facilities.

cause of World War II damage and the postwar lag in construction, a housing shortage still exists in most European countries, forcing the renting of rooms or doubling-up with relatives. This shortage causes not only a greater density of population than in American cities but also a more apparent mixture of social classes—points substantiated by the author's research in Germany. In Europe apartment sizes vary considerably within buildings, blocks, and neighborhoods, and income levels also fluctuate widely in new as well as old apartment houses. The pull of the core is still reflected in the presence there of larger apartments for the well-to-do. At the same time, the greater mobility allows different people to occupy such units on the fringe. Villas, built by wealthy families, have frequently been converted, in part, to apartments in the desire to supplement income. Large single-family housing subdivisions built for varied ranges of income as found in the United States are rare in Europe.

AXES AND NODES OF INDUSTRY. The locational association ment of codes for building, zoning, and sanitation.
and rivers is quite noticeable today. These two axes represented the primary means of not only assembling raw materials and energy (in the form of coal) but also of distributing the products. Apartment houses for workers were located nearby because of the lack of mobility in a pedes-

trian city. A third type of axis is represented by streetcar lines which were also associated with factories and apartment houses. A dense population and fewer automobiles have allowed the streetcar to persist longer in European cities.

Nodes of light industry were also associated with housing developments. In Vienna builders designed entire blocks of apartment houses with the factory in the middle courtyard *(Hinterhofindustrie)* to simplify the journey to work. The influence of these builders was so great that the zoning regulations *(Bauordnungen)* actually permitted building coverage of 85 percent. Large areas of the city were covered by monotonous rectangular blocks *(Raster* style) of apartment houses that exhibit today less than minimal standards of light, air, space, and sanitation (see fig. 10.8). Reaction to this type of housing led to rent control in Vienna in the 1920s and to one of the most elaborate programs of municipal housing which modern history records. Superblocks of apartment houses were created around large courtyards *(Hof* style), reducing the building coverage area to 30-60 percent (see fig. 10.8). This municipal housing of Vienna is one of the outstanding examples of what Berry calls public intervention to counter the human consequenes of laissez-faire industrial urbanization. In other European cities, the reaction was similar with the introduction of programs of low-income housing and the development of codes for building, zoning, and sanitation.

MIXED LAND USES.   The above historic characteristics have the overall effect of mixing land uses in European cities to a degree that makes clear demarcation of functional zones difficult. As related earlier, large urban blocks of apartment buildings combine residences with small retail shops, professional offices, and "backyard" industries. The clearest land use demarcations occur in the areas of heavy industry and the postwar residential regions. Such a mixing, of course, makes planning more difficult, especially in the applications of zoning classifications. However, the increased interaction among people that is present in West European cities under such a system of mixed land uses have led American planners to question the traditional approaches to zoning where land use types are separated.

ABSENCE OF THE ZONE–OF–DETERIORATION.   In Europe, as contrasted with the United States, no clear-cut zone of deterioration exists (à la Burgess), because centripetal forces bring people (including millions of foreign visitors) to the cores of European cities. Not the least of these attractive forces include the public buildings and parks which date from a royal period of enforced "city grandeur." However, the lack of an ethnic problem until recently (e.g., *Gastarbeiter* or migrant workers) and the mixing of social groups tend to be important in preventing the

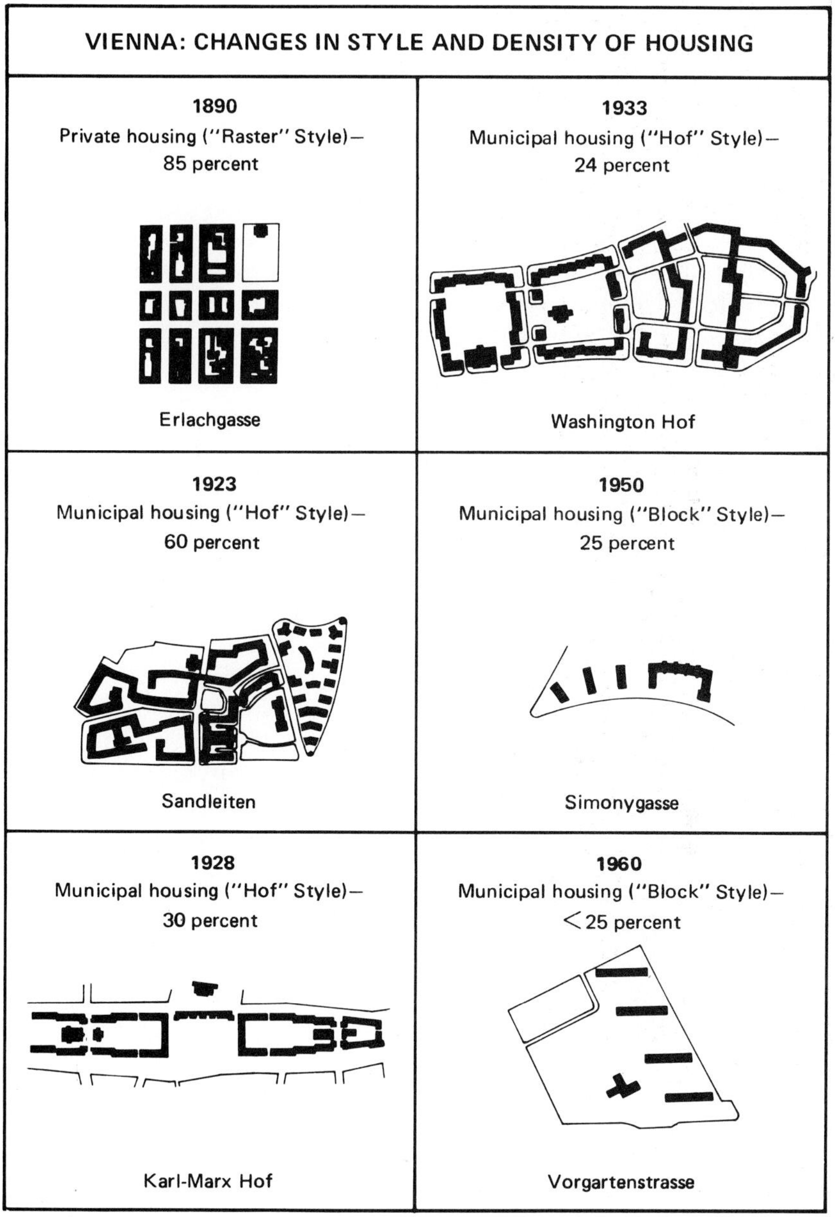

VIENNA: CHANGES IN STYLE AND DENSITY OF HOUSING

1890

Private housing ("Raster" Style)—
85 percent

Erlachgasse

1933

Municipal housing ("Hof" Style)—
24 percent

Washington Hof

1923

Municipal housing ("Hof" Style)—
60 percent

Sandleiten

1950

Municipal housing ("Block" Style)—
25 percent

Simonygasse

1928

Municipal housing ("Hof" Style)—
30 percent

Karl-Marx Hof

1960

Municipal housing ("Block" Style)—
< 25 percent

Vorgartenstrasse

FIGURE 10.8. The historical evolution of housing in Vienna reflects a decreasing density of buildings per unit of land. The pattern changes from the dense **Raster** (grid) layout to the decreasing densities permitted by the **Hof** (court) and the **Block** (freestanding) styles.

dominance of large areas of low income residents. Finally, since a short-age of housing exists, people tend to maintain what they have, and the durable construction materials assist residential stability.

RELATIVELY LOW SKYLINE. Except for a towering cathedral European cities tend to have relatively low and even profiles (see fig. 10.4). The core areas have older apartment houses of up to six floors while new apartment blocks are found in the suburbs. Apparently re-strictions on fire-fighting equipment, insecure subsoil, and the desire to let cathedrals dominate the skyline are three of the factors involved in this urban characteristic. Today, these restrictions are less significant, but large portions of cities were built while they were adhered to.

IMPORTANCE OF PUBLIC TRANSPORTATION. Europeans have long depended on public means to travel within their cities—streetcar, bus, and special intraurban transport services—occasioned in part by a lack of private automobiles. Even in the postwar period, as cars have become more evident, narrow streets and lack of parking space restrict autos for shopping and commuting purposes. Public transporta-tion networks, therefore, are dense and reach all parts of the city, pro-viding frequent service to most neighborhoods. The goal is to provide service at all costs, even at the expense of empty conveyances much of the time. In the United States, semipublic utility companies frequently jettison routes that do not pay for themselves, thereby leaving certain people, including the aged, without service. Americans may be surprised by the importance of public transport in Europe and probably will ob-serve that land uses related to the auto—gas stations, garages, and "drive-in" enterprises of all kinds—are lacking. In part, a primary stimulus to centrifugal movements—the auto—is overshadowed by the centripetal pattern of public transport. However, the pattern is changing as Europeans obtain automobiles, and certain large cities already show signs of traffic problems which, magnified by narrow winding streets, may soon rival those of American cities.

IMPORTANCE OF PUBLIC PARKS. One of the strongest legacies of the past in large European cities is the park or forest located near or in the urbanized area (see fig. 10.9). Most of these green areas originated in the Renaissance or Baroque periods when a strong ruler was able to maintain his private park or hunting retreat. An outstanding example of this land use is the Vienna Woods, a portion of a planned green belt around the Austrian capital where private construction is prohibited.

COMPACT STRUCTURE AND SHARP URBAN–RURAL BOUND-ARIES. A final noteworthy characteristic of European cities is the

FIGURE 10.9. Schönbrunn Palace in Vienna with its large park and gardens serves as a cultural center for both the Viennese and tourists.

compact built-up area delimited by a sharp urban-rural boundary. Owing to several interrelated factors—medieval tradition, population pressure and high cost of land, use of apartments, and prejudicial building codes—urban densities are generally higher in European cities than they are in American cities where single-family homes and sprawl reduce the figures. Vacant land *within* European urbanized areas is developed because residents are not mobile enough to move elsewhere and because the cities do not encourage leapfrog or strip settlements. The transition between city and country, therefore, is generally very abrupt.

20TH CENTURY ELEMENTS OF URBANISM

Although the 19th Century form elements tend to remain significant in most West European cities, 20th Century changes are evident everywhere. As in the United States, the mobility of people has increased with the automobile and a greater freedom of location exists for retail enterprise, residence, and factory. Thus, many large cities in Western Europe have a modern look with department stores, shopping centers, strip land uses oriented toward the automobile, and apartment houses and industrial parks in the suburbs. The American influence is evident in franchise enterprises like Holiday Inn, Hilton Hotel, Kentucky Fried Chicken, and McDonalds. However, superimposing these 20th Century urban forms on frameworks that are 19th Century and even medieval in origin, has caused serious problems of spatial organization. Largely for this reason, the human consequences of 20th Century urbanization in West Europe have led to greater public intervention into the private development process. This intervention is apparent first of all in the attention paid to preserving historic buildings of tourist interest. For example, in Vienna designated buildings are numbered to key with city guidebooks. However, public input is also seen in the 20th Century form elements that have appeared since World War II, especially in projects connected with renewal, subways, social housing, and New Towns.

RENEWAL OF CORE AREAS.   The core areas of major European cities today appear to be a mixture of old and new. The primary historic elements that represent strong cultural traditions and attract tourists have been maintained. Famous boulevards like the Champs Elysées in Paris and the Ringstrasse of Vienna, which with their associated buildings represent landmarks in civic planning, are significant focal points in downtown areas. However, associated with these are modern shopping areas, constructed in the last 20 years, that incorporate department stores, office buildings, and pedestrian malls. In some cities like Paris even skyscrapers have been built, often to the displeasure of the populace which objects to the distortion of a traditional low skyline. The great influx of cars in a core area with streets from the Middle Ages has resulted in public intervention to restrict the automobile. In Vienna the primary artery in the core area—Kärntnerstrasse—has been turned into a pedestrian mall of great beauty (see fig. 10.10). Such malls were pioneered after World War II in Rotterdam with the construction of the Lijnbaan, which is anchored by two department stores. Such malls exist in many other cities and are combined with "Walking Streets," where automobiles are prohibited all or part of the time. Hohestrasse and Schildergasse in Cologne are examples of the latter.

SUBWAYS. The automobile explosion, a human consequence of 20th Century urbanization in West Europe, has resulted in public intervention in the form of mass transit. Although this approach is slow to be used in the United States, the major cities of West Europe have made decisions to go underground, in great part because the high densities of urban population support it; Berry (1973, 144) states that these densities in Vienna are 60 per acre as against 10-25 per acre in North American cities. The results of subway policies have been good. Although the ex-

FIGURE 10.10. Kärntnerstrasse, a famous shopping street in Vienna, has been turned into a pedestrian mall. (Photo courtesy of Galen Saylor.)

pense has been great and temporary construction bottlenecks are a nuisance, the strong traditional pull of the core area seemingly will make the subway pay. Vienna and Munich are examples of cities which have gone this route. In Stockholm, the subway is used as a basic framework for suburban expansion with satellite communities like Vallingby and Farste oriented along the lines. The fact that Stockholm owns much of the outlying land was an aid in this policy, which has been examined with interest by many planners.

Supplementing the subway as a form of urban development are underground parking lots and shopping malls. In Vienna, for example, a large parking lot exists under the main square of Am Hof and several underground areas have been constructed below the Ringstrasse to reduce congestion aboveground. Shops line these *Passagen* ("passages") and in one of them streetcars from the outer city areas turn around for their return trip.

OUTLYING SHOPPING CENTERS. In many countries of Western Europe, suburban expansion reflects American urban development in the form of outlying shopping centers: in Ludwigsburg, a suburb of Stuttgart, West Germany, an enormous *Einkaufszentrum* dominates the landscape just off the *Autobahn.* Nearby is an *Industriegebiet,* which bears a strong resemblance to an American industrial park. However, many out-lying shopping centers are different from those in the United States. For example, they may be designed as portions of town centers for planned satellite suburbs as in Nordweststadt near Frankfurt. Here the public input is greater since community features like a hall, cinema, police and fire headquarters, town administration offices, and post office are in-cluded. The city also built the access streets and utilities plus surround-ing apartment buildings. However, most of the commercial facilities were financed by trade union funds. One can say that this outlying shopping center of Frankfurt, like many in West Europe, represents an unusual combination of public and private investments.

SOCIAL HOUSING.   Still another example of public intervention as a consequence of *laissez-faire* industrial urbanization in Western Europe is social housing. Many American planners who visit cities there have remarked about the European use of public finances to gain a greater mix in social levels of housing (McKeever, 1969, 7-8). As a result of this mix, large free-standing apartment houses, which are ubiquitous in West European cities, frequently contain dwelling units for a variety of income levels (see fig. 10.7). What is more, these buildings are often located in the outer rings of cities, thereby providing a contrast to American cities with their subdivisions of single-family houses. A considerable amount of this housing is carried out with public funds, and low interest rates are available for purchasing them. Although the public input in housing finance thus makes apartments available to a variety of groups, construction still lags, which creates a waiting period for dwelling units in most cities in spite of the extensive use of pre-fabrication processes.

NEW TOWNS.   One of the most important examples of public inter-vention in West European cities as a counter to the human consequences of urbanization is the New Town (Galantay, 1975). In contrast to American New Towns, which are privately developed, those in West Europe are developed with strong public inputs. In Britain a national urban policy is focused around some 30 New Towns which in part evolved from the Garden City movement and are designed to relieve the pressure on exist-ing large centers (see fig. 10.11). For example, eight of these are located around London to handle some of the overspill from growth in this great metropolitan area. The New Towns are backed by public funds through a Development Corporation that buys the land in advance. Both commercial and industrial areas in these Towns are built by the Corpo-rations which depend on the factories, often "growth" types like elec-tronics, to produce profits. The more recent New Towns developed

NEW TOWNS OF GREAT BRITAIN

New Towns Under Development Corporations ●

New Towns under Commission for New Towns ■

Proposed New Towns ○

100   50
Miles

Glenrothes
Cumbernauld
Livingston
East Kilbride
Irvine
Washington
Peterlee
Aycliffe
Central Lancashire
Skelmersdale
Warrington
Runcorn
Telford
Newtown
Corby
Peterborough
Redditch
Northampton
Milton Keynes
Stevenage
Welwyn
Cwmbran
Hemel Hempstead
Harlow
Llantrisant
Hatfield
Bracknell
Basildon
Crawley

FIGURE 10.11. The New Towns of Great Britain are found throughout the island with the largest concentration near London. (Source: *Town and Country Planning*, 38 [Jan. 1970]: 42.)

after 1960 are designed for the automobile, although attempts are also made to integrate Town Center with residential areas. Over 1.5 million people now live in these towns and the goal is 3.5 million by the year 2000. However, these towns have not necessarily stopped the growth of metropolitan areas and in the case of London have led to tremendous diversification of the outer-ring area. The Towns also have been criticized in terms of their inadequate connections to other cities and with regard to the emphasis on physical planning at the expense of social planning; the latter is especially evident in the lack of diversity in income groups and opportunities for interaction. Nevertheless, as the first real attempt to use New Towns as partial nodes in a national urban policy, one can say they have been successful.

Other new towns in Europe are less "national" in scope than those of Great Britain. Some, like the French towns (e.g., Evry) bear resemblance to the British ones in that they are designed to relieve congestion in the Paris area. Others, like Wolfsburg in West Germany which was built for the Volkswagon plant, are industrial towns. Finally, some like those of Sweden and Tapiola in Finland were built as satellite towns for major cities. Tapiola has received considerable attention as the most "green" of New Towns, since the design includes a park-like setting of fields, forests, and lakes. This Town was privately financed and includes housing for both blue- and white-collar workers. It is definitely a satellite in its dependence on Helsinki, and in this sense resembles the Swedish towns more than those of Great Britain.

FACTORS AFFECTING URBAN DEVELOPMENT

The sections above emphasized the impact of the medieval, Renaissance-Baroque, industrial, and modern periods on the development of the West European city. A logical supplement to this descriptive analysis is an evaluation of the specific factors which help to explain the various characteristics given above (Rugg, 1965). These factors fall naturally into four groups: historical, economic, political, and cultural. An important trend associated with all factors is the public intervention which West European cities have interjected to counteract the negative human consequences of rapid urbanization. This is particularly evident in the period after World War II when modern forms of the 20th Century are superimposed on cities that for the most part developed in the 19th Century and even earlier periods.

HISTORICAL FACTORS. Many of the urban forms persisting in European cities naturally date from the periods mentioned and are unique to them (see fig. 10.9). The old medieval core and the impressive royal sections established during the Renaissance-Baroque periods are important legacies, especially for tourism, but cannot be adapted easily to modern urban needs. Present day housing and industrial expansion reflect, in part, the traditional importance of the apartment dwelling unit and handicraft industry, respectively. Perhaps the greatest problem for municipal administrators and planners is to decide how much of the historical city-character to preserve. In the modern-day city, progress requires the provision of space and mobility for residents to work, produce, dwell, learn, and play. Therefore, old patterns of streets and buildings must be changed, frequently at the cost of historic buildings attractive to the tourist.

Today most European cities try to reach a compromise between tradition and progress. A land use plan designates those buildings and narrow streets to be preserved and those subject to change. In countries like Germany, destruction from World War II presented opportunities to reconstruct cities, preserving some parts and modernizing others. Some cities like Hanover and Kiel did this very well—both establishing new, wide arterial streets and Kiel even developing a pedestrian mall. Others for a variety of political and economic reasons did not. In many cases, the old pattern of streets and utilities, including sewers and gas lines, represented a considerable investment and, therefore, a barrier to wholesale change, especially the construction of new boulevards suitable for the age of the auto. Perhaps few European leaders in 1945 could foresee the future economic boom. Traffic problems similar to those of the United States are evident and may be hard to solve if the historical framework acts as a straitjacket. Centrifugal forces will become more apparent in the future as the auto permits greater flexibility in the location of shopping facilities, dwellings, and industrial firms.

ECONOMIC FACTORS.   The economic factors influencing urban expansion in Europe are mostly related to land development. In contrast to the United States there are a number of reasons why it is more difficult in Europe to turn vacant land into urban uses.

1. **Land Is Scarce.** In most European countries land is not easily available. Average population densities are high, thereby requiring the maximum use of land for agricultural production in order to reduce dependence on food imports. For example, the average population density in most European countries is at least three to four times higher than that of the United States, and in the Netherlands it is 16 times as high. Also, forest areas must be preserved in order to control water and to provide recreational possibilities. The result of such demands on land is that urban areas are compact, and sharp urban-rural boundaries exist around the city because planners weigh carefully every decision to convert rural land to urban use.

2. **Land Is Expensive.** Owing to the need for farm land and to a high demand for urban land as the rural-urban migration increases, land costs are quite high, much higher than in the United States. For example, Chiffelle (Clout, 1975, 286) reports that in 1974 land in central Zurich, Switzerland was worth $3.5 million per acre. Undeveloped land on the outskirts of large Swiss cities was valued at $130,000 per acre, an amount perhaps 25 times greater than similar land in American cities. Such costs have a tendency to force intensive use of the land and one indeed does not see much of the ubiquitous asphalt-covered parking lot in European cities.

3. **Land Is Fragmented.** Agricultural land on the outskirts of cities tends to exist in fragmented parcels, the result of inheritance systems which force eligible sons to divide the land. Therefore, acquiring a number of these parcels large enough for a housing development is often difficult since the refusal of one farmer to sell may block the entire plan. In some cases these European farmers exhibit a surprising tendency to remain on the land of their ancestors, even when offered tremendous financial inducements to sell.

4. **Capital For Land Development Is Lacking.** In view of the above factors, it comes as no surprise that capital is lacking for land development, especially for residential uses which may take a long time to amortize. For this reason, national and local governments often must supply part of the money which, of course, gives them a voice in the structure of the project, especially in the social composition of its residential body. In Germany *Sozialwohnungen,* or apartments for lower income groups, are generally provided in projects supported by federal funds.

5. **Rent Control Discourages Investment.** In some countries of Europe, rent control policies, which reduce the amount of capital available to landlord or developer, discourage maintenance and construction of buildings. When this factor is added to those already mentioned—shortage and high cost of land, difficulty of acquiring land, and lack of capital—it is possible to understand why housing (mainly, of course, apartments) lags behind demand, resulting in certain social aspects mentioned earlier: high densities and considerable mixture of social classes. In Vienna, the long period of rent control is largely responsible for the shabby condition of many residential areas, a situation that so amazes visitors.

6. **City Utilities Are Restricted In Undeveloped Areas.** Some cities use utilities as a brake on the development of land in order to prevent leapfrog projects (with high costs to taxpayer and city) and to preserve land for rural uses (agriculture and recreation). Therefore, gas, electricity, sewage, and water lines are not established in new areas in the urban fringe without considerable forethought having been given to the trans-

formation of precious rural land. The Federal Planning Law of West Germany prohibits any new projects in the urban-rural fringe that are not tied to the existing built-up area in a physical sense (Rugg, 1966, 332-34). Such policies, along with other factors mentioned above, help to explain the compact city areas of Europe and the rather sharp urban-rural boundaries (see fig. 10.12).

The above economic factors have emphasized some of the reasons why land is difficult to develop in West European cities. However, it is important also to stress the positive economic factors as well. One of these was the economic boom that was initiated after World War II by the Marshall Plan. Because of the traditional pull of the core areas on urban residents, both public and private finances resulting from this boom were directed into urban renewal projects. American planners have stated (McKeever, 1969, 6) that European cities have been able to channel appreciations in land values to public profit much more than have American cities. The economic boom also led to the technological developments of automobiles, larger retail outlets, and skyscrapers that have caused such an impact on traditional urban layouts.

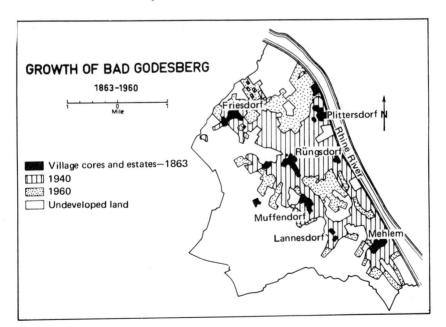

FIGURE 10.12. Bad Godesburg, an old settlement on the Rhine River, is now a part of Bonn, the capital of the Federal Republic of Germany. The city evolved around several villages which coalesced. The tendency is toward compact development as gaps are filled in and sprawl is avoided.

POLITICAL FACTORS.   In most European countries the government is involved to so considerable an extent in the lives of the citizens that a public environment can be said to exist alongside the private one. What is meant by the concept of a public environment? The average urban resident in Europe is accustomed to controls in the public interest. Because land is scarce and valuable, the national, regional, and local governments are involved in most processes of land development which transform the face of cities. For example, the government supplies capital for housing and thus has a say in its location, characteristics, and occupants. A large number of public buildings and parks are owned and maintained by the government. Finally, a considerable amount of industry and transportation may be under national control. The public has come to expect this control and often demands it. Examples of such control are frequent denials of petitions for zoning change, when the change may affect the public interest, and restrictions on sprawl of land uses owing to public costs for the infrastructure. In other words, the public interest (the majority) in densely populated Europe is often emphasized while in the United States a tendency exists to protect private interests (the minority), particularly if stimulation of private initiative is involved. Perhaps a different way of stating this idea is that Europeans are generally quite vocal in their support of good maintenance for a public urban environment since they lack the means of mobility to escape the more objectionable areas. In some cases, health hazards produce strong land control in Europe, e.g., in the Netherlands where the water table is unusually high.

Governmental influence in European cities has resulted in consolidation of political control over much of the urbanized area. Many European cities, owing to prestige and influence, increase their size at the expense of towns and rural areas surrounding them and tend to be "overbounded" in contrast to American cities, which are generally "underbounded." Much of the built-up area, therefore, is often under one control, avoiding the American problem of municipal fragmentation. This geographical advantage is most important in metropolitan areas where growth problems are greatest.

In some European countries provisions exist for the integration of city and regional planning, that is, city plans must be coordinated with those for the province, state, and nation. In Germany, much coordination is handled by three sets of legislation—Bundesbaugesetz, Landesplanungsgesetze, and Raumordnungsgesetz (Rugg, 1966). National or provincial interests can take precedence over local interests in cases where problems cross city or state boundaries (e.g., metropolitan areas) or where the national interest is paramount (e.g., defense).

CULTURAL FACTORS. It is difficult to generalize about cultural factors affecting locational patterns in European cities because they are entwined with the other factors mentioned above. It seems to this observer, however, that at least two aspects of urbanism in West Europe are culturally related and worthy of comment: attitudes towards cities and residential stability.

1. **European Attitudes Toward Cities.** Many observers have commented on the overall well-being of the West European city as against that of the American city. Coppa (1976, 168) feels that a strong factor in this contrast may be the notion on the Continent that civilization has been intimately connected with urban areas, while American society has been viewed as rural-based. From the beginning, such influential writers as Jefferson, Thoreau, and Emerson viewed large cities as detrimental to the health, morals, and liberty of Americans. Attempts to preserve features of small-town life contributed to the animosity against centralized metropolitan government while acting to support limited and fragmented local government. State legislatures, controlled by rural constituencies, enacted laws which limited the independence of cities. In short, Americans have not always appreciated cities and, in fact, have continuously tried to escape them by moving to the suburbs. This movement, facilitated by widespread automobile ownership, often included several changes of residence and led to the weakening of ties to neighborhoods. The wealthy classes of American metropolitan areas became less involved in central-city activities, unlike the aristocrats of Europe who generally possessed a *Residenz* in the city core. The values of the latter group included leisure, aesthetics, and *noblisse oblige,* all of which had an effect on European cities in terms of culture, planning, and welfare activities that are apparent today. Even the average European, however, is drawn to the central core of large cities for a variety of reasons—to shop, visit the opera or other public buildings, attend a centrally located university, or mingle socially with people. In parts of southern Europe the *paseo* or evening promenade in the "city" is a regular occurrence. These centripetal forces bring elements of stability to the central cores of European cities. Thus, one may conclude that the comparative urban geography of America and Europe must be in part explained on the basis of differences in human attitudes.

2. **Residential Stability.** European and American cities vary in the stability of residential structures. In America stability is hindered because a hierarchy of residential areas exists, and the lowest of these gradually become slums as residents successively move to better housing. Many visitors to Europe, on the other hand, are impressed by urban stability, especially in view of the many old buildings. This stability is

most noticeable in central and northern Europe, especially in Scandinavia, Great Britain, the Low Countries, Germany, Switzerland, and Austria. In Vienna, however, rent control and other factors have lowered housing quality. Making allowance for the reconstruction after World War II, residential stability in Europe is related to the following factors:

a. *"Mixing" Of Social-Economic Groups.* The "mix" of socio-economic groups in residential areas of West European cities is greater than in American cities, often because of the role the government has played in providing for low-income housing. This "social housing," which is often tied in with residential projects for middle- and higher-income groups, seems to reflect a traditional value of European urbanism that is partly related to the cost of land and to the lack of capital. In any case, the social "mix" seems to provide a degree of residential stability, perhaps because the lowest elements are more dispersed throughout the city.

This "mix" of socio-economic groups extends only to the national population and not to the immigrants. The influx of Commonwealth people into Great Britain and of *Gastarbeiter* (temporary workers) into countries of northern Europe have greatly affected the large cities. Extensive ghettos of Pakistani and other groups are found in British cities while similar areas of Italians, Spaniards, Yugoslavs, and Turks are present in continental cities. The national governments have had difficulty in absorbing and integrating these groups, especially the *Gastarbeiter* because of their temporary characteristics. In any case the residential stability of sections within large European cities have been affected and problems have emerged not unlike those in American cities resulting from migrations to urban areas.

b. *Maintenance.* The degree of maintenance on residential structures in many European cities is impressive. This upkeep is true of villas, apartment buildings, and even rural-type structures that represent old villages absorbed by the expanding city. A main factor appears to be the shortage of housing and the realization that once obtained it must be maintained as a long-term place of residence. The lack of housing mobility, therefore, assures a high maintenance rate.

c. *Permanent construction material.* Because most housing in Europe (except in Scandanavia) is constructed from permanent materials of brick or stone, good maintenance is greatly facilitated. Such materials not only reduce the fire danger and eliminate the necessity of repainting, but also add a variety and charm to the cities. The nature of the geology of an area can often be interpreted from the housing; for example, in Britain dwellings are made of granite in Aberdeen, limestone in the Cotswolds, brick in the clay vales of the Midlands, and flint in parts of East Anglia.

d. *Other factors.* This residential stability of many European cities is also influenced by other factors. Apartments are often purchased rather than rented, a key point in favor of maintenance. Owing to a long historical development, a variety of style and pattern has evolved which by itself seems to provide elements of stability; furthermore, owing to a high degree of maintenance or to the use of vegetative buffers, various architectural styles of housing or even contrasting land uses may exist side by side. Frequently, however, incompatibility of adjacent land uses is controlled and avoided by strict enforcement of zoning regulations. The physical site attributes of a city are also utilized to a greater extent in Europe by such methods as retaining steep slopes in forests, and developing river banks as park-promenade areas. Of course, the ethnic problem of segregated neighborhoods is less serious in Europe as theoretically all housing is "open."

Finally, the centripetal forces still existing in European cities tend to pull people into the center and create an atmosphere of stability. Only recently has the possession of greater mobility through the automobile created centrifugal forces which reduce stability—the ability to "escape" the center and reach the rural-urban fringe where housing has been lacking until now because of inaccessibility. Fortunately, the over-bounded nature of European cities will help to maintain city controls on housing and land use in this fringe to a greater extent than in American cities, where the comparable peripheral area is generally part of the county with fewer building, health, or zoning controls.

Obviously the generalizations presented above cannot hold true for all of Western Europe. In many parts of the area, especially in the Mediterranean countries, the controls and stability found in most northern and central European cities do not exist. Nevertheless, the effects of public intervention on West European cities are apparent in most areas and seem to represent a spatial variation in the urbanization process that should be analyzed in greater depth.

URBANIZATION IN WESTERN EUROPE

In previous sections the internal pattern of the West European city has been interpreted. Perhaps it would be useful to conclude this discussion with some remarks concerning the degree of urbanization in Western Europe. Modern industrial cities are found throughout the western portion of the continent, but in some regions the proportion of people living in cities is much greater than others. The degree of metropolitan development also differs. What sort of patterns exist?

Approximately 350 million inhabitants live in the area referred to as Western Europe, which excludes the "socialist" countries of Eastern

Europe and the Soviet Union (to be considered in the next section). Although comparable urban statistics are often difficult to secure, it is estimated that in 1970 somewhat less than one-half of this total (150 million) lived in metropolitan areas of over 100,000. Roughly one-half of this metropolitan population (75 million) lived in a broad belt extending from Western England (Lancashire) through the Low Countries and along the Rhine and its tributaries (see fig. 2.15). Many of the twenty-six agglomerations of Europe with more than 1 million inhabitants are found in this belt.

This great belt of dense urban population, concentrated in large cities, metropolitan areas, and conurbations, forms one of the most significant geographical patterns of postwar Europe. With certain exceptions like central Sweden, the Po valley of Italy, and large capital cities and ports, it includes the economic heart of the continent. Much of the heavy industry of six Common Market countries is located here and its juxtaposition to frontiers helps to explain the development of this economic union for furthering trade across traditionally antagonistic frontiers. This belt of industrial-urban population in Europe is based primarily on three things: coal, transport, and accessibility. The great coal fields of northern France, eastern and northern Belgium, and northern Germany all lie in the heart of this belt. These regions are also accessible to each other and to the other countries of the world by ocean routes and the Rhine traffic artery with its tributaries. Coal served as the original stimulus for this industrial-urban development and for the growth of cities like Birmingham, Liège, Lille, and Essen. On the other hand, cities like Newcastle, Rotterdam, Antwerp, Cologne, and Mannheim are located on the coast or on the main rivers, well situated to receive raw materials and ship out manufactured products. Oil has partially replaced coal as a source of energy for power and heat, and can be easily imported because of the accessibility of this industrial belt to water transport; however, oil pipelines from the fringes of the continent now reach central Europe and stimulate additional industrial development.

The remaining large metropolitan areas of Europe, which lie outside the great industrial belt mentioned above, fall into three categories—capital cities, ports, and old regional centers. Capital cities like Madrid and Rome are each certain to reflect something of the political, economic, and cultural importance of their respective countries. However, ports are also important because the many seas and peninsulas of Europe make accessibility a prime factor to be exploited. Finally, many of these countries originated out of separate historical regions which retain some of their importance today as provincial or state capitals. It is not difficult to find examples of the three categories of cities in European countries:

Country	Capital	Port	Regional Capital
France	Paris	Marseilles	Bordeaux (Aquitaine)
Austria	Vienna	———	Graz (Styria)
Spain	Madrid	Barcelona	Valencia (Valencia)
Italy	Rome	Genoa	Florence (Tuscany)

THE WEST EUROPEAN CITY IN PERSPECTIVE

Berry's concept of persistent public intervention in West European urban development as a consequence of the historic processes of urbanization is apparently a valid one. This intervention is especially apparent in planning for urban core renewal, transportation, New Towns, and social housing. He feels that perhaps the most significant difference emerging in the urbanization process between Western Europe and North America is the public creation or support of satellite communities with consistent architectural design, green belts and open space, specification of growth directions, and clear preference for mass transportation as opposed to private development of automobile oriented suburbs based on profit-making motives. Certainly this attempt to use New Towns and other communities as planned means of controlling the expansion of large metropolitan areas in West Europe is apparent around London, Paris, the Randstad, Stockholm, Helsinki, and Frankfurt. Perhaps it is this policy, whether national or regional in scope, that provides a lesson for North American urban development in the future.

CHAPTER 11

THE SOCIALIST CITY

THE SOCIALIST CITY

THE SOCIALIST CITY IN THEORY.   A visitor to Moscow, the capital of the Soviet Union, may be confused. He sees a city that is clean and safe to walk in at night; wires are underground; public facilities like transportation and green space are excellent; industry is often separated from residences, and the limited number of automobiles has held back air pollution; the population seems to be well fed, clothed, and housed. Yet after more than just a brief stay the visitor begins to feel that this "Socialist City" is not necessarily ideal. People live in crowded apartments and residential space per capita is small (less than one third that of the United States) with a long wait to procure it. Services are lacking in residential neighborhoods, and lengthy waiting lines to purchase food consume large amounts of time. Only 10 percent of the population possess a telephone. Consumer goods that the Westerner takes for granted are lacking. Citizens have little input in urban planning, and the cities have a drab uniform appearance. Therefore, Moscow today is a paradox to the Western visitor. However, it is important that outsiders attempt to understand this city, for as Frolic (1975, 309) states, it serves as a model for other Socialist cities in the Soviet Union and in Eastern Europe.* He seems to imply that Socialism produces a particular kind of city, and Fisher (1962) supports this thesis. Berry (1973, 165) also feels that the socialist city is different from urban centers in the non-socialist world owing to a greater degree of government intervention to cope with the human consequences of rapid industrialization and urbanization. Therefore, examining the theory of socialist urban development and analyzing to what extent reality compares with this theory is now necessary.

*One of the most complete studies of Moscow is Frolic, B. Michael, "Moscow: The Socialist Alternative," in Eldridge, H. W., ed., *World Capitals*, 1975, pp. 295-339. The author has studied in Russia and carried out research at the Harvard Russian Research Center. In 1975, he was serving as first secretary in the Canadian Embassy in Peking. Many aspects of the socialist city as exemplified by Moscow are drawn from this source. Another excellent source is Hamilton, F. E. Ian, *The Moscow City Region*, 1976.

The model (fig. 11.1) adapted from Kansky (1976, 270) is designed to represent some of the factors that relate to socialist urbanization. At least in theory, this urbanization is rooted in Communist ideology. Kansky (1976, 150), who has studied this process in Czechoslovakia, feels that a series of fundamental Marxist principles have guided the Soviet policy of urbanization, which he believes has been diffused and applied in East European countries:

1. Rapid national economic development is a necessary condition for achieving a Socialist or Communist society.
2. National development is based on rapid industrialization of the country.
3. Industrialization must be carried on evenly in all areas of the country—that is, all areas should obtain a "sufficient" amount of industrial capacity.
4. Resources and funds must be allocated and people rearranged in such a way that industrialization is evenly developed.
5. Evenly developed industrialization must be associated with evenly distributed urbanization.

MODEL OF THE SOCIALIST CITY

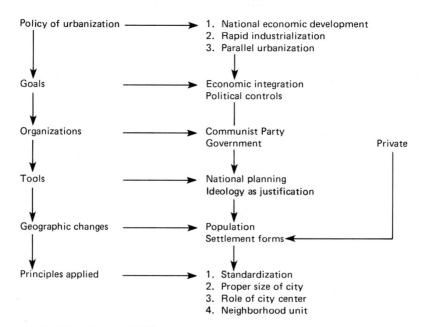

Modified from Kansky (1976).

FIGURE 11.1. A model of factors affecting the development of the Socialist City.

In brief, socialist urbanization is part of a national policy of country-wide industrialization. The goal of allocating resources for industrial and urban growth to *all* parts of the country is a key one because it permits inequalities among regions to be reduced—not only between advanced and backward ones but also between cities and countrysides. According to Marxist ideology, the reduction of these regional inequalities permits the *integration* of the country so that each area carries its share of economic development although its contribution may be less than that of other regions. In this way a true socialist society can be created in which all members benefit from collective resources. Through an integrated society the Party also can control and stimulate the people with respect to Marxism, and collective ideals can be promoted. Such ideals include an emphasis on values related to the state rather than to the individual. These concepts of economic integration and political control help to explain why the Communist leaders place such emphasis on *rational* development of all regions of a country. Integration and control of the entire state are vital to the parallel Party-State oranizations as they carry out national plans of economic development, which are supported and justified by the Marxist ideology.

Such Marxist principles then explain why communist countries have largely handled urbanization policies in connection with those of industrialization. Progress in national economic development, especially of societies that are either backward or regionally unbalanced, is based on industrialization goals which may require changes in the patterns of population and settlement, especially housing in cities. For example, factories may be established in undeveloped regions where resources and surplus labor exist but where cities are lacking. Therefore, the government is forced to manipulate population and settlement—moving people, creating cities with factories and apartments, and developing transportation facilities. In doing this, certain operational principles of urbanization have evolved which seem to be common to socialist cities in the Soviet Union and Eastern Europe. Fisher (1962, 252-5) has identified four of these operational principles that constitute the end products in our hypothetical model of socialist urbanization (see fig. 11.1).

1. **Standardization.** A visitor is quick to note the effects of standardization in the construction of socialist cities. In Eastern Europe as in the Soviet Union, the most noticeable affect is uniformity in commercial, industrial, and residential areas. Store fronts are similar, while monotonous areas of apartment blocks of five to eight stories dominate the landscape. The reasons for this standardization are practical and ideological: maximum effects from limited investments are gained by minimum designs for large areas. At the same time, uniformity should be characteristic of a "classless" society in which distinctions between so-

cial groups are theoretically nonexistent. Osborn (1967) feels that practical reasons are more important than ideological ones in establishing monotony in urban landscapes, i.e., that low economic priority for housing forces a premium on plain and inexpensive designs, mass production techniques (like prefabrication), and stereotyped layout. Architectural expressions of individuality, therefore, are generally absent. Norms of housing space are established by the state in accordance with size of family, and are small by American standards. One may conclude that although standardization of urban form is a result more of practicality than ideology, at least the effect conforms to ideology.

2. **Proper size of city.** In the early stages or urban planning of both the Soviet Union and the countries of Eastern Europe, the size and growth of cities were restricted. In any system of national urban planning, it was felt that rapid growth of particular cities would upset the integration of the country and create problems similar to those evident in capitalistic cities. So, large cities were to be limited in size and excess growth directed elsewhere, often to satellite cities (*gorada-sputnick*), e.g., Sumgait near Baku. Growth patterns of most urban areas were to be planned on the basis of their potential for "production." Thus, for example, the availability of raw materials, labor, housing, markets, and transportation facilities could be important factors in setting population limits. Among these factors, the labor element was viewed as critical. As Fisher (1962, 253) states, city size would depend on proper calculation of the basic or city-forming segments of the population. These segments would include not only industrial functions but also administrative and cultural ones. Many of the arguments for limiting urban growth in the large cities appeared to be ideologically based; for example, smaller cities are supposedly better able to not only cope with environmental problems characteristic of large "capitalistic" cities (e.g., air polluti on) but also can be located to help equalize existing differences between town and countryside. However, the planners found that setting limits to urban growth is easier to talk about than to actually carry out.

3. **Role of the city center.** A third principle of socialist planning is to create a new role for the city center. This role in theory is completely different from that in capitalist cities. In the latter, the CBD is the hub around which other functions arrange themselves in a market economy where rent and transport costs are predominant locational factors. In socialist countries, on the other hand, the city center, in contrast to the past, is being developed as a focus for political and cultural activities (Fisher, 1967, 1081). Commercial areas have been limited in size because of restricted emphasis on both the production of consumer goods and the provision of certain services. Planners, therefore, have tended to de-

centralize such activities out to the residential areas and avoid the overloading of public transport that would occur if too many people shopped in the center. Thus, the core areas of Socialist cities lack the large variety of retail enterprises so common in Western cities. However, some growth of commercial activities persists simply because the center is the most accessible location. In addition, hotels exist, especially as tourism becomes important as a means of attracting the "hard money" of the West.

National policy under a centralized-planned regime requires a focus of activity which takes the place of the Central Business District and serves to coordinate the entire urban complex, especially the commercial, service, and residential activities that have been systematically decentralized. Such a focus is political and cultural. Included in this district is a symbol of Communist Party authority, such as the Kremlin in Moscow or the Palace of Culture in Warsaw. An additional focal point is a square where the masses gather, voluntarily or involuntarily, to celebrate the "great Socialist Revolution" and other official events and to hear words of indoctrination, e.g., in Red Square in Moscow or in the Square of September Ninth in Sofia (see fig. 11.2). Other symbols of the Party, such as red stars, monuments and statues, posters, etc., are in great evidence. The street kiosk is the official outlet for state publications and certain other items. In such a planned society, it is natural that the central core be dominated by numerous government buildings; this administrative framework is supplemented by the cultural institutions which not only facilitate Marxist indoctrination but also help take the place of missing commercial establishments. The opportunities to attend operas, concerts, films, plays, circuses, and sports events in socialist countries are truly remarkable. In addition, books are cheap and easily available.

4. **Neighborhood-unit concept.** The last of the four principles of "socialist" urban planning is an attempt to stress the neighborhood-unit concept (*mikrorayon*). In the development of self-sustaining residential units, which possess shops and services for the people living there, the Communist countries followed a concept which has been significant in "Western" areas. However in Communist states, the neighborhood unit is a "social tool" for urban development as the state establishes residential areas utilizing official norms for size and services without class distinction—at least in theory. At the same time, definite economies are possible in mass construction, and cross-city transport is relieved as units become more self-contained. Neighborhood units are made up of a series of apartment houses with dwelling units of varying sizes, oriented around a core of shops, services, and culture centers (see fig. 11.3). The

FIGURE 11.2. Moscow: View of rally held in honor of Cosmonauts Valentina Tereshkova and Valery Bykovsky in Red Square. (Sovfoto.)

structure represents a way of organizing the space within a city and yet preserving uniformity since each unit is exactly like the others. The neighborhood-unit concept is related to the other three principles in that a certain number of standardized units are grouped around a political-cultural center to form a city of predetermined size.

A chief characteristic of the neighborhood units is their homogeneity in terms of socio-economic characteristics, a contrast with Western cities. Musil (1968) in his study of Prague found that such characteristics as number and age of population, sizes of families, and occupations tended to become more uniform during the postwar period, when the regime controlled the city's growth by reducing in-migration. A second factor was the absence of land value and rent determinants in the distribution of socio-economic groups. Housing is allocated by the government and thus rent does not fix the choice of housing. Land value surfaces are fairly uniform, at least in comparison with capitalist countries, and "filtering" of housing does not take place. Thus, neighborhoods tend to be socially mixed and great differences are not apparent. Only in the mid-1960's with the introduction of cooperative housing was the market factor apparent in housing as a balance to social considerations.

THE APPLICATION OF THEORY TO REALITY: MOSCOW.   This model of socialist urbanization is theoretical and must be analyzed to see how it compares with reality. Moscow represents the first real test which

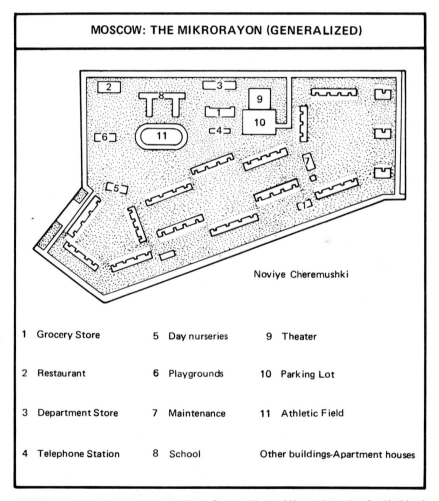

MOSCOW: THE MIKRORAYON (GENERALIZED)

Noviye Cheremushki

1	Grocery Store	**5** Day nurseries	**9** Theater
2	Restaurant	**6** Playgrounds	**10** Parking Lot
3	Department Store	**7** Maintenance	**11** Athletic Field
4	Telephone Station	**8** School	Other buildings-Apartment houses

FIGURE 11.3. A generalized *mikrorayon* in the Noviye Cheremushki area of Moscow. Integration of residential and service structures is an essential part of the plan. (Soviet source: V. Kongress mezhdunarodnovo Soyuza arkhitektorov Moskua, 1958, p. 28.)

came with the 1935 Plan. The Plan was necessary as a framework for not only dealing with immediate pragmatic problems of rapid Soviet industrialization and urbanization but also for establishing basic principles of future urban development in the country. As Frolic (1975, 309) states: "Whatever was to be done in Moscow would henceforth serve as a model for other Soviet cities." The plan represented a drastic change in Moscow's physical layout involving the limiting of population and the reduction of densities. The city was to be no larger than five million in the future and was to be spread out with a green belt added on the edge for recreation. The historic core was to be maintained as well as the radial-concentric pattern of streets but squares were to be created and certain arterials widened, e.g., the primary shopping artery of Gorki Street is now 120-150 feet wide. The subway was designed to be the means of providing mass transportation within this expanded city. Residential districts and neighborhoods were to be self-contained in terms of retail and service enterprises. Natural gas was to be the basic form of energy and wires were to be underground. In this sense, the plan was forward looking in an attempt to anticipate problems of the future.

According to Frolic (1975, 314) the influence of Stalin on the Plan of 1935 was strong. Not only was it viewed as a socialist "blueprint" but it also served political purposes such as moving troops (wide boulevards), assembling people for celebrations (Red Square), providing propaganda (world's most elaborate subway), and reflecting Party authority (massive buildings including six skyscrapers). These ideas were applied in other cities, especially in the New Towns which established (e.g., Zaporozhje and Magnitogorsk).

However, the conflict between socialist theory and reality in the Soviet Union was reflected in the national growth policy. From the beginning, Moscow as model, capital, and large industrial city, continued to attract more than its planned share of the population. Consequently, the Marxist goals of balanced regional development and socialist integration of society were difficult to attain. After World War II the pull of Moscow became even more apparent as the social (or environmental) costs of rapid industrialization were cancelled out in the minds of Soviet leaders and citizens by the immediate economic and cultural benefits of living in the great metropolis. Therefore, the population of Moscow continued to grow after World War II and by 1972 it reached 7.5 million. The primary problem facing the Party and planners as a result of this growth was housing, and Khrushchev was responsible for initiating what may have been one of the largest programs of public housing in the history of world urbanization. Hamilton (1973, 459) reports that between 1958 and 1972, 1.8 million new apartments were constructed for six million people. Much of this housing was prefabricated, a method which became a model for socialist housing. The landscape of Moscow is now dominated by large areas of standardized five to eight story apartment buildings which often suffer from poor quality and maintenance of construction, lack of nearby services, and inadequate landscaping.

As the metropolitan area increased in size and population, the problems of spatial organization multiplied. By 1960 controlling the size of Moscow was impossible and the Party made basic decisions that illustrated a major break with the theory of controlled growth. A regional concept of dispersed metropolitan development was initiated which was facilitated by extending Moscow's political boundaries to include the green belt, an area designated for mass recreation. Some of Moscow's population was to be concentrated in satellite cities in the suburban zone beyond this belt. However, this planned dispersion of a metropolitan area with links to the central city required an enlarged transport system: between 1950 and 1971 the length of the subway was increased from 18 to 85 miles. In 1970 the system carried over four million passengers daily, four times the number carried by the New York City system. Over 12 million people lived within 40 miles of the city, and the regional population was close to 30 million. Therefore, by 1971 planning decisions of regional dispersion, metropolitan government, increased housing, and subway extension all illustrate the results of a primary deviation of reality from theory by accepting the inevitability of metropolitan growth. Perevedentsev (1971, 4), an authority on population problems, justifies this change in Soviet urban policy by defending large metropolitan areas.

However, this expansion of Moscow caused further deviations of reality from theory in terms of housing. The most important one was a change in the concept of the neighborhood unit (*mikrorayon*). As Frolic (1975, 300) explains, two things happened. First, the lack of resources made it impossible to build the service facilities on the scale desired by planners while, at the same time, rapid population growth in Moscow led to even higher residential densities. Secondly, it was discovered that residents did not want to be isolated in neighborhood units and forced to build social associations with their neighbors. As a result, these units have become much larger (50,000) and attempts at developing a full range of services have been abandoned.

Another socialist approach to urban development also was modified by 1971. The concept of the self-contained satellite city (*sputnik*) like that of the *mikrorayon* was finally abandoned in favor of large-scale housing construction within city boundaries and dormitory towns in the suburban area beyond the green belt. The primary satellite example had been

Kryukovo, located about 20 miles outside Moscow and planned for 70,000. In this case the attempts to create a self-contained settlement were costly and apparently not in agreement with desires of residents to be more accessible to Moscow.

Two other changes in socialist planning represent further departures of reality from theory. Cooperative housing is now much more significant than it was in the past although it introduces private capital into the socialist city. Such housing, which makes up over 15 percent of the total dwelling units in Moscow, allows groups to sponsor housing mortgages and has the advantage of encouraging the use of private funds to ease the housing shortage. A second change has been the move from the "socialist" architecture to more modern types less reflective of a progressive ideology. The primary example of the former is the heavy, "wedding cake" style developed during the Stalin era, e.g., the skyscraper of Moscow State University. Russian architects, while admitting the lack of logic behind such a building, have still attempted to find a "socialist" style with little success. Gradually, there has been a move toward more conventional designs. For example, a project like the renewal of Kalinin Street has become a showpiece because it is both modern in function and alive with people in an urban sense. Here a series of shops, including especially those selling records and books, are associated with restaurants, a cinema, and high-rise apartment houses.

The contrast between the 1971 and 1935 Plans of Moscow illustrate the ways in which reality has affected theory in urban planning. A primary conclusion is that the Marxists now accept large cities and try to allow some degree of decentralization in management whereas originally they had tried to restrict size and to organize planning centrally. Planning in the 1970's is attempting to be more polycentric with degrees of autonomy in Moscow's eight zones, each with one million people, oriented around zonal centers with major political, economic, and social functions. These zones in turn are broken down into planning and residential districts. Present goals are to increase the housing space per unit and the services accompanying these units, problems that have been unsolved up to now. Residential units will rise to nine stories although overall population densities will be kept down by use of green space. The central city area (*Sadovoye Koltso*), which lies within the garden ring, will possess not only a smaller resident population but also a lower working one as the imbalance between jobs and labor is corrected; thus, the center of Moscow can more truly serve as an administrative and cultural center for the overall city. The subway network is to be extended to 200 miles, and will handle nearly 40 percent of all urban travel. Surprisingly, the plan is to have the number of automobiles expanded to

1.5 million by 1980, an increase which Soviet planners feel they can deal with environmentally. As recently as 1970, probably only about 20 public gas stations existed in this city of seven million. The absence of land uses related to the automobile—sales outlets, repair and service facilities, used car lots, and "drive-in" facilities—is one of the strongest contrasts between Moscow and Western cities.

A final departure of reality from theory in socialist urbanization as reflected in Moscow is the apparent abandonment of the goal of creating a new social structure in cities. Frolic (1975, 308) emphasizes, for example, that in the early planning of Moscow the transformation of social life had to be subordinated to economic and political criteria. He quotes Kaganovich who, in citing Stalin, stated in the early 1930's that "eliminating the differences between town and country meant turning peasants into town dwellers and not worshipping garden cities." In other words, it may be impossible to industrialize a society and transform its social structure at once. Reality thus forces a slow-down in theory, and, therefore, the "socialist" city might have to wait until the "industrial" city is satisfactorily developed. Kaganovich was really putting production ahead of planning and politics ahead of ideology. After World War II Communist theoreticians like Strumilin (Frolic, 1964, 285-7) advocated replacement of *mikrorayons* by *communes* in which individual and family life were to be subordinated to a collective social structure in cities. However, little is now heard of this socialist city of the future.

DIFFUSION OF THE SOCIALIST URBAN MODEL: CZECHO-SLOVAKIA. Moscow has shown that it does not exactly fit the socialist model of urbanization. The city was transformed considerably under the impact of Marxist ideology but in return Moscow itself had some effects on the theory of socialist urbanization, for it proved that the realities of urban development require some relaxation of the model. Similar interaction between theory and reality is found when the model is applied in other parts of the Soviet Union and Eastern Europe. Kansky (1976), in a penetrating study of urbanization in Czechoslovakia, shows how the socialist model as developed in the Soviet Union was diffused into this Central European country after World War II (see fig. 11.1). He feels that the most apparent aspect of this process is the way Party-State organizations follow Soviet policy in manipulating population and housing in order to industrialize and urbanize the entire country. Once again, a key goal is the reduction of differences between urban and rural areas in order to integrate them as a unit and thereby contribute to the progress of socialist development. Thus, he finds that urbanization in northern Moravia and Slovakia has expanded at the expense of Bohemia. After

1947, the former area, with its resources of coal and steel, was expanded and contributed to the establishment of a heavy industrial base in backward areas of Slovakia, where undeveloped raw materials existed. Examples of this base include the hydro-electric developments along the Vah River and the steel plant near Košice. Thus, the industrial and population gravity of the country shifted eastward as the relative importance of Slovakia in national production increased from eight percent in 1939 to 24 percent in 1967. The emphasis upon industrial growth in Northern Moravia and Slovakia is reflected in relative growth of cities as shown on the map (see fig. 11.4). Kansky (1976, 166-170) finds, for example, that these government policies changed the normal rank-size patterns of urban centers in the country. The greatest changes in urban national rank between 1950 and 1970 were found in the cities of northern Moravia where heavy industry had been promoted by the Party; in the vicinity of the great steel city of Ostrava, the new town of Havířov increased from a rank of 50 in 1950 to seven in 1970, while Karviná and Třinec also jumped by seven and eleven ranks, respectively. In Slovakia, cities like Žilina, Banská Bystrica, Nitra, and Martin all increased in rank. These manipulations of population seem to illustrate attempts by the

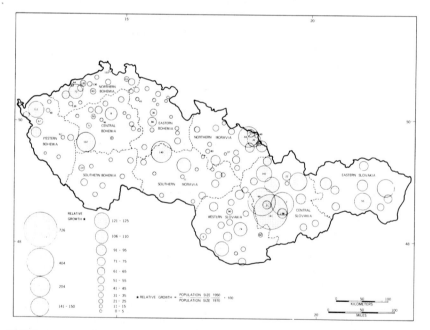

FIGURE 11.4. A map of relative population growth in the urban centers of Czechoslovakia, 1950-1970. Note the large increases in the eastern part of the country. (From Czechoslovak Republic, *Predbezne vysledky scitani lidu, domu a bytu k 1. prosinci 1970 v CSSR* (Prague: Federalni Statisticky Urad, 1971), Table 2b, pp. 20-31.)

regime to emphasize the socialist principle of a proper size for cities within a planned urban system. Such changes in rank can be contrasted with those of the American urban system described in chapter 6.

These disproportionate changes in Czechoslovakian urban populations are also reflected in the percentage of housing that was built after World War II: while only 31.5 percent of the Czech dwellings by 1970 were post 1945, 58.6 of Slovakia's units were erected in this period (Kansky, 1976, 94-6). Northern Moravia shows the highest postwar housing percentage (44.2) of all regions in Bohemia and Moravia. In the Moravian industrial city of Ostrava, 60.6 percent of dwelling units are postwar.

However, this manipulation of population and housing as a part of Socialist national policy in Czechoslovakia created serious problems. The rate of industrialization was too rapid and urbanization could not keep up. With the lack of housing in cities, the birth rate fell, a phenomenon that was also related to the large number of women working and to legalized abortions. Serious dislocations existed between industry, population, and housing, especially in the older cities of Bohemia where investment in urbanization was lacking. Even in the newer factory areas of Slovakia, housing did not keep pace. As a result, large numbers of factory workers had to remain in villages and commute to cities.

Perhaps the most significant conflict between theory and reality that Kansky found in Czechoslovakia was between government and private goals in cities, a feature that he incorporated into his model. For example, the private goal of greater per capita housing, which is emphasized in Marxist theory, was ignored by Party-State organizations in the 1950's in the interest of practical problems of economic growth. However, by the 1960's this factor became significant. As in the Soviet Union, pressure from the population forced the regime to ease the long wait for housing by state construction of more apartment houses, remodelling of older ones, and increased use of cooperative housing. For example, the number of rooms per apartment increased from 1.77 in 1961 to 2.12 in 1970; average living floor space per person increased from 34.7 to 39.4 square meters (Kansky, 1976, 87).

Czechoslovakia thus illustrates the way in which theory and reality diverge in socialist urban planning. Under Marxism, both industrialization and urbanization are emphasized, and the governmental powers feel it should be possible to create factories and cities with optimum environments at the same time. However, in reality industrialization runs ahead of urbanization and, in fact, determines it. Housing becomes a "tool" of industrialization and often is not developed to satisfy demand or help the living standard until it is convenient or necessary to do so.

Thus the right of a socialist citizen to an apartment is not always observed. Only later, when the pressure of society becomes greater, do the "private goals" of citizens have an effect on improving the social urban environment. These contrasts between theory and reality seem to be present in most socialist countries.

DIFFUSION OF THE SOCIALIST URBAN MODEL: OTHER EXAMPLES OF THE APPLICATION OF MARXIST PRINCIPLES IN EAST EUROPE CITIES.

1. **Standardization and population density: The case of Warsaw.** Many visitors to socialist countries remark on the apparent uniformity of cities in regard to housing distribution; that is to say, apartment houses of similar types are found throughout the city. This evenness may be related to definite policies of distribution, but proving this idea is difficult because of the lack of data. Dawson (1971, 108) in a study of Warsaw feels evidence illustrates increasing uniformity in population and housing density over that existing during the prewar period. The factors involved are the reduction of densities in the core as gardens and open spaces replaced tenements and factories, and the increase of densities in the suburbs with the planned construction of apartment houses and industry there. Thus, the outward decreasing density gradient of housing and population, which is typical of the North American city, is not characteristic of the Polish capital. The fact that Warsaw was 85 percent destroyed during World War II, of course, gave Communist planners the opportunity for introducing a new structural pattern.

Dawson also feels that the socialist city, as exemplified by Warsaw, is typified by an axial pattern that reflects association between suburban growth and transport routes. Since these cities are not automobile-oriented, factories and neighborhood units must be located close to the axis of public transport (e.g., the roads and railroads in Warsaw). The model illustrates the axial pattern (see fig. 11.5).

The conclusion is that although suburban densities in the socialist city have increased relative to the center, the pattern remains axial. Both characteristics contrast with the North American city where the automobile provides the mobility for suburban residents to locate in low-density single-family houses between the major radial axes.

2. **Proper size.** As in the Soviet Union, the Party in the East European countries has found difficulty in applying the principle of "proper size" for cities. This problem is particularly apparent in restricting growth of large capital cities or in encouraging growth of cities in backward areas at the expense of those in more advanced ones. In the first case, the more primate capitals like Budapest and Bucharest are still predominant in their respective countries, but this importance has de-

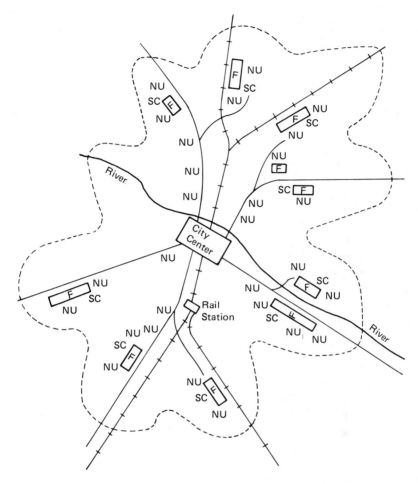

FIGURE 11.5. A theoretical pattern of development for a Socialist City (after Dawson). Abbreviations: F = factory; NU = Neighborhood Unit; SC = Service Center.

creased (Davis, 1969, I, 246). The table illustrates the varying degrees of primacy in seven countries of East Europe and the changes since 1960 (see table 11.1). There is little doubt that a city like Budapest with one-fifth of Hungary's population and an even higher percentage of its industry presents a problem in urban concentration.

However, the second case, in which cities of backward areas of a country are emphasized at the expense of those in more advanced regions, also represents problems for the Communist regimes. The rapid rise of Slovakian cities at the expense of Bohemian ones was mentioned above. Here traditional regional differences are a sensitive issue and the

TABLE 11.1
East Europe: Four-City Index of Primacy*

Country	1960	1970
Bulgaria	1.64	1.46
Czechoslovakia	1.20	1.11
East Germany	.79	.77
Hungary	4.64	4.04
Poland	.62	.55
Romania	2.32	2.05
Yugoslavia	.64	.62

*The population of the first city divided by the combined population of the next three.
From *World Urbanization 1950-1970* by Kingsley Davis and Gerald L. Fox. Reprinted by permission.

central government was aware of this. A similar situation exists in Yugoslavia where the federal government, in industrializing backward areas like Macedonia, Montenegro, and Bosnia, helped the growth of Skopje, Titograd, and Sarajevo, respectively. At the same time, this regional "subsidy" was resented in Slovenia and Croatia, whose representatives felt that disproportionate support was being parcelled out to the southern areas at the expense of developed regions where the markets were greater.

3. **City center.** In Eastern Europe reality has altered somewhat the theory regarding the role of the socialist city center as a political-cultural focus. Consumer goods and even automobiles have received more emphasis. Perhaps the most extreme example is Ljubljana, Yugoslavia, which resembles a Western city in its stores and automobile traffic. Similar changes are evident in many other large cities. Nevertheless, the core areas of socialist cities remain different from those of Western cities. More and more, one has the feeling of an attempt to hold back industrial and residential growth there in order to leave it free for specialized functions of culture, administration, and tourism.

4. **Neighborhood unit.** The changing role of the neighborhood unit (*mikrorayon*) in Moscow has been discussed above. This unit plays an important role in socialist urban planning, but the degree to which it conforms to theory, i.e., as self-contained, will vary considerably. In some cities, these units possess a considerable range of services. Generally, apartment buildings are oriented around an elementary school and green space with recreation facilities. Shops may exist on the ground floor of apartment buildings or in separate structures. Periodic needs such as clothing, drugs, post office, bank, and theater may be provided. In the New Towns like Schwedt in East Germany, reality seems to follow

theory to the greatest extent in the development of neighborhood units (see fig. 11.6).

Perhaps the greatest deviation from socialist neighborhood planning is in Yugoslavia where the impact of returning *Gastarbeiter* (migrant workers) is apparent. Some 700,000 Yugoslavs have lived and worked in West Germany, for example, and many of them have used money

1. Kindergarten and day nursery
2. School area
3. Culture Center
4. Movies, espresso, fashions
5. Administration
6. Post office and bank
7. Department store
8. Specialty shops
9. Food stores
10. Hotel
11. Inn
12. Swimming pool
13. Hospital with ambulance and pharmacy
14. Railroad station
15. Parking areas
16. Parking garage
17. Volleyball

FIGURE 11.6. The pattern of Schwedt, a new town in East Germany that developed as an oil refining center on the pipeline from the Soviet Union (after Feuerstein).

earned there to construct private dwellings on their return. This housing has not only eased the domestic shortage but has also created a landscape of dwellings that in part reflects German and other north European designs.

TWO TYPES OF "SOCIALIST" CITY.   Understandably, such a transformation of urban society will take some time and the visitor to Eastern Europe or the Soviet Union will have some difficulty identifying degrees of "socialist" urbanism. Therefore, on the basis of the degree of change along Marxist-Leninist lines, it is possible to contrast the partially-transformed city with the new urban complex that conforms more completely to "socialist" theory.

1. **Partially-changed cities.** The old historic elements are so important in the communist cities of today that it is sometimes difficult to realize change is under way. This is especially true in the large cities where a process of scrapping everything and starting anew is impossible. Besides, abolishment of everything in the past is not the desire of socialist countries. Generally a nation must have some historic foundation into which its culture is rooted, and even though communism is stated to be the society of the future, it has evolved on an older substructure of which only part is to be transformed. Recent appeals to national tradition in communist states are related to the partial fragmentation of international communism, and this rise of nationalism may add diversity to the uniformity of socialism. Romania has become a leader in the movement toward "independent roads to socialism," and historical traditions, especially in the arts, play a part in the resistance of national Party leaders to Soviet leadership. In Poland a cross section of the entire population, including Party leaders, supported the reconstruction of the "old town" of Warsaw which was destroyed during World War II. Although this quaint square plays little active part in the commercial activity of the metropolis, it stands today as a quiet backwater of the past, symbolic of the cultural persistence of the Polish people. The old cores of Poznan, Gdańsk, and Lublin in Poland also have been restored. Even in Moscow, there is no talk of tearing down the Kremlin which under Tsars and Commissars alike has been an administrative center.

The pre-"socialist" elements of *East European* cities resemble, in part, those described above for West Europe. Medieval cores of castle or palace, market square, city hall, and cathedral exist in Warsaw, Prague, Budapest, Belgrade, and many lesser cities. The mixed land uses, small shops, public buildings, and parks of the past are also noticeable. However, the urban tradition came late to East Europe, and industrial-commercial traditions are lacking except in a few places—most notably in German,

Polish, and Czech regions where German, Austrian, and Jewish influences helped to stimulate such activities. Planned standard urban sections were grafted by German settlers upon earlier Slav nuclei, and city hall and market place became important foci. In the Balkans, the long occupation by the Turks was responsible for the importance of mosques while commercial activities were restricted to bazaars except where Italian or Greek influences penetrated. The legacy of Byzantium—the Orthodox church—revived as the Turks were pushed back. In the interwar period, when national states finally emerged in Eastern Europe, urban institutions finally began to evolve, only to be cut short by World War II.

Characterizing the old elements of *Russian* cities is difficult because so many cultures are represented. The Slavic element, of course, is predominant, but Leningrad looks Western and Riga has a German appearance while cities of central Asia possess Turkic-Tatar, Persian, and even Chinese characteristics. Byzantine culture contributed through the establishment of the Orthodox church. In most cities, however, administrative-defense elements played important early roles in urban development. The *gorod* or walled city included a kremlin or fortress which still dominates certain large Soviet cities today, e.g., Moscow and Gorky. Churches and fortified monasteries, the latter having served as defensive outposts for larger cities against Tatar raids (e.g., Novo-Devichy and Donskoi for Moscow) are to be seen today. Within the *gorod* or often outside its walls was the *posad* or commercial center for artisans and merchants that evolved into the congested business district of today. As late as 1900, Russian industry was confined to Moscow, Leningrad, textile centers north of Moscow, and the Donets coal area. Even today the squalid, planless aspect of early industrial centers, especially those located on coal fields, is apparent.

Functional diversification in Russian cities, therefore, was lacking until recently. The former palaces and elegant villas of Russian nobility in Baroque style are evident, but tenements in brick, stucco, and wood line poorly cobbled streets. Perhaps most characteristic as a legacy of Russia's feudal past is the village-like appearance of sections of cities which include one-story houses of wood, small isolated shops and workshops, unpaved streets, neglected churches, outside water pumps or taps, and the "free market" now used by the collective farmers. However, such conditions are becoming harder to find each year. In the western part of the Soviet Union, street patterns are irregular while farther east and in Central Asia planned settlements, generally Russian in origin, led to a grid pattern, often superimposed upon an earlier irregular one.

In both East Europe and the Soviet Union, new socialist elements have been added to the pre-"socialist" urban forms described above. When the communists came to power, the early 5-year plans provided for industrialization programs designed to effect great changes in the cities. The new industries required labor, raw materials, and factory sites. Collectivization programs were pushed in order to mechanize farm operations and release rural labor to the cities. Transportation networks were constructed to tap the rich raw materials of the Soviet Union for use in industrial factories. The influx of labor and raw materials into Russian cities as part of "socialist" programs of industrialization led to the construction of new urban elements—apartment houses, warehouses, factories, railway stations, and transport. In Tashkent, the great regional center of Central Asia, a clear separation between old and new towns exist. In East Europe, contrasts between the pre-"socialist" and "socialist" portions of cities also are to be found, e.g., Zagreb in Yugoslavia. In most instances portions of the old towns are to be reconstructed or, in the case of primitive urban districts of Central Asia, eventually destroyed. In the meantime, Intourist does not encourage visits to and pictures of these areas because they do not represent "socialist urban progress."

The majority of the "socialist" cities, therefore, are only partially-changed along Marxist lines and the interpretation of Soviet cities today involves some reference to history.

2. **New cities.** The new socialist cities represent those constructed as a unit along the Marxist-Leninist principles mentioned above. Shkvarikov states (1964, 307) that in the Soviet Union between 1926 and 1963 over 800 new towns were built, one-third of them being constructed on vacant land, e.g., Zaporozhje, Magnitogorsk, and Komsomolsk. After World War II, the Communist governments of Eastern Europe also established industrial cities. Generally, these cities were designed as show pieces for "socialism" and often included a large iron and steel plant as a working nucleus for the self-contained project. The main examples are:

> Eisenhüttenstadt, East Germany
> Nowa Huta, Poland
> Nowe Tychy, Poland
> Havířov
> Dunaújváros, Hungary
> Gheorghe Gheorghiu-Dej, Rumania
> Victoria, Rumania
> Dimitrovgrad, Bulgaria
> Velenje, Yugoslavia
> Titograd, Yugoslavia

These new cities have risen "out of the fields" to house the growing worker class, and departures from the traditional capitalistic pattern should be complete as no previous "urban" complex existed on the site (see fig. 11.7). The cities are usually built to accomplish a single specific purpose: to house the workers of a large plant (Nowa Huta), to relieve congestion in an adjacent industrial area (Nowe Tychy), or to serve as a regional administrative center (Titograd).

Nowa Huta is an industrial satellite town for Krakow, Poland. A great integrated steel plant was constructed here after World War II to symbolize the new industrial era of socialism; unlike the steel plants of Upper Silesia, which were built largely by German technology and capital, this factory was to be completely Polish and "socialist." The capacity of the plant is over three million tons of steel, a big help to Polish industrialization. Coking coal is supplied from Polish and Czechoslovak sources, but the iron ore comes from the Soviet Union. Many of the worker-residents are of rural origin since one of the locational factors in the decision to undertake the project here apparently was the rural overpopulation which had been characteristic of the area when it was part of the Austrian Empire as the province of Galicia. Nowa Huta is a self-contained new town of 100,000 and is organized along socialist principles around a central square with shopping and collective institutions located to serve the worker-residents of the six-story apartment houses. The city is linked to Krakow by frequent train service.

FIGURE 11.7. Gheorghe Gheorghiu-Dej is a new industrial town in eastern Rumania. In ten years a city of 35,000 arose to accompany the complex of petro-chemical plants nearby.

Still another example of a new town is Schwedt in East Germany (see fig. 11.6). The town was built as an urban center near a new oil refinery on the "Friendship" Pipe Line constructed through East Europe from the Soviet Union. The plan for this center includes provision for a cultural center, residential apartment units (with parking!), and sports areas. Feuerstein (1968, 104-9) feels that overall the site gives a spacious impression which he feels is a contrast to the higher densities characteristic of similar towns in Western Europe.

NATURE OF THE "SOCIALIST" CITY.   The geographer has long been intrigued with the question of whether or not a landscape can reflect national policy. Whittlesey (1935, 90) states, for example, that central authority, acting for the whole of its territory, "tends to produce uniformity in cultural impress even where the natural landscape is diverse." In testing this hypothesis, it would seem logical to begin with a Communist country. Here the Party controls the factors of production and through national plans has succeeded in transforming the patterns of rural and urban settlement. Whether or not one is justified in calling this new landscape "socialist," however, is open to question. As Rugg (1970, 118) implies, the concept of a "socialist landscape" is difficult to support because although many forms are of socialist origin, others are either uniquely national or modern in the sense that they are present in any industrialized country. However, it is the quality of uniformity apparent in a form like the collective farm that causes many visitors to the Soviet Union, East Europe, or China to reflect upon the existence of a unique "socialist landscape." In examining the urban component of such a landscape, one finds uniformity through application of the principles of standardization, political-cultural role of city center, and neighborhood unit. Berry (1973, 164) feels that the control of urbanization reaches its maximum in the centralized command economies of socialist states where planning is utilized to handle the consequences of rapid industrialization.

What is 'socialist' about the city centre, neighbourhood unit or new town? As pointed out above, certain buildings, squares or monuments are distinctly socialist because they reflect the ideology through style, ornaments, or personification of specific individuals. The city center and neighbourhood units possess an association of forms that appear different although admittedly such a statement may be hard to prove. Finally, such cities represent the attempt to apply socialist principles of city planning. However, can we go further and make remarks about socialist architecture? The author is inclined to agree with Yurick Blumenfeld (1968, 60-1) who states that the skyscrapers of Moscow, Warsaw and

Bucharest—wedding cakes frosted with pediments and pseudo-rococo ornamentation—have a distinctive period flavour (see fig. 11.8). Although it may be resented as a Russian import, the Palace of Culture in Warsaw may have more character than the more modern structures around it. The same is true of the massive Party buildings of Sofia. Since the Stalin era, there appears to be a weakening in the influence of Marxist ideology upon architectural design. Hutchings (1968) feels that factors of technology and foreign influence were instrumental in reducing the ideological themes of "isolationism," "nationalism," "secularism," "orthodoxy," "proletarian triumph," and "doctrinal propaganda." However, the new styles, while closer to the West in some respects, also seem to reflect in their uniformity a Party-directed mass culture, devoid of much originality and based on the Plan above all: "Dreary, monotonous blocks of brick or concrete seem to be bereft of spiritual feeling or human content (Blumenfeld, 1968, 60)." The variety made possible in

FIGURE 11.8. Moscow State University is one of several skyscrapers built in the Soviet capital during the Stalin period. Note the ornamentation.

"Western" cities by varied store fronts, use of different architectural designs and materials (e.g., glass and aluminum), and presence of advertising and neon lights is lacking in "socialist" cities. Perhaps it is the lack of "character" or "personality" that most symbolizes the socialist city. Supplementing this idea are negative qualities of poor landscaping, overcrowded transportation, and inadequate services (see fig. 11.9). Even air pollution exists, derived as in Western countries from the over-emphasis on "production" at the expense of social costs connected with the environment. On the other hand, certain positive qualities are present with the frequent presence of "collective" institutions such as parks (of rest and culture), schools, nurseries or kindergartens, hospitals, youth clubs—all identified in some way with the regime. One concludes that the "socialist" character of these cities is in part impressionistic but nevertheless worthy of trying to capture.

URBANIZATION IN EASTERN EUROPE AND THE SOVIET UNION

EAST EUROPE.   The eastern part of Europe is not as industrialized as the western part. The Industrial Revolution was slow to diffuse into this part of the continent, in part delayed by the persistence of feudalism and by the lack of a middle class. The wealth that flowed into West Europe from colonies was also missing in the east. As a result, the area in

FIGURE 11.9. This new housing project in Dushanbe, the capital of the Tadzkik Soviet Socialist Republic (Soviet Union) had an unfinished aspect after completion in 1963.

the 1930s was only 35 percent urbanized and over two-thirds of this was in the northern three states of East Germany (then part of Germany), Poland, and Czechoslovakia. Actually, in these states, the concentration was most evident in Thuringia, Saxon-Anhalt, Saxony, Bohemia, Moravia, and Silesia. This urban concentration was directly related to the fact that 75 percent of the industry in East Europe was located within a triangle between the cities of Erfurt, Lodz, and Budapest (Hamilton, 1971, 176-9).

After World War II, Communist programs focused on collectivization and rapid industrialization had great impact on the growth of manufacturing and on cities. Large rural to urban migrations developed as surplus agricultural labor was released. Marxist attempts to develop backward areas also had the effect of evening out the industrial and urban patterns. For example, the triangle by 1970 possessed only 50 percent of East European industry, and manufacturing employment in the Balkans increased from 16 percent of the total in 1939 to 39 percent in 1967. These industrial changes are directly related to urban ones. In 1970, 48 percent of the 120 million people in East Europe were considered urban by official sources (Kosinski, 1974, 135). The northern states still dominated (62 percent of the total), but in the Balkans changes were more rapid (e.g., Bulgaria from 21 to 46 percent urban). Percentages in the 1960s ranged from 28 in Yugoslavia to 73 in East Germany with Czechoslovakia and Poland in the middle at 50. Within countries, differences were still apparent, e.g., Bohemia over Slovakia, and Slovenia over Serbia and Macedonia. Nonetheless, all areas exhibited cities where none had existed before.

However, it is well to point out that the rural landscape of villages still dominates over large areas of Eastern Europe. In contrast to Western Europe where 46 percent of the population lived in cities over 100,000 in 1970, this proportion in Eastern Europe was only 24 percent (Davis, 1969, I, 132-3).

Urban centers in East Europe can be grouped as follows (see table 11.2):

1. **Capital Cities.** In each of the eight East European countries the capital city is important (see table 11.1). However, it is of relatively lesser importance when the country is composed of several historical regions or has regional industrialization or commerce that is significant. In Hungary, Bulgaria, and Albania, the capital is predominant, for older regional capitals are less significant and industry is either located to a considerable extent in the capital (e.g., Budapest) or is little developed.

2. **Regional Centers.** In the other five countries, regional centers of historic importance help to reduce the preëminence of the capital and

TABLE 11.2
Eastern Europe: Important Urban Centers

Country	Capital	Regional center and region	Port	Industrial city
East Germany	East Berlin	Leipzig (Saxony) Dresden (Saxony) Erfurt (Thuringia)	Rostock	Magdeburg Halle Karl Marx Stadt (Chemnitz) Eisenhüttenstadt
Poland	Warsaw	Poznan (Great Poland) Wroclaw (Silesia) Krakow (Little Poland)	Gdańsk Szczecin	Katowice Lódź
Czechoslo-vakia	Prague	Brno (Moravia) Bratislava (Slovakia)		Liberec Plzeň Moravská Ostrava
Hungary	Budapest	Debrecen (Great Plain)		Miskolc Dunaújváros Györ
Rumania	Bucharest	Cluj (Transylvania) Iaşi (Moldavia) Timişoara (Banat)	Constanţa	Ploieşti Hunedoara Reşiţa
Bulgaria	Sofia	Plovdiv (Rumelia)	Varna	Dimitrovgrad
Albania	Tirana	Elbasan	Dürres	Qytet Stalin
Yugoslavia	Belgrade	Zagreb (Croatia) Ljubljana (Slovenia) Sarajevo (Bosnia-Hercegovina) Skopje (Macedonia)	Split Rijeka	Zenica Jesenice

account for a larger number of true cities. Since historic areas like Saxony, Silesia, Moravia, Croatia, and Moldavia were once independent kingdoms or duchies, their principal cities of Dresden, Breslau (Wroclaw), Brno, Zagreb, and Iaşi each attracted certain political, cultural, and economic functions that give them urban status today.

3. **Industrial-commercial cities.** Each of the East European countries has certain industrial or port cities, which tend to be of greater relative importance in the northern states. The historical development of these centers was greatly affected by external influences since industry was established by German or Austro-Hungarian interests. The cities of the Ore Mountains (e.g., Dresden and Chemnitz, the latter now Karl Marx Stadt) reflect a medieval iron-working tradition in Saxony, while the

great complex of Upper Silesia was developed largely under Prussia, based on the large coal field. Within the Austrian Empire, metallurgical centers evolved at Plzeň and Moravska Ostrava (now both in Czechoslovakia), Miskolc-Diosgyör (now Hungary), Reşiţa (now Rumania), and Jesenice and Zenica (now both in Yugoslavia). The great port of Danzig (Gdańsk) developed under Prussia while the ports of Trieste and Fiume (now Rijeka in Yugoslavia) served the Austro-Hungarian Empire. One important exception to the German-Austro dominance in industry was Łódź in Poland, a planned center established in Congress Poland to produce textiles, largely for the Russian Empire.

Under communism the industrial influence is altering the urban pattern of Eastern Europe. New factories and residential areas have been added not only to the old industrial centers but to capitals and regional centers as well. East Europe's largest conurbation, Upper Silesia, is now completely Polish and the six major towns plus suburbs include over 3 million inhabitants. Planners in all these countries are attempting to arrest the concentration of functions, including industry, in the older centers. Therefore, new "socialist" cities (mentioned above) are being created, and satellite cities for industry and residence are increasing in size. This urban influence is spreading also to village and town as small industries are added and the rural aspect is less predominant.

SOVIET UNION. Urbanization in the Soviet Union has been influenced by the great emphasis on industrialization. The two processes generally work together so it is not surprising that during the sixty years since the Revolution, the share of urban inhabitants in the total population increased from about 15 percent to over 55 percent. Although this percentage is less than the figure of over 70 percent for the United States, the rapid change in Soviet society is probably unparalleled in the history of urbanization for any large nation.* The number of cities of over 100,000 population increased from 31 in 1926 to 201 in 1970. In absolute terms, urban population increased by 55 million in the years 1926-62, a remarkable expansion especially in the light of wartime losses. Over two-thirds of this increase resulted from a large-scale migration from rural to urban areas while population increase and changes in settlement classification accounted for the remainder.

Soviet urban growth is based on the development of certain functional specialties (see table 11.3). Many cities are administrative centers for political areas. Others act as regional economic centers or are ports.

*Comparisons of Soviet and American cities are difficult because the former tend to be "overbounded" and therefore will include more of the real built-up area than the "underbounded" cities of the United States.

TABLE 11.3
Major Urban Centers of the Soviet Union With Over
300,000 in Population

National capital—Moscow

SSR capitals—Moscow (RSFSR); Kiev (Ukraine); Baku (Azerbaydzhan); Tashkent (Uzbek); Tbilisi (Georgia); Riga (Latvia); Minsk (Belorussia); Yerevan (Armenia); Alma-Ata (Kazakh); Tallin (Estonia); Vilnyus (Lithuania); Frunze (Kirghiz); Dushanbe (Tadzhik); Kishinev (Moldavia); Ashkhabad* (Turkmen)

Other regional centers—Leningrad; Kazan; Perm; Ufa; Lvov; Irkutsk; Khabarovsk; Krasnodar; Barnaul; Izhevsk; Orenburg; Bryansk

Ports—Odessa; Vladivostock; Zhdanov; Archangelsk; Nikolayev; Murmansk; Kaliningrad

Coal fields and associated undustries—
Donets: Donetsk; Makeyevka; Gorlovka; Lugansk
Karaganda: Karaganda
Kuznetsk: Novokuznetsk; Kemerovo; Prokopyevsk
Tula: Tula

Other resources—
Urals—Sverdlovsk; Chelyabinsk; Nizhny Tagil; Magnitogorsk
Iron—Krivoy Rog

Volga River centers—Gorky; Kuibyshev; Volgograd; Saratov; Yaroslavl; Astrakhan; Ulyanovsk

Trans-Siberian railroad centers—Novosibirsk; Omsk; Krasnoyarsk; Tomsk

Other industrial centers—Kharkov; Dnepropetrovsk; Rostov; Voronezh; Zaporozhye; Ivanovo; Kalinin; Penza; Kirov; Grozny; Ryazan; Kaunas

*under 300,000 population

Resources and industry are the main functions of a large number of newer cities while still others are based on transportation arteries like the Volga River and the Trans-Siberian railroad.

The geographical aspects of the urbanization process are enlightening and pertinent. Most Soviet cities, large or small, are located in the so-called "fertile triangle," the area enclosed between lines drawn from Leningrad to Odessa to Irkutsk (see fig. 2.15). This area, comprising some 12 percent of the country, is estimated to have nearly 80 percent of the population. North of this triangle the climate is too cold for many permanent settlements of any size, especially since the growing season is less than 100 days, while to the south it is too dry, with annual rainfall under 12-15 inches. In 1970, 108 cities had over 200,000 inhabitants, but only 27 were located any distance outside the triangle, and 20 of these were to the south. To the north and east of the triangle, only seven large cities exist—Murmansk and Archangelsk in the northwest and Ulan-Ude, Chita, Khabarovsk, Komsomolsk, and Vladivostok, all located to the east on the Trans-Siberian railroad. The 20 cities in the area south of the triangle are not only ports and political capitals of republics but also industrial centers such as Grozny, Krasnodar, and Karaganda. Therefore, the conclusion is that the large cities of the Soviet Union are confined to a particular belt in spite of the attempts of Soviet planners to widen the area of settlement. Not only do most of the people in the Soviet Union live in the "fertile triangle" but also the majority of the urban areas are located here, especially in the area west of the Ural Mountains. The persistence of settlement in this "triangle" reflects the overall harshness of the Siberian environment which, in spite of its resources, repels people and the development of larger markets. In recent years, attempts to even out, at considerable cost, the geographic distribution of industry have diminished and profit motives have become apparent.

Does this mean that Soviet economic development has not made progress in the areas of harsh environment? No, it does not, but simply reflects the fact that *large-scale* urbanization will probably never be extensive in the areas east of the Urals. Within the narrow portion of the triangle are a number of large cities, situated near or on the Trans-Siberian railroad, which serve as industrial cores of the Ural-Lake Baikal zone. The relative and absolute growth of these cities in the past 20 years has been exceptional and reflects Soviet attempts to even out economic development in spite of distances from markets. Away from this belt, however, cities are smaller and fewer in number. One may point to Norilsk (140,000) on the Yenesei River and Yakutsk (95,000) on the Lena River as examples of isolated regional centers in the north. The urbanization of Siberia undoubtedly will continue through existing "growth centers," but the difficulty of attracting settlers to this area may slow down the process. In spite of special inducements in the form of wages, many Russians are unwilling to help "build socialism" in an area of rigorous climate, chronic shortages of consumer goods, and limited housing facilities.

The degree of urbanization in various regions of the Soviet Union depends on several factors including historical tradition, agricultural possibilities, and availability of industrial raw materials. Thus Moscow and Leningrad have expanded as enormous metropolitan areas based in part on tradition and the presence of skilled labor. The Ukraine is Russia's most important agricultural area but, owing to coal and iron resources, it also contains the largest centers of heavy industry—factors which explain an urbanization of nearly 50 percent. On the other hand, Belorussia is predominantly rural (in fact, backward) and only 30 percent of the population lives in cities. The regions of Eastern Siberia and the Far East are over 50 percent urban largely because agriculture is of minor importance.

The emphasis on industrialization has had an effect on the composition of the urban population. Russian administrators and engineers are increasingly evident in the non-Slavic republics while ethnic groups from these areas attend school and work in the Russian cities. Overall, the population is becoming much more cosmopolitan. For example, the Kazakh Republic is now less than 50 percent Kazakh.

The slowdown in industrial-urban dispersion means that the metropolitan trend will probably accelerate. In spite of Soviet efforts to avoid over-concentration, there are more than 35 cities in the country that possess over 500,000 inhabitants and 10 with over 1 million. Several of the latter are multi-million centers or conurbations. Moscow now includes over 7 million people as its administrative, cultural, and industrial functions attract residents from all over the country. Each day over 500,000 commuters come into the city from the surrounding area and the city accounts for 15 percent of Soviet industry. Leningrad now has over 3 million inhabitants while the industrial cities of the Ukraine and Urals are increasing steadily. In many cases, major conurbations have developed, as in the Donets Basin where 6 million people live in a series of coalescing cities. Apparently practical factors of industrial efficiency, improved climate, better housing, and cultural amenities serve to keep people in large cities of western Russia, counteracting the ideological effort to develop a more even spread of industry and settlement.

THE SOCIALIST CITY IN PERSPECTIVE

Is there such a phenomenon as the Socialist city? Urban specialists seem to feel that the strong degree of central control which exists in communist states is reflected in uniformity in terms of size, architectural style, and roles of city center and neighborhoods. In part, these differences between Socialist and Capitalist cities seem to be related to the Marxist ideology. However, a comparison of theory and reality as applied to Moscow and Czechoslovakia reveals that the Party has had to make many concessions to practicality over ideology in city and regional planning. Although public intervention in the form of manipulation of population and settlement is perhaps greater in communist countries than in other areas of the world, Marxist planners apparently find it difficult to hold down the size of cities or even prevent pollution problems. Nevertheless, the comparison of theory with reality in Socialist cities offers unique opportunities for constructing and testing cross-cultural models of urban development.

THE PREINDUSTRIAL CITY

THE PREINDUSTRIAL CITY

AN URBAN CONTRAST. A primary contrast drawn today in comparative urban study is between industrial and preindustrial cities. Such a contrast has been furthered since 1945 by interest in the "developing" countries where industrial and urban progress is taking place unevenly. In these countries the largest settlements generally appear quite different from cities in industrialized areas although they may possess a "Western" portion derived from the colonial period. Several scholars, including especially sociologists and anthropologists, have attempted to make generalizations concerning the preindustrial city. Sjoberg's (1960) attempt to develop a preindustrial urban model is based on the premise that such cities and the feudal societies that support them, whether past or present, share an imposing number of similar structural characteristics.* This model is also cross-cultural, i.e., the preindustrial city has similarities in different cultural areas.

Sjoberg feels that the most significant variable explaining differences between industrial and preindustrial cities is technology, which includes energy, tools, and know-how. The level of technology differentiates folk, feudal, and industrial societies. In the folk society the lack of any real food surplus prevents specialization in nonagricultural functions so that agglomerated settlement is restricted to villages, and the paucity of specialization inhibits the development of a class system. On the other hand, the more advanced agricultural technology of feudal society makes possible the production of sufficient food surpluses to support specialized functions and a social organization dominated by a "leisured," literate elite. The technology is sufficient for limited craft industry and commercial activities, but is almost solely based on animate, i.e., human and animal, energy. The degree of urbanization is low in feudal society—generally less than ›10 percent of the total population—but the primary points of spatial organization are recognizable as cities—called preindus-

---

*Gideon Sjoberg. *The Preindustrial City* (New York: Free Press, 1960). Many details on the preindustrial city model are taken from this source.

trial cities. Distinct from the folk and feudal societies is the industrial society, utilizing inanimate sources of energy, a complex set of tools, and specialized knowledge in the production of goods and services. To attain these, it becomes virtually imperative that large portions of an industrial society live in cities.

Since preindustrial cities are developed within feudal societies, a closer look at these societies and their social, political, and economic characteristics will make it easier to interpret them.

FEUDAL SOCIETY.   Socially, feudal society is characterized by a rigid class structure comprising a small elite or upper class, a large lower class, and certain outcastes. The elite, though small, forming perhaps less than 5 to 10 percent of the total social order, dominates both city and society. At the minimum, Sjoberg states, this literate group comprises the upper ranks of the governmental, military, religious, and educational bureaucracies and exerts the necessary social power to integrate all the specialized activities (e.g., collection and distribution of surpluses) that arise as technology changes. In such matters as extended family ties, lack of manual work, and distinct manners, dress, and speech, members of the elite are to be contrasted with the largely uneducated lower class, composed of minor government officials, merchants, lower military personnel, artisans, unskilled laborers, and part-time farmers. Still farther down the social hierarchy are the outcastes, either slaves or certain segregated groups carrying out defiling tasks, e.g., midwives, prostitutes, dancers, religious groups, etc. Mobility between classes is low, often impeded by the barrier of birth, and no real middle class can develop. Even the merchant, although necessary, is restricted in his capacity to rise, because as a potential disseminator of new and heretical ideas, he may disturb the status quo.

The primary function carried out by the elite class within feudal society is political organization. The supreme ruler and his ministers and advisors are drawn from this group, often from a few extended families that have dominated the society for generations. Political organization of state territory is facilitated by use of family ties—intermarriage if necessary—in maintaining the power structure in regional capitals. Rule of the elite is made legitimate by appeals to absolutes, i.e., "divine right" to rule by birth, e.g., the former ruler of Ethiopia, Haile Selassie. Such a position is reinforced by religious, military, and intellectual groups who are members of the elite class and dedicated to perpetuating rather than criticizing it. This pattern of authority is difficult to upset when all the elements of criticism or opposition—press, radio, assembly, and political parties—are lacking. No real functional specializations exist except those sponsored and controlled by the elite. Members of the feudal bureaucracy, instead of forming elements of balance between government and governed as they do in industrial societies, use their positions as means of self aggrandizement through promotion and graft. In such a society, social and political change are difficult. Murphey has pointed out (1954) the contrast between the West European and Chinese cities as centers of change; in the former the merchant class led a movement establishing new liberal institutions which never developed in China. Current feeling against the rule of an elite in "developing" countries of Latin America, Africa, and Asia is more understandable in the context of feudal society and its inertia with respect to change.

Owing to the dominance of the elite class and to a simple technology, economic activity in feudal society is generally quite limited. Agriculture predominates as most of the people are peasants. The elite class, although located in preindustrial cities in order to maintain control of the society, owns most of the rural land. In many feudal societies, this class chooses to invest its money in land rather than in industry or trade. No *independent* merchant class develops since capital and market are lacking; furthermore, the elite group is suspicious of people who may represent an ethnic or religious minority, handle money, and maintain frequent contact with lower classes. Entrepreneurial activity remains small scale in nature, undertakings confined usually to the home of craftsmen or to small shops in the market place. Sjoberg states that small size reflects a technology that sets barriers to capital formation, prohibits the development of a mass market for goods, and has little need for a concentration of workers on one spot. The craftsman does not specialize in one step of the mass production of a product, as he does in industrial societies, but carries the production through from beginning to end. Furthermore, he may have purchased the raw materials and marketed the product as well—often through a time-consuming process of haggling. The market for crafts is small, in great part local, with a large number of cheap items for the lower class and a small number of luxury items for the elite group. Only the latter group constitutes support for distant trade and for tertiary service activities, e.g., import of Western goods or use of professional personnel and servants. This group also subsidizes certain types of economic activity, e.g., industries or public works. Other aspects that restrict the scope of economic activities include fluctuating prices, a barter system, nonstandardization of goods, and lack of any credit system. Credit is particularly lacking in a society where the elite group feels that the accumulation of capital through profit-making and money lending for interest represent opportunities by other groups to gain power and, therefore, is a potential threat.

The above summary of the feudal society in terms of its social, political, and economic characteristics serves as an introduction to the spatial aspects of preindustrial cities—the focal points for the organization of this society.

EXTERNAL ORGANIZATION OF SPACE. The external relations of cities in feudal societies are dominated by three characteristics: concentration of functions in a primate city; significance of the administrative function; and predominance of short-range central-place activities.

When the political, social, and economic functions of one state are concentrated in a single city, it becomes "primate" at the expense of the others. Such a condition generally is helped not only by the social power of the elite class in one city but also by the lack of industrial and commercial development that might lead to the rise of other cities. Instead, the elite group tends to direct the location of government buildings, state industries, and cultural activities to the capital city. Such a pattern of concentration was continued by colonial powers and has been retained since independence. One can think of many examples of primate cities in "developing" countries, e.g., Bangkok, Nairobi, and Lima, but naming the second and third cities of these countries is not easy.

In a society where political functions dominate over economic ones, the elite group establishes the hierarchy of urban centers on the basis of regional administrative control. The primary functions represented in these cities are governmental affairs related to such things as agricultural distribution, communications, education, social services, military garrisons, and even state industry. The regularly spaced network of walled cities in China serves as a good example of this pattern of spatial organization. Generally, external relations based primarily on administration are not reciprocal; the cities influence the countryside, but the rural area has very little impact on the urban centers. Overall the transport system is poorly developed, but the best accessibility is provided from the primate city to the regional administrative centers which have less contact with one another. As exemplified by the early rise of imperial Rome, food and raw materials feed into the primate city, and there is little basis for separate regional development unless sponsored by the controlling elite class. Attempts to change this pattern are often opposed because the elite fears the rise of regional opposition. The civil war of Nigeria, although based in great part on ethnic differences between the people, illustrates the problem of regional antagonisms in a "developing" country.

The economic segment of external support for preindustrial cities is dominated by central-place functions that are too limited to maintain large cities. Within the feudal society are small cities or towns that serve as places of administration and as marketing centers for food and craft articles; some of these towns also serve as transfer points for shipping goods to the large cities. City populations may fluctuate greatly during the course of a week, increasing on special market days—when farmers pour in from the rural areas to sell their goods to the city resident and to buy things in the markets—only to be drastically reduced the rest of the week; the role of religious celebrations also influences this population influx. Many of the political functions mentioned above are actually central-place activities and provide indirect economic support for the preindustrial cities; examples include the regional drawing power of school, dispensary, police or post office, and court. However, certain regional service functions—financial, professional, and recreation—are lacking. In contrast to the small market towns, which are administrative centers first of all, stand the large primate cities that possess rather specialized central place functions for the country as reflected in shopping district, church, university, and cultural attractions. In rare cases, certain cities exhibit rather unusual drawing power as religious centers, e.g., Mecca or Benares.

INTERNAL ORGANIZATION OF SPACE. Few geographers and other specialists have analyzed the organization of space within the pre-industrial city. An interesting conceptual approach to this problem has been developed by Paul English (1968) and is based on the perception by individuals in a preindustrial society of what the urban environment should provide: security and privacy, separation of private and public areas, and rational use of space. In looking at Herat, Afghanistan, English analyzes these three qualities of the urban environment and concludes that elements of order and control exist in this preindustrial city.*
—The plan and architecture of Herat were devised to provide citizens with enclosure, protection, and privacy (see fig. 12.1). At great cost and effort high walls were constructed around the old city to insulate it while contacts with the outer world were carefully filtered through the five gates in the walls. Inside the walls the three main large structures are the citadel, mosque, and granary, all of which provided security and comfort to residents in one form or another. In the residential quarters space is also organized for security and privacy. Streets and lanes are narrow and twisting with many sharp turns and frequently a cul-de-sac; the lack of traffic and the impracticality of using street addresses add to the privacy.

*Paul Ward English, "The Preindustrial City of Herat, Afghanistan," paper given at the Annual Meeting of the Association of American Geographers, Washington, D.C., August 1968. Many of the details on internal structure are taken from this source.

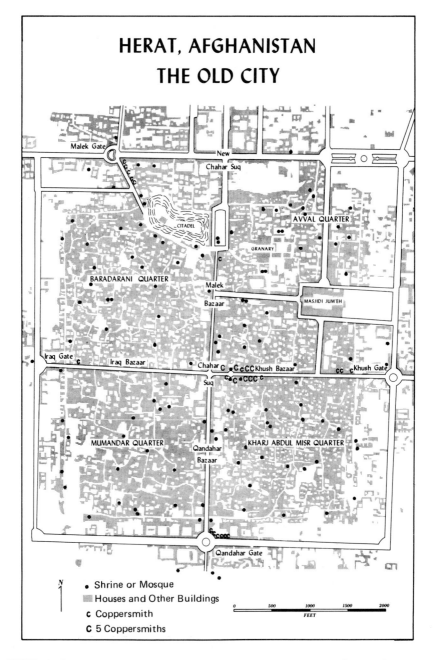

HERAT, AFGHANISTAN
THE OLD CITY

Malek Gate

New
Chahar Suq

CITADEL

AVVAL QUARTER

GRANARY

BARADARANI   QUARTER

Malek

Bazaar

MASJIDI JUM'EH

Iraq Gate

Iraq Bazaar

Chahar

Khush Bazaar

Khush Gate

Suq

MUMANDAR QUARTER

Qandahar

Bazaar

KHARJ ABDUL MISR QUARTER

Qandahar Gate

N

• Shrine or Mosque

▓ Houses and Other Buildings

c Coppersmith

C 5 Coppersmiths

0   500   1000   1500   2000

FEET

FIGURE 12.1 The old city of Herat, Afghanistan illustrates many of the features of the preindustrial city. On this map are noted the walls, gates, bazaars, quarters, concentrations of coppersmiths, and religious buildings. (Courtesy of P. W. English, 1968.)

These neighborhoods are divided into cell-like compounds with doors studded and barred and windows small, inaccessible, and covered by grills. Outside the old city, the perception of environment is different as new apartment houses reflect a changing mentality and attitude.

—Public and private space are clearly differentiated in Herat. Conventional institutions—city hall, court house, library, playgrounds, fire stations, etc.—are nonexistent except for a mayor's office and police station, and points of spatial organization for the community are restricted to four bazaars, a few parks and gardens, and the courtyards of the mosques (see fig. 12.1). English states that here the men of the city practice their trades, barter for goods, worship together, drink tea, and converse. Such public space is cared for by the government with the daily hiring of men to clean the water channels in the bazaar, dampen the main roadways, and protect and tend the flower gardens. On the other hand, private life and space is centered in the residential quarter. However, the narrow lanes and alleyways are mutual ground and are cared for by no one resulting in constricted, smelly areas full of garbage and sewage. The water supply is directed by gravity through the city along these lanes and is generally polluted, especially at the lower levels of the system. Adequate public services in terms of sewage, water, and even power apparently are not generally characteristic of the preindustrial city. The absence of street lights is noticeable too.

—Space in Herat is actually used rationally, being well adapted to the climate, economy, and social practices of the city. The overall design for the old city is the Hellenistic quadrilateral split by four major avenues that provide access to the core for wheeled vehicles and marching men (see fig. 12.1). "Medinas," the old, walled inner cities of Muslim areas in Africa and the Near East are examples of this plan. The bazaars with shops and stalls of artisans and traders are located along the major avenues. Space is organized to enable residents of the quarters in the old city to walk to a bazaar in ten minutes or less. Daily necessities, such as bread, sugar, and tea can be purchased almost anywhere along these avenues, but more expensive and permanent goods like copper pots and cloth are sold at the central bazaar—the Chahar Suq—the point of minimum travel for most people in the city. Under this system of organizing space, Herat has 5,500 shops within easy walking distance of 80,000 people and still provides for the minimal wheeled traffic that exists in this pedestrian society. The lanes of residential quarters, despite their odors, also represent a rational use of space since they are adequate for their purpose, provide some shade, and are not wasteful of land. The houses which lie off these lanes in a maze of walls are small (about 30 feet square) and are built of sun-dried brick faced with mud. Such dwellings are adapted to the large diurnal temperature ranges of Herat's desert climate and maximize the amount of courtyard space available for use.

Urban space in Herat, therefore, has been organized to maximize security and privacy, provide public areas, and, most important, maintain contact between individuals in a pedestrian society. The use of walls, narrow streets, and a close distribution of focal points such as mosque and bazaar all serve these goals. It is not difficult to assume a similar perception of space in other preindustrial cities.

The result of such use of space is high population densities and a compact internal structure. The old central portions of Calcutta and Delhi have densities up to 450,000 persons per square mile or 650 to the acre; by contrast, Jones states (1966, 106) that in Britain the densities of industrial slums are only 250 persons per acre. Such densities are even more notable when the low profile of preindustrial cities is considered. The concentration of urban functions in the core of preindustrial cities leads to centripetal forces which are reflected by the elite class being located near the center with access to other members of this group. Although their dwellings may be larger and include a courtyard, this group is small, and high densities among other residents in the center are maintained by the combination here of workplace with residence. Large-scale centrifugal expansion is not yet feasible for urban residents, and new migrants to cities cluster on the edge in dense squatter settlements. Therefore, population density gradients for preindustrial cities exhibit much more uniform spatial patterns from core to fringe than do "industrial" cities, a feature pointed out by Berry and his colleagues (Berry, Simmons, and Tennant, 1963).

The primary organizing points of life in Herat, as in most preindustrial cities, are the quarters and bazaars (see fig. 12.1). Although they have been mentioned above as part of the general discussion of space in Herat, it is helpful to examine them in more detail.

—The preindustrial urban *quarter* is generally a social unit where people are bound together by ties of ethnic group, religion, occupation, family, or common origin. Each quarter may form a nearly independent community isolated by walls, and have its own church, market, customs, and laws. In the Near East different Muslim sects, Jews, Armenians, and Christians are often identified with a distinct section of the city. This segregation by ethnic groups, which are generally associated with specific occupations, often leads to a unique social organization within that quarter for matters of leadership, education, and welfare. Relationships between government and quarter are handled by appointed officials who collect taxes, select draftees for the army, and record such things as sales of property and vital statistics. As English explains, the residential quarter has been a common organizing principle of preindustrial urban life. The absence of distinct social groups in the quarters of

Herat leads him to the conclusion that several variables account for the pattern of residential location in preindustrial cities: supplementing the normal factor of segregation by social or economic group are others such as availability of space, access to work, and nearness of family or friends.

—The *bazaars* of preindustrial cities are organizing points for commerce and transportation in the city and the region in which it is situated. Herat is a regional marketing center for the million or so people who live in the Hari Rud valley of western Afghanistan, and the bazaars serve both the periodic and regular needs of this external area in addition to those of the city itself (see fig. 12.2). Each morning peasants from neighboring villages set up temporary stalls in the open places of the bazaars and sell melons, tomatoes, and fruits to the urbanites. On Sundays and Wednesdays, periodic bazaars are held near two of the gates where the more valuable merchandize—woven silk, hides, wheat, and animals—are brought to market.

Supplementing the temporary stalls set up during the daily and biweekly markets are the more permanent shops of the bazaars. English has provided us with some details on these shops of which there are 5,500 along six linear miles of bazaar. This number amounts to one shop for every 15 urban residents. Such shops provide the basic staples of life with one out of three selling either candy, cloth, spices, fruit, or a cup of tea. The traditional artisan skills are also represented with the most

FIGURE 12.2. A main street in Herat, Afghanistan, showing bazaar areas. (Courtesy of P. W. English.)

numerous types being shoemakers, tailors, carpenters, ironsmiths, and coppersmiths (see fig. 12.1). Although the preindustrial technology is dominant, imports of modern technology have begun to appear, e.g., precolored yarn and factory-woven cloth.

Commercial land use in Herat shows some degree of areal differentiation within the cities and bazaars. English finds that central location is highly valued and the best shops are found near the intersection of the four bazaars and adjacent to the mosque. The latter section of the bazaar had a domed roof (until 1930) and is occupied by dealers in high-value, permanent goods such as cloth, copper, jewelry, carpets, leather, and books. As in many cities of the Near East, each trade is not only localized, with producers and retailers of the same type of good occupying adjacent stalls, but is also located in particular streets or districts convenient to the clientele (e.g., coppersmiths and grain sellers). More ubiquitous services mentioned above (e.g., candy) are widely distributed. The turnover in shop occupants is rapid as the proprietors have varying success in paying the higher rent of the center ($10 per month) plus the "key money" necessary to initially rent a shop. Many shopkeepers may move to fringe areas of the bazaar where rent and key money are much less. It appears, therefore, that the bazaars of Herat are organized on the basis of economic factors like land rent and type of market. The traditional locational factors of preindustrial cities—religion, status, and guild organization—appear to be less important here. Most crafts are still hereditary and guilds exist, but only to act as liaison between government and artisan rather than to regulate marketing through monopolies. Furthermore, the central position of most guilds in training and social activities is lacking in Herat.

THE COLONIAL CITY.   The contrast between industrial and preindustrial cities is theoretically significant, but such a division is not inclusive enough for urban typology. Many of the largest cities in states dominated by feudal societies possess external relationships and internal patterns that are alien to this society. In most cases these characteristics developed during the colonial period when various industrial powers superimposed their political, social, and economic patterns on portions of the feudal societies. This impact was most often felt in one or more major cities, often seaports, where the zones of contact were greatest and entrepreneurial activity was generated for the first time—although under European supervision. Colonial powers viewed their cities primarily as bases for administration or commercial activity and only secondarily as centers of production or cultural change.

Murphey points out (1968) that with the coming of colonialism a Western type of city was in effect imported by way of the expanding European nuclei as they developed trade bases on the maritime fringes of Asia. These coastal settlements are well illustrated through cities like Shanghai, Saigon, Bangkok, Rangoon, Calcutta, and Karachi. As these Asian cities evolved, existing domestic patterns of economic activity— formerly focused inland and on many small points of external contact—were reoriented through a process of concentration; the most accessible places (mostly ports) became the nuclei of modernizing trends and the gates to the Western world. Virtually all of the largest coastal or near-coastal cities in Asia owe the bulk of their growth and essential characteristics since the seventeenth century to Western traders. In Africa and Latin America, coastal cities did not serve as overall points of economic and cultural organization of space as they did in Asia except in certain cases like Capetown, Rio de Janeiro, and Buenos Aires.

The most significant internal urban pattern that emerged from this series of colonial contacts was the "dual city," where the preindustrial portion, described above, contrasted with the new Western area established by residents of the alien European society. The latter community possessed a regular plan, with broad, tree-lined streets separating neat compounds, and bungalows interspersed with public institutions such as law courts, clubs, churches, and hospitals. A commercial section was also present. Densities of population were relatively light in comparison to those of the preindustrial portion of the city. Such a sharp cleavage between preindustrial and industrial portions of colonial cities were developed in China and India. However, the number of European settlers in Asia was relatively small and it was no real problem to separate Western and indigenous groups. On the other hand, European settlers in parts of Africa and Latin America were more numerous, and the problem of separating them from indigenous groups in cities was handled quite differently in the two areas. Differences in the colonial cities of Asia, Africa, and Latin America are illustrated by four examples.

—Many of the coastal cities of China were transformed through foreign impact as treaty ports. Through conflict or Western pressure a rather large number of cities including Shanghai and Canton became commercial cities as special privileges were given to various western countries. Commercial and dock sections of these cities were constructed together with rather extensive residential districts. The Shanghai "bund" or waterfront with port facilities, warehouses, banks, and offices, became a symbol of this external influence.

—The impact of Britain on urban areas of India was perhaps more widespread than in most colonies because of the many functions that were carried out. British sections of towns not only included the commercial, port, and railroad areas, but also residential sections for British administrative (civil lines), military (cantonments), and railway personnel. A buffer zone such as a park or railroad separated these attractive residential quarters from the irregular preindustrial portions of great cities such as Karachi, Delhi, and Calcutta. In the postwar period of independence these areas have been taken over by Indian residents, often employed in the same occupations.

—In Africa, colonial cities of Britain, France, Belgium, and Portugal exhibited varying degrees of cleavage between industrial and preindustrial functions and forms. However, the preindustrial city was generally less evident in the tribal societies of Subsaharan Africa, and two special urban forms evolved to house the indigenous peoples who migrated to the Western cities—the "location" and "compound." The former represented the section of the colonial city where Negroes lived after migrating from the tribal village. A "compound," on the other hand, was a special living area for Negro employees of large companies, e.g., the gold and copper mines of South Africa and Rhodesia, respectively. Although the living conditions in the "compound" were generally better than in the "location," the average Negro migrant apparently preferred to live in the latter because the social aspects of tribal life were preserved there.

—Latin American cities present still another problem for the student developing an urban typology (see fig. 12.3). Only a few pre-Columbian cities existed in Latin America and of these apparently only the Aztec centers may have influenced later colonial urban development. Earlier urban traditions of the Maya and Toltec, if they existed, had died out. Therefore, most Spanish and Portuguese cities in Latin America were subsequently laid out in planned form. The focus of the grid layout was a square flanked by cathedral or church (Violich, 1962, p. 177). The market was established nearby and several wide avenues linked the more important buildings. Residential areas for the well-to-do were built near the center with outside walls of the dwellings built to the street line and concealing patios, gardens, and interior dwellings. In this type of arrangement, which is similar to that found in Europe, the quality of the house or apartment is not revealed to the passerby in the streets. The elite colonial group lived near the center because of the necessity for contacts with each other in controlling society.

The geographical characteristics of colonial cities mentioned above seem to correspond to varying relationships between colonizers and the colonized. Basically, all relationships in the colonial city represented the

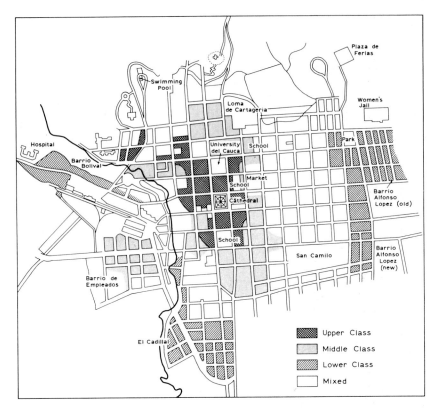

FIGURE 12.3. The city of Popayán, Colombia in 1950. This city illustrates how the pattern of residential structure in Latin American cities is often reversed from that of the North American city as upper classes tend to cluster near central institutions. (From *Andean City* by A. H. Whitford. Reprinted by permission of Michigan State University.)

domination of one society by another, often reflected spatially in the presence of a foreign urban group within an indigenous hinterland. Horvath (1968), however, has established three aspects of domination that appear to affect the internal spatial patterns of such cities:

—China, India, and many of the colonies of Asia and Africa: imperialistic colonialism dominated in these areas where the mother country made *little attempt to allow settlers to enter*. In these colonies, the foreign portion of the city was small as compared with the preindustrial section, although in India the British group was unusually large.

—South Africa, Rhodesia, and certain other African colonies: colonization in these areas exhibited *no attempt at assimilation* of the indigenous people. Since preindustrial cities were small or lacking, associations between colonizer and colonized are marked by special urban settlements like the "location" and "compound."

—Latin American colonies: colonization in these areas was characterized by settler colonization with an emphasis on *assimilation* of the indigenes. These colonial cities were generally laid out as newly planned units and all groups—Spanish or Portugese, Indian, and mestizo—were part of the urban unit without the sharp separation recognized in the dual cities of Africa and Asia; the elite group, however, did tend to be segregated near the center of the city.

In all colonial cities, a social structure evolved which included the elite colonizers, other foreigners (e.g., Indians in East Africa), and the educated and noneducated indigenous people. The wide differences within and between these groups led to great urban variations. The fact that the European elite group differed more in language, education, wealth, and way of life from the educated indigenous people (the elite in a preindustrial city) than the latter did from the noneducated indigenous group led to the sharp "Western" and non-"Western" contrasts. After independence these relationships between colonizer and colonized altered and the cities reflect these changes.

The differing spatial patterns of colonial cities are also related to the nature of the particular colonial group. The British group was composed of state and business interests, both reflected in the railroad, administrative, military, and commercial land uses. On the other hand, the Spanish urban class was based on the integrated institutions of state, church, and land; the conservative nature of these groups is still evident in Latin American cities as wealth is invested in land rather than commercial or industrial ventures, and urban functions may exhibit a lack of diversification.

THE INDUSTRIALIZING CITY

In the years since World War II, preindustrial cities, differing in the degree to which they were altered by colonial influence, have undergone considerable transformation. As growth centers within independent "developing" states, these cities have attempted to initiate programs of industrialization. In China a planned "socialist" solution to the transformation of society has been attempted which bears similarities to the process carried out in the Soviet Union. In most countries of the "developing" world, Western help for industrialization and urbanization has been provided for a variety of reasons. In some cases the motive for this help has been political, as communist and non-communist ideologies sought to influence the "Third World." More often, the interest is economic as Western states recognize the interdependence of world trading units.

Overriding both of these has been the social attempt to assist "developing" people to gain the benefits of modern technology.

How has this process of transformation of preindustrial cities been carried out? Obviously the colonial cities that are now under indigenous control underwent some transformation in the past, particularly in their commercial and residential patterns. The preindustrial section of such cities often had already expanded beyond the walls of the old city where "suburbs" began to develop. In the postwar period, however, a series of new processes have taken place which together help to explain urban transformation in an industrializing city. All of them have contributed to making the preindustrial city what it has not been before—a center of production and cultural change. Three of the most significant of these processes are: technological change; migration of rural residents to form squatter sections on the edges of cities; and locational changes in the decision-making process.

TECHNOLOGICAL CHANGE   As mentioned earlier, the preindustrial city is dominated by central-place functions, generally the provision of marketing and other ubiquitous services for the surrounding area. In the past limited technology permitted very little specialization of functions, especially manufacturing. However, with independence the situation changed in most "developing" countries as external support began to flow in through investments by former colonial powers, exploitation of resources, and foreign aid. Much depended on the resources available. Some raw materials like copper exhibited price fluctuations and a country like Chile had problems. Other countries with oil possessed a resource that became more and more important. Fox has pointed out (1968, 14) that a major impetus to postwar urban transformation in Iraq, especially that in Baghdad, was the expansion of the oil industry. Revenues from oil were placed in the hands of a board, appointed by the King, which distributed the funds for various development processes; in Baghdad streets were paved and lighted, sewage services expanded, industries added, and flood protection provided. In most of the preindustrial countries the primary result of the industrialization trend is rapid changes in technology. The primary cities of the "developing" world now exhibit many Western characteristics such as high-rise apartment houses, office buildings and hotels, power lines, public utilities, factories, cinemas, and consumer goods. Automobiles and buses appear on the streets although they are usually imported. Industrial cities like Monterrey in Mexico and Jamshedpur in India illustrate city specialization in steel production. New districts of apartment houses have been built, often for certain governmental, professional, or factory groups that display varying degrees of heterogeneity. However, residents of these new districts frequently lack shopping facilities or means of transportation to work.

These attempts at technological change are superimposed upon a feudal society. The elite class is under considerable external and internal pressure to alter the old colonial pattern through modernization of the urban structure. Such changes, however, threaten the existence of feudal society, as a middle class, composed of technicians, administrators, and skilled workers, emerges. The actual change of the feudal society may be very slow as is evidenced by the continued existence of such elite groups in most of the "developing" states; in Africa, independence often led to new forms of elite control as certain Black rulers established dictatorships in which the benefits of modernization were not felt by most people. Social change thus lags behind technology in most preindustrial cities of the world, the result often being considerable political instability as liberal groups agitate for reform of society.

MIGRATION OF RURAL RESIDENTS TO FORM SQUATTER SECTIONS ON THE EDGES OF CITIES (Mountjoy, 1976). Perhaps the most important result of the modernization trend in preindustrial cities is the development of a large rural-urban migration. Villagers, often males, from all over the country are attracted to the larger cities by employment and promises of a better life. This rural-urban migration is responsible for urbanization rates in "developing" countries that dwarf the speed of this process when it occurred in the "developed" countries (see table 12.1). In 1920, for example, the latter had two-thirds of the world's urban population but this total only amounted to 180 million people. By 1960, urban population in the two areas was relatively even at about 380 million each. In 2000, however, the projection is that the "developing" countries will possess two-thirds of the total and the amount will be 1.5 billion! It is apparent that urbanization is increasing at a geometrical rate and that the "developing" part of the world is the chief factor. Furthermore, these countries are still relatively low in urbanization! In other words, they may have only 20-40 per cent of population in cities and yet because the few cities are increasing so fast, urban numbers are larger than ever before. United Nations statistics show, for example, that since 1950 the number of cities in the "developing" world possessing over one million inhabitants rose from 80 to 150. Evidently only the largest cities are usually able to offer the economic opportunities that attract the rural migrants. In some cases only the capital city can do this and primacy, discussed in Chapter 6, becomes characteristic of the urban system. Certainly the urban hierarchy is unbalanced in contrast to that of "developed" world countries.

The contrast between "developed" and "developing" worlds in terms of rate of urbanization is supplemented by another difference that is

TABLE 12.1

World urban population:	1920		1960		2000	
	No. (mill.)	Percent of world urban population	No. (mill.)	Percent of world urban population	No. (mill.)	Percent of world urban population
Total urban pop.	267		760		2,337	
Developed area	180	67	389	51	784	33
Europe	113	42	188	25	290	12
N. America	48	17	115	14	253	10
S. Union	16	7	78	11	222	10
Other	3	1	8	1	19	1
Developing areas	87	33	371	49	1,553	67
East Asia	40	14	147	18	425	17
South Asia	27	11	118	15	568	24
L. America	13	5	69	11	342	16
Other	7	3	37	5	218	10

Source: United Nations, *Population Studies*, No. 44, 1969.

much more serious: urbanization in Europe and the United States *followed* industrialization while in the Third World it *precedes* it (Dwyer, 1968, 358). Thus the early diffusion of the Industrial Revolution created the employment which could absorb the rural migrants released when the inefficient three-field system was replaced by one based on rotations. It was possible, therefore, for the standard of living to rise not only for the fewer people remaining in rural areas but also for the migrants to cities. In the case of the latter groups, birth rates gradually began to fall. This situation is impossible however, in "developing" areas today. Here population pressure in *both* country and city is great. Owing to high rural birth rates, these populations continue to increase in spite of outmigration to the cities. Therefore, population pressure on the land is persistent and fuels the migrations. On the other hand, the cities lack the industry to absorb migrants who are subsequently forced into tertiary tasks such as domestic servants.* Underemployment as well as unemployment then becomes a characteristic of these groups. If a factory should be added, the rate of rural-urban migration only increases and the rate of unemployment stays the same. Finally, the spread between death rates and birth rates is greater now than in earlier days of urbanization in

---

*An exception to the pattern is Singapore. In this city state, the rural-urban migration is reduced while birth rates are also much lower through public education, free contraceptives, and skillful use of incentives. Finally, industry is present to absorb surplus population.

Europe and the United States. Medical technology today permits death rates to be reduced rapidly while birth rates fall more slowly among the rural migrants once they reach cities since village mores still prevail. This contrast between urban processes in "developed" and "developing" areas is illustrated by figures from Austria and India. In 1890, Austria had only 12 per cent of its population in cities and yet that portion of the empire was 30 per cent industrialized, thus providing a basis for absorption of future rural-urban migrants. In 1951, however, India, also 12 per cent urbanized, was only 11 per cent industrialized. This lag of industry behind urban development is a major dilemma of the "developing" world.

Given this rapid growth of "developing" world cities from rural-urban migration, where do these people live? The answer is simple: in squatter settlements which now form significant portions of most large cities of the "developing" world (see fig. 12.4). Their importance makes them perhaps the major new settlement form of the second half of the 20th Century. The extent of this phenomenon is shown in the table which illustrates the magnitude of these uncontrolled settlements (see table 12.2). They are frequently located on the periphery of these cities and/or on steep land which is generally unattractive for other uses; they are not unorganized, as reports show that most possess systems of government, often a carryover from the rural village. Many are developed by rural migrants who go to the site directly but others are the result of organized movements by groups who have spent earlier periods in the slums of the city. These settlements are known by different names in different countries, e.g., *ranchos* in Caracas and *favelas* in Rio de Janeiro. Structures in these settlements are shanties built largely of scrap material—timber, oil drums, zinc sheets, planks, palm, adobe, and straw. Services like water, sewage, electricity, and streets are generally lacking.

Some urban specialists feel that the squatter settlements could be the norm of the future for "developing" world cities, since they appear to be increasing in size; causative factors make them almost inevitable. A logical question is whether or not they should be legalized and assisted by the authorities. In other words, if they are inevitable anyway, why not improve their environments as much as possible? The squatter settlement appears to be the only method by which rapid urban growth with low-income families can be accomplished. At the same time, it must be kept in mind that this urbanization is really ruralization in a concentrated form. Villages are, in a sense, recreated and the residents remain part of a folk society. If this is true, it would appear that these cities in the future have less opportunity to become "centers of change" than European and American cities did. Certainly the rapid urbanization is hindering attempts at national planning.

FIGURE 12.4. A squatter settlement in Bogota, Colombia. The hillside location is often related to the fact that such areas are not yet occupied by other dwellings and to the better natural drainage.

TABLE 12.2
Developing Countries: Extent of Uncontrolled Settlement in Various Cities

Country	City	Year	Uncontrolled settlement Total (000s)	% city pop.
Turkey	Ankara	1970	750	60
Iraq	Baghdad	1965	500	29
Afghanistan	Kabul	1968	100	21
India	Calcutta	1961	2,220	33
Indonesia	Djakarta	1961	725	25
Philippines	Manila	1968	1,100	35
Tanzania	Dar es Salaam	1967	98	36
Mexico	Mexico City	1966	1,500	46
Venezuela	Caracas	1964	556	35
Brazil	Rio de Janeiro	1961	900	27
Peru	Lima	1969	1000	36

Source: UN General Assembly, *Housing, Building and Planning: Problems and Priorities in Human Settlements,* Annex III, p. 55, 1970.

*LOCATIONAL CHANGES IN THE DECISION-MAKING PRO-
CESS* A third major process found in the industrializing city is a
change from extra-national to local orientation in the decision-making
that is fundamental to the growth and prosperity of these cities. Larimore has shown (1968) how replacement of Europeans at all levels of
employment by Africans is changing the external and internal relations
of cities in Uganda, Kenya, and Tanzania. Not only is the locus of political, social, and economic control shifted from foreign areas to cities in
these countries, but also the internal patterns are altered as well. Although such replacements of personnel are costly and represent a loss of
efficiency, the political factor of nationalism remains predominant. Political functions have been Africanized most rapidly, affecting governmental offices in all but the smallest urban areas. Religious and social
institutions are also rapidly coming under the control of indigenous personnel. On the other hand, privately controlled economic establishments
have made the least rapid changes as many firms remain in the hands of
Europeans and Asians; only in the small centers have changes been observed.

Larimore states that frontal attack by governmental policy on retail
establishments owned by Asians in small centers of East Africa began
some years ago. In these *duka* retail centers, specific national plans have
been implemented to increase substantially the African share of this
trade, either by direct subsidization and expanded training of traders or
by setting up cooperatives and state retail chains. Apparently, this policy
has already caused a drift of Asian traders to the towns and cities, and in
a few years the ubiquitous *dukawalla* (*duka* proprietor) may cease to be a
feature of the landscape in small urban centers; only the large businesses
owned by Asians will continue to have a future in East Africa.

The large economic establishments in the primary cities, especially in
the capitals, generally remain under the direct control of overseas owners. Therefore, indigenous *direction* of trade in agricultural surpluses for
overseas markets and of the production and distribution of manufactured products is a matter of the future; however, local authorities may
have an effect on the *distribution* of commercial and industrial land use.

The change to indigenous control of political and economic activity
in the cities of East Africa illustrates a key process of an *industrializing*
city, which may represent a significant variation of the models of the
preindustrial and *colonial* cities in other areas. Before independence, the
British colonial elite controlled the political and economic decision-
making positions by limiting access to necessary schooling and training.
Certain economic positions that were not monopolized by the colonials
were open to the Asians. Lastly, various African groups maintained cer-

tain institutions in their own particular residential quarter of the city. These quarters, therefore, exhibited a cohesiveness reflected in a common ethnic and occupational status. After independence this pattern of monopoly of position was discarded as the foreign colonial elite was replaced by an indigenous group of decision-makers. According to Larimore, equal access to positions by all citizens appropriately trained by a mass educational system has now become national policy. Individuals attaining positions of political, social, and economic control will be selected primarily by achieved rather than ascribed status within the national society. Thus, increasing numbers of governmentally educated Africans challenged the preponderance of Europeans and Asians in these positions. Larimore finds that this new class of Africans is heterogeneous because it comes from all portions of the former feudal society rather than through quotas set by existing tribal groups. Such changes in employment through national policy will probably have great effects in altering the existing pattern of society, reducing not only the dependence on foreigners but also the indigenous class barriers. These changes are bound to affect the city as the old homogeneous quarter is broken up, and commercial and industrial areas replace the bazaar and handicraft districts.

THE PREINDUSTRIAL CITY IN PERSPECTIVE

The above generalizations concerning the preindustrial city and its variations are made with the knowledge that this model has been criticized on several counts. Wheatley (1963) has questioned many aspects of such a theoretical construct, especially the static nature of Sjoberg's city. The point is well made and, therefore, the concepts of the colonial and industrializing cities are introduced to provide a more dynamic aspect. Sjoberg's lack of attention to the urban hierarchy, also mentioned by Wheatley, illustrates a questionable subordination of economic concerns to things political-religious and ignores the city as a system in space with a specific series of functional interrelationships. Finally, Sjoberg's reliance on secondary European sources for much of his empirical data covering such a broad model increases the possibilities of overlooking significant cultural differences such as the role of guilds, position of merchants, and the importance of geomancy. Nevertheless, Sjoberg's contribution should not be minimized as it represents the first real attempt to develop a cross-cultural model of the preindustrial city upon which other scholars can build.

CHAPTER 13

GENERALIZATIONS
ABOUT CITIES

A primary purpose of this book is to emphasize the spatial foundations that cities have in common. Although it is true that cities differ from each other and that each is unique in certain characteristics, a more fundamental way of understanding them geographically is to ask what spatial traits they have in common. Once a common framework of urban spatial organization is established, comparisons between cities can be made and the differences recognized and explained. This focus on common urban models and how they fit in the real world has been utilized in the 12 preceding chapters. Even the chapters on comparative urban geography, while dealing with differences between American, West European, Socialist, and preindustrial cities, illustrate elements they also share. It is logical then to summarize this book by asking the following question: What *selective* generalizations concerning the spatial attributes of cities can be made about all cities that have a population of over 20,000, pointing out where possible the variations represented by different cultures?

CITIES ARE DIFFICULT TO DEFINE

Cities represent but one level of the continuum of agglomerated settlement designated by the terms hamlet, village, town, city, and metropolis. Although large size and a high skyline are sometimes indicative of a city, political, economic, and social characteristics are more commonly used as criteria. A city has legal status, generally through incorporation and possession of a charter giving the citizens power to govern, levy taxes, and provide services for the inhabitants. However, a city also implies a degree of functional specialization and "way of life" that are not apparent in the village. As the city enlarges its interaction with external areas, specialization of activities increases: for example, goods are not only exchanged but also stored, sold, processed, insured, advertised, and distributed. Furthermore, the interaction of people provides for those advances in engineering, technology, education, religion, and the arts which we call civilization. At the same time, the people living in cities become more heterogeneous and the pattern of social relationships becomes quite complex in contrast to that of a village. Although the residents of a city may find it difficult to identify and participate, they benefit from a wide variety of cultural and economic opportunities.

URBANIZATION APPEARS TO BE A UNIVERSAL TREND THROUGHOUT THE WORLD

Everywhere in the world the degree of urbanization is increasing, and more and more people are living in larger agglomerated settlements. These changes are most evident in the United States where a whole series of new terms exist to describe the changing urban landscape. The single city has grown beyond its legal limits as an "urbanized area" composed of a variety of suburbs, whose components consist of space-eating subdivisions, industrial parks, and airports. The total urbanized area and its zone of influence is referred to as a metropolitan area and when two or more of these coalesce we have a conurbation. A series of adjacent conurbations is called a megalopolis. This increasing degree of urbanization is also affecting the lower ends of the agglomerated settlement continuum as the hamlet, village, and town establish more permanent contacts with cities and their forms are altered accordingly.

Therefore, larger and larger percentages of American population are living in cities, especially in the larger cities referred to as metropolitan areas and conurbations. In 1975 over two-thirds of the United States population lived in Standard Metropolitan Statistical Areas. In other parts of the world, the same trend of urbanization is evident but to a lesser degree. In 1900 only 5.5 percent of world population lived in cities over 100,000 while in 1975 the figure was over 20 percent. In certain countries of Europe 50-60 percent of the population is considered urban, and conurbations are increasingly evident, especially in Britain, Benelux, and West Germany. In the developing countries, the percentage of population living in cities remains small but it is increasing rapidly and is marked by a concentration in single primate cities and by continued high urban birth rates.

HISTORICAL CHANGES IN URBAN SPATIAL ORGANIZATION REFLECT IN GREAT PART THE DEGREE OF CONTROL EXERCISED BY COLLECTIVE VS. ELITE GROUPS

An intriguing theme of urban history for the geographer is the way in which control of spatial organization in the city has fluctuated between collective and elite groups. It appears that the contributions of the two groups to urban growth were different. The elite group was better able to organize the technological forces of urban expansion, both in terms of external means of support and in internal design. On the other hand, the collective group represented interaction between people and participation in community affairs.

Thus, one way of looking at the different periods of urban development is to view each in terms of the interplay of collective and elite control, particularly with reference to spatial organization. As an aid to this approach, a series of sub-hypotheses are tested in Chapter II of this book. These tests reveal that collective control was most apparent in the early village, Greek city state, medieval city, and suburb. In all of these cities participation was facilitated by the limited size of urban unit and the balance between controlling groups. In the case of the Greek city state, participation was increased by the status of citizenship and was reflected in urban forms like the agora and theater. The medieval city, on the other hand, was responsible for the first real municipal organization of space backed up by town law which gave the middle class certain rights as reflected in city hall and market square.

The other periods of urban history illustrate the power of elite groups to organize external and internal space although perhaps at the cost of collective participation. The early Mesopotamian rulers, for example, were able to exploit a river plain environment for food surpluses, thereby creating support for perhaps the first real urban specialization as seen in forms like palaces, temples, graneries, and barracks. External control of space by elite groups reached even greater heights under Rome when the engineer created roads (still seen today) that bound together the first continental empire directed by a single city. In the Renaissance and Baroque periods, strong absolutist kings had the power to completely redesign city areas to reflect their own grandeur. Finally, the industrial city reflects the urban control exerted by a new group—the bankers, entrepreneurs, industrialists—who were able to mass the forces of production in creating new urban forms like factory, tenement, Central Business District, and skyscraper.

The modern city seems to reflect both groups. In the United States many major decisions on urban development are made by an elite group of businessmen and government officials who frequently are isolated from collective citizen input. This separation between elite and collective decision-making is most evident in the overall balance of services available in a city. Frequently, only those services that make a profit are emphasized and the public environment, which includes parks and recreation, utilities, and civic centers, may suffer. However, sometimes even these services are turned down by the collective group because of tax increases. This imbalance between private and public environments, which is often found in American cities, is less evident in West European and Soviet cities. In these areas the public environment is stressed because most people are more dependent on civic center, parks, and utilities that exist in the central city. They lack the mobility to escape to the suburbs to live, work, and play—thus they help to provide a degree of stability to the central city that is lacking in America. The cities of the Developing World exhibit further contrasts between private and public environments, but the rapidity of growth makes any balance between them precarious. In these cities the elite group plays a strong role although the lack of mobility does create population densities that force improvements in public services. One concludes that although describing spatial aspects of urban history in terms of elite versus collective control is perhaps simplistic, the theme does provide one means of explaining the forms that developed and persisted through time.

CITIES ARE PARTS OF URBAN ECOSYSTEMS IN WHICH MAN AND ENVIRONMENT ARE INTERDEPENDENT

Everything in an urban area is related to everything else. This general principle of environmental unity expresses the basic idea behind all ecosystems that the elements and processes of environment are interrelated and interdependent, and that a change in one will lead to a change in the other. Thus, cities are parts of urban ecosystems which cannot function independently of the rest of the world. A primary characteristic of such an ecosystem is the series of feedbacks which result from man's activity. He chooses a location for a city that possesses site and situational attributes that will affect its later development. He also changes the surface or subsurface terrain, produces a microclimate, and alters the patterns of vegetation and noise. All of these actions are interrelated to some extent. For example, the action of man in paving over large portions of cities increases the runoff of water which in turn changes the quality and quantity of streams. The surfaces also contribute to the development of an urban microclimate and disturb the earlier patterns of drainage and vegetation. The feedbacks are obvious: greater water and air pollution, possibilities of floods, a hostile environment for vegetation, and increased noise. As the size of urban area increases, the consequences of such actions in terms of feedbacks have become even more apparent. As a result, environmental controls have been instituted which vary in their degree of acceptance in world cities. Nevertheless, the ecosystem principle is now a fact of urban life.

CITIES HAVE DEVELOPED A COMPLEX SERIES OF RELATIONSHIPS WITH EXTERNAL AREAS

Man organizes space around a series of nodes called cities for the purpose of carrying out political, economic, and social activities. For example, he must form governments, exchange goods, and establish universities. Thus, the support for these nodes is external and the basis for this support is the interaction between them. This interaction in time is both regular and irregular in pattern. The more regular movements involve the provision of ubiquitous goods and services on a frequent basis. The nodal points for such services must be central to populations and so we call them central places. On the other hand, the more irregular patterns of interaction represent specialized activities like manufacturing. In these cases, nodal points may cluster together for mutual advantages of resources, labor, and markets. When these specialized activities are superimposed on those providing the regular goods and services, we have an urban system. The series of relationships which cities have with external areas, therefore, can be broken down into interaction or movement, central-place patterns, and the urban system itself.

Geographers have made considerable progress in developing theory and concepts within these three topics. In dealing with interaction the gravity model has been used to establish theoretical patterns of movement between and around cities. Perhaps the best example of theory is represented by models dealing with regularities of movements around central places and the hierarchy that emerges. The Christaller theory of central places is the best known of these, and served as the basis for testing of settlement hierarchies in a variety of situations and using a diversity of methods. Considerable progress in the use of quantitative methods in geography has been associated with analyzing the regularities of the central-place model and especially in isolating the spatial behavior that lies behind the regularities. Finally, the third approach to external relations of cities—analysis of the urban system—represents a logical attempt to combine the regularities of central-place theory with the irregularities of specialized functions. Here again progress has been made in developing theory or at least concepts which can be tested in the real world. The rank-size rule and primacy, for example, which reflect hierarchies with all settlements included, illustrate factors that distort urban systems such as colonial or imperial background, degree of industrialization, and size of country. Vance's mercantile model and certain industrial principles show how wholesaling and industry also can distort the urban system. Lastly, the economic base concept and Pred's model of circular and cumulative causation focus on the more dynamic aspects of urban growth, especially metropolitan areas, and on why some of these grow faster within the urban system than others. Although the concepts utilized here to illustrate external relations of cities represent only a sample of those available, they do seem to illustrate that individual cities do not develop independently of the urban system of which they are a part.

SPATIAL ORGANIZATION WITHIN CITIES REFLECTS CENTRIPETAL AND CENTRIFUGAL FORCES AROUND A SERIES OF NODAL POINTS.

The spatial organization of land uses in a city today reflects the presence of two sets of forces. The Central Business District, for example, illustrates the centripetal ones where a single node or core dominates internal organization. These forces, which include access to the entire city, functional linkages between enterprises when they are close together, and the prestige of a "downtown," have been apparent in cities throughout history. They were evident in the juxtaposition of palace, temple, and granery in the first "urban area" and they were present in the medieval city when castle, cathedral, market square, and city hall all grouped together for mutual advantage. Even the close location of railroad, factory, and tenement in the first industrial cities illustrates centripetal forces. Only recently, when man's mobility has been increased by use of automobile, truck, and bus, have the centrifugal forces become important. These forces of transport have reduced the friction of space and enabled man to move out to the outskirts of cities or fill in the gaps between the tenacles represented by fixed rail lines. Thus, he has been able to overcome the disadvantages of a central core or node which include congestion, nuisances like pollution, high cost of land, and legal and tax restrictions. At the same time, however, other problems have emerged. The most serious of these is the cleavage between central city and suburbs, a pattern most apparent in America where more affluent people, generally white, have escaped to the fringe. It is as if two cities exist—a decaying central core surrounded by a sprawling urban fringe. Each needs the other but they tend to go their own way.

These two sets of opposing forces form a framework for geographical analysis of internal urban patterns. Man organizes space within cities around a series of nodes and thus centripetal and centrifugal forces come into play in three ways. In the first place, *movement* within cities occurs between and around these nodes. Geographical models of residential location and consumer behavior illustrate both permanent and temporary movements in which these forces play a role, especially as they are affected by man's perception of urban space. Secondly, cities *grow* concentrically and by sectors around these nodes or multiple-nuclei on the basis of centripetal and centrifugal forces. These growth patterns are responsible for the three classical models of urban spatial structure. Finally, individual land uses in a city seem to bear a strong relationship to the costs of friction which represent the advantages of *location* around nodal points. Location within a node like the CBD reflects good accessibility to people and thus high rents, while locations away from it represent higher transport costs and reduced rents. Man seems to trade off these two costs, and this trade off is evident in the degree to which he is affected by centripetal or centrifugal forces. At the same time, the economic aspects of these forces are affected by distorting factors such as history, political fragmentation, and governmental influence. The effects of these factors can be tested in the real world against the model of the costs of friction.

COMPARISONS BETWEEN CITIES IN DIFFERENT CULTURAL AREAS SEEM TO BE FACILITATED BY EMPHASIZING THE FACTOR OF PUBLIC INTERVENTION.

Geographers have only begun to analyze the differences that exist between cities in contrasting cultural areas. Most research, however, has revealed that public intervention in urban development is greater in most areas of the world than it is in the United States. Berry, in fact, has developed a model in which he emphasizes a spectrum of public intervention in cities in order to combat the human consequences of urbanization. This spectrum of intervention runs from a peak in the communist countries through substantial amounts in the welfare economies of Western Europe to reduced influence in the Developing World. Geographers have developed models which reflect these differing public inputs.

In this book the author has either developed or modified models that emphasize public intervention in explaining cross-cultural aspects of urban spatial organization. For the socialist world, three models have been modified and combined: 1) one for Moscow, originated by Frolic, illustrates the pattern of internal planning for this large metropolitan area that has served as a blueprint in socialist countries; 2) one for Eastern Europe by Fisher focuses on several principles of internal structure and planning, and 3) one for Czechoslovakia by Kansky is regional in nature in portraying how the communist regime manipulates population and settlement to carry out policies of industrialization and urbanization. In dealing with West Europe, the author has put together an evolutionary model which illustrates the contribution of different periods to the present city of this era. In all of these periods the influence of public control is evident, most recently through national policies of growth which often involve the establishment of new towns. Finally, models of the preindustrial city by Sjoberg and English reflect limited public intervention. The former provides one conceptual base for this type of city while the latter represents a framework for internal urban structure based on Herat, Afghanistan. In all of these world areas where public intervention is seemingly greater than it is in the United States, the centripetal forces in urban development remain significant. This phenomenon reflects both the lower degree of mobility and the greater expense of land. However, in all areas modernization is evident and certain changes in the direction of the North American model are apparent. Nevertheless, it appears to this writer that in spite of similarities in urban modernization around the world, certain cultural differences are difficult to erase.

CONCLUSION

The above generalizations illustrate the approach used in this book. The focus throughout has been on the spatial characteristics that cities have in common under the assumption that they are the product of systematic processes. Thus, theory regarding these processes can be established as a framework against which urban reality can be measured. When theory and reality are considered together, the former serves as the basis for regional comparisons. The geographer's concern with areal differences is actually facilitated because there is some common basis against which comparisons can be made, something that has not always been true in the past. Naturally, the models which serve as the basis for comparison must be continuously tested to see if they can serve to explain the real world. This is particularly true of those established to analyze urban problems, e.g., the decline of the Central Business District. In this book, the theory introduced, while not comprehensive, was designed to introduce the introductory student to some of the ways that geographers have studied urban problems. Although many of these spatial models are derived from the North American city, cross-cultural comparisons are made and three chapters are devoted to models from other parts of the world. In this way the book hopefully has served to clarify some of the spatial foundations of urbanism.

References Cited

Abler, Ronald. "Distance, Intercommunications, and Geography," *Proceedings of the Association of American Geographers,* 3 (1971), 1-4.

Adams, John. "Directional Bias in Intra-urban Migration," *Economic Geography,* 45 (1969), 302-323.

Adams, John. "Residential Structure of Midwestern Cities," *Annals of the Association of American Geographers,* 60 (1970), 37-62.

Alexander, John. "The Basic-Nonbasic Concept of Urban Economic Functions," *Economic Geography,* 30 (1954), 246-261.

———. *Economic Geography* (Englewood Cliffs, New Jersey: Prentice-Hall, 1963).

Alexandersson, Gunnar. *The Industrial Structure of American Cities* (Lincoln, Nebraska: University of Nebraska Press, 1956).

Alonso, William. *Location and Land Use* (Harvard University Press, 1964).

Belser, Karl. "Misuse of Land in Fringe Areas and Inadequate Subdivision Standards," *Decentralization in Metropolitan Areas* (Berkeley: Department of City and Regional Planning, 1954), 21-5.

Berghinz, F. Carlo. "Venice Is Sinking into the Sea," *Civil Engineering,* 41 (1971), 67-71.

Berry, Brian. "City-Size Distributions and Economic Development," *Economic Development and Cultural Change,* 9 (1961), 573-588.

———. "Internal Structure of the City," *Law and Contemporary Problems,* 3 (1965), 111-119.

———. *Geography of Market Centers and Retail Distribution* (Englewood Cliffs, New Jersey: Prentice-Hall, 1967).

———. *The Human Consequences of Urbanization* (New York: St. Martin's Press, 1973).

Berry, Brian and Garrison, William. "Alternate Explanations of Urban Rank-Size Relationships," *Annals of the Association of American Geographers,* 48 (March, 1958), 83-91.

———. "Functional Bases of the Central Place Hierarchy," *Economic Geography,* 34 (April, 1958), 145-154.

———. "A Note on Central Place Theory and the Range of a Good," *Economic Geography,* 34 (October, 1958), 304-311.

Berry, Brian, et al. "Retail Location and Consumer Behavior," *Papers, Regional Science Association,* 9 (1962), 65-106.

Berry, Brian, Simmons, James, and Tennant, Robert. "Urban Populations: Structure and Change," *Geographical Review,* 53 (1963), 389-405.

Berry, Brian, Tennant, Robert, Garner, Barry, and Simmons, James. *Commercial Structure and Commercial Blight* (University of Chicago: Department of Geography Research Paper 85, 1963).

Blumenfeld, Hans. "The Modern Metropolis," *Scientific American,* 213 (1965), 64-74.

———. *The Modern Metropolis* (MIT Press, 1967).

Blumenfeld, Yurick. *Seesaw: Cultural Life in Eastern Europe* (New York: Harcourt, Brace and World, 1968).

Boal, Frederick. "Technology and Urban Form," *Journal of Geography,* 67 (1968), 228-236.

Bobeck, Hans and Lichtenberger, Elisabeth. *Wien: Bauliche Gestalt und Entwicklund seit der Mitte des 19. Jahrhunderts* (Vienna: Verlag Hermann Böhlaus, 1966).

Boyce, Ronald. "Residential Mobility and Its Implications for Urban Spatial Change," *Proceedings of the Association of American Geographers,* 1 (1969), 22-26.

Breese, Gerald (ed.). *The City in Newly Developing Countries* (Englewood Cliffs, New Jersey: Prentice Hall, 1969).

Brown, Lawrence and Moore, Eric. "The Intra-urban Migration Process: A Perspective," in Bourne, Larry, *Internal Structure of the City* (New York: Oxford University Press, 1971), 200-209.

Brunhes, Jean. *Human Geography* (Chicago: Rand McNally Co., 1920).

Brush, John. "The Hierarchy of Places in Southwest Wisconsin," *Geographical Review,* 43 (1953), 380-402.

Burgess, Ernest. "The Growth of the City: An Introduction to a Research Project," *The City* (University of Chicago Press, 1925), 47-62.

Burghardt, A. F. "A Hypothesis about Gateway Cities,"*Annals of the Association of American Geographers,* 61 (1971), 269-285.

Carrothers, Gerald. "An Historical Review of the Gravity and Potential Concepts of Human Interaction," *Journal of the American Institute of Planners,* 22 (1956), 94-102.

Carter, Harold. *The Study of Urban Geography* (London: Edward Arnold, 1972).

Chapin, F. Stuart. *Urban Land Use Planning* (University of Illinois Press, 1965), 142.

Chicago Area Transportation Study, Vol. I, 1959.

Chiffelle, Frédéric. "Switzerland," in Clout, Hugh, ed., *Regional Development in Western Europe* (London: Wiley, 1975).

Childe, V. G. "The Urban Revolution," *Town Planning Review,* 21 (1950), 3-17.

Chisholm, Michael. "Must We All Live in Southeast England?," *Geography,* 49 (1964), 1-14.

Christaller, Walter. *Die zentralen Orte in Süddeutschland* (Jena, Germany: Gustav Fischer Verlag, 1933). Translated by C. W. Baskin and published by Prentice-Hall, 1966.

Clark, Philip and Evans, Francis. "Distance to Nearest Neighbor as a Measure of Spatial Relationships in Populations," *Ecology,* 35 (1954), 445-453.

Colby, Charles. "Centrifugal and Centripetal Forces in Urban Geography," *Annals of the Association of American Geographers,* 23 (1933), 1-20.

Converse, P. D. "New Laws of Retail Gravitation," *Journal of Marketing,* 14 (1949), 379-384.

Coppa, Frank. "Cities and Suburbs in Europe and the United States," in Dolce, Philip, *Suburbia* (Garden City, New York: Anchor Books, 1976), 167-191.

Dacey, Michael. "Analysis of Central Place and Point Patterns by a Nearest Neighbor Method," in Norborg, K., ed., *Proceedings of the IGU Symposium in Urban Geography, Lund, 1960* (Lund, Sweden: Gleerup, 1962), 55-75.

Davie, Maurice. "The Pattern of Urban Growth," in Murdock, G. P., ed., *Studies in the Science of Society* (Yale University Press, 1937), 133-161.

Davies, W. K. D. and Lewis, C. R. "Regional Structures in Wales: Two Studies of Connectivity," in Carter, H. and Davies, W. K. D., *Urban Essays: Studies in the Geography of Wales* (London: Longman, 1970), 22-48.

Davis, Kinsley. "The Urbanization of the Human Population," *Scientific American*, 213 (1965), 41-53.

———. *World Urbanization, 1950-1970*, I-II (Berkeley: Institute of International Studies, 1966 and 1972).

Davis, Ross. "The Location of Service Activities," in Chisholm, Michael and Rodgers, Brian, *Studies in Human Geography* (London: Heinemann Educational Books, 1973), 123-171.

Dawson, A. H. "Warsaw: An Example of City Structure in Free Market and Planned Socialist Environments," *Tijdschrift voor Economische en Sociale Geografie*, 62 (1971), 104-113.

Deskins, Donald. "Interaction Patterns and the Spatial Form of the Ghetto," *Special Publication*, No. 3 (Department of Geography, Northwestern University, 1969).

Detwyler, Thomas and Marcus, Melvin. *Urbanization and Environment* (Belmont, California: Duxbury Press, 1972).

Dickinson, R. E. *The West European City* (London: Routledge and Kegan Paul, 1951).

Dwyer, D. J. "The City in the Developing World and the Example of Southeast Asia," *Geography*, 53 (1968), 353-364.

English, Paul. "The Preindustrial City of Herat, Afghanistan," paper given at the Annual Meeting of the Association of American Geographers, Washington, D.C., Aug. 1968.

Evans, David. "Man-made Earthquakes in Denver," in Tank, Ronald, *Focus on Environmental Geology* (New York: Oxford Press, 1973), 76-87.

Feuerstein, Günther. "East Germany: Residential Construction and Urban Design," in Feuerstein, Günther, *New Directions in German Architecture* (New York: George Braziller, 1968), 103-113.

Firey, Walter. "Sentiment and Symbolism as Ecological Variables," *American Sociological Review*, 10 (1945), 140-148.

———. *Land Use in Central Boston* (Harvard University Press, 1947), 87-135.

Fisher, Jack. "Planning the City of Socialist Man," *Journal of the American Institute of Planners*, 28 (1962), 251-265.

———. "The Reconstruction of Skopje," *Journal of the American Institute of Planners*, 30 (1964), 46-48.

———. "Urban Planning in the Soviet Union and Eastern Europe," in Eldredge, H. W., (ed.), *Taming Megalopolis* (Garden City, New York: Doubleday and Co., 1967), Vol. II, pp. 1068-1099.

Fizer, Webb. *Mastery of the Metropolis* (Englewood Cliffs, New Jersey: Prentice-Hall, 1962), 117-125.

Fox, William. "Baghdad, a City in Transition," paper given to the Annual Meeting of the Association of American Geographers, Washington, D.C., Aug. 1968.

Freeman, T. W. *The Conurbations of Great Britain* (Manchester University Press, 1966).

Frolic, B. Michael. "The Soviet City," *Town Planning Review,* 34 (1964), 285-306.

———. "Moscow: The Socialist Alternative," in Eldredge, H. W., ed., *The World Capitals* (Garden City, New York: Anchor Press, 1975), 295-339.

Galantay, Ervin. *New Towns: Antiquity to the Present* (New York: George Braziller, 1975).

Galbraith, John. "To My New Friends in the Affluent Society—Greetings," *Life* (March 27, 1970), 20.

Gallion, Arthur and Eisner, Simon. *The Urban Pattern* (Princeton, New Jersey: D. Van Nostrand, 1963).

Garner, Barry. "Models of Urban Geography and Settlement Location," in Chorley, Richard and Haggett, Peter, *Socio-Economic Models in Geography* (London: Methuen University Paperbacks, 1968), 303-360.

Garner, Barry and Yeates, Maurice. *The North American City* (New York: Harper and Row, 1976).

Getis, Arthur and Getis, Judith. "Christaller's Central Place Theory," *Journal of Geography,* 65 (1966), 220-226.

Getis, Arthur. "Residential Location and the Journey to Work," *Proceedings of the Association of American Geographers,* 1 (1969), 55-59.

Golledge, R. G., et al. "Some Spatial Characteristics of Iowa's Dispersed Farm Population and Their Implication for the Grouping of Central Place Functions," *Economic Geography,* 42 (1966), 261-272.

Gottmann, Jean. *Megalopolis* (New York: Twentieth Century Fund, 1961).

———. "Why the Skyscraper?," *Geographical Review,* 56 (1966), 190-212.

———. "Urban Centrality and the Interweaving of Quaternary Activities," *Ekistics,* 29 (1970), 322-331.

Green, F. H. W. "Urban Hinterlands in England and Wales: An Analysis of Bus Services," *Geographical Journal,* 116 (1950), 64-88.

———. "Urban Hinterlands: Fifteen Years On," *Geographical Journal,* 132 (1966), 263-266.

Green, Howard. "Hinterland Boundaries of New York City and Boston in Southern New England," *Economic Geography,* 31 (1955), 283-300.

Griffin, Donald and Preston, Richard. "A Restatement of the Transition Zone Concept," *Annals of the Association of American Geographers,* 56 (1966), 339-350.

Hadden, Jeffrey and Borgatta, Edgar. *American Cities: Their Social Characteristics* (Chicago: Rand McNally, 1965).

Haggett, Peter. *Locational Analysis in Human Geography* (New York: St. Martin's Press, 1966).

Haig, Robert. "Toward an Understanding of the Metropolis: The Assignment of Activities to Areas in Urban Regions," *Quarterly Journal of Economics,* 40 (1926), 402-434.

Hall, A. Stuart. "Taxation, Urbanization and Property," unpublished paper given at the Conference on Urbanization, Nebraska Center for Continuing Education, Lincoln, Nebraska, Feb. 1967 (7 pp.).

Hall, Peter. *The World's Cities* (New York: McGraw-Hill, 1966).

Hallenbeck, Wilbur. *American Urban Communities* (New York: Harper and Brothers, 1951).

Halvorson, Peter. "The Income Factor in the Journey-to-Work: Attitudes and Behavior," *Professional Geographer,* 25 (1973), 357-362.

Hamilton, F. E. Ian. "The Location of Industry in East-Central and Southeast Europe," in Hoffman, George, ed., *Eastern Europe: Essays in Geographical Problems* (London: Methuen, 1971), 173-213.

———. "Muscovites Move Away from the Centre," *Geographical Magazine*, 45 (1973), 451-459.

———. *The Moscow City Region* (Oxford University Press, 1976).

Harris, Chauncy. "A Functional Classification of Cities in the United States," *Geographical Review*, 33 (1943), 86-99.

———. "The Market as a Factor in the Localization of Industry in the United States," *Annals of the Association of American Geographers*, 44 (1954), 315-348.

Harris, Chauncy and Ullman, Edward. "The Nature of Cities," *Annals of the American Academy of Political and Social Science*, 242 (1945), 7-17.

Hart, John Fraser. "The Changing American Countryside," in Cohen, Saul B., (ed.), *Problems and Trends in American Geography* (New York: Basic Books, 1967), 64-74.

Hauser, Philip and Schnore, Leo. *The Study of Urbanization* (New York: John Wiley and Sons, 1965).

Heyman, Mark. "The End of Classic City Planning," *Landscape*, (Winter 1965-1966), 18-20.

Horvath, Ronald. "In Search of a Theory of Urbanization: Notes on the Colonial City," paper given at the Annual Meeting of the Association of American Geographers, Washington, D.C., Aug. 1968.

———. "Machine Space," *Geographical Review*, 64 (1974), 167-188.

Horwood, Edgar and Boyce, Ronald. *Studies of the Central Business District and Urban Freeway Development* (Seattle, Washington: University of Washington Press, 1959), 19-26.

Hoyt, Homer. *One Hundred Years of Land Values in Chicago* (University of Chicago Press, 1933).

———. *The Structure and Growth of Residential Neighborhoods* (Washington, D.C.: Federal Housing Administration, 1939).

———. "Structure and Growth of European and Asiatic Cities as Contrasted to American Cities," *Urban Land*, Sept. 1959, 3-8.

———. "Recent Distortions of the Classical Models of Urban Structure," *Land Economies*, 40 (1964), 199-212.

Huff, David. "A Topographic Model of Consumer Space Preferences," *Papers, Regional Science Association*, 6 (1960), 159-173.

———. "A Probability Analysis of Shopping Center Trading Areas," *Land Economics*, 53 (1963), 81-90.

Hurst, Michael. *I Came to the City: Essays and Comments on the Urban Scene* (Boston: Houghton Mifflin, 1975), 286-292.

Hutchings, Raymond. "The Weakening of Ideological Influence upon Soviet Design," *Slavic Review*, 27 (1968), 71-84.

Isard, Walter. *Location and Space Economy* (New York: Wiley, 1956).

Jefferson, Mark. "The Law of the Primate City," *Geographical Review*, 29 (1939), 226-232.

Johnston, R. J. "On Spatial Patterns in the Residential Structure of Cities," *Canadian Geographer*, 14 (1970), 361-367.

———. *Spatial Structures* (New York: St. Martin's Press, 1973).

Jones, Emrys. *Towns and Cities* (London: Oxford University Press, 1966).

Kansky, Karel. *Urbanization under Socialism: The Case of Czechoslovakia* (Prague: Praeger, 1976).

Kenyon, James. "The Industrial Structure of the New York Garment Center," in Thoman, Richard and Patton, Donald, *Focus on Geographic Activity* (New York: McGraw-Hill, 1964).

King, L. J. "The Functional Role of Small Towns in Canterbury," *Proceedings, Third New Zealand Geographical Society Conference,* 1961, 139-149.

————. "A Quantitative Expression of the Pattern of Urban Settlements in Selected Areas of the United States," *Tijdschrift voor Economische en Sociale Geografie,* 53 (1962), 1-7.

Kolars, John and Nystuen, John. *Human Geography: Spatial Design in World Society* (New York: McGraw-Hill, 1974).

Kolb, J. H. *Service Relations of Town and Country* (University of Wisconsin, Agricultural Experiment Station, Research Bulletin 58, Dec. 1923).

Kolb, J. H. and Brunner, E. *A Study of Rural Society* (Boston: Houghton Mifflin, 1946).

Kosinski, Leszek. "Urbanization in East-Central Europe after World War II," *East Europe Quarterly,* 8 (1974), 129-153.

Landsberg, H. E. "The Climate of Towns," in Thomas, W. L., ed., *Man's Role in Changing the Face of the Earth* (University of Chicago Press, 1956), 584-606.

Larimore, Ann. "The Africanization of Colonial Cities in East Africa," paper given at the Annual Meeting of the Association of American Geographers, Washington, D.C. Aug. 1968.

Legget, Robert. *Cities and Geology* (New York: McGraw-Hill, 1973).

Leopold, Luna. *Hydrology for Urban Land Planning: A Guidebook on the Hydrologic Effects of Urban Land Use* (Washington, D.C.: U.S. Geological Survey, Circular 554, 1968).

Llewellyn, Richard. *How Green Was My Valley* (New York: Macmillan, 1940).

Lösch, August. *The Economics of Location* (New Haven: Yale University Press, 1954).

Lovelace, Eldridge. "Control of Urban Expansion: The Lincoln, Nebraska Experience," *Journal of the American Institute of Planners,* 31 (1965), 348-352.

Lowe, John and Moryadas, S. *The Geography of Movement* (Boston: Houghton Mifflin, 1975).

Lowry, William. "The Climate of Cities," *Scientific American,* 217 (1967), 15-23.

Mackay, J. R. "The Interactance Hypothesis and Boundaries in Canada: A Preliminary Study," *Canadian Geographer* 11 (1958), 1-8.

Madden, C. H. "On Some Indications of Stability in the Growth of Cities in the United States," *Economic Development and Cultural Change,* 4 (1956), 236-252.

Mahoney, Daniel. "Property Taxation and the Underuse of Land," unpublished paper, Department of Geography, University of Nebraska, 1975.

Marshall, J. U. *The Location of Service Towns: An Approach to the Analysis of Central Place Systems* (University of Toronto, Department of Geography, 1969).

McKeever, J. Ross. *What's New in Europe's Urban Development* (Washington, D.C.: Urban Land Institute, 1969).

McNee, Robert. *A Primer on Economic Geography* (New York: Random House, 1971).

McPherson, M. B., *Hydrological Effects of Urbanization* (Paris: UNESCO Press, 1974).

Merritt, Richard. "Infrastructural Changes in Berlin," *Annals of the Association of American Geographers,* 63 (1973), 58-70.

Metropolitan Toronto and Region Transport Study (Toronto: Parliament Building, 1966).

Morrill, Richard. *The Spatial Organization of Society* (Belmont, California: Wadsworth Publishing Co., 1974), 69-92, 191-202.

Moser, C. A. and Scott, W. *British Towns: A Statistical Study of Their Social and Economic Differences* (Edinburgh: Oliver & Boyd, 1961).

Mountjoy, Alan. "Urbanization, the Squatter and Development in the Third World," *Tijdschrift voor Economische en Sociale Geografie,* 67 (1976), 130-137.

Müller, Karl (ed.) Dicaearchus in *Geographi Graeci Minores* (Paris: 1855), Vol. I, p. 97.

Mumford, Lewis. *The City in History: Its Origins, Its Transformations, and Its Prospects* (New York: Harcourt, Brace, and World, 1961).

Murdie, Robert. "Cultural Differences in Consumer Travel," *Economic Geography,* 41 (1965), 211-233.

————. *Factorial Ecology of Metropolitan Toronto, 1951-1961* (University of Chicago, Department of Geography, Research Paper 116, 1969).

Murphey, Rhoads. "The City as a Center of Change: Western Europe and China," *Annals of the Association of American Geographers,* 44 (1954), 349-362.

————. "Traditionalism and Colonialism: Urban Roles in East Asia from Da Gama to Chiang Kai Shek," paper given at the Annual Meeting of the Association of American Geographers, Washington, D.C., Aug. 1968.

Murphy, Raymond and Vance, James. "Delimiting the CBD," *Economic Geography,* 30 (July 1954), 189-222.

————. "A Comparative Study of Nine Central Business Districts," *Economic Geography* 30 (Oct. 1954), 301-336.

Murphy, Raymond, Vance, James, and Epstein, Bart. "Internal Structure of the CBD," *Economic Geography,* 31 (1955), 21-46.

Musil, J. "The Development of Prague's Ecological Structure," in Pahl, R. E., *Readings in Urban Sociology* (Oxford: Pergamon, 1968), 232-259.

Nelson, Howard. "A Service Classification of American Cities," *Economic Geography,* 31 (1955), 189-210.

————. "Some Characteristics of the Population of Cities in Similar Service Classifications," *Economic Geography,* 33 (1957), 95-108.

Northam, Ray. *Urban Geography* (New York: Wiley, 1975).

Olbricht, K. "Die Vergrosstädterung des Abendlandes zu Beginn des Dreissigjährigen Krieges," *Petermanns Geographische Mitteilungen* 85 (1939), 349-353.

"One Way to Better Cities (film)," Robert Schalkenbach Foundation, 50 East 69th St., New York, N.Y., 1971.

Osborn, Robert. "How the Russians Plan Their Cities," *Ekistics,* 21 (1967), 75-78.

Ottoson, Howard. "Urbanization and the Rural Community," unpublished paper given at the Conference on Urbanization, Nebraska Center for Continuing Education, Lincoln, Nebraska, Feb. 1967 (11 pp.).

Perevedentsev, V. "Population Migration and Utilization of Labor Resources," *Current Digest of the Soviet Press,* 23 (No. 2), Feb. 9, 1971, 1-6.

Pirenne, Henri. *Medieval Cities* (Princeton University Press, 1925).

Poland, J. F. and Davis, G. H. "Land Subsidence Due to Withdrawal of Fluids," in McKenzie, Garry and Utgard, Russell, *Man and His Physical Environment* (Minneapolis: Burgess, 1972), 79-82.

Pred, Allen. "Industrialization, Initial Advantage, and American Metropolitan Growth," *Geographical Review,* 55 (1965), 158-185.

Prentice, Pierrepont, ed. "The Great Urban Tax Tangle," *Fortune,* 71 (1965), 106-107, 188-198.

Preston, Richard. "The Zone in Transition: A Study of Urban Land Use Patterns," *Economic Geography,* 42 (1966), 236-260.

———. "Recent Changes in the Size and Form of the Southern California Metropolis," *California: 1970, Problems and Prospects* (Association of American Geographers, 1970), 83-144.

Proudfoot, Malcolm. "City Retail Structure," *Economic Geography,* 13 (1937), 425-428.

———. "Public Regulation of Urban Development in the United States," *Geographical Review*, 44 (1954), 415-419.

Ratcliff, Richard. "The Dynamics of Efficiency in the Locational Distribution of Urban Activities," in Fisher, Robert, ed., *The Metropolis in Modern Life* (New York: Doubleday, 1955), 125-148.

Reilly, William. *Methods for the Study of Retail Relationships* (Austin: Bureau of Business Research, University of Texas, 1929; reprinted in 1959).

Risser, H. E. and Major, R. L. "Urban Expansion: An Opportunity and a Challenge to Industrial Mineral Producers," reprinted in Tank, Ronald, *Focus on Environmental Geology* (New York: Oxford University Press, 1973), 441-454.

Rossi, P. H. *Why Families Move* (Glencoe, Illinois: The Free Press, 1955).

Rugg, D. S. "Comparative Aspects of the Urban Geography of Alexandria, Virginia and Bad Godesberg, West Germany," *Economic Geography,* 41 (1965), 157-181.

———. "Selected Areal Effects of Planning Processes upon Urban Development in the Federal Republic of Germany," *Economic Geography,* 42 (1966), 326-335.

———. "Aspects of Change in the Landscape of East-Central and Southeast Europe," in Hoffman, George, ed., *Eastern Europe: Essays in Geographical Problems* (London: Methuen, 1971), 83-122.

Russell, Josiah. "Late Ancient and Medieval Populations," *Transactions of the American Philosophical Society,* 48 (Part 3, 1958), 59-63, 105-129.

———. "The Metropolitan City Region of the Middle Ages," *Journal of Regional Science*, 2 (1960), 55-70.

Sanders, W. T., and Price, B. *Mesoamerica: The Evolution of a Civilization* (New York: Random House, 1968).

Schoustra, Jack and Lake, Thomas. "Los Angeles Hillside Developments," *Civil Engineering,* 39 (1969), 39-42.

Scofield, William. "Values and Competition for Land," *A Place to Live,* Department of Agriculture Yearbook, 1963 (Washington, D.C.: Government Printing Office, 1963), 64-72.

Shevky, E. and Bell, W. *Social Area Analysis: Theory, Illustrative Applications, and Computational Procedures* (Stanford University Press, 1955).

Shkvarikov, V., et al. "The Building of New Towns in the USSR," *Ekistics,* 18 (1964), 307-319.

Sinclair, Robert. *The Face of Detroit* (National Council for Geographic Education, 1970).

Sjoberg, Gideon. *The Preindustrial City* (New York: Free Press, 1960).

———. "The Origin and Evolution of Cities," *Scientific American*, 213 (1965), 55-63.

Skinner, G. William. "Marketing and Social Structures in Rural China, Part I," *Journal of Asian Studies,* 24 (1964), 3-43.

Smailes, Arthur. "The Urban Hierarchy in England and Wales," *Geography*, 29 (1944), 41-51.

Smith, R. D. P. "The Changing Urban Hierarchy," *Regional Studies*, 2 (1968), 1-19.

Smith, R. H. T. "Method and Purpose in Functional Town Classification," *Annals of the Association of American Geographers*, 55 (1965), 539-548.

Smith, William. "Trees in the City," *Journal of the American Institute of Planners*, 36 (1970), 429-436.

Taaffe, Edward. "Air Transportation and United States Urban Distribution," *Geographical Review*, 46 (1956), 219-238.

Travis, Richard. "Reinterpreting the Urban Landscape: Location vs. the Content of Places," *Geographical Survey* (Mankato, Minn.: Blue Earth County Geographical Survey, Jan. 1972), 25-35.

Ullman, Edward. *Mobile: Industrial Seaport and Trade Center* (University of Chicago Press, Department of Geography, 1943).

———. "The Role of Transportation and the Basis for Interaction," in Thomas, W. L., ed., *Man's Role in Changing the Face of the Earth* (University of Chicago Press, 1956), 862-880.

Ullman, Edward and Dacey, Michael. "The Minimum Requirements Approach to the Urban Economic Base," in Norborg, K., ed., *Proceedings of the IGU Symposium in Urban Geography, Lund, 1960* (Lund, Sweden: Gleerup, 1962), 121-143.

Ullman, Edward, Dacey, Michael, and Brodsky, Harold. *The Economic Base of American Cities* (Seattle: University of Washington Press, 1969).

United Nations, "Growth of the World's Urban and Rural Population, 1920-2000," *Population Studies*, No. 44, Department of Economic and Social Affairs, 1969.

———. *Skopje Resurgent,* 1970.

Vance, James. "Emerging Patterns of Commercial Structure in American Cities," in Norborg, K., ed., *Proceedings of the IGU Symposium in Urban Geography, Lund 1960* (Lund, Sweden: Gleerup, 1962), 485-518.

———. *Geography and Urban Evolution in the San Francisco Bay Area* (Berkeley: Institute of Governmental Studies, University of California, 1964.

———. *The Merchant's World: The Geography of Wholesaling* (Englewood Cliffs, New Jersey: Prentice-Hall, 1970).

Vining, R. "A Description of Certain Aspects of an Economic System," *Economic Development and Cultural Change*, 3 (1955), 147-195.

Violich, Francis. "Evolution of the Spanish City," *Journal of the American Institute of Planners*, 28 (1962), 170-179.

Warner, Sam. *Streetcar Suburbs* (Harvard University Press, 1962).

Weber, Adna. *The Growth of Cities in the Nineteenth Century* (New York: Macmillan Co., 1899).

Wheatley, Paul. "What the Greatness of a City Is Said to Be," *Pacific Viewpoints*, 4 (1963), 163-188.

Whiteford, A. H. *Andean City at Mid-Century* (Michigan State University, 1977).

———. *Two Cities of Latin America* (New York: Doubleday and Co., 1964).

Whittlesey, Derwent. "The Impress of Effective Central Authority upon the Landscape," *Annals of the Association of American Geographers*, 25 (1935), 85-97.

Wirth, Louis. "Urbanism as a Way of Life," *American Journal of Sociology*, 44 (1938), 1-24.

Wolfe, R. I. and Mumford, Lewis. "On Freedom, Freeways, and Flexibility—The Private Correspondence of Messrs. Wolfe and Mumford," *Journal of the American Institute of Planners,* 27 (1961), 74-77.

Wolpert, Julian. "Behavioral Aspects of the Decision to Migrate," *Papers, Regional Science Association,* 15 (1965), 159-169.

Woolley, Sir Leonard. *Excavations at Ur* (New York: Thomas Y. Crowell, 1954).

Zanarini, Roger. "A Shopping Center Exploration: Las Vegas, Nevada," *Great Plains-Rocky Mountain Geographical Journal,* 2 (1973), 99-104.

Zipf, G. K. *Human Behavior and the Principle of Least Effort* (Cambridge, Mass.: Addison-Wesley Press, 1949), 364-376.

INDEX